Histor

History Museums in the United States

A Critical Assessment

Edited by

Warren Leon
and
Roy Rosenzweig

University of Illinois Press
Urbana and Chicago

© 1989 by the Board of Trustees of the University of Illinois
Manufactured in the United States of America
1 2 3 4 5 C P 5 4 3 2 1

This book is printed on acid-free paper.

Library of Congress Cataloging-in-Publication Data

History museums in the United States : a critical assessment / edited
    by Warren Leon, Roy Rosenzweig.
        p. cm.
    ISBN 0-252-01400-6 (cloth : alk. paper). ISBN 0-252-06064-4
(paper : alk. paper)
    1. Historical museums—United States.   2. Historic sites—United
States.   3. Historic sites—United States—Interpretive programs.
I. Leon, Warren.   II. Rosenzweig, Roy.
E159.H73 1989
973—dc 19   88-27883
                                                           CIP

To the memory of

Stephen Botein
(1941–1986)

Contents

Acknowledgments

Over the four years during which this book has taken—and changed—shape, we have acquired a number of debts. Our largest thanks go to the authors of the essays included here. They stuck with the project despite the absence of financial support, particularly for travel. As all of us (including those who dropped out along the way) discovered, the critical evaluation of museums and historic sites takes a great deal of time, commitment, and perseverance.

In addition to writing one of the essays, Gary Kulik has been a source of advice and encouragement throughout. The interest and support of Richard Wentworth, Director of University of Illinois Press, was crucial to sustaining our efforts. David Glassberg provided a perceptive commentary on the entire manuscript, while Mary Alexander, Deborah Kaplan, Barbara Melosh, and Cynthia Robinson offered helpful comments on the introduction. Herbert Hyde expertly copyedited the final manuscript.

Finally, we have dedicated the book to the memory of Stephen Botein, a brilliant historian, teacher, and friend with whom we studied and collaborated during our years in graduate school. Steve had nothing to do directly with the development and editing of this particular volume. But we would like to think that it has been influenced by the insights and values that we learned from his remarkable teaching and inspiring example.

W.L. & R.R.

Introduction

Warren Leon and Roy Rosenzweig

In 1976 the Smithsonian's National Museum of History and Technology (now the National Museum of American History) opened "A Nation of Nations," its bicentennial exhibition on America's immigrant heritage. Since then, millions of visitors have seen the exhibit, which was mounted by an eleven-person exhibit committee, a sixteen-member design team, and numerous volunteers, consultants, and support staff.[1] Given the expense and effort involved in organizing "A Nation of Nations" as well as the enormous number of people who have seen it, the lack of sustained critical attention that either museum- or university-based historians have devoted to the exhibition is remarkable. No professional history or museum journal has ever included a full-scale review of it. Indeed, few published works of any kind discuss it at all.[2]

By way of comparison, consider the critical attention lavished on a widely circulated history book on a similar topic and of similarly large scope and scale: Oscar Handlin's *The Uprooted: The Epic Story of the Great Migrations that Made the American People*, a Pulitzer Prize–winning work first published in 1951 and reissued in an enlarged second edition in 1973 about the time work began on "A Nation of Nations." The original edition received reviews in at least twenty scholarly journals; more than a dozen mass-circulation periodicals (including *The New Yorker*, *The New York Times Book Review*, and the *Nation*) also commented. Even more important, Handlin's evidence, thesis, and approach have been praised, criticized, and modified in literally dozens of dissertations, articles, and monographs.[3]

Neither example is atypical. The attention accorded Handlin's book, while more than that given an ordinary monograph, is not unusual for a prize-winning synthesis with an original interpretation. Indeed, even a specialized work in American history, which might sell fewer than fifteen hundred hardcover copies, is likely to receive more than ten reviews in scholarly journals.[4]

The critical neglect of "A Nation of Nations" is also typical. In general, a blanket of critical silence has surrounded such presentations, and it has rarely been pierced by museum professionals, academic historians, or newspaper and magazine critics. Some would no doubt anticipate the lack of commentary on the displays of local historical societies, short-term temporary exhibits, out-of-the-way historic houses, and profit-making wax museums. But it is harder to explain or justify the reluctance to address historical presentations that affect the perceptions of literally millions of Americans.[5]

Few, if any, critics have appraised the historical presentation at such a well-known site as Mount Vernon, even though more than one million people visit each year. The lack of attention devoted to less well-known institutions is less surprising but no less lamentable. Although the Frederick Douglass Home in Washington, D.C., attracts only thirty-six thousand visitors per year, the site's organizers thought of it as the "black Mount Vernon," and many of its visitors, 95 percent of whom are black, probably share this view.

To proceed with further examples would only repeat the same theme: the absence of critical scrutiny of museum-based historical presentations. It would also highlight another theme: the importance of these sites in shaping the public's perception of the past. It is rare, for example, for a scholarly monograph in black history to sell 36,000 copies in a year. Similarly, the 350,000 visitors to Plimoth Plantation probably exceed the cumulative readership of all the new scholarly works in colonial history in a typical year. By any standard, the 100 million or so annual visitors to history museums and historic sites constitute a massive public audience for the past.[6]

Very recently, however, there have been signs this critical silence about history museums is being broken. For many years, *Technology and Culture* was the only historical journal to offer regular reviews of museum exhibits, although a few other publications (*Winterthur Portfolio*, *William and Mary Quarterly*, and *Radical History Review*, for example) have, at times, included reviews.[7] Yet in 1987 and 1988, five major historical publications—*Journal of American History*, *American Quarterly*, *The Public Historian*, *History News*, and the American Historical Association's *Perspectives*—began (or announced plans to begin) museum-exhibit review sections. Around the same time, the "Common Agenda for History Museums" program, sponsored by the American Association for State and Local History and supported by the Smithsonian Institution and the National Endowment for the Humanities, has made museum criticism and evaluation a major objective.[8]

But the recent efforts at evaluation and criticism remain limited and scattered. Indeed, no doubt the largest body of critical "literature" is the oral tradition of commentary passed among museum workers at professional meetings and other encounters. In contrast to the history-museum community's general neglect of collective appraisal, other professional groups regularly reflect upon the state of their fields. In 1971, for example, the American Academy of Arts and Sciences sponsored a volume of essays titled *Historical Studies Today*; a decade later Michael Kammen edited *The Past Before Us: Contemporary Historical Writing in the United States* for the American Historical Association.[9] But no analogous volumes exist for history museums.

It is because of this gap, as well as our strong conviction that history museums are central means of presenting history to a variety of publics, that we have organized this volume, the first book-length critical assessment of historical museums in the United States. But given the dearth of previous evaluative work, no single volume can provide an overall judgment on the vast practice of the nation's history museums. Thus, this book does not offer either a comprehensive or a definitive survey of the history-museum field. Rather, it seeks to initiate formal, critical discussion of historical interpretation at museums and to stimulate additional efforts at professional dialogue.

Any consideration of the history-museum field—even one, like ours, that is avowedly nonsystematic—must confront the interrelated problems of first defining and then embracing such a vast and heterogeneous arena. Museum visitors and even museum workers are often unsure what is and is not a history museum. The general public probably has no difficulty identifying an institution like the National Museum of American History as a museum, but people become more confused when visiting a place like Old Sturbridge Village, a re-created 1830s community in Massachusetts. Sturbridge's outdoor setting suggests a park, its animals summon up a farm or a zoo, the role playing by staff members evokes a theatrical performance, and the organization of the experience seems to parallel a theme park.[10]

Museum professionals themselves are sometimes unsure of the contours of the field in which they labor. On the one hand, such research libraries as the National Archives and the Pierpont Morgan Library in New York often include exhibits but do not label themselves as museums. On the other hand, such historic districts as South Street Seaport in New York and Old Town San Diego identify themselves as museums, but some museum workers wonder whether their real purpose is not expressed by the stores, restaurants, and other commercial operations that dominate their sites.

Previous museum surveys have varied in their definitions of the field. When the National Endowment for the Arts prepared its 1973 report *Museums: USA*, it counted only institutions with a collection and at least one full-time employee with academic training. Based on this definition, it found 1,821 museums in the United States: more than one-third of these (683) were purely history museums; another 10 percent (186) combined history with art; still more combined history with other subjects.[11]

In 1978 the Institute for Museum Services sponsored its own "museum universe survey." In this broader survey, a museum was "an institution organized on a permanent basis for essentially educational or aesthetic purposes, which, utilizing a staff, owns or uses tangible objects, whether animate or inanimate, cares for those objects and exhibits them to the public on a regular basis." This definition may seem rather sweeping, but the IMS surveyors actually eliminated close to half of the responses they received as "clearly not museums." Nevertheless, they still concluded that there were more than 4,400 museums in the United States, with half of them defined as history museums.[12] A still broader criterion, self-selection, has been used by the American Association of Museums in its *Official Museum Directory*, which lists more than 6,500 museums. But even this list is not complete. Certain commercial institutions (for example, Plymouth National Wax Museum, which claims a half-million visitors a year) are not included since their owners do not identify closely with the museum profession. (Their profit, rather than educational or aesthetic, orientation also eliminated them from the IMS survey.) And such multisite institutions as the Minnesota Historical Society, with 24 locations throughout the state are listed only once.

For the purposes of this book, we define history museums as institutions that display historical artifacts, or even reproductions or representations of artifacts, in the formal effort to teach about the past. Yet even this definition (which is close to that offered by IMS but includes profit-making institutions) raises some further questions: the meaning of such terms as *institutions*, *artifacts*, and *teaching*, for example. Moreover, it still leaves us with something like three thousand museums to consider—a rather formidable body of historical institutions.

No single person is likely to visit all these places. And even if someone did embark on such an exhausting and compulsive journey, he or she would still not have a full picture of history-museum presentations at any one point. When the last museum was reached (and at the rate of one per day, it would take close to a decade), much of the information about the first stops on the itinerary would be outdated, since museum exhibits change so frequently. In a field where a permanent exhibit may remain in place for as little as five years, change is the norm.

The remarkable diversity of history museums makes it even harder to comprehend the field as a whole. There are historic houses, interpreted battlefields, living-history farms, re-created communities, and museums of local, state, and national history as well as specialized museums covering the history of such different subjects as whaling, broadcasting, politics, toys, tools, and trains. Ethnic groups, religious bodies, corporations, and professional organizations all have their own museums, as do fans of everything from baseball to snowmobiles to Liberace. Moreover, specific categories of museums can embrace a wide range of possibilities. Local-history museums in adjoining communities may not use any of the same exhibit techniques or cover any of the same general subjects.

Some individual organizations are so complex that it is hard to summarize all their activities and approaches to history. The state-supported Ohio Historical Society, for example, was born in 1885 out of interest in the region's Indian mounds. Initially, it concentrated on archaeology and gathered more than one million artifacts from its excavations. The society's Columbus museum, now called the Ohio Historical Center, and such society-run Indian sites as Serpent Mound and Fort Ancient continue to show the influence of the organization's heritage, but striking diversification has occurred, especially since the 1950s. The society now operates thirty-three museums or sites: such historic houses as the Ulysses S. Grant birthplace in Point Pleasant, the Dayton home of black poet Paul Laurence Dunbar, and Glendower (a site more noteworthy for its Greek revival architecture than its former inhabitants); a living-history museum called Ohio Village; the National Road/Zane Grey Museum; restored Fort Meigs; the Neil Armstrong Air and Space Museum in Wapakoneta; the National Afro-American Museum and Cultural Center in Wilberforce; and a planned industrial and labor museum in Youngstown.[13]

Despite the size, diversity, and lack of definition of the history-museum field, some generalizations are possible. Most history museums are new, especially when compared to other educational institutions like colleges. Even such seemingly well-established and venerable institutions as Plimoth Plantation, Old Salem, and the Museum of the Rockies are forty years old or less. The IMS 1978 survey discovered that 47 percent of history museums had been founded after 1960; only 9 percent could trace their origins to the nineteenth century.[14]

Unsurprisingly, institutions that focus on aspects of local history are generally smaller than those presenting state, regional, or national history. And, as one also might expect, the local-history museums tend to vary in size with the size of their communities. Perhaps less predictably, those in large communities are often older than those in small towns.[15] But unlike art and science museums, where the largest institutions are almost always in the largest cities, the biggest history museums often have nonurban locations. Many major historic houses, such as Monticello and Hearst Castle, are removed from large cities. Outdoor history museums, a category that includes some of the most heavily attended and best-known history museums, require large tracts of land away from urban centers. Colonial Williamsburg's location in a town of ten thousand helps account for its attracting less than half the annual visitation at New York's Metropolitan Museum of Art, Bronx Zoo, or American Museum of Natural History despite comparable promotion efforts and national visibility. But a location away from major population centers ensures that most of Williamsburg's visitors stay longer than city dwellers do at their local art or science museums.

Although there are more history museums than all other kinds of museums combined, history-museum attendance is not quite as large as this figure would indicate. The average history museum is smaller than the average art or science museum; hence, only about one quarter of all museum visits are to history museums. Moreover, a surprisingly small number of the largest American museums are history museums: only 9 percent of those with budgets over $1,000,000 at the time of the 1973 NEA survey. In contrast, two-thirds of the surveyed history museums had budgets under $50,000.[16]

Nevertheless, the IMS survey still counted 86 million annual visitors to history museums. And its category of specialized museums (with 9 million annual visitors) includes institutions that could be called historical (e.g., costume, gun, and transportation museums) and many of its general and park museums have historical presentation as one of their central purposes. Not surprisingly, larger institutions get a disproportionate share of total attendance. The NEA survey showed that just one-fifth of its 683 history museums received more than three-fifths of the visitors.[17] The Henry Ford Museum/Greenfield Village, with 1 million visitors each year, has a larger attendance than either 200 of the smaller local-history museums or a dozen midsized history museums of the size and prominence of the Strong Museum, Strawbery Banke, Historic Deerfield, and the Hagley Museum.

Because the history-museum field is so large and complex, no one has adequately traced its history. Charles B. Hosmer's series on historic preservation and Walter Muir Whitehill's examination of independent historic societies have provided useful material on related subjects, but no general survey of the entire field exists. The available surveys, such as Edward P. Alexander's *Museums in Motion* and Michael Wallace's "Visiting the Past: History Museums in the United States," offer important (albeit not always congruent) frameworks for understanding the history of museums, but many of their generalizations apply only to a limited number of institutions.[18] The complex and diverse universe of history museums cannot be traced back through a direct linear path to a relatively few simple origins.

A full history would instead need to consider a large number of only occasionally related paths to the present. For example, historic houses more than other museums have been strongly influenced by the first two major preservationist efforts: the conservation of the Hasbrouck House (George Washington's headquarters in Newburgh, New York) and the creation of the Mount Vernon Ladies' Association to save the president's home in the 1850s. Later preservationists converted other great men's homes into museums, most often in the quest to memorialize the Revolutionary War era. In the late nineteenth and early twentieth centuries, other criteria for establishing historic-house museums emerged when various groups, most notably the Society for the Preservation of New England Antiquities, began opening houses to the public based not on the fame of their inhabitants but on their antiquity and architectural significance.

The story becomes more complicated as other categories of museums—and other specific institutions—are considered. Such museums as Hartford's Wadsworth Atheneum and the Museum of the City of New York are heavily indebted to the art-museum tradition. Others, such as Richmond's Museum of the Confederacy and the Abigail Adams Smith Museum in New York City, still show the influence of nineteenth-century cabinets of curiosities. For local-history museums, however, different influences have been crucial: the efforts of late nineteenth-century nativists to "protect" their communities against immigrant newcomers; the effects of the New Deal's WPA projects, which encouraged Americans to examine their own communities; the upsurge in popular interest in grass-roots history around the time of the American Revolution bicentennial; and revived scholarly interest in social history in the late 1960s and the 1970s. Local-history museums—indeed, virtually all museums—have also felt the powerful, recent effects of the National Endowment for the Humanities, the funding guidelines of which have strongly encouraged more interpretive exhibits.

The conventional history of outdoor history museums emphasizes Scandinavian antecedents and the giant shadows cast by the dominant early American versions at Colonial Williamsburg and Greenfield Village. Yet the less familiar living-history-farm movement, commercial theme parks, and state and local government tourist-development efforts have had at least as much influence on the large number of outdoor museums established since 1960.

Like outdoor history museums, some American museums have been influenced by trends in vacationing and travel, whereas other institutions seek a purely local audience. Yet whatever the category of museum, some institutions remain unaffected by developments shaping other museums of the same type or even the same locale. A trolley museum, for example, is likely to be untouched by interpretative changes at a neighboring historic house; the staff and governing board may even be uninterested in what is done in other trolley museums.

Because change comes so unevenly to history museums and because so many institutions remain outside the professional mainstream, the exhibit techniques of many different eras coexist. Some history museums are still using methods pioneered by George Brown Goode at the Smithsonian Institution in the 1880s, while others feature futuristic high-tech multimedia exhibitry. Given the breadth and unevenness of the history-museum field, any single evaluative volume, no matter how ambitious, can cover only a portion of the terrain. Nevertheless, the essays cumulatively address a broad range of questions of importance to understanding what museums say about the past, how they say it, and why they say things in the ways they do.

In looking at the historical content and interpretation of museums, our authors are especially concerned with how recent historical scholarship has and has not been translated into museum presentations. This concern reflects, in turn, a particular moment in the history of museums, a moment stretching over the past two decades, in which the so-called new social history has had enormous influence. Yet that influence has not spread evenly over the museum landscape; its effects have varied according to the size, purpose, and focus of differing institutions. The authors represented here generally applaud the appearance of the new social history as a positive force in the life of museums. They note the ways in which it not only has forced the attention of museums on neglected subjects (the lives of women, blacks, workers, and immigrants, for example) but also has led to the reconceptualization and revitalization of traditional museum topics (for instance, the histories of technology, agriculture, and domesticity).

Yet while welcoming the new social history's much-heralded arrival in the museum world, some of our authors caution against an uncritical embrace. Like critics of new-social-history scholarship, they note that close studies of the culture of subordinate groups can neglect the larger (and often oppressive) contexts of economic and political power in which those groups must carve out their lives. Moreover, "history from the bottom up" can wind up producing the same sort of celebratory history found in traditional great-man accounts. To argue that museums need to incorporate better and newer historical scholarship into their exhibits is thus to beg the more difficult questions: Which historical scholarship? Using what analytical framework?

In the rush to bring the latest historical scholarship to the public, museum-based historians also need to pause and ask whether such efforts are invariably worthwhile, whether all historical subjects are equally amenable to museum presentation. Are some topics simply best left to the printed page? In part, the answer to this question hinges on another: Should museum exhibits be driven by artifacts or ideas? Although most would reject this either/or formulation, different authors in this collection (like different practitioners in the field) place unequal priorities on the historical object or the historical concept in organizing exhibits and other public presentations.

It is a mistake, then, to assume that the problems of museums lie solely in knowing what history to present, to assume that the "correct" historical interpretation will make a good museum. Although these essays are more concerned with the *what* of history museums (interpretation) than the *how* (technique), it is impossible to separate content and form. Indeed, form can have a shaping effect on content; the medium can become the message. Because the exhibit is in many ways a more complex mode of communication than the book or article, it is more difficult to control meaning. A single powerful artifact or image, for example, can overwhelm the carefully crafted message spelled out on dozens of labels. Given the enormous perils and possibilities of museum-based presentations of the past, matters of exhibit design and strategy must be part of any serious evaluation of the work of history museums.

Just as form cannot be separated from content, museums cannot be isolated from the complex social, cultural, and historical contexts in which they are situated. Any effort to understand (and possibly change) museum presentations of the past must consider the constraints under which they operate. In other words, an examination of what they display and how they display it must also ask *why* museums tend toward certain representations (and sometimes misrepresentations) of the past.

The authors of the essays in this volume seek to explicate the *why* of history exhibits by considering three sets of constraints that shape museum presentations. The most obvious constraints are institutional and political. Considerations of staffing, financing, and sponsorship affect what museums say in obvious and not-so-obvious ways. For example, the volunteer docents at a historic house may not have the time, interest, or skill to develop a sophisticated historical understanding. They may (consciously or unconsciously) present their own version of the past, one that is at odds with the institution's official message. In addition, museums are leery of material that might offend either major donors or the communities in which they are located. To say that an exhibit idea is not "fundable" may mean that it is not politically acceptable. Such financial and institutional concerns may produce distorted or sanitized versions of the past. Or, more commonly, they result in museums avoiding anything that might provoke controversy.

Museum operating revenues often come from gate receipts as well as from wealthy individuals, large corporations, and government agencies. That means museum audiences also serve as an important constraint on how museums portray the past. Although the boom in tourism in the twentieth century has fueled the explosive growth of museums, it has also restricted the form and content of museum presentations. An exhibit on slave whippings or industrial accidents might be deemed inappropriate because it would shock or disturb museum visitors out to enjoy a breezy summer Sunday.

Yet, as some of our authors make clear, the nature and expectations of museum audiences need not be taken as a given. The composition of museum audiences is itself a political question that museums need to face. Museums that expand their constituency—by attracting more Afro-Americans, blue-collar workers, and recent immigrants, for example—find themselves with new sets of audience expectations. Black visitors are much more likely to want to see depictions of the painful story of slavery, just as blue-collar workers might prove to be more interested in exhibits on the hazards of industrial work. Indeed, a more inclusive vision of the past is often the key to bringing new audiences into the museum in the first place.

At the same time, as some of our authors indicate, the populist goals of an expanded and more inclusive audience can be in tension with the professional goals of a more scholarly and up-to-date historical interpretation.

For understandable reasons, blacks, women, and workers, for example, have wanted their histories publicly affirmed and legitimized. Hence exhibits involving these groups often have employed the same hagiographic and celebratory modes as those presenting the lives of great white men. Is it possible, then, to promote both a history that nonspecialists find inspiring and engaging as well as the agenda of a more professionalized history that harshly judges such presentations, regardless of their appeal? Or, to frame the problem in its broadest terms, for whom are we presenting history? What are the larger goals of public presentations of the past? One irony of the new social history may be that it has helped press forward a professionalization of museums that ultimately makes them more independent of audience. Indeed, one definition of professionalization is that standards are set more by peer review than by clients (audiences). Somewhat uneasily, this book can be said to participate in that process of professionalization.[19]

There is no easy solution to this dilemma of simultaneously listening to a diverse public audience and presenting a sophisticated and critical view of the past. After all, the expectations of museum audiences are shaped not simply by their social composition; visitors bring with them what they have learned from the larger culture about the nature of history. Thus, as these essays suggest, historical museums need to consider their relationship to other purveyors of the past, from television docudramas to commercial theme parks. Indeed, they may need to confront directly the "misinformation" and "misinterpretations" that people receive from these commercial media if they hope to convey their own information and interpretations successfully. At the same time, they need to confront what may be their own misinformation about their audiences, since most discussions of the composition, inclinations, and knowledge of museum audiences have been based more on loose speculations than on systematic investigations. Consequently, museums must build their audiences, not simply by attracting new constituencies, but also by actively engaging those constituencies in the process of rethinking the past and its public presentation.

Museums, then, operate in a social and cultural matrix that includes the bureaucratic politics of individual institutions and the larger politics of private and public financing as well as the nature and expectations of museum audiences. These forces shape and constrain (but do not determine) museum presentations. A final constraining force on history museums is history itself. As many of the following essays make clear, museums can be understood only in relationship to their pasts.

Forms of presentation that originated in particular historical moments carry on into later periods. The exhibit genre, for example, tends to force historical material into certain conventional modes—celebrations of technological progress, nostalgic evocations of a simpler time, lionizations of individual or community achievement—sometimes despite curators' intentions to the contrary. Nonexhibit modes of presentation have their own shaping conventions. New living-history museums, for example, assume they must feature craft demonstrations, since that has always been a dominant feature of their predecessors. Part of the reason the past exerts such a powerful force within museums is, of course, the fact that historical objects are their stock in trade and past collecting practices determine what museums have available to display and interpret. In addition, the objects' mere historicity can make them seem valuable and significant. Indeed, the structures in which museums operate (or the ground on which they are sited) are themselves often historical. In this literal and figurative context, museums find it difficult to overcome the powerful tendency to present themselves, and for audiences to perceive them, as shrines.

In addressing these questions about the what, how, and why of museums —their interpretations, techniques, and contexts—our authors have used as their model, at least in part, the review essay, the essay that broadly considers the state of a particular field and suggests the most important directions for the future. But the review essay is not an easy model for museum reviewers to follow. One problem is temporal. Museum exhibits are intrinsically more ephemeral than books. Exhibit reviews are, perhaps, more comparable to dance or theatre reviews than to book reviews. Yet the evanescent, transient quality of the exhibit heightens the significance of the exhibit review: it documents the exhibit and at the same time critically responds to it.

The second problem is geographic. Book-review essayists can pile the relevant volumes on their desk and then consider the individual works as well as the overall state of a particular field. Such a sedentary approach obviously will not work for the author of the museum-review essay. Such reviewers must get out of their offices and into the field, a process that involves huge expenditures of time and money and limits the degree of comprehensiveness of any resulting essay—a problem compounded by the absence of previous critical works. As a result, the essays in this book consider only a small percentage of the history museums in the United States. But since they tend to focus on the largest, most influential, and best-attended museums, they discuss a much larger percentage of those museums and exhibits that have influenced both the public and museum practices.

The essays in Part One explore some of the basic types of history museums and museum presentations. In the first, Gary Kulik examines the most prevalent form of museum presentation, the gallery exhibition. By explicating four critical moments in the evolution of the history exhibit, he explains not only the evolution of current museum practices but also the past's powerful legacy in the museum present. He notes signs of progress, such as the rise of the interpretive social-history exhibit and more willingness to incorporate conflict and tragedy into exhibits. But he also cites persistent problems: the failure to "blend objects and ideas into a well-designed whole" and the continuing tendency to treat museums as "places of celebration, even veneration."

Michael Frisch follows Kulik with a look at a particular setting for gallery exhibitions: the big-city museum. By investigating these institutions' formal versions of their cities' history, Frisch similarly identifies an inclination toward boosterism and celebration that is common to most local-history museums. But he argues that the conventional urban-biographical narrative can be a "real resource" for sophisticated and appealing presentations if it is infused with the new social history's "concrete insights and vivid details about the lives of identifiable common people" and makes effective use of "that most fundamental and venerable of museum functions—the collection and the display of meaningful artifacts." At the same time, Frisch points out, even the best combination of narrative, scholarship, and artifacts will fail unless museums "respect the audience's own experience" as "a force supporting and propelling complex interpretation."

The other five articles in Part One concentrate on history-museum presentations outside the gallery. Warren Leon and Margaret Piatt highlight the agrarian, middle-class, Protestant bias of living-history museums, which use costumed staff members to enact historical activities in restored or re-created settings. While noting the constraints under which such institutions operate (for example, the difficulty of finding and training a skilled staff and the reliance on revenue from admission fees provided by tourists seeking entertainment rather than education), they also point up the advantages that living history has over other museum forms.

John A. Herbst looks at what is generally one of the smallest museum settings, the historic house. Often through volunteer efforts in hundreds of communities across the country, Americans have preserved notable homes as museums. Herbst shows how such institutions can and should be reinterpreted to bring their public presentations in line with current scholarship.

Although some of the museums David Lowenthal discusses are historic houses or use living history, he is not concerned with either of these conventional categories. Instead, he shows the utility of analyzing as a group those museums that share "a unique set of ideas and values" centering on the concept of the "pioneer." In so doing, he emphasizes the particular importance of examining museums in relation to their audiences and their histories. Pioneer museums, he notes, "owe meaning and appeal to that moment when the living memories they portray are just passing away."

Two concluding essays in the first section of the book are case studies. By focusing on the complex history of the Gettysburg battlefield, John S. Patterson shows the many factors that can shape the appearance and public perception of a historic site. Through his historical analysis, we see, for example, how the federal takeover of the site in 1895 shifted its interpretation from a celebration of Northern bravery and triumph to a statement that the "war is over" and that it was time to celebrate *American* valor on the battlefield.

Whereas Patterson examines one of the nation's oldest historical tourist sites, Michael Wallace considers one of the newest: EPCOT Center at Disney World. He traces the evolution of "Mickey Mouse History" from the simple optimism of Disneyland (which retrospectively tidied up the past) to the more inclusive but still highly selective historical vision of EPCOT Center. However skewed the message, Wallace argues, the technological glitz of Disney World exerts a powerful influence on the way millions of Americans perceive not just the past but also museums themselves.

The five essays in Part Two of the book consider how museums have presented categories of historical scholarship, especially those shaped by the new social history. Some of the most creative and vibrant social-history research has been directed towards illuminating the history of women and identifying gender as a decisive historical category. By looking closely at recent women's-history exhibits, Barbara Melosh shows that although museums have seldom been innovators in women's-history scholarship, they have not been passive borrowers. She finds that "exhibits both facilitate and contain the reconsideration of women's lives that feminists demand" and suggests ways for museums to overcome the sometimes stifling conventions of the exhibit genre, the limitations of "museum speak," and the dearth of surviving material evidence.

Museums that present Afro-American history, James Oliver Horton and Spencer R. Crew note, also face the problem of limited artifactual evidence. But their broad-based examination of that topic, rooted in a historical narrative, a survey of the entire current field, and visits to representative sites, argues that the crucial constraint on adequate presentations of black history is institutional. For example, those museums that have recruited black staff members have been most successful at making Afro-American history central to their exhibit programs.

At the same time that the new social history has broadened the scope of historical inquiry, new interdisciplinary approaches, new questions, and new research techniques have transformed more traditional fields of scholarship —economic history and the history of technology, for example—and these changes have had a significant but uneven effect on history museums. In assessing museum presentations of the history of technology, Joseph J. Corn dissects the strengths and weaknesses of the four primary ways that technological artifacts have been displayed to the public: the internalist, the celebratory, the social historical, and the cultural historical. Although he gives the highest marks to those modes of presentation that interpret and analyze rather than merely display the artifact, he also cautions against producing exhibits that ignore the fundamental artifactual basis of museums. "If artifacts cannot help tell the story," Corn asks, "why do an exhibit?" In addition, he points up some general problems (the difficulty of displaying very large artifacts and black-box technologies, for example) that confront most historical museums of technology regardless of their interpretive framework.

Whereas Corn ranges across the museum landscape, Mary H. Blewett focuses her inquiry on a more limited geographical area. By examining museums that interpret a central strand in the history of industrialization, the rise and fall of the New England textile industry, she shows the reshaping potential of recent scholarship. But despite her admiration for these museums' depiction of the details of industrial transformation, Blewett challenges them to undertake an even more difficult task: retaining dense (and intrinsically local) social history while simultaneously eschewing local boosterism; connecting the local experience to regional, national, and international developments as well as to the rise of capitalism generally; and linking past experience to present dilemmas.

The past two decades of scholarly ferment have caused historians to search for new primary sources to study. The academic discovery of material culture has been especially important in bringing academic historians and museum professionals together. In our concluding article, Thomas J. Schlereth explores the ways museums have collected, described, and preserved material culture for scholarly use and public display. He proposes some new directions for museums that would build on recent material culture scholarship.

In evaluating and explaining history museums, the authors of the twelve chapters in this book use a variety of methods. Two (by John S. Patterson and Michael Wallace) present extended and historically grounded case studies of a single institution. Most of the others take readers through a series of briefer case studies but select their examples in different ways. Joseph J. Corn, for example, chooses one or two representatives of each major approach to the history of technology. By contrast, Mary H. Blewett picks one aspect of the vast subject of industrialization and then examines all the major institutions that interpret that topic. James Oliver Horton and Spencer R. Crew use a questionnaire to analyze their subject quantitatively, and Thomas J. Schlereth relies on secondary literature as well as many site visits to survey his topic broadly. Given their backgrounds as historians, it is not surprising that many of the authors find historical analysis to be an especially useful tool in evaluating and understanding museums. They show that one cannot fully understand current practices without uncovering their origins.

Of course, these different approaches are not mutually exclusive, and a number of the authors combine several of them. Collectively, they offer a variety of models for others to follow or modify. Far from establishing some new orthodoxy, either in terms of research methods or conclusions, it is our hope that this volume will open debate on a wide range of questions. Just as we have critically assessed history museums in the United States, so do we urge our readers to scrutinize the utility of our methods and the validity of our conclusions.

NOTES

1. See Peter Marzio, ed., *A Nation of Nations: The People Who Came to America as Seen Through Objects and Documents Exhibited at the Smithsonian Institution* (New York: Harper & Row, 1976).

2. In one very recent exception, Michael J. Ettema discusses "A Nation of Nations" as an example of a thoughtful, analytical exhibit that has had only mixed success in conveying its concepts to visitors. "History Museums and the Culture of Materialism," in *Past Meets Present: Essays About Historic Interpretation and Public Audiences*, ed. by Jo Blatti (Washington: Smithsonian Institution Press, 1987), 77–83.

3. See, for example, Colin Greer, "Remembering Class: An Interpretation" in *Divided Society: The Ethnic Experience in America*, ed. by Colin Greer (New York: Basic Books, 1974), 1–35; Rudolf J. Vecoli, "Contadini in Chicago: A Critique of *The Uprooted*," *Journal of American History* 51 (December 1964), 404–17. There is even a study guide to *The Uprooted* directed at students: Frederic Jaher, *Oscar Handlin's The Uprooted: A Critical Commentary* (New York: American R.D.M. Corp., 1966). Three decades after its publication, *The Uprooted* is still regularly cited by scholars, based on a check of the *Humanities Citation Index*.

4. It is impossible to calculate precisely how many reviews specialized monographs receive, since there is no comprehensive index to scholarly book reviews. Ten is probably a low estimate.

5. In noting the lack of attention paid to such sites, we are obviously excluding the large number of travel articles, which are almost always celebratory in tone.

6. The Institute for Museum Studies estimated eighty-six million annual visitors to history museums in 1978. Given continued increases in attendance over the past decade and our broader definition of museums, one hundred million seems like a reasonable guess. Lewis C. Price, Lisa DiRocco, and Janice D. Lewis, *Museum Program Survey, 1979* (Washington: National Center for Educational Statistics, 1981), 64.

7. *Technology and Culture* announced its policy of reviewing exhibits with Thomas W. Leavitt's "Toward a Standard of Excellence: The Nature and Purpose of Exhibit Reviews," *Technology and Culture* 9 (January 1968), 70–75. *Winterthur Portfolio* has now begun regular reviews. Exhibit reviews have also appeared recently in the *Oral History Review* (see, for example, vol. 14, 1986) and *International Labor and Working-Class History* (see, for example, no. 33, Spring 1988). For other recent calls for regular exhibit reviews, see Barbara Melosh, "Museum Exhibits: Breaking the Silence," *Organization of American Historians Newsletter* 13 (May 1985), 23–24; Thomas J. Schlereth, "The History Behind, Within, and Outside the History Museum," *Curator* 23 (December 1980), 257–60; Jo Blatti, "Past Meets Present: Field Notes on Historical Sites, Programs, Professionalism, and Visitors," in *Past Meets Present*, 10–13.

8. On the "Common Agenda," see Lonn W. Taylor, ed., *A Common Agenda for*

History Museums: Conference Proceedings, February 19–20, 1987 (Nashville, Tenn.: American Association for State and Local History, 1987).

9. *Daedalus* 100 (Winter 1971); (Ithaca, N.Y.: Cornell University Press, 1980). See also John Higham, *History: Professional Scholarship in America* (New York, 1965).

10. Thomas Angotti discusses the blurring of the line between museums and "amusement-park replicas, recreational villages and ad hoc tourist traps" in "Planning the Open-Air Museum and Teaching Urban History: The United States in World Context," *Museum* 34 (1982), 179–88.

11. National Endowment for the Arts, *Museums USA* (Washington: National Endowment for the Arts 1974); National Research Center of the Arts, *Museums USA: A Survey Report* (Washington: National Research Center of the Arts, 1975).

12. Price, *Museum*, 3–9. The report, which was carried out by the National Center for Educational Statistics for IMS, estimates there are 156 for-profit museums in the United States, but it did not include these in the survey. The findings are summarized in Lee Kimche, "American Museums: The Vital Statistics," *Museum News* (October 1980), 52–57.

13. Walter Muir Whitehill, *Independent Historical Societies: An Enquiry into Their Research and Publication Functions and their Financial Future* (Boston, 1962), 282–88; Ohio Historical Society, *Annual Report, 1986*.

14. Kimche, "American Museums," 54. Using a slightly different set of criteria, the American Association of State and Local History survey *A Culture at Risk: Who Cares for America's Heritage* (Nashville, Tenn.: American Association for State and Local History, 1984) concluded that more than half of the nation's state and local historical organizations had been founded since 1960, while close to 30 percent were less than thirteen years old (p. 27).

15. *A Culture at Risk*, 29, 38.

16. *Museums USA: A Survey Report*, xi. See also Price, *Museum*, 9, 29.

17. Price, *Museum*, 64, Appendix A; *Museums USA: A Survey Report*, 130–31.

18. Charles B. Hosmer, Jr., *The Presence of the Past: A History of the Preservation Movement in the United States Before Williamsburg* (New York, 1965); *Preservation Comes of Age: From Williamsburg to the National Trust, 1926–1949* (Charlottesville: University of Virginia Press, 1981); Whitehill, *Independent Historical Societies*; Alexander, *Museums in Motion: An Introduction to the History and Functions of Museums* (Nashville, Tenn.: American Association for State and Local History, 1979); Wallace, "Visiting the Past: History Museums in the United States" in *Presenting the Past: Essays on History and the Public*, ed. by Susan Porter Benson, Stephen Brier, and Roy Rosenzweig (Philadelphia: Temple University Press, 1986), 137–61.

19. Our thanks to Barbara Melosh for her help in formulating the problem discussed in this paragraph.

Part One

The Museum and Historic Site
in Context

Charles Willson Peale, *The Artist in His Museum,* oil on canvas, 1822. (Pennsylvania Academy of the Fine Arts, Philadelphia. Gift of Mrs. Sarah Harrison. The Joseph Harrison, Jr., Collection.)

Designing the Past: History-Museum Exhibitions from Peale to the Present

1

Gary Kulik

Peale's Museum

In 1822, Charles Willson Peale painted a self-portrait. He captured himself lifting a theatrical crimson curtain to reveal the Long Room of the Philadelphia Museum—his museum. On the two visible walls stood cases of stuffed birds, stacked four high, surmounted by a double row of portraits of Revolutionary heroes and statesmen. Barely visible behind the curtain stood the museum's principal object, the skeleton of a large mastodon exhumed in 1801. In the foreground was the museum's first object, an Allegheny River paddlefish, along with a stuffed turkey from the Long Expedition, a taxidermy kit, a painter's palette, and several large mastodon bones. In the far background, sharply reduced in scale, Peale painted his audience; a contemplative man musing over birds, a father instructing his child, a well-dressed woman with her arms raised in astonishment as her eyes met the mastodon. Peale had captured the order, diversity, and pedagogical intent of America's first serious museum.[1]

Peale faced three questions that all subsequent history museums would face: what to collect, how to display it, and how to teach. The answers he arrived at were a product of his own time and place, as would be the answers of those who came after him. This is an essay about those answers. It presents case studies of four influential museums: Peale's, George Brown Goode's late-nineteenth-century Smithsonian Institution, the American Wing of the Metropolitan Museum of Art of 1924, and the New York State Historical Association at Cooperstown from the 1920s through the 1950s. Each of these institutions was a leader in its time. Each addressed the questions of display, taxonomy, and educational intent differently. The first two were natural-history museums with ambitions to represent all human knowledge, including history. Both elaborated an approach to history exhibitions that had an impact well into this century. The last two were more specialized, one being an art museum and the other a history museum. Each developed a distinctive aesthetic of exhibition and a distinctive collections policy. The overall path we will follow is one that will take us from the collecting of the associational and the exemplary to the collecting of the commonplace; from taxonomic exhibitions to thematic ones, from museums run by natural scientists to museums run by historians. The essay concludes with a discussion that brings us to the present, but we begin with Peale.

Peale was deeply committed to popular education. A portrait painter and former saddlemaker, he was closely tied to Philadelphia's radical artisan culture with its strong emphasis on self-education. He intended his museum to serve democratic purposes. It was to be a "school of useful knowledge," with lectures and publications accompanying his exhibitions. Peale supported, for example, the magnificent nine-volume study of American birds by Alexander Wilson, the Scottish weaver-poet who had been imprisoned in Scotland for his labor-protest poems. The purpose of Peale's museum was to diffuse knowledge of the natural world and to serve the public as a center of "rational amusement." It was to be a "Great School of Nature." [2]

Inspired by a deistic sense of nature's order, Peale sought to display the wonderful work of divine creation. He wanted to provide a visual experience that would bring his visitors "nearer to the Great-First-Cause." To that end, he collected the odd and the curious—a cow of five legs, six feet, and two tails; a petrified nest; a devilfish—but less as an end in itself than as testament to the Creator's awesome capacity for order amidst diversity. Peale was aware that such items would attract the paying public, no small benefit given his consistent failures to attract state support. But his focus was always on Linnaean order, and his collection policy, his educational intent, and his exhibitions reflected that order.[3]

Consider again Peale's self-portrait. The Long Room was a precise statement of classical order. Its pristine white wall cases contained row on row of birds, each labeled as to genus and species. In the top row were the predators, in the middle the songbirds, and nearest the floor ducks, pelicans, and the earthbound penguins. In an earlier watercolor done by his son Titian Ramsey Peale as a background study for the self-portrait, these cases faced a series of free-standing white cabinets containing minerals, insects, and fossils. Perched atop the cabinets was a series of busts of scientists by William Rush, along with Houdon's *Washington*. They stared directly across to the portraits of Revolutionary heroes that hung in a double row just below the ceiling. The first historical objects in Peale's museum, the busts and the paintings occupied places of honor and were intended to evoke reverence. Placed as they were at the highest point of the room, they also evoked an Enlightenment version of the "great chain of being," with statesmen and scientists presiding over the natural order of a new age.[4]

Peale was an innovator in exhibit design. Instead of displaying his birds in front of a white background, as was common in Europe, he used painted backgrounds to suggest naturalistic settings. He also placed birds on tree branches and small mammals on little landscaped hills. He arranged his ducks "in Various attitudes on Artificial ponds[,] some Birds and Beasts on trees and some Birds suspended as flying." His were among the first contextual natural-history displays, precursors of the dioramas that would become popular later in the century. He also experimented with the use of waxwork manikins arranged in tableaux, with trompe l'oeil paintings to arouse visitors' interest, and with what we would now regard as interactive exhibit devices: a speaking tube (in a mounted lion's head) that ran between rooms and allowed visitors to talk back and forth. For a time, he employed "Moving Pictures" (or "Perspective Views with Changeable Effects"), experiments in light, sound, and clockwork motion, offering his visitors views of nature, technology, naval battle, and scenes from Milton's *Paradise Lost*.[5]

Peale's concern for effective and entertaining presentation was both principled and economically necessary. The museum supported itself through paid admissions. A silhouette maker, "Magic Mirrors," and evening entertainments were all designed to draw the crowds necessary to support the museum. With Peale's retirement in 1811, his sons focused even more sharply on entertainment. Tattooed human heads, "anatomical preparations," freaks of nature which Peale had collected but not displayed came out of storage. Monkeys done up as blacksmiths, carpenters, coopers, and shoemakers parodied artisan culture.[6]

The Peale family's final failure to attract public funds sealed the museum's fate. In 1821 it was incorporated as a joint-stock company. After Peale's death in 1827, the stockholders became insistent about turning a profit. The museum turned to live-animal shows, to Siamese twins, to the "Virginia Dwarfs," to the "Big Children" (two large and unfortunate girls from Poughkeepsie), to the "Belgian giant" and the "Automaton Musical Lady." Peale's educational vision was lost. His effort to create a museum that was both serious and popular had foundered. By 1850 the building and collections had become the property of Moses Kimball and P. T. Barnum.[7]

Barnum and Kimball brought a new meaning to the word *museum*. Entrepreneurs of the bizarre, they tapped the voyeurism of the American people. Moving far beyond the Peales, they blurred the boundaries between museums and carnival sideshows, between the theatre and the circus, between the real and the contrived. Museums of the odd, the curious, and the fake proliferated in antebellum America, in Boston, Albany, New York City, and Cincinnati, museums that sacrificed everything to effect, to titillation, to entertainment. Even before Barnum's purchase of Peale's collection, such museums exerted an appreciable pressure on Peale and his sons that in some part accounts for the drift of the Philadelphia Museum in the years after 1810.[8]

It was Peale's genius to imagine a world in which scholarship and entertainment were compatible, in which museums were the great instruments of democratic education, in which the apparent disorder of the world revealed itself in Linnaean order. It was a worthy vision but flawed even in its own terms. Peale's pedagogy and taxonomy were better suited to birds and mastodons than to history and human culture. Peale's effort to order the human past denied the bloodshed of the Revolution and the political disorder of its aftermath. It was the latter, the personal and ideological disputes, that marked Philadelphia's post-Revolutionary politics, that had driven him away from politics and toward his museum in the first place. His gallery of heroes made the Revolution tamer, more respectable, and more orderly than it ever could have been. He never succeeded at integrating historical artifacts into his museum. His collecting in these areas never rose above the purely associational and the patriotic, and Federalists would claim his was a peculiarly Jeffersonian patriotism. His educational endeavors were only rarely designed to shed light on the human past. The phrase *cabinets of curiosity* has come to define early American museums as collections of random and unconnected objects. As a characterization of Peale's efforts, it is inaccurate and misleading, but it comes closest to describing Peale's history collections.[9]

Yet in the end, Peale deserves credit for articulating a vision bolder and more encompassing than those of any of his peers. His was the first great museum in the age of democracy, the first to combine scientific system with a broad educational intent. With his failure, the museum movement bifurcated. Scholarship became divorced from public education, not absolutely, but far more sharply than it had been in Peale's day. For a generation, popular education became the preserve of the Barnums and the Kimballs. The first great historical societies, the American Antiquarian Society (1812), the New-York Historical Society (1804), and the Massachusetts Historical Society (1791) among them, had little interest in the kind of public education that Peale had fostered. Retreating from anything that smacked of entertainment, some societies even retreated from public exhibitions and the collection of antiquities other than books and paintings. That had not always been the case. The American Philosophical Society, for example, had once had an active object-collecting program, but by the middle years of the century the focus had shifted to books and manuscripts.[10]

Listen to Christopher Columbus Baldwin, librarian of the American Antiquarian, express his disdain for the kinds of collections that Peale cherished. His comments followed a visit to the New-York Historical Society in 1833.

There were very few objects of curiosity or antiquity in the collections. This is correct taste. A library should contain nothing but books, coins, statuary and pictures. . . . how absurd to pile up old bureaus and chests, and stuff them with old coats and hats and high-heeled shoes. The true history of all these things are handed down by painting. And besides, if they are once received there will be attempts to fool somebody with the 'Shield of Achilles.'[11]

To avoid the risk of fakery and the taint of Barnum, Baldwin narrowed his collecting vision. He and his peers would quietly build their library collections and stuffily protect them from the public. As late as 1900, no less a Brahmin than Samuel Eliot Morison, then a Harvard graduate student, was denied permission to use the card catalogue at the Massachusetts Historical Society.[12]

George Brown Goode's Smithsonian Institution

Peale's vision of a museum of universal history of wide popular appeal, combining history, art, and the natural sciences, was revived in the late nineteenth century. The new visionary was George Brown Goode, son of an Indiana merchant and natural scientist trained at Harvard by Louis Agassiz. Goode worked briefly as the curator of Orange Judd Hall of Natural Science at Wesleyan University in Middletown, Connecticut, before coming to the Smithsonian Institution in Washington. He organized the Smithsonian's exhibits at the Philadelphia Centennial in 1876 and three years later assumed full charge of the U.S. National Museum.[13]

By the 1880s the U.S. National Museum had emerged as a major component of the Smithsonian. It had its own new building, and its collections had expanded enormously. More than forty freight cars of items had arrived from the centennial to add to the miscellaneous collections that had been accumulating slowly since the 1840s. The new Arts and Industries Building was a major presence in Washington, a clear expression of the Smithsonian's commitment to public education.[14]

That commitment had not always been so clear. James Smithson's half-million-dollar bequest to the United States had been a political football ever since the money arrived in 1835. It had been Smithson's wish "to found at Washington, under the name of the Smithsonian Institution, an establishment for the increase and diffusion of knowledge among men." At various times during the next decade, Congress debated proposals to use the money for a national university, a museum of natural history, an observatory, a library, and a school to train teachers of science. The Smithsonian's first secretary, Joseph Henry, had waged a long political struggle to maintain the bulk of the Smithson endowment for scientific research, for the increase of knowledge. His efforts clearly paralleled those of Baldwin and others who preferred pure research to public education. It was not that Henry opposed museums, but that he cared about research more and was determined that Congress should foot the bill for the additional costs associated with collections and display. Congress did so, appropriating $250,000 for the new building in 1879.[15]

Goode brought to his new task the classificatory habits of the natural scientist. At Philadelphia he had devised his own classification for cultural and historical objects, based loosely on Linnaean order. The tools of the hunt, for example, fell under ten headings and fifty subheadings. In Washington he refined his system. Every object could find its home in one of eight major divisions and sixty-four subsections. His desire for system and for taxonomic schema took him beyond Peale and well beyond the cabinet of curiosities. The authority of the natural sciences would put history in its place.[16]

Goode, asserted one of his memorialists, was an "apostle of scientific knowledge." He had come to intellectual maturity in the great age of evolutionary positivism. Like others of his generation, he believed that science was the motor of history and scientific method the key to truth. History was progressive, its advance was incremental, if inexorable, and it moved in stages from the primitive to the civilized. The growth of knowledge was the key to progress. Museums, as places of research and education, had a key role to play. Goode's mission was nothing less than the creation of "an illustrated encyclopedia of civilization." [17]

In pursuing that goal, Goode developed a new taxonomy and new principles of history collecting. He collected portraits and busts and personal items of America's heroes, but he was as interested in acquiring objects that signified "permanent land-marks of the progress of the world." And so Tiffany lamps, the Slater spinning and carding machines, and the John Bull locomotive would find their places along side Washington's tea service. Goode was intent on developing a "museum of record," combining the type specimens of the natural sciences with objects of cultural and industrial achievement. The latter too became specimens, a term that lingers to the present in some history museums, evoking the ghosts of white-coated scientists presiding over the exemplary relics of American civilization.[18]

In addition to the exemplary, Goode encouraged the collecting of the ordinary and the commonplace. Taking his cues from the extraordinary revival of interest in the colonial past that was taking place around him and from the development of museums in Europe, with their interest in the "folk," Goode carefully articulated new collecting principles. He played a key role in bringing the Copp family collection, a rich trove of housewares, clothing, and textiles from a middling Connecticut family, to the Smithsonian. There was nothing populist about any of this. Goode was a genealogical activist, an officer in several national ancestral societies, and the author of his own genealogy. He was proud of his English ancestry and prouder yet of the Aryan race, "the most illustrious in the world." His were the purest of Anglo-Saxon genes. No more than 10 percent of the marriages in his line, he reported, had been with people whose paternal ancestors had arrived in America later than 1725. Goode collected the "humble and simple objects" of the American past as an act of filiopietism. Substantial attention had been lavished on American Indian collections, Goode asserted, when "much that is of equal or greater importance belonging to our own ancestors has been allowed to go to destruction." [19]

The Smithsonian's history exhibits, however, were expressions of a collecting policy based not on the commonplace but on both the exemplary and the associational. Goode must share credit with A. Howard Clark, the National Museum's history curator, a Wesleyan University graduate and *Mayflower* descendent. Clark was committed to the preservation and display of "relics of important national events or of persons prominent in the history of our country." A plaster cast of the Statue of Freedom, more than nineteen feet high, presided over the museum's history hall. This dramatic icon of patriotism looked out over cases full of ship models (the *Sally Constant* and *Mayflower* among them), Revolutionary War relics, and autographed papers and personal items of Washington, Jefferson, Adams, Grant, and other presidents, soldiers, and statesmen. Other cases contained coins and paper money, maps, commissions bearing presidential signatures, and military orders and decorations. Visitors could gaze at the pocketknife of Daniel Boone, the hair of fourteen presidents, "from Washington to Pierce, inclusive," and a variety of cannonballs, bayonets, and presentation sabers. The emphasis was on great men and patriotic acts. Like Peale's gallery of Revolutionary heroes, Goode's history museum was a shrine.[20]

The Smithsonian's display of natural history and anthropology reinforced the meaning. Its overriding message was progressive and evolutionary. All life proceeded, as the exhibition handbook asserted, in a "steady progression . . . from the simple to the complex." The inorganic world, the world of rocks and minerals and the uses to which they were put—mines, quarries, and smelters —constituted one section. The organic world of plants and animals, arranged to reinforce the central message, constituted another. Humanity emerged front and center in the third section. Here Goode presented the primitive and the exotic, from Neanderthal skulls to the Catlin portraits of American Indians, from Japanese porcelains to a model of the Zuni pueblo. This exercise in evolutionary anthropology merged into a substantial section on comparative technology. The focus here was on fisheries, medicine, transportation, food, and architecture. All objects of like function—all weapons, all tools, all boats —were grouped together. The exhibits thus opened with the "simplest type" and closed with "the most perfect and elaborate object of the same class." The message could not be clearer. In Goode's time, the museum had become a temple to secular progress, an affirmation of the happy confluence of moral and material well-being.[21]

Goode cared about public education. He sought to bring to museum exhibitions a new clarity of purpose. Mere curios had no place. System was everything, for Goode's museum was designed to express the systemic linkages among otherwise disparate phenomena. Labels would be clear; connections between exhibit elements would be apparent. Exhibit cases would be flexible, capable of being moved to articulate more than one theme. Such was Goode's intention.[22]

Reality never matched intention. Goode's exhibitions were dense, cluttered affairs, in keeping with the dominant aesthetic of high Victorianism. Row on row of "glass-covered boxes of uniform size" greeted the public, arranged, as space permitted, to express Goode's complex schema. His labels were principally of interest to scholars and specialists. The array of educational techniques that Peale developed and employed lay unused. Even as other museums were beginning to experiment with contextual displays, dioramas, and period rooms, Goode stuck resolutely with the taxonomic exhibit. A limited number of "environmental groups" featuring the use of manikins in native dress occupied space in the natural-history and anthropology halls, though not in history. Goode was wary that too many such displays would detract from that "dignified and systematic order, which should be characteristic of every museum." The specter of Barnum lingered.[23]

The taxonomic exhibit expressed the intellectual preeminence of the natural sciences at the end of the century. It was a form poorly suited to explicating history, and Goode never succeeded in subsuming history under the natural sciences. The history hall of the Smithsonian remained a reliquary, a hall of disconnected personal items and stray oddments where the Washington relics coexisted beside a section of oak tree shot down at the Battle of Spotsylvania. Goode's positivist and evolutionary schema worked best for the technology hall, where it was capable of order and precision. The contrast between the history and technology halls was striking. Goode's separation of these realms would have long-term consequences for the Smithsonian, the first history museum of which, opened in 1965, expressed the separation in its name: Museum of History and Technology. In Goode's Smithsonian, history had become a residual category, the repository for collections that did not fit the elaborate natural-science model that Goode championed.[24]

Ironically, all this happened precisely at the moment that a distinct history profession emerged in America. Despite the close formal ties between the Smithsonian and the new American Historical Association (1884), trained historians had little influence on Goode's collecting and exhibition philosophy. There were points of agreement. Like Goode, many of the first recipients of history Ph.D.'s were committed Anglo-Saxonists. The history they wrote, with its stress on statesmen, generals, and politicans, paralleled the Smithsonian's fascination with the personalia of the rich and famous. Fur-

History of the United States Hall with the Statue of Freedom in the background, Arts and Industries Building, Smithsonian Institution. (Smithsonian Institution)

ther, many historians thought of themselves as scientists, and their focus on institutional development echoed the naturalists' interest in the evolution and development of species. But the first professional historians had no interest in things. They were preoccupied with words—constitutions, charters, treaties —and they defined their subject in ways that precluded the study of ordinary people. In collecting technology, consumer goods, and the commonplace, Goode placed the Smithsonian several generations ahead of the historians of the academy. But neither he nor anyone else had any way of articulating such leadership. In a meandering speech to the American Historical Association, Goode frankly admitted there was no connection between the research interests of the Smithsonian and those of academic historians. Unlike the expansive intellectual role the Smithsonian played in the development of both the natural sciences and anthropology, its role in history was limited and insignificant. It would not hire its first history Ph.D. until after World War II.[25]

Goode had elaborated the form Peale first developed in America. In his ambition to subsume the artifacts of history, technology, and anthropology under the rubric of the natural sciences, Goode went much further than Peale. In attempting to rescue the museum exhibition from Barnumesque frivolity, Goode sought to combine sound scholarship with the goals of public education. Under the thrall of the natural sciences, Goode had brought the museum exhibition to its highest stage of development. Though he was far less imaginative and less effective in presentation than Peale, there was no mistaking Goode's meaning. The Smithsonian's exhibitions confirmed the pieties of the age. In an age of cultural imperialism and mass production, the Smithsonian gloried in its objects. The cluttered nature of its displays, not unlike the Victorian parlor, became a measure of its moral worth. Its appropriation of the exotic and the primitive was baldly culminated by its insistent nationalism. In less-skilled hands and in spaces less grand than the Arts and Industries Building, Goode's techniques would produce the dull, dark, and lifeless museum of early-twentieth-century popular imagination: mausoleums of the old explicated in the arcane language of their increasingly professional staffs.

R. T. H. Halsey's American Wing

Goode failed to explore the possibilities of the only nineteenth-century innovation in exhibit design, the period room. With its origins in the Sanitary Fairs of the Civil War and in the New England kitchen of the Philadelphia Centennial, the period room found its first museum expressions in Oakland, California, and Salem, Massachusetts. During the course of the twentieth century, it would become one of the principal elements in the vocabulary of history exhibits. At its best it was a device designed to establish context, to put back together the chairs, the tables, the china that collectors had once separated.

The period room offered a brief glimpse of everyday life in the American past, and millions of Americans would experience the past by peering through glass barriers or leaning over velvet ropes.[26]

Period rooms became popular at a time when significant numbers of "old stock" Americans turned to the past for solace and inspiration. In retreat from cities crowded by immigrants, from the "smoky modernism" that afflicted Henry James, these Americans sought in the past the sense of rootedness they could not obtain in the present. Images of hearth and home, of a simpler and nobler past, proliferated. Local history blossomed, preservationists asserted an ethic at odds with the aggressive commercialism of the day, and historic houses began to assert themselves on the American landscape.[27]

The period room may have brought a new form to the history exhibit, but its uses reinforced the filiopietism of the day. Most of the early collectors, Cummings Davis of Concord the most prominent, were driven to save and display the ancestral possessions of local worthies. Some room assemblers made no pretense to serious scholarship. They sought instead to create an aura of charm and romance, a snug haven from the forces of modernism that lurked outside. Even those rooms based on the best contemporary scholarship —George Francis Dow's efforts at Salem, for example—were overfurnished; they were grander and more elegant than the rooms of common folk had ever been.[28]

The rooms appealed to and reinforced the new aesthetic of simplicity that was only then gaining popularity. In conscious revolt from Victorian convention, from overstuffed parlors, heavily draped windows, and the bizarre excesses of Victorian furnishings, a new generation of artists turned to the colonial and preindustrial past for inspiration. They would come to value Windsor chairs, blue and white porcelain, and claw-footed breakfronts for reasons different from those of previous collectors. Their aesthetic values would have a powerful effect on twentieth-century history museums. Under the sway of art, the period room would reach an extraordinary stage of refinement and popularity.[29]

A key moment was the opening in 1924 of the American Wing at New York's Metropolitan Museum of Art. Its curator, R. T. H. Halsey, a wealthy stockbroker, could trace his American lineage to the 1630s. Its benefactors were Robert W. de Forest and his wife, Emily Johnston de Forest. She was a collector of early Americana; he was an affluent lawyer and had been the Metropolitan's president since 1914. Its facade was that of the United States Branch Bank, built on Wall Street between 1822 and 1824. Within, like so much bullion, lay three stories of period rooms and associated displays: a seventeenth-century parlor from Ipswich, Massachusetts; the elegant chamber of Samuel Wentworth of Portsmouth, New Hampshire; the Assembly Room from Gadsby's Tavern in Alexandria, Virginia; the entry hall from the

The Baltimore dining room, exhibited in the American Wing, Metropolitan Museum of Art, 1924. (The Metropolitan Museum of Art)

Van Rensselaer manor house of Albany; an Adams-style dining room from Baltimore. The sixteen rooms provided stage sets for the best of high-style furnishings—Revere silver, Steigel and Amelung glass, Phyfe chairs, and Philadelphia highboys—and established the canon for early American taste and elegance. The American Wing drew upon several European precedents, notably the Swiss National Museum (1893–1898) in Zurich. The latter displayed period rooms along with a series of architecturally harmonious galleries containing objects also grouped by period. Its purpose was to explicate and reinforce a nationalist vision of craft design. In philosophy and technique, the American Wing followed the Swiss example. No other American museum had ever used period rooms in this way. The museum visitor was led from the seventeenth century to the early nineteenth, following a path that traced the history of design and good taste. Glass vitrines contained what the rooms could not: "a comprehensive collection of American decorative arts . . . displayed against appropriate backgrounds and in systematic groupings." Halsey clearly differentiated his work from that of history museums. He sought to display only those "things which have class." "The furnishings should be restrained and no semblance of crowding permitted," he wrote. "[T]he exhibition of the quaint and the curious should be left to our historical museums." [30]

The American Wing promoted new standards of display. The period room became an art object in its own right. The blend of colors, the arrangement of furniture, the display of rugs and draperies revealed Halsey's taste as much as his research. This is not to argue that the rooms were inauthentic in any gross sense, but in the absence of countervailing evidence Halsey and his many successors were free to indulge their own taste, and indulge it they did. These early period rooms were almost always overfurnished by colonial standards, yet by contemporary standards they were elegantly spare. Equally elegant were the well-lighted cases displaying silver, glass, and ceramics. Enshrined as art, such objects assumed a luster they could never have in history museums. [31]

The Metropolitan collected the exemplary, aesthetically beautiful objects of exquisite style, but it was not above playing to the associational value of its rooms. The American Wing, Halsey wrote, contained "a room where Washington danced with Franklin's daughter, and another where Lafayette was given two historic dinners." But the Metropolitan succeeded as no other institution had at investing early American objects with the aura of art. Even wholly commonplace items—andirons, pewter mugs, and betty lamps—became, under the Metropolitan's influence, art objects. Although Halsey's definition of exemplary objects differed from that of Goode, the American Wing helped to define a new taxonomy for historical objects. Its categories of value —metalwares, ceramics and glass, textiles and costumes, furnishings—came to parallel precisely the antiques market and would eventually determine the curatorial slots that history museums would feel compelled to fill. [32]

The American Wing's influence was formidable. Other art museums began to collect and display American decorative arts. Historic-house museums did the same, becoming four-sided stage sets for elegant furnishings. The American Wing brought a new panache to antique collecting, encouraged the continuing revival of colonial styles, and decisively influenced the design of department-store rooms. The work of Halsey and his many successors ultimately produced two generations of history-museum curators of the decorative arts and designers whose notions of taste and composition came directly from art museums.[33]

Halsey's American Wing had a self-conscious educational intent. The wing was a shrine, not just to the American past, but to the aesthetic taste and sensibility of the old elite. Halsey portrayed the founding fathers as connoisseurs and patrons of the arts. Moreover, the virtues of the founders—honesty, forthrightness, simplicity, craftsmanship—could be read in the objects themselves. No less than Peale's Philadelphia Museum and Goode's Smithsonian, the American Wing was a patriotic shrine.[34]

Patriotism was an urgent issue in the early 1920s. A small but significant segment of the white Anglo-Saxon Protestant upper middle class had lost its faith in America's capacity to assimilate immigrants. In 1924, the same year the wing opened, Congress passed the most restrictive and racist immigration bill in this century. The new law reflected the fear that the newest immigrants, those from southern and eastern Europe, were unassimilable and harbored radical and un-American ideas. Halsey openly played to those fears while promoting the American Wing as a patriotic antidote. "Many of our people are not cognizant of our traditions and the principles for which our fathers struggled and died," he wrote. "[T]he tremendous changes in the character of our nation and the influx of foreign ideas utterly at variance with those held by the men who gave us the Republic threaten, and unless checked, may shake, the foundations of our Republic." A journey through the American Wing "can not but fail to revive those Memories and bring with it a spirit of thankfulness that our great city . . . has a setting for traditions so dear to us and invaluable to the Americanization of so many of our people to whom much of our history has been hidden in a fog of unenlightenment."[35]

If the American Wing taught patriotism, it did so only indirectly. There was little connection between intent and practice. Its labels were largely descriptive, the language often technical. The *Handbook of the American Wing* used such terms as *bombe base, simulated cabriole legs,* and *girandole* without defining them for the uninitiated. Halsey and others believed the wing would teach the true principles of design, but if it did, it did so only implicitly and only to those visitors who brought with them considerable knowledge. The exhibition and its related educational materials contradicted the stated intent. Its subtle message was that it was far easier to inherit good taste than to acquire it.[36]

For more than a century, the natural sciences had dominated history museums. With the success of the American Wing, art history would exert an increasing influence on the public presentation of the past. The art museum redefined the purpose of collecting while establishing a new form of taxonomy. The new standards were aesthetic, and the new categories were those hallowed by the antiques market. The new experts were not trained scientists or historians, but amateur collectors of Anglo-Saxon origin and upper-middle-class to upper-class background. Their expertise lay in a mystical connoisseurship that neither could be easily taught nor readily learned. And their sense of the past, unlike that of Peale and Goode, was fundamentally nostalgic.[37]

The American Wing severed the connections between past and present. Peale and Goode, in the service of a thoroughly Whiggish approach to history, had tried to maintain those connections. But the Metropolitan asserted the superiority of the past, extolling the "craftsmen's age." It was the past that contained the secrets of good design, of honest workmanship, of understated elegance. Halsey decried the present as an "age of materialism" and, like countless curators since, retreated to the past for solace and inspiration. The American Wing was a self-conscious assault on the modern. Ironically, modernist artists and architects would attempt to appropriate the Metropolitan's version of the colonial past to their own purposes, justifying their starkly barren designs as inspired by the "functionalism" of the colonial. For both Halsey and the modernists, the past was a weapon to wield against the present.[38]

The Cooperstown of Stephen C. Clark, Sr., Dixon Ryan Fox, and Louis C. Jones

There were other forces at work. In Newark from 1901 to 1929, John Cotton Dana demanded that museums take education and exhibition more seriously. With the rise of the automobile, the number of historic houses and outdoor museums increased significantly. The collecting of commonplace items became more prevalent, and by the 1930s some of that collecting had freed itself from the strictures of filiopietism. Museums began to collect such items out of a genuine interest in the history of ordinary men and women. In general, history museums began to assert their own identity, gradually freeing themselves from the natural-history and art-history models that had so constrained their development. Trained historians began to take a more active role in the development of museums. And there came to be a much more self-conscious approach to exhibition and public education that would gradually yield a new form of history exhibit. These trends are exemplified in the history of the New York State Historical Association.[39]

The New York State Historical Association (NYSHA) was founded in 1899. Unlike the public historical societies of the Midwest, it was a private organization. Its purpose was to promote the history of the state, with special emphasis on the military and Indian history of the Lake George region. Gradually it expanded its intellectual scope to include politics, religion, and general cultural history. Initially, its programs were limited. It held annual meetings, published a quarterly journal, and occasionally lobbied the state legislature on issues of preservation. It took an active interest in the teaching of history, encouraging the use of visual aids as early as 1911. But it had no headquarters, no library, no museum.[40]

That would change in 1926 with the construction of Headquarters House at Ticonderoga, financed by Massachusetts paper manufacturer Horace Moses, who summered in the Lake George region. Modeled on John Hancock's house in Boston, which had burned in 1863 after a failed effort to preserve it, Headquarters House contained both a library and a museum. With an endowment (also provided by Moses), the association published a ten-volume history of New York, along with eight specialized monographs. In these years NYSHA came to exert impressive local and national influence, and with the publication of Arthur C. Parker's *Manual for History Museums* in 1935, it took a leadership role in the history-museum business.[41]

Parker was director of the Rochester Museum of Arts and Sciences and had established a reputation for imaginative exhibits. His book proposed independent history museums strongly committed to public education. Historical societies typically focused their energies on their libraries and archives and gave their object collections short shrift, he argued, and history museums were shrines to their donors or "costly showcases" with the "dust of death in the air," so funereal and inactive had they become. Still others exhibited their collections with no semblance of order, thereby surrendering the opportunity to teach. The great art museums employed the past for the benefit of the few; they merely reinforced "previously acquired knowledge and tastes." Parker sought history museums that would "revisualize the past for the benefit of the whole community," museums that would be places of activity, drama, and clarity of purpose. Parker's arguments were not new ones. John Cotton Dana had made similar ones earlier, but Parker was the first to focus exclusively on the problems and opportunities of history museums, and his recommendations had an important influence, especially on the practice of exhibitions.[42]

Parker wanted history exhibits to tell a story. The story should be clear and explicitly presented, and each section should advance the main story. Parker used an exhibit from his own museum as an example. The exhibit told a conventional story of the early history of Rochester through portraits, maps, deeds, graphics, objects, period spaces, and several small models. No particular category of object was privileged over any other. The point was to tell a simple story in a visually appealing way. Parker's approach, commonplace today, was sufficiently novel in the early 1930s to warrant detailed exposition.[43]

Parker could not, however, free himself from the patriotic pieties that remained ingrained in American history museums. One of his exhibits at Rochester was called the Shrine of the Citizen. "It depicted the scene of the signing of the Declaration, and," wrote Parker, "as an allegory, displayed an altar of liberty upon which rested the Constitution." A ballot box, the scales of Justice, a sword, a plow, and the flag of the new constellation completed the scene. It was designed for its emotional effect, and Parker proudly reported its success. Men took their hats off while approaching it, and "several women knelt in prayer before it." [44]

Parker articulated no specific collecting philosophy. It was clear, however, that he was skeptical of associational collecting; too much of it was of "little historical importance." He discouraged the display of local "relics," disparaged indiscriminate collecting, and thought that museums which defined their purpose solely in terms of preservation were not doing their job. By the mid-1930s the collecting of the commonplace was just that and required no defense; Parker offered none. He urged museums to adopt a simple taxonomy, one developed in part by the National Research Council, one far more suited to history museums than the taxonomies derived from art or natural history. [45]

Dixon Ryan Fox, a prominent professor of history at Columbia and later president of Union College, wrote the introduction to Parker's book. Columbia University Press published it. Never before had the worlds of university scholarship and history museums been closer. Fox, a student of Charles Beard and James Harvey Robinson, was an important figure in the development of the "new History," an effort to transcend the categories of political and diplomatic history to encompass the history of ordinary life. With Arthur M. Schlesinger, Sr., he coedited the twelve-volume History of American Life Series, a pioneering effort to promote social and cultural history. Like his mentor Beard, he sought to communicate with an audience outside the academy. Fox was born in upstate New York and had a deep commitment to writing the state's history, so he threw himself into the work of NYSHA, becoming a trustee in 1919. Ten years later he became the association's president and guided it through its most important period of change. [46]

Fox wanted museums to be both popular and scholarly, and he apparently saw no conflict between the two missions. He understood his debt to Peale and, though critical of Peale's neglect of history, grasped that their educational intentions were similar. He saw the museum serving the twentieth century in the same way that the public library served the nineteenth: as a great educational institution. Dismayed at what he saw around him, at the failure of museums to educate, he sought to promote clear visual education. "Hundreds of thousands of visitors," he wrote, "leave museum rooms each year choked with confusion, still hungry . . . for understanding." A new career was open to those who could master its techniques, but Fox clearly believed it demanded commitment to both scholarship and historical training. NYSHA continued to publish scholarly books and articles, and the first three directors—Julian Boyd, Edward Alexander, and Clifford Lord—had Ph.D.'s in history from Columbia.[47]

Fox's vision was impressive, but it would be more than matched by Stephen Carlton Clark, Sr., heir to the Singer sewing-machine fortune. Fox approached Clark in search of an endowment for a chair in fine arts, not for NYSHA, but for Union College. An art collector and a trustee of the Metropolitan Museum of Art, Clark was a likely candidate for Fox's request, but he had other ideas.[48]

Clark had a summer home in Cooperstown, a nineteenth-century resort village on the southern tip of Lake Otsego. In the 1850s his grandfather Edward, Isaac Singer's partner, had settled in Cooperstown, where he built a grand house and indulged a curious medievalism in constructing Kingfisher Tower, a miniature castle that stands today as a testament to his paternalism. Stephen's brother, Edward Severin Clark, continued the family tradition. The Squire, as he was known locally, erected a huge hotel, the Otesaga; a community gymnasium; and an extraordinary stone barn, his "cow palace," burnishing his image as gentleman farmer and village patriarch. And then, just a year before his death in 1933, he completed Fenimore House, a magnificent neo-Georgian mansion, tearing down a house formerly occupied by James Fenimore Cooper. At Edward's death, Stephen assumed the mantle. In the midst of the Great Depression, he sought to do something for the village's economy. The Clark-Singer fortune, however, would not be used to foster industry or anything else that might spoil the preindustrial charm of Cooperstown.[49]

By the late 1930s, Stephen Clark was committed to making the village both a cultural center and a major tourist attraction. He was the prime mover in the establishment of the Baseball Hall of Fame, which opened in 1939, and he persuaded Fox and his fellow trustees to move NYSHA from Ticonderoga to Cooperstown. Clark paid for the move, and the new headquarters opened in 1939. From then until his death in 1960, Clark would finance and oversee the development of a new museum complex. Though Fox would retain the title of board president, Clark came to assume the real authority. It was he who saw the potential for an outdoor museum composed of vernacular structures and who moved the association into the forefront of folk-art collecting.[50]

By all accounts, Clark was an exceedingly private man, not given to grand public gestures. There was little in his background that marked him as different from other East Coast patricians. He was a graduate of Yale and the Columbia Law School, a staff officer during World War I, a corporate and foundation director, a club man. In the familiar trinity of *Who's Who* entries, he was a Republican, an Episcopalian, and a Mason. Conservative in his politics but unconstrained by past museum practice, he was prepared to act boldly and imaginatively. He apparently saw little to emulate in the museums around him. And so this conservative and wealthy Republican would come to preside over one of the most explicitly populist museums in America and hire New Deal Democrats to implement his vision.[51]

The new museum, located first in temporary quarters in the town, displayed art, furniture, and farmers' tools and devoted a special exhibit to James Fenimore Cooper. In 1945, NYSHA established the separate Farmers' Museum in Edward Severin Clark's elaborate barn; it was a challenge to the American Wing and its imitators. The museum was devoted, not to the high-style products of the "craftsmen's age," but to tools, the "implements of the worker." "The sponsors of this new museum," wrote Clifford Lord, then director, "are convinced that a better picture of American life . . . can be had from the production tools and implements of the common man than from the most elaborate furniture, the best art, the finest luxury goods." Lord contended that the focus of the Farmers' Museum "is useful in a democracy in order to produce a truer appreciation and a healthier respect for the dignity and accomplishments of those who practiced agriculture or a trade." [52]

However innovative in intent, the Farmers' Museum was wholly traditional in exhibit technique. The order was taxonomic. On the first floor, blacksmith tools comprised a facsimile smithy, carpenter's tools made up another section, spinning and weaving implements a third. The barn's great loft displayed row upon row of farm implements: harrows, plows, threshers, and scythes. The arrangement was orderly if not artful. There was little label copy and little explicit teaching. The objects were not in cases, and the period rooms were craft shops. Otherwise, this was a wholly conventional museum.[53]

The 1940s brought important changes in the association's leadership. With Dixon Ryan Fox's death in 1945, Clark assumed the title of chairman of the board, combining titular authority with the effective power he already had achieved. Director Clifford Lord was called to military service in 1943, and curator Janet MacFarlane became acting director. A former staff member of Arthur Parker's museum in Rochester, she would capably preside over the planning for the new outdoor museum and remain as an important and effective curator after Clark selected a new director in 1946. Among her accomplishments was Cooperstown's clear and accurate depiction of women's work. When Lord chose to take the directorship of the Wisconsin Historical Society at war's end, Clark began looking for a new director.[54]

He chose Louis C. Jones. Whether Clark realized it or not, it was an inspired choice. Like all of Fox's directors, Jones was a Columbia Ph.D.; unlike them, he was not a historian but an English professor and folklorist. As such he had an openness to the culture of ordinary people and to material culture that was about to become increasingly rare among trained historians.[55]

The late 1940s and early 1950s saw movement away from the new history championed by Fox and others. Younger historians became captivated by intellectual history, and if they showed any interest in the culture of workers, farmers, and craftsmen, it was to argue that such groups were culturally indistinct from the entreprenurial middle class. The politically inspired progressive synthesis that shaped the new history would be replaced, not by an alternate theory, but by a scholarly style that prized complexity, irony, paradox, and indeterminacy. The new dispensation put a premium on the close reading of words. The study of things was pushed further to the edges of scholarly respectability, and the close connection between history museums and university history departments, which Fox had fostered, would be threatened.[56]

Jones brought a different sensibility to Cooperstown. As an undergraduate he supported Norman Thomas, and later he became a New Deal Democrat. A scholar of folk culture, he had a deep commitment to the history and culture of ordinary people. He came to believe that his audience at Cooperstown consisted mostly of workers and farmers, and he wanted them to go away with a "new sense of the historic importance of the American working classes, a sense of the historic importance of the American farmer and the American craftsman." Few museum directors had ever talked that way.[57]

Jones took his teaching responsibilities seriously and surrounded himself with an able staff. In addition to Janet MacFarlane, George Campbell, self-taught agricultural historian and knowledgeable collector of farm tools, remained on the curatorial staff. Jones later hired Frederick L. Rath and Per Guldbeck.

Rath had done graduate work in history at Harvard under Arthur M. Schlesinger, Sr., and had worked for the National Park Service in the late 1930s, where he learned the lessons of what he called roadside history. Convinced of the importance of history museums to popular education, he shared Jones's educational vision, and, like Jones, he had been influenced by the leftist political currents of the 1930s. He had been a pacifist who performed alternative service during the early stages of World War II, and he was a supporter of Franklin Delano Roosevelt. After the war he served as the first historian at FDR's home and later became the first director of the National Trust for Historic Preservation. He would serve as Jones's principal deputy overseeing the Farmers' Museum from 1956 to 1972.

Guldbeck had an M.A. in anthropology from the University of Denver and brought to Cooperstown the skills of a scholar, artist, conservator, and designer. Like Rath, he had served his apprenticeship in the National Park Service and came to Cooperstown dedicated to effective museum education. Like Jones, he shared a deep respect for the experience of ordinary people. His parents were immigrants from Denmark, his mother a farm woman, his father a photographer who worked for advertising agencies. Guldbeck blended his parents' experiences in ways that enhanced Cooperstown's programs as he became the principal figure behind Cooperstown's best and most-celebrated exhibit.[58]

Under Jones and his new team, the outdoor museum was completed, the folk-art collections expanded, and so did the library and archives. Jones created the popular summer Seminars on American Culture and in 1964 supervised the creation of the Cooperstown Graduate Programs in collaboration with the State College at Oneonta (now SUNY, Oneonta), one of the first graduate programs designed to produce history-museum professionals and a self-conscious rival to the Winterthur program, then devoted almost exclusively to the decorative arts. The program had two tracks, one in history-museum studies and the other in American folk culture. In addition, Jones and his colleagues brought a new approach to the Farmers' Museum: they banished all the do-not-touch signs, introduced interpreters to demonstrate how things worked, and began to rethink their approach to exhibition.[59]

That rethinking would result in "The Farmer's Year," an exhibit on the seasonality of rural life curated and designed by Per Guldbeck with the help of George Campbell and other staff members. It opened at the Farmers' Museum in 1958. Wilcomb Washburn, reviewing it in 1963, described it as "one of the most brilliant evocations of the past ever achieved in an American museum." "The Farmer's Year" went well beyond the appeals of Arthur Parker. It not only told a story, it had a theme and as such was one of the first interpretive-history exhibits. Its theme was simple: the importance of the seasons to the work of preindustrial farmers. More than a decade before E. P. Thompson's seminal article "Time, Work Discipline, and Industrial Capitalism," Guldbeck explicated a theme central to the understanding of rural culture, which he elaborated in twelve sections corresponding to the months of the year. Each section contained characteristic tools, graphics, and brief explanatory labels. Large earth-toned wall panels defined each section. Guldbeck attached objects to the panels or placed them directly in front; there were no cases. By the standards of traditional history museums, including Cooperstown itself a few years earlier, the use of objects was spartan. Some lessons clearly had been learned from the art museums. The arrangement of objects and images, the placement of labels, the use of main headings—all communicated a sense of self-conscious design. Washburn prized it for its simplicity and the absence of gadgets or the kind of high-powered lighting that was only then coming into vogue. Its genius lay in its studied simplicity and the extraordinarily effective fit between content and design.[60]

"The Farmer's Year" was the product of diverse influences. As a form of pedagogy, it sprang from Arthur Parker's manual, reinforced by the exhibit work of the National Park Service in the 1930s. The Park Service played a key role during those years in developing simple and effective exhibit designs, and its influence deserves closer study. In the 1950s, other history museums, notably the historical societies of Detroit, Nebraska, Colorado, and Ohio, began to experiment with new forms of exhibition. Science centers and natural-history museums also started to experiment with new forms of exhibition, with color, with the placement of objects outside cases. The design influences were even more diverse. Advertising, industrial trade shows, and even shop windows had come to express an aesthetic based on a sharp delineation of ideas and images. The simplicity and clarity of much of modern design would come to exert a demonstrable influence on history-museum exhibits, and "The Farmer's Year" would come to have its own impact.[61]

That impact was the result of several factors. Washburn's review helped, coming as it did at a time when exhibition reviews were exceedingly rare. It also helped that Jones, Rath, Guldbeck, and several others on the staff had national stature in the museum and historical-agency community. NYSHA's stature and visibility in the profession enhanced the exhibit's stature. But it was the Cooperstown's graduate program that ensured the exhibition's influence. Scores of graduates would carry its lessons to their first museum jobs. "The Farmer's Year" was likely not the first thematic history exhibit, nor even the first to successfully blend content and design. But no other exhibit from that era had its visibility or its impact. No other exhibit lingers so in professional memory. Several years after its dismantling, it remains, for many museum people, a bright example of what a thematic exhibit can be.

For three decades NYSHA had been a leader among the history museums and historical societies of America. No other museum came closer to expressing Peale's belief in the essential unity of high scholarship and popular education. Other organizations, particularly the publicly supported historical societies of the Midwest and Great Plains, had established reputations for good scholarship, for close ties to university historians, and for strong commitment to public education. Most had excellent libraries and archives. Some had innovative museums. Their history and influence deserve closer study. NYSHA certainly was not alone. Yet it was special, in the quality of its leadership, in its collections, in its approach to exhibitions. It was among the very first museums to establish the importance of the commonplace and the everyday. It was among the very first to establish the possibilities of the thematic exhibit, decisively breaking with the taxonomic exhibition derived from natural history and from the well-lighted period rooms and vitrines of art history. Through its seminars, its graduate program, and its presence in the profession, it exerted a strong influence.

NYSHA established the importance of common people in ways that few American museums ever had. Its essential story was the manner in which "the plain people of yesterday, in doing their daily work, built a great nation where only a great forest had stood." Hardiness, pluck, and craft skill were the emphasized traits. The Farmers' Museum stressed the realities of daily life. Fenimore House, with its displays of folk art, opened a window into the realms of culture and imagination. To its credit, NYSHA's staff attempted to

"The Farmers' Year" exhibition at the Farmers' Museum, 1958. (New York State Historical Association, Cooperstown)

present the past without blinders, without romanticism. Toil was unremitting, fireplaces were inefficient, barnyards smelled, taverns were fly filled.[62]

Much of this worked, though the beauty of the site undercut the message. Fenimore House was an imposing mansion, the Farmers' Museum an extraordinary barn. An attractive and well-kept golf course, bordering the site, and a gorgeous lake view asserted a strong visual presence. The simple clapboard structures of the outdoor museum, the steepled church reflected in a small pond, the farmstead and craft shops blended into the setting harmoniously. More than a century of nostalgic calendar views of rural villages had prepared the visitor. Cooperstown was a postcard, and its museum buildings communicated a cumulative sense of order, grace, and prosperity that was not what the interpretive staff intended.

The larger message could not help being celebratory. Cooperstown had its hero, and its hero was, in a now increasingly archaic phrase, the common man. The staff's antiromanticism surprisingly reinforced the message. Life was hard, and wresting a livelihood from the soil was especially difficult, yet our rural ancestors not only did so but left us with simple yet handsome buildings, well-made tools, and an occasional quilt or painting of surpassing beauty. Their hardiness created a civilization where only a forest had stood. It was not that such a belief was grieviously wrong, but it clearly did not promote the sort of skeptical and critical intelligence that is necessary to historical understanding. To their credit, the staff at Cooperstown never surrendered to the kind of cold-war rhetoric that was increasingly common in 1950s history museums. Yet despite their accomplishments, they were not able to break decisively with the long tradition of the museum as shrine.[63]

Toward the Present

NYSHA had played a direct role in accelerating three of the principal twentieth-century trends in history museums: collecting the commonplace, developing the interpretive exhibit, and introducing trained historians at museums. Some history museums would continue to collect the associational and the exemplary, but it was the ordinary and the everyday that increasingly would engage their time. This was especially true of outdoor museums, such as Old Sturbridge Village, an organization decisively influenced by NYSHA, and the small regional-history museums established since the 1960s, such as the Conner Prairie outdoor museum in Noblesville, Indiana. The importance of the history of everyday life had been kept alive by NYSHA in the 1940s and 1950s, even as historians turned increasingly to intellectual history. With the great revival of interest in social history in the 1960s and 1970s, the academy would reinforce the directions that NYSHA had pioneered.[64]

Trained historians long had played key roles at Cooperstown, and by the

1950s they were found in increasing numbers as the directors of museums and historical societies. The great influx of historians into museums and, in particular, into curatorial and interpretive positions did not occur, however, until the 1970s. There were three reasons for such timing. History and American-studies graduate programs, taking advantage of new forms of government aid, had expanded during the 1960s. The academic job market had not. A good many Ph.D.'s who had intended to pursue careers as teachers found better opportunities in museums. At the same time, the rise of social history narrowed the distance separating historians of the academy from historians who practiced their craft in museums. The research agendas of museums and university history departments had never been closer. In addition, some of the new museum historians brought with them a strong commitment to public education, a desire to educate beyond the conventional boundaries of academe. This was a commitment that had been nurtured, like the new social history, by the leftist currents of the 1960s and 1970s.[65]

These trends were reinforced, at times self-consciously, by the policies of the National Endowment for the Humanities. During the 1960s and 1970s, the endowment became a major force in the financing of museum exhibitions and other public programs. True to its congressional mandate, it expected museums and historical societies to use the best and most recent humanities scholarship. In practice, this meant the endowment offered its resources contingent upon the willingness of museums to seek the advice of academic consultants. The quality of useful advice museums received from consultants varied greatly, but the endowment did bring university historians and museum staffers into closer and often more fruitful contact. Hundreds of historians would serve as consultants and panelists and in the process rub shoulders with their museum counterparts. Their presence would help to affirm the increasing importance of the interpretive exhibition.

With its thematic character, the interpretive exhibit embodied an intellectual form familiar to historians. The stress on ideas gave historians a voice in the creation of exhibits that they would not have received had the taxonomic exhibit or the art-museum exhibit remained dominant. This created tension. The focus on ideas and themes tended to disenfranchise traditionally trained (often self-trained) curators; they saw the new social historians as knowing little about objects and even less about exhibitions. Historians might know how to write books, according to one well-known refrain, but exhibits were not books. For their part, historians saw curators as defensively turf-conscious when they were not simply anti-intellectual. These, of course, were caricatures, but there was enough truth in both positions to wound.

Politics compounded the tension. Many social historians were leftists, while curators tended to be apolitical, though a few were explicitly conservative. Most curators brought to their work a reverence for the objects under their care that made a truly critical stance difficult. It was easier to see the cotton gin as a great technical achievement than to see it as an instrument of oppression, for example. Such tensions were present in virtually every history museum in the 1970s in one form or another. But the interpretive exhibit would, by the 1980s, be the principal form for the expression of ideas in history museums, and exhibitions and interpretive programs influenced by the new social history would come to exert a powerful presence from Oakland to Williamsburg.

The interpretive exhibit needed broadly trained historians, but it needed designers even more. Once objects came out of cases, they had to be arranged. Once the arrangement was no longer taxonomic, the form that exhibitions took became an issue in ways that it never had before. The use of color, of light, of audiovisual programs required specialized expertise. Only a few museum professionals could combine the skills of curator and designer in the manner of a Per Guldbeck. And so, in the 1960s and 1970s, museums came to rely increasingly upon designers, hiring them as permanent members of the staff, establishing design departments for the first time, and contracting with designers on a project-specific basis. There were enough such contracts during this period to foster the growth of exhibition design firms, the most important of which would play an influential role in the elaboration of the interpretive exhibit.

By the early 1970s, a recognizable aesthetic had emerged. Its sources were diverse. The interpretive-history exhibit, as it had developed in the 1960s, was one source. Trade shows, world's-fair pavilions, and science centers offered additional inspiration. The architectural use of space, the use of color, the placement of objects outside cases all reflected some of the lessons learned in history museums. But the new form rebelled against modernist simplicity and thus implicitly against "The Farmer's Year." The new form was characterized instead by a dense overlay of objects, graphics, and text. Objects were suspended in midair, sometimes overlapping other objects. The use of time lines, offering a profusion of information, became common. This was a form that embraced more of everything: objects, graphics, and words.

Charles and Ray Eames, furniture designers, filmmakers, exhibit designers, were the principals behind this new form. The Eameses and those influenced by them put their mark on major traveling exhibitions, such as the "The World of Franklin and Jefferson" (designed by the Eameses for the Grand Palais and other museums, 1975–77), and on permanent installations in the Chicago Historical Society (Staples and Charles, 1978), the Oakland Museum (Gordon Ashby), and the National Museum of History and Technology (Nation of Nations, Chermayeff and Geismar, 1976). The great profusion of both objects and information that characterized these exhibitions offered visitors multiple levels of meaning. The basic style of the exhibits—their sparing use of exhibit cases, their nondidactic presentation, their apparent accessability—was clearly a product of their time, of a piece with the effort to make museums less forbidding, more interactive, more accessible and democratic, which was itself part of the cultural politics of the late 1960s.[66]

The Eames style in history exhibits was not without its critics. Traditional curators tended to dislike the style, correctly seeing it as one that diminished the importance of individual objects. Others were offended by the density, the clutter of presentation or by the absence of a clear and effective educational intent. This was a style that sacrificed clarity to inclusiveness and content to design.

By the 1980s, most designers had moved away from the Eames style, though without declaring explicit rebellion. Exhibits had become cleaner and less dense, objects had regained some of their luster and singularity. A good many history exhibits had come to look more and more like art exhibits. The sense of democratic accessibility that pervaded the Eameses' exhibitions—a visual approach that undercut the notion of the museum as shrine—was less evident. The only real innovations were in audiovisual programs and interactive computer games; technique and content only rarely meshed.

History museums had a profusion of design possibilities during these years but no articulate way of choosing among them. Some museums had lively internal debates about the meaning of design, but the debates did not inform the profession as a whole. Was the Eames style better suited for certain kinds of exhibits? Was the style of the "The Farmer's Year" appropriate only for exhibits of carefully circumscribed theme? Why had designers embraced the Eames style at one moment only to move away at another? It was not the absence of consensus on such questions that hurt history museums, it was the absence of discussion.

The emergence of designers changed the internal politics of museums. Historians and curators still found themselves in disagreement, but they sometimes found common ground in opposition to designers. All this was further complicated by the simultaneous rise of museum education specialists, often defending their own professional agendas. During the 1970s and 1980s, the history of a particular exhibit's development was often the history of shifting alliances between and among curators, designers, historians, and education specialists. In retrospect, the success of Cooperstown in the 1950s may have had something to do with the relative absence of these divisions. The position of social historians was especially paradoxical. Never had they been more important to the intellectual life of museums, yet they shared the fate of curators in having less influence than curators had enjoyed a generation earlier in determining what the public actually saw. As a result, some historians came to see designers as lacking seriousness and historical understanding, too given to gimmicks, while the former saw the latter as pedants lacking interest in real education, wanting to put books on the wall. Again these were caricatures,

"A Nation of Nations," National Museum of American History, 1976. (Smithsonian Institution)

but again with enough truth to wound. There were notable exceptions, but successful collaborations between historians and designers were rare.

A full generation after "The Farmer's Year," the interpretive social-history exhibit still seems to flounder from one exhibit style to another. Museums do not yet know how to blend objects and ideas into a well-designed whole. This is not simply a matter of conflict among the principals, though that is part of it. It is also the case that there is no organized way of learning from the past practices of museums, for there are few journal reviews, few professional schools, few conferences. Some of this is changing, but not at a rate to ensure a consistent discourse on exhibitions. The National Endowment for the Humanities, for example, continues to make major financing decisions entirely on the basis of written proposals; there is no requirement that museums submit models or even slides. Typically, discussions center on content, not on the relation of design to content or on the effectiveness of the interrelationship. We cannot have a real discourse on museum exhibitions until these issues become part of the discussion.[67]

Most museums remain shrines. That part of Peale's legacy has not been transcended. Some museums have made notable progress in the past several years in their willingness and ability to confront conflict and tragedy, but it remains to be seen whether these efforts genuinely presage a new direction or are exceptions whose very presence as exceptions helps to legitimize the museum as shrine even more. For too many visitors, and even staff members, museums remain places of celebration, even veneration. Yet the presence of historians in museums will mean nothing unless it means that the same critical standards that suffuse books and classroom lectures find their way into exhibits as well.

NOTES

1. On the portrait, see Roger B. Stein, "Charles Willson Peale's Expressive Design: The Artist in His Museum," *Prospects* 6 (1981), 129–85; Edward P. Alexander, *Museum Masters: Their Museums and Their Influence* (Nashville, Tenn.: American Association for State and Local History, 1983), 45; and Charles Coleman Sellers, *Charles Willson Peale* (New York: Charles Scribner's Sons, 1969), 402–3. On the connections between presentation and collecting, I have learned from Richard Rabinowitz's "Learning in Public Places," an unpublished address delivered at the meeting of the American Educational Research Association in 1973.

2. On Peale's life, see Charles Coleman Sellers, *Charles Willson Peale: Early Life* (Philadelphia: American Philosophical Society, 1939), 151–281, and *Mr. Peale's Museum: Charles Willson Peale and the First Popular Museum of Natural Science and Art* (New York: W. W. Norton and Co., 1980), 1–114, 203–6. See also the profiles of Peale in Edward P. Alexander, *Museum Masters*, 43–77, and Joseph J. Ellis, *After the Revolution: Profiles of Early American Culture* (New York: W. W. Norton and

Co., 1979), 41–71. The Peale quotes are cited in Charles Coleman Sellers, *Charles Willson Peale: Later Years* (Philadelphia: American Philosophical Society, 1947), 229, and Alexander, *Museum Masters*, 24, 26. For the Peale papers, see Lillian Miller, ed., *The Selected Papers of Charles Willson Peale and His Family*, vol. 1, *Charles Willson Peale: Artist in Revolutionary America, 1775–1791* (New Haven, Conn.: Yale University Press, 1988), and vol. 2, *Charles Willson Peale: The Artist as Museum Keeper, 1791–1810* (New Haven, Conn.: Yale University Press, 1988), pts. 1 and 2.

3. "Broadside, Peale's Museum," 1 February 1790, in Miller, *Selected Papers*, I:580; Sellers, *Mr. Peale's Museum*, 36–37, 111–12, 152–53; Sellers, *Peale: The Later Years*, 224–51; Sellers, *Peale* (1969), 331–52; Richard P. Ellis, "The Founding, History, and Significance of Peale's Museum in Philadelphia," *Curator* 9 (1966), 235–58; Charles Coleman Sellers, "Peale's Museum and 'The New Museum Idea,'" American Philosophical Society *Proceedings* 124 (1980), 21–34.

4. Peale, "Broadside, my design in forming this Museum," 1792, in Miller, *Selected Papers*, vol. II, pt. 1, 12–24; letter, Peale to William Findley, 18 February 1800, in ibid., 276–81; Sellers, *Mr. Peale's Museum*, 121, 162–63. Sellers, *Peale* (1969), 331–41; Edgar P. Richardson, Brooke Hindle, and Lillian Miller, *Charles Willson Peale and His World* (New York: Harry N. Abrams, 1983), 79–86.

5. Letter, Peale to John Beale Boardley, 5 December 1786, in Miller, *Selected Papers*, I:460–61; Peale, "First Advertisement for the Museum," *Pennsylvania Packet*, 7 July 1786, in Miller, *Selected Papers*, I:448; Sellers, *Mr. Peale's Museum*, 26–31; Sellers, *Peale* (1969), 212–24; Alexander, *Museum Masters*, 60–61.

6. Sellers, *Peale* (1969), 329, 336–37. Sellers, *Mr. Peale's Museum*, 36–37, 50–51, 111–12, 195–97, 207, 215–16; Alexander, *Museum Masters*, 63–64.

7. Sellers, *Mr. Peale's Museum*, 255–314, 320–21; Neil Harris, *Humbug: The Art of P. T. Barnum* (Chicago: University of Chicago Press, 1973), 38–40.

8. Harris, *Humbug*, 33–57. Whitfield J. Bell, Jr., et al., *A Cabinet of Curiosities: Five Episodes in the Evolution of American Museums* (Charlottesville: University of Virginia Press, 1967).

9. Sellers, *Peale* (1969), 212–13, 256–57, 350–51, 380–81; Sellers, *Mr. Peale's Museum*, 331–35; Ellis, *After the Revolution*, 32, 58–59.

10. Miller, introduction to *Selected Papers*, vol. II, pt. 1, xxviii; Harris, *Humbug*, 33–57; Walter Muir Whitehill, *Independent Historical Societies* (Boston: Boston Athenaeum, 1962), 3–131; Bell et al., *A Cabinet of Curiosities*; Leslie Walker Dunlap, *American Historical Societies, 1790–1860* (Madison: University of Wisconsin Press, 1944).

11. Quoted in Clifford K. Shipton, "The Museum of the American Antiquarian Society," in Bell et al., *A Cabinet of Curiosities*, 40–41.

12. Whitehill, *Independent Historical Societies*, 20.

13. On Goode's life, see Alexander, *Museum Masters*, 279–309, and G. Carroll Lindsey, "George Brown Goode," in Clifford Lord, ed., *Keepers of the Past* (Chapel Hill: University of North Carolina Press, 1965), 127–40.

14. Lindsey, "George Brown Goode," 286.

15. Wilcomb E. Washburn, "Joseph Henry's Conception of the Purpose of the Smithsonian Institution," in Bell et al., *A Cabinet of Curiosities*, 106–66; Nathan

Reingold, "New York State Roots of Joseph Henry's National Career," *New York History* 59 (April 1973), 132–44; Joel J. Orosz, "Disloyalty, Dismissal, and a Deal: The Development of a National Museum at the Smithsonian Institution, 1846–1855," *Museum Studies Journal* 2 (Spring 1986), 22–33; S. Dillon Ripley and Wilcomb E. Washburn, "The Development of the National Museum at the Smithsonian Institution, 1846–1855: A Response to Joel Orosz's Article," *Museum Studies Journal* 2 (Spring–Summer 1987), 8–11. Orosz, "In Defense of the Deal: A Rebuttal to S. Dillon Ripley's and Wilcomb Washburn's 'Response,' " *Museum Studies Journal* 3 (Fall–Winter 1987), 7–12.

16. George Brown Goode, *Catalogue of the Collection . . . Exhibited at Philadelphia in 1876 . . .* (Washington: Government Printing Office, 1879), 4–13; Smithsonian Institution, *Annual Report, 1875*, 58–71, *1876*, 70–83, *1881*, 117–22; James McCabe, *The Illustrated History of the Centennial Exhibition* (Philadelphia, 1876; reprinted in Philadelphia by National Publishing Co., 1975); Robert C. Post, ed., *1876: A Centennial Exhibition* (Washington: National Museum of History and Technology, 1976); Smithsonian Institution, *Annual Report, U.S. National Museum, 1895*, 74–92.

17. Henry Fairfield Osborn, "Goode as a Naturalist," in Smithsonian Institution, *Annual Report, 1897*, pt. 2, *A Memorial of George Brown Goode*, 23; George Brown Goode, "First Draft of a System of Classification for the World's Columbian Exposition," 656 (RU70, Box 42, SI Archives); George Brown Goode, "America's Relation to the Advance of Science," *Science* n.s. 1 (4 January 1895), 4–9. See Michael Lacey, "George Brown Goode and the Idea of the Museum in the Late Nineteenth Century," a working paper prepared for the Conference on Collections and Culture: Museums and the Development of American Life and Thought, Woodrow Wilson Center/National Museum of American History, October 1987. See also Michael Lacey, "The Mysteries of Earthmaking Dissolve: A Study of Washington's Intellectual Community and the Origins of American Environmentalism in the Late Nineteenth Century," doctoral dissertation, George Washington University, 1979.

18. Smithsonian Institution, *Annual Report, 1881*, 82, *1883*, 177. See also George Brown Goode, "The Principles of Museum Administration," in Smithsonian Institution, *Annual Report, 1897*, pt. 2, 195–240.

19. George Brown Goode, *Virginia Cousins: A Study in the Ancestry and Posterity of John Goode of Whitby* (Richmond, Va.: J. W. Randolph & English, 1887), xviii–xix; John Brenton Copp Collection Files, No. 28810, Office of the Registrar, National Museum of American History; Grace Rogers Cooper, *The Copp Family Textiles* (Washington: National Museum of American History, 1971); Smithsonian Institution, *Annual Report, 1881*, 86; *1895*, 90.

20. *Visitors Guide to the Smithsonian Institution and the U.S. National Museum* (Washington: Government Printing Office, 1886); Smithsonian Institution, *Annual Report, Report of the U.S. National Museum, 1896*, 320.

21. Smithsonian Institution, *Annual Report, 1884*, 54; *Visitors Guide to the Smithsonian*, 1886; Curtis M. Hinsley, Jr., *Savages and Scientists: The Smithsonian Institution and the Development of American Anthropology, 1846–1910* (Washington: Smithsonian Institution Press, 1981), 91–94.

22. George Brown Goode, "The Museums of the Future," in Smithsonian Insti-

tution, *Annual Report, 1897*, pt. 2, 243–62; see also Alexander, *Museum Masters*, 286–305.

23. Smithsonian Institution, *Annual Report, 1881*, 94; *1890*, 18–19; *1893*, 56.

24. *Visitors Guide to the Smithsonian*, 1886 and 1890; Marilyn Sara Cohen, "American Civilization in Three Dimensions: The Evolution of the Museum of History and Technology of the Smithsonian Institution," doctoral dissertation, George Washington University, 1980.

25. George Brown Goode, "Museum-History and Museums of History," *Papers of the American Historical Association* 3, no. 2 (1889), 251–75, reprinted in Smithsonian Institution, *Annual Report, 1897*, pt. 2, 65–81; John Higham, *History: The Development of Historical Studies in the United States* (Englewood Cliffs, N.J.: Prentice-Hall, 1965); Barbara Miller Solomon, *Ancestors and Immigrants: A Changing New England Tradition* (Chicago: University of Chicago Press, 1956); David D. Van Tassel, "From Learned Society to Professional Organization: The American Historical Association, 1884–1900," *American Historical Review* 89 (October 1984), 929–56.

26. Melinda Young Frye, "The Beginnings of the Period Room in American Museums: Charles P. Wilcomb's Colonial Kitchen, 1896, 1906, 1910," in Alan Axelrod, ed., *The Colonial Revival in America* (New York: Winterthur-Norton, 1985), 217–40; Rodris Roth, "The New England, or 'Olde Tyme,' Kitchen Exhibit at Nineteenth-Century Fairs," in Axelrod, *Colonial Revival*, 159–83; Dianne H. Pilgrim, "Inherited From the Past: The American Period Room," *American Art Journal* 10 (May 1978), 5–23; Anne Farnum, "George Francis Dow: A Career of Bringing the 'picturesque tradition of sleeping generations' to Life in the Early Twentieth Century," *Essex Institute Historical Collections* 121 (April 1985), 77–90.

27. Henry James, *The American Scene* (New York: Charles Scribner's Sons, 1907), 270.

28. Elizabeth Stillinger, *The Antiquers* (New York: Alfred A. Knopf, 1980), 4–26, 149–54.

29. See Kenneth L. Ames, introduction to Axelrod, *Colonial Revival*, 1–14, and Harvey Green, "Popular Science and Political Thought Converge: Colonial Survival Becomes Colonial Revival, 1830–1910," *Journal of American Culture* 6 (Winter 1983), 3–24.

30. On Halsey, see Wendy Kaplan, "R. T. H. Halsey: An Ideology of Collecting American Decorative Arts," *Winterthur Portfolio* 17 (Spring 1982), 43–53, and Kaplan's master's thesis of the same title, University of Delaware, 1980. The Halsey quote comes from a letter to Robert W. de Forest, 21 January 1918, Metropolitan Museum of Art Archives, cited in Kaplan's article, 52. R. T. H. Halsey and Elizabeth Tower, *The Homes of Our Ancestors* (Garden City, N.Y.: Doubleday, Page & Co., 1925); R. T. H. Halsey and Charles O. Cornelius, *Handbook of the American Wing*, 2d ed. (New York: Metropolitan Museum of Art, 1924). Henry Watson Kent, "The American Wing in Its Relation to the History of Museum Development," *Metropolitan Museum of Art Bulletin* 17 (November 1922), pt. 2, 14–16.

31. On changing furnishing plans, see Donald C. Pierce and Hope Alswang, *American Interiors: New England and the South, Period Rooms at the Brooklyn Museum* (Brooklyn, N.Y.: Brooklyn Museum, 1983).

32. R. T. H. Halsey radio address, "The Character and Nature of Colonial Art," p. 2, typescript, Halsey Papers, Winterthur.

33. Stillinger, *Antiquers*, 204–14; Robert W. de Forest, *Art in Merchandise: Notes on the Relationships of Stores and Museums* (New York: Gilliss Press, 1928); Neil Harris, "Museums, Merchandising, and Popular Taste: The Struggle for Influence," in Ian M. G. Quimby, ed., *Material Culture and the Study of American Life* (New York: Winterthur-Norton, 1978), 140–74.

34. R. T. H. Halsey, "George Washington and the Humanities" and "Washington's Print Collection," typescripts, Halsey Papers.

35. R. T. H. Halsey, "Address," in Metropolitan Museum of Art, *Addresses on the Occasion of the Opening of the American Wing* (New York: Metropolitan Museum of Art, 1925), 9–10.

36. Halsey and Cornelius, *Handbook of the American Wing*.

37. Stillinger, *Antiquers*, 188–282.

38. R. T. H. Halsey, *American Silver* (Boston: Museum of Fine Arts, 1906), 9–10.

39. On history museums in the early twentieth century, see Michael Wallace, "Visiting the Past: History Museums in the United States, *Radical History Review* 25 (1981), 63–96; Laurence Vail Coleman, *The Museum in America*, 3 vols. (Washington: American Association of Museums, 1939); Charles B. Hosmer, Jr., *Preservation Comes of Age: From Williamsburg to the National Trust*, vol. 1 (Charlottesville: University of Virginia Press, 1981). On Dana, see Alexander, *Museum Masters*, 379–411, and the special issue of *The Museologist*, 51 (Winter 1988), devoted to Dana.

40. Hosmer, *Preservation Comes of Age*, vol. 1; *The New York State Historical Association and its Museums: An Informal Guide* (Cooperstown, N.Y.: NYSHA, 1968), 10; James A. Roberts, "Introductory Address by the President," *Proceedings of the New York State Historical Association* (1901), 24–27.

41. "Dedication of the Hancock Building of the NYSHA," *Quarterly Journal of the New York State Historical Association* 7 (October 1926), 259–84; *The New York State Historical Association and its Museums*, 11; Arthur C. Parker, *A Manual for History Museums* (New York: Columbia University Press, 1935).

42. Parker, *Manual*, 13–15.

43. Ibid., 52–67.

44. Ibid., 65.

45. Ibid., 52–89.

46. Ibid., vii-x; Robert V. Remini, introduction to the Torchbook Edition of Dixon Ryan Fox, *The Decline of Aristocracy in the Politics of New York, 1801–1840* (New York: Harper & Row, 1965), xi–xxviii; John Allen Kraut, "Dixon Ryan Fox," in Lord, *Keepers of the Past*, 67–77.

47. Dixon Ryan Fox in foreword to Parker, *Manual*, ix; Hosmer, *Preservation Comes of Age*, 1:97–109; *The New York State Historical Association and its Museums*, 9–13.

48. Hosmer, *Preservation Comes of Age*, 1:99.

49. Louis C. Jones, *Cooperstown*, 5th ed. (Cooperstown, N.Y.: NYSHA, 1982), 47–57.

50. Ibid., 59–105.

51. *Who Was Who in America*, vol. 4 (Chicago: A. N. Marquis, 1968), 177.

52. Clifford Lord, "The Farmers' Museum," *New York History* 41 (January 1943), 4–14.

53. Ibid.; postcard views of the Farmers' Museum exhibits, NYSHA Archives.

54. Hosmer, *Preservation Comes of Age*, 1:104–5.

55. Ibid., 105–6; Louis C. Jones, *Three Eyes on the Past: Exploring New York Folklife* (Syracuse, N.Y.: Syracuse University Press, 1982), xi–xxxvi; Louis C. Jones, "The Trapper's Cabin and the Ivory Tower," *Museum News* 42 (March 1962), 11–16.

56. John Higham, *Writing American History: Essays on Modern Scholarship* (Bloomington, Ind.; Indiana University Press, 1970).

57. Interview with Louis C. Jones; Louis C. Jones, "Folk-Culture and the Historical Society, *Minnesota History* 31 (March 1950), 11–17.

58. Interviews with Louis C. Jones, Frederick Rath, and Jan Guldbeck; see also Rath, *The Cost of Freedom*, president's address, pamphlet, 1962 (Madison, Wis.: American Association for State and Local History, 1962).

59. Jones, *Cooperstown*, 83–105; *The New York State Historical Association and its Museums*, 14–16; interview with Jones; Jones, *Three Eyes on the Past*, xi–xxxvi; Louis C. Jones, "A Decade of History, 1947–1956: The Director's Report," Farmers' Museum Minutes, 1957, 53–120 (NYSHA Archives); George R. Clay, "The Lightbulb Angel: Towards a Definition of the Folk Museums at Cooperstown," *Curator* 3, no. 1 (1960), 43–65.

60. Wilcomb E. Washburn, "The Dramatization of American Museums," *Curator* 6 (1963), 109–24; *The New York State Historical Association and its Museums*, 17–23; interview with Frederick Rath; E. P. Thompson, "Time, Work Discipline, and Industrial Capitalism," *Past and Present* 38 (December 1967), 56–97.

61. Interview with Frederick Rath; interview with Daniel Porter, current director, NYSHA; on the National Park Service's approach to exhibitions, see Ned J. Burns, *Field Manual for Museums* (Washington: U.S. Government Printing Office, 1940). Lothar P. Witteborg, "Design Standards in Museum Exhibitions," *Curator* 1 (January 1958), 29–41; Witteborg, "*Curator* Looks at 'Expo '58,' " *Curator* 4 (Autumn 1958), 41–48; Leon Gordon Miller, "The Industrial Designer: New Member of the Museum Team," *Curator* 6 (1963). Walter Muir Whitehill, *Independent Historical Societies*, 243–320, offers a survey of the whole field as of 1959–60. On 1950s history exhibitions, see "History in the Show Window," *History News* 7 (September 1952), 43; Herbert Fisher, "The Exhibit: And How Not to Avoid the Public," *History News* 10 (August 1955), 39–40, continued in September 1955, 43, and October 1955, 47. On the Nebraska Historical Society, see *History News* 9 (May 1954), 25, and on the Detroit Historical Museum, *History News* 9 (September 1954), 42.

62. *The New York State Historical Association and its Museums*, 17, 27, 38–64.

63. See Samuel Chamberlain and Henry N. Flynt, *Historic Deerfield: Houses and Interiors* (New York: Hastings House, 1952; reprinted in 1979), 1–19, and E. H. Cameron, *Samuel Slater: Father of American Manufactures* (Portland, Maine: Bond Wheelwright, 1960), a book commissioned by the founder of the Slater Mill Historic Site.

64. Much that follows is based on my own experience in museums during the past decade. On some of these issues, see Cary Carson, "Living Museums of Everyman's History," *Harvard Magazine* (July–August 1981), 22–32.

65. Carson, "Living Museums;" Wallace, "Visiting the Past;" Thomas J. Schlereth, ed., *Material Culture Studies in America* (Nashville, Tenn.: American Association for State and Local History, 1982).

66. Frederick S. Wight Art Gallery, *Connections: The Work of Charles and Ray Eames* (Los Angeles: UCLA Art Council, 1976); Harold K. Skramsted, Jr., "Interpreting Material Culture: A View from the Other Side of the Glass," in Quimby, *Material Culture and the Study of American Life*, 175–200.

67. There are hopeful signs. See Thomas J. Schlereth, "Causing Conflict, Doing Violence, *Museum News* 62 (October 1984), 45–52; Susan Porter Benson, Stephan Brier, and Roy Rosenzweig, eds., *Presenting the Past: Essays on History and the Public* (Philadelphia: Temple University Press, 1986); Jo Blatti, ed., *Past Meets Present: Essays about Historic Interpretation and Public Audiences* (Washington: Smithsonian Institution, 1987).

The Presentation of Urban History in Big-City Museums

2

Michael Frisch

A growing number of major American cities now have museums, whether public, private, or somewhere in between, that offer to citizens, visitors, and schoolchildren a formal version of the city's history, a civic "presentation of self." This essay considers some of the problems and opportunities of this very particular dimension of public historical practice. Its aims can also be more general, however, because the urban history museum stands at the precise intersection of a complex of distinct concerns that, taken together, define the current moment in the evolution of public historical presentation. These concerns include meeting the obligations of a museum to its diverse and often conflicting public constituencies, fixing the role of modern historical scholarship and scholars (often but not exclusively academic), and resolving the tension between the need to develop and display collections and the need to focus on broader didactic or thematic historical conceptions. Every history museum confronts one or more of these issues to a certain degree, but for the urban history museum, for reasons to be explored here, they are all central and interconnected.

The usefulness of the big-city museum as a context for engaging broader issues is coming to be widely recognized. At the 1984 Past Meets Present Conference—organized by the New York Council for the Humanities as a first attempt at bringing historians, designers, and museum professionals together to crystallize an emerging discourse about common concerns—the most productive discussions focused on conference field trips to urban and community history exhibits, ranging from the Chinatown History Project and the Museo del Barrio in New York to the Silk City project that linked several museums in Paterson, New Jersey. At the same time, there is a sense that urban museums very much need to draw on a wider perspective; at the next major meeting to engage such issues, the 1987 Common Agenda Conference, an influential working paper argued that city museums were "only beginning to explore urbanization and urbanism as explanatory paradigms, the potential of the urban museums as possibly a unique history museum type, or the responsibilities of such an institution in documenting and collecting contemporary city life." In consequence, one of the few specific implementation steps proposed in the final report of Common Agenda was that "a coalition of urban-based North American museums should interpret the story of how we became an urban-suburban civilization on a scale unprecedented in the twentieth century." [1]

Such a task force has now been formed with imaginative and knowledgeable museum professionals from institutions already providing fine examples of imaginative new approaches to urban historical exhibition. Over the next few years the results of this collaboration should be evident, a testament to how much of the energy for the reimagining of history museums is being generated from within the profession. Given that such concentrated effort and expertise is being brought to bear on the challenge of the urban history exhibit and collection by informed museum professionals, there may be some complementary value in offering here a view not only from the outside, but from the bottom up, which in museum terms means from the vantage of the visitor strolling through the galleries in more or less casual curiosity.

In such a spirit, this essay considers some major-city history museums with special attention to the formal urban-biography core exhibits. Resources precluded anything approaching a representative sample of city or exhibit types, but in any event my aim is neither to survey and typologize the many nor to select an exemplary few. Rather, I want to explore a vocabulary for discussing what is going on in the standing major-city biography exhibit, based on visits made without prior discussion with museum personnel or investigation of the collections or institutional background of any exhibit. My approach sought to approximate the perspective of visitors who encounter these exhibits with little preparation—an audience that can be presumed to be interested in the history *in* the museum but is not likely to be aware of or concerned with the exhibition history *of* the museum. These examples will lead us to consider a few more intentionally chosen exhibits representing what I identify as some important directions in current interpretation. Discussion of these directions, I hope, may help close the circle, linking this outsider's perspective to the insights of the Common Agenda group and other professionals currently so active on this very lively interpretational frontier in cities across the country.

Our tour begins with the permanent exhibits, in 1987, at the Museum of the City of New York, the Atwater Kent Museum in Philadelphia, and both the Missouri Historical Society and the Old Courthouse in St. Louis. And like a tour guide struggling to hold visitors in the orientation center or on the bus before releasing them to the exhibition itself, let me suggest that our survey will prove more useful if we first consider a number of themes central to the challenge of the municipal history exhibit at this specific moment of public historical museum development.

Challenges in Three Dimensions

Each of the three general concerns noted above has a particular meaning for the official or semiofficial city history exhibit, making its challenge both especially problematic and especially interesting. First is the form and content implied by the commitment to municipal self-portraiture. In the American context in which city identities have long been commonly projected in terms of economic growth and progress, the frame for urban biography has been almost necessarily deductive, a linear, heroic form into which a city's growth and development must fit. This process has tended to harness the narrative of the past to an optimistic assessment of a city's present and future.

This tendency is reinforced by the official or semiofficial sponsorship of many such museums, since it comes to seem natural that a core exhibit should offer a municipal history with meaning and direction, constructively leading to the collective future for which the city sponsors are in some sense responsible. Such an instrumental approach to collective mythobiography is reinforced as well by the complex audiences such museum exhibits characteristically are expected to address: a regular procession of local schoolchildren presumed to need a simplified, graspable story line; visiting tourists, dignitaries, and businessmen for whom it seems desirable to put a best municipal foot forward; and a diverse general population that many museums have sought to gather under a unifying historical umbrella, building and reinforcing community through the act of celebrating it historically. In practice if not in theoretical necessity, the narrative form, the self-promotional purpose, and the evocation of a presumptive community have long been almost impossible to distinguish in conventional municipal exhibits.

The celebratory impulse is an obvious obstacle to good historical interpretation, as is the all-embracing fictive community. But the narrative form is different in that, less obviously, it may be a real resource, as much part of the solution as part of the problem. Much recent social history has been held vulnerable to the charge that its findings have fragmented even academic understanding by failing to generate coherent narrative, the story structures that ultimately should be built from the products of all the toil in the forests and quarries of historical research. Whatever the academic validity of this criticism (it often has masked a rear-guard assault on the political implications of recent scholarship), it does represent a pressing concern for museum presentation, where the public's right to a graspable, engaging, and coherent exhibit should be axiomatic. In this sense, the inherited story-line structure of the municipal portrait offers a solid, audience-supportive foundation, if only its dimensions can be stretched to support the kind of edifice implied by modern urban historical scholarship.

More particularly still, the urban biographical narrative perspective inevitably involves some mix of broad economic and political forces; of regional, national, and even international relationships; and of a complex of social groups and relations across the racial-ethnic and class spectrum, however prosaically approached. Even proponents concede that the new social history has focused on neglected groups and particular subcultural experiences at the frequent expense of precisely these broader systemic perspectives. Thus the conventional frame of the municipal biography may offer a useful structure for realizing that elusive presentational synthesis of particular social experiences with broader political and economic analysis.

In informing this structure with contemporary scholarship, we encounter a second dimension requiring attention: the particular content, form, and meaning of urban historical scholarship as a subcategory of the new social history and its implications for museum interpretation and presentation. Urban history was arguably the first evolving new speciality to climb from the hothouse swamp of intellectual ferment in the late 1960s onto broadly recognized historiographical ground. Responding to both the social-political urban crisis of that period and the new historical awareness of social-scientific methods and approaches, the so-called new urban history had an enormous impact, especially in its focus on social and geographic mobility through analytically retracing the lives of the actual inhabitants of the nineteenth-century city.

The enterprise has foundered somewhat of late, however; much of its energy has been drawn into the broader concerns of the new social history, and critics have recurrently noted that the promise of a coherent analysis of urban structure and processes has not been realized. And even the milestones of intellectual progress mark a road that would seem to lead away from the museum, a road paved with a formidable macadam of statistics, quantification, historical data banks, and complex economic and planning models. As with the narrative tradition, then, modern urban scholarship would not seem to offer an encouraging base for innovation in public historical scholarship. But here too the liability may offer some surprising advantages in that, however ironically, these forbidding methods have produced some of the most concrete insights and vivid detail about the lives of actual, identifiable common people, those usually invisible and certainly silent in the artifact collections and documentation drawn on for conventional exhibits.[2]

Finally, we need to reflect on the relation between collection and interpretation, between displayed artifact and didactic design, as this defines the terrain within which effective urban historical-museum exhibits, as distinct from illustrated academic lectures, can be mounted. Recent commentary has tended to see modern scholarship as a kind of populist knight riding to rescue history from tradition-bound, elite-serving museums. Often quite correctly, critics have faulted the museums for having confused cart and horse—for permitting an obligation to display their "things" to overwhelm interpretation, imprisoning it within airless display cases. Accordingly, feverish imagination has been devoted to opening up the museum so that new ideas, values, and subject matter might ventilate the intellectual space of the exhibit. In the process, however, historians have often undervalued the artifactual base of most museum collections and what these artifacts contribute to the museum experience. Indeed, scholars have often proved quite insensitive to the whole notion of how and why a museum exhibit is interesting to its visitors.

This is not simply a matter of academics casting the exhibit process in their own intellectual image. The problems are real enough, and the critique intimidating enough, that the academic approach has been largely internalized by many museum professionals seeking to modernize their exhibit approaches. Relatively less attention is being paid to the collections and how the interest they hold for visitors may serve as a resource for new approaches to historical interpretation. Instead, inordinate emphasis has often been placed on the "script" content and the conceptualization behind it, as if the point were to present the "right" message "to" the public, its points "illustrated" by artifacts, rather than to offer an environment within which historical materials and ideas were discussed "with" visitors, however implicitly.

This is a subtle but important distinction that is just beginning to be recognized more widely. In Edward Alexander's classic overview *Museums in Motion*, for instance, there is virtually no attention to how history museums and their audiences interact, aside from a rule-proving exception: a discussion of communications theory, feedback loops, and behavioral objectives that has no particular relation to historical communication as such. And at the vanguard Past Meets Present Conference, for all the exciting dialogue between historians and museum professionals, there was almost no discussion linking the two on questions of presentational choices involved in effectively reaching an audience with a given historical thematic exhibit. Those talking about space, display, and design issues tended to be the professional designers, who quite naturally approached these questions in terms of flow, imagery, and audience psychology, not as matters with implications for historical content and interpretation.[3]

Recent experience on a National Endowment for the Humanities (NEH) museum panel suggests that there is something more general in this indifference. The panel I served on examined some thirty-five proposals, most of them professional, sophisticated, and well prepared. Yet scarcely *any* spoke at all, much less in depth or precision, to what I would term the strategic challenge of the proposed exhibit: how it intended to work with and for the kind of audience anticipated; how this context informed what could and could not be displayed or communicated; how content and design were related to hoped-for responses and reactions, and to what effect. Almost totally missing was any consideration of the collections approach and the design challenge of the particular theme or content and the proposed solution offered by the exhibit interpretation and plan. Rather, the grant writers were relentlessly drawn to elaborate demonstrations of the intellectual pedigree and scholarly provenance of exhibit concepts and affirmations of the importance of bringing them to a wide public. But the process of actually doing this was rarely discussed as complex or demanding in any serious intellectual sense; this was implied to be something the design consultants and collection people would take up later.

Some of this may trace to the fact that these were applications to NEH, after all, and that such an intellectual focus is what applicants thought they were expected to advance. But NEH's Museum Division panels are generally composed equally of museum professionals and academics, and even if correct the guess as to what was expected of applicants only underscores the point that academic historical discourse and the museum's traditional concern with the uses of collections and the power of artifacts remain on separate tracks. The two dimensions ultimately need to be joined in and for the visitor, of course, and in doing so I think that the degree of attention to the audience role in how an exhibit actually works may turn out to be a crucial variable.

In the area of formal municipal history exhibits, the problem of audience extends across the conventional academic-museum divide, yet each side has real resources that can be mobilized to address it. There is much in the new social and urban history that could generate innovative ways for helping visitors see their own lives and experiences reflected in the narrative flow of city history. And since the conventional municipal exhibit is usually not about a focused collection but must use a wide range of objects to tell a broader story far from explicit in the artifacts themselves, it rests to a real extent on precisely the inquiry-driven approach to the use and development of collections that the Common Agenda group, for instance, sees as one of the most promising bridges for linking museums and historical scholarship.[4] Indeed, as we shall see presently, important clues to how artifacts can figure in presentation and interpretation can be rescued from even the most parochial, pedestrian, and pompous exercises in historical puffery.

Thus alerted to some of the barriers to and opportunities for innovative public-historical presentation in the large-city urban history exhibit, let us move out of the interpretation center into some of the museums themselves.

A Visit to Some Current Core Exhibits

Founded in 1923, the Museum of the City of New York claims to be the first museum in the nation explicitly dedicated to the history of a major city. Housed in an imposing Georgian building at Fifth Avenue and 103rd Street, it is somewhat off the visitor's beaten path in Manhattan, and it gives the impression of a sleepy, old-fashioned facility with rich, traditional collections, just beginning to show some vitality and to struggle for broader relevance and scope in its offerings and programs. The featured exhibit on my 1987 visit was "Bellevue Hospital: 250 Years in Service to New York," and it was smartly designed and quite professional, mixing artifacts, well-chosen photographs, and a sophisticated text. While it contains little that might disturb the Bellevue alumni whose grant supported it, this exhibit does offer historical insight into the complexity of defining and providing institutional welfare, medical, and psychiatric services in a growing metropolis.

The formal, permanent city history exhibits, however, are very dated. They stem from an era in which history largely meant the colonial and Revolutionary periods, and in which maps, a few tools and artifacts, and a great deal of furniture were arranged to evoke a long-departed urban milieu. The two major galleries focus on Dutch New Amsterdam and English-Revolutionary New York City. The latter consists mostly of furniture, costumes, and Gilbert Stuart Washingtons. The Dutch gallery is an imposing example of an old-fashioned form: there is a replica of a fort whose steps and balustrades one can walk. And there is a marvelous diorama surrounding an elaborate model of Lower Manhattan with corresponding maps. But there is nothing that really suggests the nature or process of urban growth, nor is there any clear interpretation of why this city, in this place, at this time, had this particular form or history.

Beyond that, the museum's exhibits are explicitly collection focused rather than historically interpretive: there are a number of period rooms from actual elite homes, an Alexander Hamilton room, silver displays, a map and print collection, and two small galleries focused on the Stock Exchange and the port, both concerned more with display of memorabilia, models, and the like rather than extensive historical interpretation. These exhibits (as well as the famous dollhouse, toy, and costume collections on the third floor) are quite interesting in the different ways that such artifacts can engage one's historical curiosity, but they do not pretend to a coherent urban historical statement.

For this purpose, the museum relies on a relatively new centerpiece: a splashy multimedia audiovisual show titled "The Big Apple" (the museum's new logo is based on the same), sponsored, quite prominently, by ITT and evidently directed at schoolchildren. In an object-bordered gallery room stands a huge red apple; as the show starts, it opens to reveal multiple slide screens. The show that follows is in constant visual motion, accompanied by narration spiced with music, sound effects, and periodic snippets of dialogue by actors.

The script is embarrassing as advertising, much less as history. It races from landmark to landmark—Verrazano, the Dutch, the Revolution, Robert Fulton, the clipper ships, Central Park, the Statue of Liberty, and so on—stitching the whole together with predictable homilies: New York City illustrates the American trinity of vigorous commercial development, technological growth, and individual opportunity; success rewards "energetic, hard working people, creative, ingenious, and inventive people from all over the world"; New York is a melting pot for groups such as the Irish (who, "after a difficult period of adjustment due to shortages of jobs and housing and religious discrimination . . . are assimilated and become another important part of New York"). For the twentieth century, the pacing becomes incoherently frenetic ("By 1930, the time of the great economic depression, the population reaches nearly seven million. And as New York's population rises to enormous heights so do its buildings."), punctuated by mention of Puerto Ricans and a hollow tribute to Harlem, where "the entire scope of Black America's unique culture survives and flourishes." This permits the conclusion that "New York City is a city of all nations. A city of all peoples and for all peoples. . . . A city for the young and a city for the old. A city for the rich and a city for the not-so-rich." [5]

The show is more instructive as a display of presentational techniques. Interestingly, the jazziest are the least effective: much of the visual material is impressive but gains little from the rapid-fire split-multiple-screen projection. And it is hard to imagine even young schoolchildren finding the theatrical moments anything but ludicrous: "There's talk our new Director-General, Peter Minuit, will offer, in the name of our Dutch West India Company, to buy legally the Island from the Indians!" and then "Governor! Governor! The English ships are entering the harbor!" giving us New York, where a man exclaims, "Life is harder here than in England, but this is a place to grow, a place for the future!" The dialogue doesn't get much better under American auspices.

Where it is grounded more in the traditional strengths of the museum, however, the Big Apple show is surprisingly effective. Its greatest contribution is housing the show not in a theater but in a museum gallery, for just as one is getting used to the barrage of slides and music, a new dimension opens up: "In 1613, Block moors his ship, the *Tiger*, near the southern tip of the small island the natives call 'Manhattan.' Unfortunately, the ship catches fire, burns, and sinks in the harbor. High on the wall, to your left, are some of the actual charred timbers of the *Tiger*, discovered fifty years ago." As heads turn, the timbers are picked out by the beam of a spotlight. The technique is used repeatedly: "Behind you, back here on your right, this fourteen-passenger horsecar and others like it help to meet the internal transportation needs of the growing community. . . . This is the era of the great clipper ships. Look to your left: that's a carved figurehead from a British East Indian ship. Sailing the Seven Seas from China, Africa, Europe, and the Spice Islands, these ships bring their cargoes to South Street, on the East River."

Even when the text is corny there is something powerful about the way the spotlight stills the breathless motion of the slide show. It provides a moment for silent concentration on a real artifact and does so far more effectively than would the pointing finger of a walking-tour guide. This reminds us of the most traditional virtue of museums: the unconstrained imaginative power of objects from the past, if we can be encouraged to pause and look at them closely.

The Museum of the City of New York, then, seems a representative embodiment of the strengths and weaknesses of very conventional approaches to city history. Its attempt to make a Great Leap Forward via technology indicates how unpromising is this effort in the absence of an accompanying effort to rethink the history itself. But it also suggests, more usefully, that the strengths of traditional collections need not be jettisoned and may actually provide substantial support for more innovative techniques, approaches, and interpretation.

The Atwater Kent Museum in Philadelphia, occupying an imposing Greek Revival building that was once the Franklin Institute, dates from 1939, which makes it the second-oldest formal city museum in the country. It is trimmer and more focused than its Manhattan predecessor and is currently undergoing substantial revitalization and redevelopment by an ambitious staff. The major exhibit, "Philadelphia, 1680–1880," was designed in the late 1970s, when the Atwater Kent attempted to interpret far more systematically than the Museum of the City of New York the process of historical development in a major city. This core installation captures well the intellectual and presentational content of a serious museum approach on the eve of the current wave of innovation and reflection.

The exhibit is traditional in style and tone: it occupies a large terraced room through which the visitor walks past a chronological-thematic sequence of artifact displays, most in cases, supplemented by a few large graphics and hangings. The most unusual interpretive display technique, in fact, dates from the 1938–40 WPA project out of which the museum itself evolved. This is a large-scale model of Elfreth's Alley, Philadelphia's most famous eighteenth-century street, oriented around a view from the complex of back-alleys and yards; a cleverly placed mirror permits a good view of the neat brick frontage of the rowhouses as well, suggesting through its refraction the contrast between the serene neat image and the more complex social reality of eighteenth-century neighborhood life. More generally, while organized around the displayed collection, the exhibit is not quite artifact driven: it follows a logical sequence of topics grounded in a reasonably clear if conventional narrative conception.

A panel at the start sets the tone: Philadelphia "germinated from a seed" planted by Penn and the Quakers, "flowered" into a commercial and cultural center, and (the botanical metaphor gives out at that point) "became a dynamic industrial metropolis" by the late nineteenth century. The displays, we are told, intend to depict what "shaped the city, guided its development, and made it unique."

The first displays deal well with the geographic setting and overall growth patterns, displaying a series of population distribution charts for the entire time period and maps illustrating the role of rivers and land in shaping Philadelphia's development. They represent a rather aggressive frame-setting start. The exhibit then settles to a more conventional movement relying on dramatic artifacts and familiar topics—a number of cases on Penn, the 1682 city plan, and the Quaker way of life, both domestic and commercial, followed by a sequence focused in eighteenth-century life—taverns, home life, and particularly artisan crafts and culture, discussed as central to understanding, both as cause and effect, Philadelphia's increasingly cosmopolitan economic role in the colonies and in Atlantic commerce. But the momentum generated here is not seized to help explain the evolution of a city or its role in broader changes. A series of cases on the Revolution loses a sense of Philadelphia almost entirely, choosing instead to highlight evocative curiosities (Liberty Chairs, carved eagles, the requisite grapeshot and river chains) not connected to any urban narrative.

The remainder of the exhibit is organized around promising thematic headings—"Maritime Philadelphia" and "By Industry We Thrive"—that suggest the evolution from a mature commercial economy to an industrial city. The artifacts, a number of them reclaimed through urban archaeology, are especially good at illustrating a range of industries identified with Philadelphia, from engines to lace and cigars and pharmaceuticals. But the limited stock of interpretive energy, it seems, is expended entirely on a number of well-taken points about the processes of growth. Nothing else gives the visitor much sense of the structure, population, space, or feel of either a commercial or industrial city, much less how one shifted into the other. Strong on some of the things that happened in the city, the exhibit makes little attempt to describe, much less interpret, the processes of city growth and life as these change over time. The exhibit seems to have lost its focus and energy near the end, presenting some topics (like transportation) out of any helpful sequence and closing with a surprisingly thin evocation of the 1876 centennial.

In sum, the exhibit is reasonably coherent and substantive, avoiding the heroic mode and approaching the process of growth with some sense of its complexity. But ultimately it remains caught in the paradox announced at the start, trying at once to show Philadelphia as unique while also more analytically interpreting it as an example of more general dynamics and processes of urban growth in the context of American history. It avoids too much of a plunge in either direction, which leaves it solidly balanced on the strength of its artifactual display: a straightforward and engaging exhibit, but not particularly inspired on either the design or conceptual level.

Other standing exhibits at the Atwater Kent focus on particular aspects of municipal institutional history—gas and water, fire, and police. A similar approach is more productive here because the artifacts are particularly interesting in human terms (leaves from police mug books, for instance) and because the way services link people, environment, and institutions makes even a brief treatment a base for interesting reflection on the workings of an actual city. These rooms provide something of a bridge between the traditional cast of the major exhibit and newer special projects just taking shape, to be discussed a little further on.

There are two museums in St. Louis offering permanent exhibits on the history of the city. As a complement to its elaborate Museum of Western Expansion underneath the mammoth waterside Gateway Arch, the National Park Service has opened the magnificent Old Courthouse nearby as an exhibit and interpretive center devoted to St. Louis's more particular role in the process and how this in turn shaped the city and its people. Several miles away, there is a similarly conceived permanent display, titled "Where Rivers Meet," in the Missouri Historical Society's Jefferson Memorial Building in Forest Park. While still essentially traditional in historical conception, both exhibits suggest some of the new currents beginning to shape presentation in the last ten years.

The Old Courthouse presents urban history in four rooms, each representing a distinct era: "St. Louis: The Early Years, 1764–1850"; "St. Louis: Becoming a City, 1850–1900"; and "St. Louis Entering the Twentieth Century, 1900–1930" are explicitly historical, while "St. Louis Revisited: 1930–present" is a pastiche of evocative current and retrospective materials, dealing mostly with architectural history.

Perhaps because the Old Courthouse is more interpretive center than museum, hence weaker on artifacts, the exhibit is heavy on design and graphics. There are dramatic photo blowups and document extracts on several of the surrounding walls, time-line charts, and kiosks featuring period-specific portraits of St. Louis people, ordinary as well as famous. These are added cumulatively so that each period kiosk is more full and varied in every sense, a quiet way of making the usually heavy-handed point about an American city's pluralistic composition. But many artifacts are displayed, with considerable imagination, to evoke larger environments: each room features a large, impressive triangular platform in the center, arranged so that it displays an exterior environment from two sides and a corresponding interior as one circles around.

The logic of historical explanation is clear if schematic: early St. Louis is a matter of the fur trade, river traffic, and the French-American transfer. Within this frame, the exhibit works hard to evoke the role and character of the Mississippi waterfront town, an evocation made more necessary because, ironically, Gateway Arch and the Expansion Park of which this museum is a part have obliterated that historical environment almost entirely. If frontier urbanization derives from larger economic settlement patterns, the maturing city is presented in terms of the shift from commerce to industry and a consequent reorganization of the nation's economic space and urban network, here aptly symbolized by the 1874 Eads Bridge that at once suggested the triumph of steel, the triumph of rails over the river and its steamboats, and the necessity of St. Louis's finding another role in the emerging modern industrial era. The twentieth century is handled less coherently: it is a tougher problem, and the lure of the 1904 fair, Lindbergh, and nostalgic domestic artifacts proves irresistible.

An accompanying orientation film, *Gateway to the West*, mirrors the strengths and weaknesses of the exhibit. More an illustrated lecture than a narrated film, it features a professor as a "walking head" posed before a sequence of attractive backdrops, telling St. Louis's story. Among his better moments are a description of how early prosperity owed less to frontiersmen than to the European "accident of fashion" that raised the price of beaver pelts so high, and a discussion of the steamboat era focused on the city's role as an outfitting and transfer point for westward movement. But the gateway theme proves exhausted once the railroad ends this era; the film leaps to a formulaic tribute to resurgent St. Louis in the late twentieth century.

The Missouri Historical Society's exhibit "Where Rivers Meet" is conceptually quite similar and follows a parallel rhythm, though it is more conventional in layout and more solidly grounded in a rich artifactual collection. The early section is excellent geographically, featuring some helpful schematic maps that clarify St. Louis's centrality in an elaborate river system extending through the Midwest and West—something not very obvious to modern audiences. But it is less sophisticated than the Old Courthouse on the dynamics of trade in the fur and steamboat eras, relying instead on boat models and an elaborate wheelhouse platform-cum-diorama, and it is equally unhelpful in dealing with railroading, beyond the Eads Bridge (neither exhibit mentions the struggle of St. Louis and Chicago interests for railroad control of the West, for instance). At the end there is a modest attempt to link social history to municipal history: the effects of turn-of-the-century immigration are treated more extensively, with attention to the process by which some stayed on rather than passing through, and their patterns of settlement in the city.

An accompanying audiovisual slide presentation retraces the story and carries it through the twentieth century in predictably heroic terms: the community spirit of 1904, later fanned by Lindbergh, flickers through the era of slums and skyscrapers, in which St. Louis was left behind by progress, "gasping its last breath" until a "newly ignited fire of pride" revives the city and makes it once again "a meeting place for all." Within this frame, however, the presentation underscores the point that urban development involves the complex intersection of "people, buildings, and history," a model not inconsistent with more sophisticated interpretation than it receives here and a good one with which to arm visitors heading into a conventional narrative exhibit.

Finally, at the Missouri Historical Society, as at the Atwater Kent, the most exciting urban history presentations are in ancillary exhibits focused on aspects of municipal life: a magnificent room on firefighters is as rich in curious artifacts as one might wish while also managing to present the process of firefighting, the relation of firehouses and water systems to the social geography of the city, and the long struggle between the volunteer system and professionalization. Equally interesting if idiosyncratic is a permanent tribute to a St. Louis curiosity, the Veiled Prophet, a pseudomythic Mardi Gras–like masked ball created by Victorian boosters and soon crystallizing as an elite ritual with a prominent debutante as queen each year. Many costumes are displayed, and the gallery is ringed by pictures of each queen from 1878 on, the implicit effect of which is cumulatively fascinating: though all are portraits of rich young women of debutante age, there is enormous variation in the social statements implicit in their dress, expression, and posture. There is also description of the form's more recent experimentation with various street and civic festival incarnations, especially after heavy political criticism; that blacks could not participate until 1979 tells us perhaps more than St. Louis boosters might wish the exhibit to reveal.

To the extent that the St. Louis, Philadelphia, and New York exhibits can be taken as defining something of a point of departure for contemporary efforts to reimagine urban historical museum presentation, what can be said more generally about this established interpretive approach? Perhaps it can best be summed up in the thematic concerns discussed at the start of this essay.

The narrative approach to framing the life story of a city in anthropomorphic terms, a city whose birth, growth, troubles, dreams, and triumphs can be set in the context of the national history within which it acts—this construct has manifest deficiencies as a way of understanding historical change. But it also has some less-obvious virtues. In addition to providing a ready framework for organizing exhibits with focus and narrative flow, the device has, in the exhibits we have seen, proved reasonably effective at handling some kinds of systemic change, such as the sequence of economic bases through which a city can move in conjunction with technological, structural, and political changes in the world around it, matters quite relevant to a public that needs to understand similar changes in urban America today. The construct has seemed able to deflect the fatal temptations of both a heroically individualized "city fatherism" on the one hand and technologically deterministic forces of change on the other, conceptions which in so many other contexts exert an irresistible pull on exhibit designers. The anthropomorphized urban biography thus stands as something of a countervaling force to approaches even further removed from historical reality.

Our examples suggest, however, that this approach is less frequently or comfortably applied to modern history, including most of the twentieth century. In part this is because only recently have traditional museums felt pressured to extend the realm of the historical towards the present; more deeply, it is tempting to speculate that the kinds of statements that seem acceptable when applied to distant periods would beg too many questions, would be too transparently inadequate as descriptions of a world viewers know at closer hand.

Taken together, these considerations suggest that rather than casting the narrative biographical story line aside as obsolete by definition, it may be worthwhile to seek ways of modernizing it, to rethink how it might still be used as a framing element that would help us discuss in broad terms how urban communities have functioned in the context of equally generalized historical constructs, forces, and systemic structural changes.

As for the second concern, neither social-scientific urbanological insights nor the new social history, by the evidence of our survey, have made much of a dent on interpretive content or design, unless one counts very modest efforts to suggest that the city population and the chamber of commerce are not exactly the same. The occasional references to blacks, immigrants, labor, women, and ordinary people in general are just that—not much more serious than the frantic compensatory acknowledgments towards the end of the Big Apple media show. Perhaps the reason for this neglect is not that more analytic or social-historical approaches are that unacceptable in their own terms, but, rather, that it has proved so hard to imagine them within the heroic narrative, hence the greater ease with which we found a refreshing variety of perspectives animating the special exhibits on urban services and institutions, exhibits that do not labor under this narrative burden and thus seem to find accessible the materials from which very different notions of urban structure and life can begin to be imagined and evoked.

Finally, there seem to be few clear patterns by which this or that approach to exhibit content and design imply consistent understandings about what will generate audience involvement and reflection. The more aggressive and conceptual modern exhibit designs seem engaging in concept but are often curiously patronizing; the older ones are the opposite in that tired concepts never quite suffocate the fascination of the richly varied things on display, sometimes quite imaginatively set forth. By and large, however, the exhibits we have examined, including the ancillary films and media materials, rely on the classic combination of a relatively unmediated display of artifacts, to which the response can be open ended and unpredictable, and an authoritative historical voice intoning the seamless narrative of a city's biographically coherent movement through time.

It remains to be seen whether newer approaches to urban historical analysis, to social history, and to the very purposes and structure of museum exhibits can combine to reach audiences in deeper and different ways, whether innovative programming can both generate and arise from a less didactic approach to interpretation, whether it can reach genuinely diverse audiences with complex relationships to the embrace of the presumptive community of the city, and whether, more generally, it is possible to be more sensitive to the needs, responses, and contributions viewers make, if only in the imagination with which they receive and digest historical exhibits.

To this end, let us turn to brief consideration of a number of current developments, both planned and realized: new approaches at the Atwater Kent; recent developments in Baltimore, both at the city-history Peale Museum and the ambitious young Museum of Industry; and in New York City, where South Street Seaport is designing an ambitious new central museum space and permanent exhibition to anchor its interpretation of the site and artifacts of the Port of New York. Though, again, my own recent visits represent only slightly more than random samples, there will be little in what follows to suggest that these are unrepresentative or anomalous.

The Emerging Shape of Presentation and Interpretation

At today's Atwater Kent, welcoming text in the entry vestibule suggests a significant reorientation: the museum formally announces its dedication to preserving, collecting, and interpreting the history of the city but defines this as explicitly including Philadelphia's complex social history and popular culture. It also moves away from the heroic stress on uniqueness and urban pride, declaring that "although the Museum's interpretive focus is on the Philadelphia experience, it depicts the city's history within the context of the broad patterns and trends of American life. . . . [It] seeks to reach a large general audience by presenting Philadelphia's history as representative of our nation's development."

The clearest departure from tradition is the way the museum, in this same vestibule, invites visitors to approach and experience historical collections, using their own authority as interpreters. Rather than assuming, as conventionally, that visitors are tabula rasa on which history is to be inscribed, the Atwater Kent asks them to think about how artifacts can reflect their own experience and knowledge of the city and to critique the exhibits from this vantage. Moreover, as the details of daily life and culture have historical meaning and as the present is soon to be history itself, visitors are asked to help the museum decide what artifacts of contemporary Philadelphia life ought to be collected now, and why. Alongside a modest display of once ordinary but now historical artifacts from the recent past (a Flexible Flyer sled, Stetson hatbox, and Philco radio, all important local products), the museum provides notebooks in which visitors can contribute suggestions, comments, and critiques.

Perhaps more in tone than in substance, this welcome touches on all of the themes noted above: it announces an intention to move the narrative mode away from the narrowly urban biographical, to refashion historical content through exploring the social history of urban life and processes, and to make the relation between museum and its audience reciprocal, open-ended, and alive—a central element in both collection development and exhibition design.

It is too early to say how these ambitions will work out in practice, as redesigning a museum is a slow process involving much more than the articulation of a new policy direction. Current steps, however, are encouraging: a staid gallery of Philadelphia paintings and prints has now been transformed into a room titled "The City Beneath Us," where changing exhibits will relate the process and findings of urban archaeology in Philadelphia to the contemporary city; another exhibit will aim at helping audiences understand "the way in which the Museum develops, cares for, and uses its collections"; and the core urban history installation is slated for total reconception and redesign.[6]

The major new exhibit at the time of my 1987 visit, "Made in Philadelphia, 1830–1930," is also an improvement. Its attention to the evolution of industrial Philadelphia omits none of the major foci that would have dominated such an exhibit in the past, from Baldwin Engine, Disston Saw, Stetson Hat, and Cramps Shipyard of the nineteenth century to G. E. and Rohm-Haas of the twentieth. But the text is far more sophisticated in discussing the process of industrial development, providing an anchor for discussion and documentation of wider patterns of economic change, of the relation of production to complex commercial and consumption patterns, and of the links between industrial work and workers—their backgrounds, skills, families, and neighborhoods.

The exhibit draws on up-to-date scholarship, particularly Philip Scranton's and Walter Licht's *Work Sights: Industrial Philadelphia, 1890–1950* (Philadelphia: Temple University Press, 1987); both authors were involved in developing the exhibit text, and excellent use is made of some of the most dramatic illustrations from their volume: large photo blowups complement specific artifacts, often picturing the context of operation by workers. While in form it attempts few dramatic presentational innovations, the exhibit's linking of economic development and daily life does suggest how socially grounded economic history can recast the story of urban growth in ways open to innovative development. And some final panels hint at how a different conception of the audience's role can energize the gallery experience. The exhibit closes by recalling that entry-vestibule request in helpfully specific terms, asking visitors to think about their own family history of work, tools, neighborhoods, businesses, and industry and to think of things the exhibit might have missed, things that might actually be in their own attics. The point is only superficially to invite donations; the effect is rather to stress that if today's personal can be historical, then urban history, process as well as artifact, can be understood as alive and real in the present, a point nicely implicit throughout the exhibit.

In Baltimore, the relation between history and the present has been seized upon as an instrument and expression of the city's current rebirth. This renaissance has been an inspiring process somewhat uncomfortably propelled by the enormously successful Harbor Place waterfront mall-boutique complex and associated gentrification. In this context, the turn to history implies a certain search for legitimation. Whatever its sources and the uses to which it is put, however, the impulse has taken on a life of its own, with generally impressive results. A constellation of City Life Museums offers a comprehensive perspective on Baltimore history and material culture. Most of this is in one complex of buildings: the Carroll Mansion, memorializing in conventional ways the longest-surviving signer of the Declaration of Independence; the 1840 House, in whose hands-on nonartifacted interiors living-history performances attempt to evoke the mid–nineteenth century; the Center for Urban Archeology, featuring actual workshops and an exhibit explaining the process of such work; and the new Courtyard Exhibition Center.

The main burden of formal urban historical display and interpretation has been taken up by the Peale Museum, a short distance away, which in 1978 began to shift dramatically from its largely artistic orientation (housed in painter Rembrandt Peale's 1814 mansion, it based its early collection on the Peale family's work and related Baltimore prints and maps). Its rebirth has involved major rebuilding, reorganizing, and a new approach to collecting, display, and audience development. All this surfaced in 1981 in its dramatic permanent exhibit, "Rowhouse: A Baltimore Style of Living," which has deservedly attracted national attention and praise.[7]

The rowhouse installation is remarkable in that although nominally about a specialized topic, it offers a strikingly inclusive social, economic, and institutional profile of Baltimore's overall history, one grounded in the most prosaic details of ordinary life and in the very buildings that still house a large proportion of Baltimore's residents (and of the museum's visitors.) That a museum whose role is to be the formal expression of Baltimore history presents this refreshing vantage as its major defining exhibit is an extraordinarily powerful statement, even before the specific content is considered.

That content is not disappointing. The show sets chronological narrative, organized in several major phases, against a sequence of dramatic period settings that display and analyze both exterior detail and interior rowhouse life. Without any sense of breathless rushing or clutter, the frame somehow permits intensive examination of architectural history, broad urban economic development patterns, complex legal financial mechanisms, the links between real estate developers and their clients, and the relation of all these to neighbor-hood, work, family life, ethnicity, and class.

At every point, such themes are reflected in a fascinating variety of graphics, documents, and illustrative artifacts. Indeed, much of the remarkable vitality of the installation seems grounded in this resonance between themes and things, and I was not surprised to learn that this relationship had been perhaps the central concern of a staff intent on revitalizing an institution. Resisting the temptation to see imported academic concepts and dazzling design techniques as ends in their own right, as the redemptive knights saving the museum from its stodgy self, the curators consciously used them for resuscitation: as one commented later, they had deliberately sought a topic that would require them to collect new artifacts, intending to show how "exhibit-driven collecting" could be used as a way "to refocus and re-energize the collecting process."

By thus expanding the symbiosis between modern interpretation and the traditional collecting and display functions of museums, the exhibit has suc-ceeded at being at once enormously popular and deeply instructive: it leaves visitors with new tools, ideas, and understandings (of everything from style to the complex social and developmental influence of Baltimore's unusual ground-rent tradition) with which to examine the city they encounter upon emerging from the museum. "Rowhouse" is hardly beyond criticism in its decisions and emphases, but as an approach to urban biography, to exploring social and urban complexity, to interpreting collections so as to help visitors to reflect on the relation of history to their own world, it is light years ahead of anything we have seen so far in this essay.[8]

Other developments in Baltimore suggest some additionally salient direc-tions. The remarkable new Baltimore Museum of Industry, for example, is gathering in an abandoned factory a spectacular collection of industrial tools and machines, assembled into re-created work environments that support not only demonstration by skilled workers but more ambitious programming about their lives and environments. The museum thus provides a powerful counter to the gentrifying impulse that would render the industrial environment anti-septically and nostalgically distant, something appropriate only to a boutique design or a condo marketing strategy.[9]

But there are also some warning signs in Baltimore, for history as a tool of civic revitalization is not history in necessarily reliable hands. Some of these dangers are evident in the City Life Museums' Courtyard Exhibition Cen-ter, whose premier exhibit, "Rebuilding an American City: Baltimore Today" traces the historical roots and processes of the current municipal vitality over some thirty or forty years. This exhibit bravely takes on some complex topics, from the intricacies of urban-renewal legislation to the workings of city, state, and federal politics to the role of neighborhood activists and organizations and the issue of race in modern America. This is ground rarely engaged by public presentation yet central to understanding modern American cities. And the exhibit approaches its topics with state-of-the-art techniques: oral history tape loops accompany a slide show featuring a diversity of political actors and community activists; we see shocking video footage of a major racial disturbance within a civic event in 1970; and there are dramatic graphics, carefully drawn maps, a place for visitor suggestions, and an elaborate electronic display titled "It's Your Choice!" offering policy options on a number of issues, with the display dependent on which choice the visitor selects.

Unfortunately, in this heady atmosphere the air of municipal self-congratulation can be suffocating. For all the attention to complex policy issues and interactive display design, the narrative seems driven to tell a story scarcely translated from its inherited nineteenth-century form, a story of civic will triumphant, of virtuous leadership, of community consensus arising out of conflict, and so on. The video of the 1970 racial disturbance, for example, is bracketed with another video of a successful civic celebration in 1972, featuring happy, strolling, racially mixed crowds: evidently Baltimore's racial problems had been handled with brisk dispatch. And the "It's Your Choice!" board works like this: if the question is whether urban renewal should focus on neighborhoods or downtown, visitors choosing the latter are told that Baltimore understood the importance of downtown and acted decisively to revitalize it; visitors choosing the former learn that Baltimore did not sacrifice its communities in favor of downtown, but, rather, acted decisively to combat neighborhood decay.

In Baltimore, then, a somewhat hyperactive but genuine and broadly grounded municipal revitalization is providing the major impetus to a broad range of museum and public historical activities, which in turn are conceived as playing a major role in sustaining this civic momentum. The moment is one of enormous potential for the urban historical museum, with both the opportunity for and the access to exciting new ideas and techniques opening up considerably. That this carries with it some reasonably obvious problems and dangers does not make the opportunity less interesting, but rather more —the struggle to turn this energy in new directions seems very much worth engaging.

This image describes well the mood at the relatively new South Street Seaport Museum in New York City, where we will focus not on an existing exhibit but on the planning process that confronts a situation exaggerating enormously the risks and opportunities of the present interpretive juncture, thereby helping to clarify the challenge faced less dramatically elsewhere.

The challenge in this setting is not so much latter-day boosterism as new-model commercialism in the form of the mammoth South Street Seaport project developed by James Rouse, which is well on its way to becoming New

York City's biggest tourist complex, with an estimated fifteen million visitors yearly. The museum itself originated as something of a tiny, underfinanced dog wagged by the enormous commercial tail of this development, for which it helped provide a legitimizing historical pedigree. This Rouse enterprise is different from his own Baltimore Harbor Place project, not only in scale, but in that history is far more explicit in the overall commercial conception—evoked in the signs and boutiques, invoked by strolling costumed hawkers and a variety of ersatz community events, and provoked by a spectacularly overdone commercial multimedia extravaganza, "The Seaport Experience," where "a surprise-filled theater" takes you back to the time "when ships were tall, men were bold, and even a kid in Nebraska could hear the call of the sea." Notwithstanding some attempts at lashing down the script with historically responsible lines, the show sails out on the romantic seas that lap the seaport as well: this is history as commercial concept, history in the hands of "interpreneurs."

The young museum set amidst all this faces a Faustian dilemma: it is temptingly provided with millions of curious visitors strolling nearby, alerted to and attracted by at least the aura of history; it sits on a genuinely important site whose fascinating story is central to one of the world's most important cities and to the entire development of modern society over the past several centuries; and it has a growing collection that ranges from maps and artifacts to spectacular dockside ships to historical buildings just revealing their treasures under restoration (an upper-floor door was recently opened to reveal a virtually intact nineteenth-century seaman's hotel, for instance). But the very forces creating the opportunity seem likely to overwhelm it entirely. Even if it cannot pretend ever to wag the tail, can this pup of a museum find a way to stand on its own and offer something of genuine historical value to those who are drawn to notice it, a huge number, in museum terms, if only a minuscule proportion of the millions eating, drinking, networking, and buying their way through the Rouse arcades?

The approach to date has been the "Museum Without Walls," described as "an accumulation of encounters and events" involving ships, guided tours, self-guided walking tours, lectures, small exhibits, and so on, beyond this essay's focus on major installations. Interestingly, however, the institution's recently approved master plan recognizes that the site and context require a "Museum *With* Walls," a "highly visible, very tangible response to the visitor's inquiry, 'Where is the Museum?' " Accordingly, it proposes, and is currently designing, a major 25,000-square-foot exhibit and support space to occupy three floors of a landmark building at the very center of the district— "a presence strong enough to compete with the surrounding activity." [10]

The 1985 master plan outlined an initial conceptualization for the proposed major permanent exhibit, and the museum is moving slowly and deliberately to develop it, aware that its margin of error is very small: the situation requires a precise combination of historical insight and imagination with great sensitivity to the interpretive requirements of the setting. To this end, the museum recently convened a daylong conference involving some twenty historians. This conference can provide the stopping point for our tour, as it brings the academic-museum dialogue to the surface in an appropriately unfinished form well capturing the open-endedness of the current moment.

It would be easy, but unfair, to see the six hours of discussion as a kind of caricature, with academics and museum people running true to stereotype and proving predictably frustrating to each other. Certainly, talk careened back and forth across the same set of topics, with no discernible resolution in sight at day's end. Nevertheless, the discussion did develop a certain focus, hopefully useful to museum planners; its contours, in any event, are quite relevant to the themes we have been following.

In the first place, the scholars—quite diverse in terms of intellectual orientation and standing at a variety of points in relation to the politics of the new social history—were close to unanimous in seeking to steer the museum's ship away from the route charted in the master plan. This had organized prospective exhibits around five chronological-thematic phases drawn initially from Robert Albion's 1939 classic *The Rise of New York Port, 1815–1860* and from a sequel volume being completed now under museum auspices. The segments were to be "Predestination, 1640–1815"; "Entrepreneurship, 1815–1860"; "Revolution, 1860–1914"; "Institutionalization, 1914–1965"; and "The Modern Port, 1965–present." To this didactic strategy was wedded a proposed interpretive one: each period would be "personified" through concentration on an "appropriate exemplar or series of witnesses."

In this scheme the historians sensed the hold of precisely the traditional conceptions the museum has a tabula rasa opportunity to transcend. The periodization seemed the most dated and misleading, obscuring any number of important historical themes and relationships behind a progression that in the early periods was fundamentally wrong in several respects and in the later periods so generalized as to provide little interpretive guidance. In the impulse to personalize, almost everyone sensed an approach that would be counterproductive in the extreme, one reinforcing the heroic implications of the narrative structure rather than counterbalancing the academic reach of the text, and one that would be interpretively retrograde by assuming audiences require human detail that could best be provided through exemplary personalities, mainly individual, powerful history makers and a few more ordinary "witnesses" thrown in for new-social-history balance.

As a result of this critique, most of the day was spent brainstorming alternate approaches. Many agreed that bottom-up historical perspectives represented a major responsibility and opportunity not yet developed in the museum's plan, implying interpretation focused more on the lives of seamen and port people and on economic growth and change as both made by and experienced from their vantage point. But it was more widely felt that such a reorientation would not itself suffice, that social history alone could tend to obscure the larger currents of change, the way the Port of New York represented a complex historical ecology, a city-building force, and an element in the complex web of world economic and political relationships, all of which were in important and distinct historical motion.

To this extent, most of the group sensed that the proper target of interpretation would be found at the intersection of two axes: one involves the way in which individual experience and local structures can be related to broad-scale systemic changes, and the other involves the way in which the past's relation to the present can be understood and expressed, that paradox by which people need to find the past recognizable, as textured and as human as the present, in order to appreciate its complexity and reality, while at the same time they need to appreciate that history means differences as well—in how things worked, how people lived and thought, and what they valued. If the crosshair of these axes could be trained just right, an exhibit strategy would have a chance to present a very different conception of what and who was relevant to the history of New York Port and what that had to contribute to an understanding of the present.

This approach presumes an implicit dialogue with the audience, and not surprisingly this was the least-developed aspect of the discussion. There was relatively little discussion of how to define, much less make, particular choices about precisely what to exhibit and how in order to reach and involve the audience. Both museum staff and historians seemed to assume that clarifying their historical message *to* the public was a necessary first step; it was harder, in this context, to discuss how thinking of that audience in more active terms, as people coming with implicit questions to be answered, assumptions to be challenged, experience to be drawn on, and ideas to be engaged might itself provide some important direction in locating the best target for our crosshair sights.

Towards a Fourth Dimension

In several senses, the South Street seminar can be taken as a good summary of this essay's examination of current urban historical museum exhibition, poised as the field is on the edge of an exciting new period of development and experiment.

The narrative structure of a city's story, we have seen, is a warhorse that needs less to be retired than to be reshod, so that its thematic strength can be used to pull very different wagons. Our visits suggest as well that the lessons of social, economic, and political history, all the newer ways scholars have been exploring or expressing what and who a city is, and how its structure, processes, and culture evolve historically for all its people—these need not be inconsistent with such stories and in fact must be turned to if we are to imagine newer forms of narrative that are effective. And finally, we have detected a perhaps underappreciated power in that most fundamental and venerable of museum functions, the collection and display of meaningful artifacts.

This constellation suggests how requisite it has become to join such notions and bring them to bear on the problem of historical interpretation. Urban and social historians have developed a wealth of exciting new insights, but they have not yet been able to present these consistently in publicly engaging ways. Historical museums have always known something about drawing and even satisfying audiences, but these audiences have traditionally been somewhat narrow, and it is not clear how meaningful and interesting their museum experiences have been. As the Common Agenda and Past Meets Present conferences suggested, there is a swelling interest in discovering how academic historians and museum professionals can help each other shape a new kind of historical dialogue with the public precisely at a time when there is a broader appreciation of how imperative it has become to deepen public awareness of our place in history and history's place in the dynamics of our lives and communities today.

But this dialogue promises more than merely another response to this recently discovered crisis in cultural and historical literacy. The urban historical museum perspective suggests more deeply a recasting of the problem. For as Larry E. Tise, the director of the American Association for State and Local History, has observed, whatever the supposed indifference to history in schools and however great the collapse of historical memory revealed by tests, there has been "an almost unbelievable explosion of interest in history" in museums, tourist sites, popular literature, and the media in "the vast arena . . . where Americans of their own free choice make decisions about what they will see, do, and read." The issue for museums and historians who care about them would seem to be less a matter of generating interest than of learning more about what drives an existing interest and thereby finding ways of meeting it with historical interpretation on mutually meaningful common ground.[11]

And this suggests, finally, the broader importance of the fourth dimension we have been able to track in the above examples, beyond the roles of narrative, scholarship, and artifact: the underappreciated capacity of the audience itself to help resolve dilemmas of presentation or interpretation of urban historical complexity. We are just beginning to explore what this might mean for a broad interpretive strategy. In the Common Agenda report, for instance, L. Thomas Frye calls for a broadened conception of how informants and sources, not excluding the actual visitor standing before an exhibit, can contribute to interpretation a special "historical specificity through direct knowledge and experience" while the museum retains responsibility for "interpreting the objects within the context of a broader shared cultural experience." [12]

Such a model is promising, but it does not really involve a very different distribution of interpretive authority, as Frye reveals in his well-intentioned but somewhat imperious advice that museums become more involved in "collecting the people along with their objects." Perhaps closer to what I have in mind is the observation by Barbara Melosh and Christina Simmons that "exhibits necessarily embody assumptions about what audiences already know; like other social texts, they carry on an implicit dialogue with an imagined audience." [13] In this essay's selective tour, we have seen the importance of this dimension for understanding precisely how the surveyed exhibits do or do not work as intended for the diverse audiences that come to big-city urban history museums; our examples suggest the importance of making the dialogue more explicit than implicit, for audiences that are more tangible and particular than imaginary.

Perhaps one final example will help make the implications of such an approach even clearer. Planners at the Brooklyn Historical Society are using an audience-sensitive approach to resolve otherwise immobilizing problems in capturing a complex social history within an attractive exhibit narrative, especially given a very small available space: after much struggle, they decided to abandon an overall chronological approach and to build the exhibit around a series of popular symbols at the center of the visitors' initial image of Brooklyn and its history: the Brooklyn Bridge, Coney Island, the Navy Yard, the Dodgers, and the Brooklynites themselves as colorful characters. These were chosen quite deliberately so that concise interpretation of each could develop a different dimension of a broader history, from social and cultural to economic to political, and link past and present. The exhibit will be enterable at any point, literally and figuratively, and the visitor's interest in these symbols of Brooklyn (and the artifact-rich displays that illustrate and interpret them) will provide a comfortable base of competence and involvement from which new historical materials and understandings can be engaged.

This is only one way in which respect for the audience's own experience might become a force supporting and propelling complex interpretation. The more general point is that involving the audience as a strategic element must mean something well beyond the already familiar tokenism in exhibit content or the shallow gimmicks that offer the illusion of active participation and involvement. Rather, our survey has suggested that we need to broaden not only techniques and historical concepts but the very way we understand audiences to be engaged in the communicative process itself, and to make this understanding a more active resource in historical exhibits. In this regard, the urban historical setting provides special and substantial opportunities for sophisticated dialogue if we can become better at respecting our visitors' very real knowledge and experience and learn how to turn both presumed certainties and areas of ignorance into the energy of activated curiosity. In the final analysis, this is the only force capable of permitting an exhibit to come alive for the people who happen to visit it, and to stay with them after they have left.

NOTES

1. See the book resulting from the New York conference, Jo Blatti, ed., *Past Meets Present: Essays About Historic Interpretation and Public Audiences* (Washington: Smithsonian Institution Press, 1987), especially the introduction summarizing the conference format, issues, and "expeditions": Jo Blatti, "Past Meets Present: Field Notes on Historical Sites, Programs, Professionalism, and Visitors," 1–20. See also Thomas J. Schlereth, "Defining Collecting Missions: National and Regional Models," and the conference's recommended specific actions in Lonn W. Taylor, ed., *A Common Agenda for History Museums: Conference Proceedings, February 19–20, 1987* (Nashville, Tenn.: American Association for State and Local History and Smithsonian Institution, 1987) 24, 13.

2. I have discussed these general intellectual developments in "American Urban History as an Example of Recent Historiography," *History and Theory* 18, no. 3 (1979), 350–77, and I consider some of the public historical implications of the new urban history in "Public History in Urban Celebratory Contexts: The Example of the 'Philadelphia's Moving Past' Project," in my book *A Shared Authority: Essays on the Craft and Meaning of Oral and Public History* (Albany: State University of New York Press, 1989).

3. Edward P. Alexander, *Museums in Motion: An Introduction to the History and Functions of Museums* (Nashville: American Association for State and Local History, 1979), 169–71; Blatti, *Past Meets Present*, includes conference papers and postconference reflections on these issues in Section II, "Design and Technique in the Realization of Interpretive Programs," 95–130.

4. "Collections Working Group"; Schlereth, "Defining Collecting Missions," in Taylor, *Common Agenda*, 9, 26–27.

5. Quoted from the full text of the script, available at the museum on request as "Classroom Study Guide For the Big Apple, a multimedia presentation of the history of New York in the Museum of the City of New York, funded by the International Telephone and Telegraph Corporation."

6. My thanks to Atwater Kent Executive Director John V. Alviti for discussing these plans with me after my unannounced 1987 visit. The museum has subsequently initiated a lively newsletter discussing its ongoing development in detail; see, for example, Atwater Kent Museum *News and Notes* 1 (April 1988).

7. See, for instance, the extensive and thoughtful review-critique by Roger B. White, "Whither the Urban History Exhibit? The Peale Museum's 'Rowhouse,' " *Technology and Culture* 24 (January 1983) 76–90.

8. Visitors receive an elaborate souvenir handout in the form of a tabloid newspaper, *The Rowhouse Times*, which summarizes the exhibit, reproduces some of its text and

graphics, and offers additional background information on rowhouses in history and as a contemporary urban concern. This is available on request from The Peale, Baltimore's Historic Museum, 235 Holliday Street, Baltimore, MD 21202.

9. This museum regularly publishes a newsletter, *Nuts and Bolts*, describing its collections, exhibits, programs, and plans. Copies are available from the Baltimore Museum of Industry, 1415 Key Highway, Baltimore, MD 21230.

10. Peter Neill, "Report From the President: The Master Plan, 1985–1990," *Seaport: The Magazine of the South Street Seaport Museum* 19 (Fall 1985), 4–9.

11. Larry E. Tise, "Organizing America's History Business: A New Ethic and Plan of Action," Special Report, Technical Information Service, American Association for State and Local History, n.d. but 1987. I discuss some of the broader issues implied by the current cultural-literacy debate in "American History and the Structures of Collective Memory," in *A Shared Authority*.

12. L. Thomas Frye, "Museum Collecting for the Twenty-first Century," *Common Agenda*, 35–36.

13. Frye, "Museum Collecting," 36; Barbara Melosh and Christina Simmons, "Exhibiting Women's History," in Susan Porter Benson, Stephen Brier, and Roy Rosenzweig, eds., *Presenting the Past: Essays on History and the Public* (Philadelphia: Temple University Press, 1986), 203.

Living-History Museums 3

Warren Leon and Margaret Piatt

Ninety years after the Essex Institute in Salem, Massachusetts, began dressing guides at the John Ward House in period costumes, living history remains controversial. This teaching approach, which uses costumed staff members who enact historical activities in restored or re-created settings, is praised for the extensive historical research it often requires but damned as frivolous show-business entertainment. Living-history museums are lauded for presenting the everyday lives of average Americans yet criticized as elitist monuments to the worldview of the dominant classes. Some critics object to the focus of living-history museums on the gritty, mundane reality of the past; others complain that they prettify and sanitize history.

All these perspectives contain elements of truth. The greatest strengths of living-history museums are sometimes also their greatest weaknesses. They are complex institutions whose problems and advantages differ from those of other museums. This essay examines both their possibilities and their limitations.

We start by profiling living-history museums as a group to show some clear and troubling biases rooted in their collective history. We then examine the constraints on an individual site's ability to present accurate and meaningful history. Such museums face structural constraints produced by physical settings and audience expectations, as well as staffing constraints, since they rely so heavily on people to teach visitors. Living history's two main teaching techniques—first-person interpretation and third-person interpretation—also embody distinct advantages and disadvantages. Finally, having set out the quite considerable obstacles to effective living history, we conclude by explaining why it remains a compelling way for museums to present history to the public.

Living-history museums are a broad and varied lot. But we will narrow the field by focusing our attention on those institutions using living history as their primary interpretive tool and eliminating those sites—historic houses

—incorporating living-history techniques as an adjunct to a different form of presentation.

The Contours of a Lopsided Field

Living-history museums show an unrepresentative sample of past Americans. With few exceptions, they depict the lives of middle- and upper-income Protestants in agrarian settings. Nineteenth-century Shakers, for example, are well represented by living-history museums, but Irish immigrant laborers, black slaves, coal miners and Polish-American steel workers are not. Jay Anderson's recent listing of sixty living-history museums in the United States includes none that focus on twentieth-century urban industrial life.[1] The largest number, thirty, featured working farms and rural farmsteads. Five forts memorialized the French and Indian War; none recalled domestic preparations for World War I or re-created the Civil War.

Some critics have charged that this tendency to focus on a seemingly simpler agrarian past merely reflects the sponsorship of living-history museums by powerful members of a corporate elite who wished to appropriate the past, but the story is actually more complicated.[2] True, prominent industrialists sponsored the largest and most popular living-history museums—John D. Rockefeller, Jr. and Colonial Williamsburg, Henry Ford and Greenfield Village, and the Wells Brothers (American Optical Company) and Old Sturbridge Village — yet most smaller living-history museums have quite different origins. State and county governments account for twenty-three of Anderson's sixty sites. The National Park Service, which was bitten by the living-history bug in the 1960s, runs seven. Groups of middle-class Americans without the support of any single dominant individual have founded others.

Hence the pre-twentieth-century agrarian bias of living-history museums reflects not just their sponsorship but also their history.[3] Historians of the living-history movement generally trace it back to European open-air museums and especially to Artur Hazelius, founder of the Swedish museum Skansen, which opened in 1881. Yet for American living-history museums, historic-house museums and historic-preservation efforts had much more influence than European precedents.

By 1910, patricians, civic leaders, and middle-class professionals anxious to protect what they viewed as traditional American values and cultural styles from the threat of more recent European immigrants had preserved one hundred historic houses. Because these native-born Americans wished to preserve and restore the "best" examples of their culture, these historic houses were either connected with prominent early Americans or represented distinguished architecture. For members of the Sons of the American Revolution, the Mount Vernon Ladies' Association, the Society for the Preservation of New England

Antiquities, and other similar groups, seventeenth- and eighteenth-century architecture became, as historian Michael Wallace has noted, "something of a cultural emblem" that symbolized the preimmigrant social order.[4]

Living-history museums emerged from this movement to preserve distinguished architecture and to glorify Anglo-Saxon cultural values. Living history began with the 1685 John Ward House in Salem, Massachusetts, which the Essex Institute had targeted for preservation and restoration in 1909. Over the next few years, the organization's secretary, George Francis Dow, experimented with re-creating a lived-in atmosphere in the house. He placed objects in casual arrangements and selected three women "dressed in homespun costumes of the time when the house was built" to show the house to visitors. Dow also moved several other structures to the site, including a shed, a store, and an apothecary shop.[5] In subsequent years, other historic houses incorporated such nascent living-history techniques.

Even some quite recent living-history museums are traditional historic houses that later expanded into living-history interpretation. Pennsbury Manor in Morrisville, Pennsylvania, for example, began in the 1930s as an effort by the Pennsylvania Historical Commission to reconstruct the architecturally distinguished country estate of a prominent colonist, William Penn. It opened to the public during the next decade as a typical historic house.[6] In the 1970s, the staff made living history its primary interpretive tool. Yet such an institution continues to be shaped by the origins and early history of the historic-house movement.

The most influential living-history museum, Colonial Williamsburg, also has strong roots in the historic-house and historic-preservation movements. William Goodwin, rector of Williamsburg's 1715 Bruton Parish Church and later professor of religion at the College of William and Mary, had supervised a conventional early-twentieth-century restoration project, that of his own church. But he gradually began to advocate a larger project, the restoration of an entire community, Williamsburg, which he considered the "Cradle of the Republic" and "the birthplace of her liberty." Goodwin realized that such an ambitious project would require significant financial resources, and he approached several influential people and groups before convincing John D. Rockefeller, Jr. in 1926 to finance an architectural plan for a restored Williamsburg. Rockefeller, who already had demonstrated an interest in architectural preservation by helping to finance the repair of Versailles and other French architectural masterpieces, was attracted to the challenge of preserving "the beauty and charm of the old buildings and gardens of the city." He contributed seventy-nine million dollars during the next decade towards the physical restoration and reconstruction of the colonial town of Williamsburg. To create a pure, eighteenth-century atmosphere, more than seven hundred buildings that postdated 1790 were demolished and a railroad was rerouted. Although the site began using costumed guides in 1932 and added craft demonstrators and other incipient living-history techniques soon after, Goodwin, Rockefeller, and their collaborators had provided Colonial Williamsburg with a heritage that emphasized the preservation of distinguished architecture and viewed seventeenth- and eighteenth-century cultural values as particularly admirable and worth emulating. As Rockefeller claimed, the restoration "teaches of the patriotism, high purpose, and unselfish devotion of our forefathers to the common good." [7]

The other major outdoor museum of the interwar period, Henry Ford's idiosyncratic Greenfield Village, owed less to the historic-house and architectural-preservation traditions but also had much less influence on the development of living-history museums. Williamsburg, not Greenfield Village, became a major national cultural symbol in the 1930s and set the standard for other outdoor history museums. Williamsburg helped enshrine the colonial era as one especially appropriate to museum restoration projects.

The next wave of outdoor history museums, which by the 1950s included the New York State Historical Association's Farmers' Museum, Old Sturbridge Village and Historic Deerfield in Massachusetts, Old Salem in North Carolina, Mystic Seaport in Connecticut, and the Shelburne Museum in Vermont, all preserved or re-created more modest communities than the colonial capital of Virginia. Yet the Williamsburg model influenced them as well; they selected structures partly for their architectural significance and considered early America a time especially worthy of re-creation. As these sites grew, they then used one another as models and developed along parallel paths.[8]

The public's response to what was presented played a major role in shaping living-history museums and, for example, encouraged the spread of craft demonstrations. Museum visitors loved to see craftspeople make products by hand. At a time when modern technology had made production processes incomprehensible and invisible to most Americans, there was something comforting and appealing to seeing a broom, chair, blanket, or andiron created by the skilled hands of the patient craftsperson. To many visitors, such demonstrations symbolized what was lost in the transition to the modern urban-industrial world and infused living-history museums with a nostalgic atmosphere.[9]

Craft demonstrations not only attracted visitors but brought in needed revenue through the sale of the resulting products. In the case of Williamsburg, the demand for such products quickly became so great that dozens of workers were employed behind the scenes to make additional reproductions. In other outdoor museums, craft demonstrations also received disproportionate public attention and museum resources. Old Sturbridge Village, for example, which claimed to show life in an inland New England community between 1790 and 1840, did not initially include a farm, even though most New Englanders were farmers. Yet the museum featured four craft shops when it opened in 1946 and several more by the 1950s.

By the 1960s, Williamsburg, Sturbridge, and the other living-history museums had created a popular model that included costumed staff members, craft demonstrations, early American buildings, period rooms, and informal settings. The interpretation focused on the decorative arts, architecture, craft processes, and the glorification of early American values. Individuals and groups who admired these living-history museums decided consciously and unabashedly to copy this model and produced smaller versions in their own communities. Without the financial or human resources of the larger institutions, the younger sites often incorporated aspects of the more established museums that were completely inappropriate to the new settings, regions, and time periods. A new museum might make the same brooms as the broom shop at Old Sturbridge Village without ever researching whether the same style of broom was used in the region the museum represented or even whether any brooms were produced there at all.

By the 1970s, as the older museums increased their attendance—with Williamsburg attracting more than a million visitors each year—and as the upcoming American Revolution Bicentennial and the vogue for "history from the bottom up" drew attention to daily life in the past, more municipalities, state governments, and individuals found it attractive to copy the living-history model that had been established at the major institutions in the 1950s.

Old Bedford Village in Bedford, Pennsylvania, was typical. Local officials saw the museum, which grew out of the community's bicentennial efforts, as a way to build a tourist industry and revive the town's failing economy. For the city of Bedford, in an economically depressed section of the state and isolated from major population centers, tourism seemed a logical route to economic redevelopment. Old Bedford Village offered a way to attract travelers who drove by on the Pennsylvania Turnpike. Unfortunately, local funds did not provide enough resources to present accurate history. Impressive community involvement enabled the museum staff to identify and transport fascinating and unusual examples of vernacular architecture to the site, but the small three-member administrative staff had neither the time nor the skill as historians to install appropriate activities in the buildings or to research fully the region's history. They placed candle making, for example, in a new structure without historical prototypes as a chandlery because it seemed to be a mainstay of other living-history museums and was popular with visitors.[10]

Ironically, as little Williamsburgs, Old Sturbridge Villages, and Plimoth Plantations sprang up across the country, changes in the museum field and historical scholarship forced changes in the very institutions that were the object of emulation. More specialized and professionally trained staff members joined the large museums. At the same time, "new social historians" turned to subjects that living-history museums had long depicted. As Williamsburg's director of research, Cary Carson has noted, the museums' "collections of ordinary, everyday activities re-created the basic life experiences that serve[d] as focal points for the new social history—birth, education, work, marriage, death, disease, and the provision of clothing, housing, and material possessions." Museum professionals used academic historians' findings and conducted their own studies so that the larger living-history museums moved from demonstrations and discussions of buildings, antiques, and processes to the interpretation of people's lives and to the themes of the new social history. Old Sturbridge Village, for example, organized its interpretation around the themes of family, work, and community, while St. Mary's City in Maryland focused on the process of historical change.[11]

By the 1980s many of the larger and better-established living-history museums saw their mission as the re-creation of an entire community and sought to explain to visitors how that community functioned. Craft demonstrations, for example, were linked to one another to show the complex web of economic and social relationships within a community. Interpreters in a pottery shop now discussed not just how a pot was made but described the potter's economic status, trading network, family life, social standing, education, work history, political activities, and religious beliefs.[12] Living-history museums in the 1970s and 1980s continually added new subjects to their repertoire, from childbirth to widowhood and old age, from religious revivals to phrenology and tavern life.

Living-history museums' functional approach, which showed visitors how a community worked, tended to downplay aspects of community life that were dysfunctional or produced conflict. Consequently, at roughly the same time Elizabeth Fox-Genovese and Eugene Genovese attacked academic social history for ignoring power relationships, social conflict, and politics, Thomas Schlereth accused living-history museums of depicting "peaceable kingdoms" that ignored conflict. Schlereth called on museums to incorporate violence, vigilantism, family discord, labor conflict, minority political movements, and other evidence of conflict into their interpretation of community life.[13]

Although historical conflict and unpleasant subjects remain strikingly underemphasized in living-history museums, in the 1980s an increasing number of institutions introduced previously uninterpreted aspects of the nondomestic sphere and widened their definition of appropriate subject matter. Conner Prairie in Noblesville, Indiana, for instance, treated controversial subjects through the re-creation of funerals, temperance meetings, and pauper auctions. Old Bethpage Village Restoration on Long Island re-created political elections. Old Sturbridge Village focused on conflict over slavery and the antislavery movement in the rural North and used town meetings to show a variety of deep cleavages in the community. Unfortunately, most living-history museums still do not interpret such subjects, and even the programs that exist reach only a small minority of an institution's visitors. Nevertheless, over time the number and range of these programs will likely increase as more living-history museums work to make their depiction of community life more comprehensive.[14]

The new social history's scholarship was not the most important influence on living-history museums' presentations during the past two decades, however. The concurrent living-historical-farms movement was even more influential. It too caused museums to raise their standards. But while closer links to academic social history encouraged individual living-history museums to broaden their interpretation of the past, the living-historical-farms movement unintentionally caused the field as a whole to restrict its scope.

The concept of working historical farms was not new. As early as 1945, Herbert Kellar had urged Agricultural History Society members to build "living agricultural museums" across the country, and other members of the society discussed at length the need for a national museum of agriculture. The Farmers' Museum at Cooperstown and Old Sturbridge Village began to keep a few head of livestock in the 1950s, but no outdoor museum re-created a fully operational farm. In 1965, when Marion Clawson again urged the members of the Agricultural History Society to establish what he called "living historical farms," he could cite several contemplated projects but no concrete accomplishments.[15]

During the next few years, however, a living-historical-farms movement spread among agricultural historians, museum professionals, and agriculturists with astonishing speed. John Schlebecker, curator of agriculture at the Smithsonian Institution, played a key role in promoting the idea by establishing the Living Historical Farms Project at the Smithsonian, which studied what various museums were already doing and developed proposals for a nationally coordinated program. Although his proposals for a special Living Historical Farms Extension Service and seven hundred thousand dollars in national funds went unheeded, Schlebecker built momentum for the movement. By trumpeting the few embryonic attempts to establish working farms and by showing the value and logic behind the concept, Schlebecker made the establishment of such museums seem both desirable and inevitable.[16]

The incipient movement coalesced about 1970. At Old Sturbridge Village, geographer and agricultural historian Darwin Kelsey began converting the Freeman family homestead into an operating farm.[17] He proved that small-scale preindustrial farming was ideally suited to living-history interpretation. The popular appeal of Freeman Farm—with its varied sounds, smells, and sights and its ever-changing seasonal activities—was apparent as soon as it opened. But the project also received unusual support from a wide range of scholars and museum professionals. A 1970 symposium in Sturbridge on American agriculture, 1790–1840, sponsored by the Agricultural History Society, the Smithsonian Institution, and the United States Department of Agriculture, gave an implicit seal of approval to the Freeman Farm project; the published proceedings of the symposium spread the idea to others.[18]

The Freeman Farm project quickly became the model for others wishing to incorporate a living historical farm into an existing outdoor history museum. At about the same time, Living History Farms in Des Moines, Iowa, showed how to create an entire new institution for interpreting agricultural history. In 1969, Iowa State University agriculture professor William Murray founded Living History Farms, where he envisioned three different farms: an 1840s pioneer homestead, a 1900s farm, and an experimental "farm of the future." In this way, visitors could see how Iowa agriculture had changed over time.[19]

Building on these efforts, twenty-seven participants at the 1970 Sturbridge symposium formed the Association for Living Historical Farms and Agricultural Museums (ALHFAM).[20] Through annual meetings and its *Bulletin*, ALHFAM provided a forum for the exchange of ideas among the growing number of operating farm museums. By 1981, 222 institutions had living historical farms.[21] Since ALHFAM was the only organization directed specifically at institutions doing any kind of living history, it became a powerful vehicle for promoting agricultural history within living-history museums in general. It meant that new ideas in agricultural interpretation were disseminated more quickly and effectively than were ideas and methods for presenting other historical subjects.

The dramatic success of the living-historical-farm idea helped to strengthen and solidify the preindustrial bias of living-history museums. Existing living-history museums sought ways to add working farms, not only because the public had shown much enthusiasm for the animals and activities on such farms but also because the leaders of the movement were successful in convincing museum professionals and boards of trustees that it was educationally important to give modern urbanites and suburbanites "a sense of farming and farm life." [22] Even such a well-established institution as the Henry Ford Museum made a working farm the centerpiece of its efforts to improve its presentation in the mid-1980s.[23]

As operating farms spread in museums, they ensured that living-history museums would continue to ignore the twentieth century. Even though, as John Schlebecker has admitted, many of the most important agricultural changes occurred after 1940, almost all living-history farms focus on the period before 1870. To attempt to re-create farming for any later time requires enormously expensive and time-consuming restoration or reproduction of machines and implements. "A pioneer period is always favoured," Schlebecker writes, "for the nostalgia is greater. More importantly, pioneers seldom had advanced machinery." [24]

These practical reasons for avoiding modern agriculture also help explain why living-history museums have avoided tackling any large-scale, complex modern communities. The more complex the community or work setting, the more difficult the task of restoration and re-creation. It is far cheaper and easier to re-create a two-story wood house than a twelve-story apartment building. It is hard enough for a museum to stock the shelves of a small rural store without trying to replicate the interior of a mammoth department store of the 1920s—or a shopping mall of the 1960s. A living-history museum showing a meatpacking district in 1915 Chicago would require complex factory equipment that has not been manufactured for more than seventy years. Could the era's telephone systems, streets, water faucets, gas appliances, trolleys, cars, and horse-drawn carriages all be restored and used? To show factory life, could the museum ask hundreds of staff members to re-create unsafe work practices in working environments that have long since been abandoned as unhealthy?

Because of costs and the inherent problems of such endeavors, living-history museums will probably retain their preindustrial agrarian bias. Still, living-history techniques *are* beginning to be incorporated into museums of urban and industrial history. The national and state parks in Lowell, Massachusetts, integrate role players into tours of an industrial city and may use costumed staff members in the weaving room of the Boott Mill, which is being restored. But several costumed staff members demonstrating a few looms in a space formerly occupied by dozens of machines and workers will not adequately re-create the work environment. Living-history methods will remain only a small part of the entire presentation. Museums seeking to use costumed staff members in such settings will need to supplement them with audio and visual presentations to give visitors a sense of the entire social system.

House museums, with their contained spaces and manageable furnishings costs, will probably have the easiest time incorporating living-history methods into an urban setting. The Baltimore City Life Museums are already using actors who perform tightly scripted scenes in the 1840 House to show working-class immigrant life.[25] Living history will gradually spread to a wider range of institutions without losing its essentially rural, preindustrial identity.

Coping with a Heritage of Incomplete Landscapes and Escapist Audiences

A single living-history museum cannot alone overcome the biases of the entire genre; it can only try to present its chosen subject fully and accurately. But even the best living-history museums generally fall far short of this goal. In fact, they are limited both by the physical plants they have inherited from their predecessors and by expectations and preferences the visiting public has built up over several generations. An extended case study of the largest living-history museum, Colonial Williamsburg, shows the difficulties all such museums face.

With a yearly budget five to ten times larger than such other well-known living history museums as Plimoth Plantation and Conner Prairie, Colonial Williamsburg has significantly greater resources at its disposal. Its joint sponsorship of the Institute of Early American History and Culture, active publication program, and impressive roster of scholars, currently including historian Cary Carson and archaeologist Ivor Noël Hume, have helped place it in the forefront of research on colonial America. The institution has openly admitted the weaknesses in its historical presentation and has worked hard to eliminate them. The public programs and physical setting of Colonial Williamsburg are continually revised and modified to bring them in line with current research findings. Extensive training programs ensure that the institution's front-line staff is familiar with the latest scholarship.

Williamsburg has also benefited from considerably more critical scrutiny than other history museums. Its preeminent place among living-history museums and its influence on the broader culture through the colonial revival movement have encouraged critics to study its message and meaning.[26] Although Colonial Williamsburg has received its share of praise, two recurring criticisms stand out: that it presents a sanitized version of the past and that it underestimates the role of slavery and slaves in colonial Virginia. Neither new programs, additional buildings, nor revised interpretation have enabled Colonial Williamsburg to respond fully to this criticism.

In the mid-1960s, critics of urban renewal projects and suburbia saw similarities between the sterility of such modern housing and Colonial Williamsburg. "For all its scholarly verisimilitude," David Lowenthal complained, "Williamsburg has the flavor of a well-kept contemporary suburb." Influential *New York Times* architectural critic Ada Louise Huxtable accused Williamsburg's overly neat and orderly museum village of sapping the vitality and sense of reality from the past. Walter Muir Whitehill, the venerable historian of the historical-society movement, was even harsher, calling Colonial Williamsburg "an entirely artificial recreation of an imaginery past," nothing more than a "fantasy in which the more pleasing aspects of colonial life are evoked, with the omission of smells, flies, pigs, dirt and slave quarters."[27]

A few years later, with renewed interest in Afro-American history and more open criticism of establishment institutions by black activists, Williamsburg's interpretation came under attack as incomplete and racist. For a museum that claimed to embody the concepts of "opportunity," "individual liberties," "self government," "the integrity of the individual," and "responsible leadership," slavery was an unwelcome embarrassment. The lives of that half of Williamsburg's population consisting of black slaves were consequently ignored by interpreters and hidden from visitors. Moreover, in a region where segregated workplaces were still common into the 1960s, virtually the only blacks that visitors encountered were the waiters, waitresses, and busboys in the cafeteria and restaurants. "A visit to Williamsburg," Zora Martin Felton, the director of education at the Anacostia Neighborhood Museum, charged in 1974, "reinforces the antiquated belief of minimal black participation and smiling faces. It is imperative that a true perspective of the people, the time, and the place emerge." [28]

Such attacks helped convince the staff and management at Colonial Williamsburg to change their presentation of the past. The emergence of the new social history helped provide them with sound models for reconsidering the history of eighteenth-century Williamsburg, and they began the task of modifying interpretive training, publications, and the physical environment of their living-history museum.

When confronting the charge that Williamsburg had prettified and sanitized the past, the Williamsburg staff and management openly admitted most of the inaccuracies in the museum's landscape, since they realized it would take time to eliminate or at least reduce them. As early as 1972 the *Official Guidebook* acknowledged that the restoration was much tidier than the original community, with "houses better painted, greens more smoothly cropped, and gardens spruced up and adorned with more flowers." Moreover, the site lacked the eighteenth-century community's "pungent smells of animal manure, rooting hogs, backyard privies, and unwashed humanity." [29]

Fifteen years later, the most noticeable changes are in the way Williamsburg's interpreters describe their historical community.[30] They are quick to point out the problems with sanitation in eighteenth-century Virginia and more openly discuss the era's social conflicts and economic dislocations. More subtle are such physical changes as the refurnishing of exhibit interiors, outbuildings that are no longer painted yearly, and grass that is not kept like a golf-course fairway.[31] But most vacationers who casually walk down Duke of Gloucester Street without examining guidebooks or conversing at length with the staff probably still go away with memories of a well-ordered, attractive community with few social problems. Even less-casual visitors probably absorb this older message, since what people see and experience in living-history museums is generally more important than what they read or hear. Costumed staff members may talk about contentious Virginians, some of whom had to struggle to attain the simplest necessities of life and to maintain basic human dignity, but the visitor is likely to remember contented, friendly, well-fed and well-clothed men and women who live in an unusually pleasant and pretty town.

To change its message dramatically, Williamsburg would need to fundamentally alter its physical environment. But an accurate re-creation of the least-pleasant aspects of eighteenth-century life would endanger visitor safety, create intolerable staff working conditions, and, most important, sharply reduce ticket sales. Williamsburg, like other leading living-history museums, has marketed itself as a holiday destination, a place for a relaxing, entertaining, even romantic, vacation. Unpleasant subjects, unappetizing smells, and ugly sights would only destroy this carefully developed promotional appeal.

Colonial Williamsburg's publicity thus downplays the newer interpretations and emphasizes the institution's older image. A widely circulated 1987 brochure, for example, begins by describing Colonial Williamsburg as "a peaceful world" with "peaceful gardens, stately government buildings, elegant colonial homes, and busy craft shops." It presents the community as idyllic and physically attractive, with "acres of beautifully landscaped gardens of colorful flowers, stately boxwood, fruit trees and berry bushes." The only odors mentioned are "the fragrance of herbs, spices, and pomanders at the apothecary." To promise tourists amenities that make for an enjoyable vacation, the brochure further blurs eighteenth-century reality with descriptions of elegant lodging ("hospitality with eighteenth-century style"), fine food ("dine in the atmosphere of gracious Virginian hospitality"), and shopping opportunities ("In eighteenth-century Williamsburg, many fine shops and stores lined Duke of Gloucester Street. Nine of these bustling retail stores operate today for you to sample both the gracious atmosphere and exceptional assortment of merchandise.").[32]

By billing themselves as popular tourist destinations, institutions like Williamsburg have reached large audiences, but those audiences have included many visitors who neither want nor expect to learn disturbing information about the past. Such vacationers seek escape from their normal concerns and cares. Living-history museums, which charge higher admission prices and rely more on tourist dollars than other history museums, cannot afford to alienate this hard-won tourist audience.

Even the modest changes to the Williamsburg landscape have offended some visitors. One such traveler explained to *Historic Preservation* why he had stopped his biennial trips to the colonial capital: "We are not at all interested in peeling paint, bare, lye-scrubbed floors and walkways paved with garbage. We can see all the dust and lint balls we want without ever leaving home."[33] Williamsburg's influence on the colonial-revival movement makes it particularly vulnerable to this sort of complaint. Many visitors who have decorated their homes in the colonial-revival style go to Williamsburg for design inspiration and think of the museum as a sort of three-dimensional *Better Homes and Gardens*. They do not want to see the warts of the past, but, rather, wish to draw inspiration from its most attractive and appealing objects and styles.

Consequently, Williamsburg has taken a cautious approach to adding new historical interpretations—one that tries to retain the institution's traditional

Duke of Gloucester Street at Colonial Williamsburg. (Colonial Williamsburg Foundation)

appeal. The new additions have had limited effect and are probably most successful at reaching the minority of visitors who participate in special programs or take special tours on economic life, women's roles, and black life.

Despite Williamsburg's considerable financial resources, it would be hard pressed to re-create the eighteenth-century community fully and accurately, even if it chose to do so. Vast sums have been invested in the current physical plant and in the arrangement of streets, buildings, and exhibit spaces. These cannot be easily changed to reflect recent historical interpretations. Unlike gallery exhibitions, which easily can be replaced by newer installations, living-history exhibits tend to be long lived. The Colonial Williamsburg staff is still coping with the implications of the 1929 decision to reconstruct the well-documented colonial capitol that had burned in 1747 rather than the architecturally less interesting but more appropriate second capitol that stood in the town at the time Colonial Williamsburg seeks to represent.[34] To reverse this decision now would be costly and time consuming. Similarly, the staff is left with the array of houses and work spaces it has inherited from previous generations of museum officials and can only gradually add buildings that might be more appropriate to an institution seeking to reflect the town's complete social and economic structure. Currently, Williamsburg still has way too many homes of prominent residents and too few dwellings of the poor.

This problem is accentuated by the peculiar nature of the Williamsburg setting, in which only a minority of the buildings in the historic district are exhibit buildings. The need to share the landscape with gift shops, restaurants, and the homes of museum staff members dilutes the flavor of the eighteenth-century community even as it gives a more accurate picture of that town's scale.[35]

Not surprisingly, attempts to improve Colonial Williamsburg's presentation of Afro-American history have focused on changing the museum's messages, staffing, training, and teaching techniques rather than its buildings, furnishings, and landscapes. In 1979, a program of "character interpretation" recruited college students with theatre experience to develop dramatic role-playing presentations to be performed that summer in the Williamsburg streets. Six of the twelve resulting characters were either slaves or free blacks. The museum abandoned this program several years later because the characters often produced confusion or anxiety in visitors who encountered them in unexpected places. But it provided a foundation for future efforts and signaled Colonial Williamsburg's commitment to the presentation of Afro-American history.[36]

The current Williamsburg programs on black history are sophisticated in content and creative in presentation. A two-hour "Other Half" tour examines black social and kin networks, religion, the laws and practices of slavery, and relations between blacks and whites. A splendid program on black music combines performance with discussion to show "how diverse African peoples created distinctive Afro-American musical forms in the New World and the forces shaping this emergent American art form." Storytelling and a play present other aspects of Afro-American culture. With a recent four hundred thousand-dollar grant from the AT&T Foundation, the programs on black history will continue to expand at Colonial Williamsburg, which is now in the forefront of using living history to present Afro-American history.[37]

Despite the quality of these new programs, Williamsburg continues to seriously underrepresent the role of black Americans in colonial Virginia. Even the museum's official images continue to downplay blacks and slavery; in 1985 and 1986, for example, the pictures in the institution's magazine, *Colonial Williamsburg*, showed 126 people in the period landscape in colonial costume, but only 5 of them were black. Moreover, most existing programs are directed at small elective audiences. The average visitor still need not confront fully the reality of slavery in Williamsburg's past, since, as Colonial Williamsburg President Charles Longsworth has admitted, "blacks are not represented physically in the Historic Area in terms of homes and room furnishings."[38]

To correct this problem, five sites "have been selected to exhibit articles representative of the material culture of black residents in Williamsburg," and major archaeological research is going on at the Brush-Everard site preparatory to reconstructing slave quarters and more fully interpreting Afro-American family life.[39] These efforts will ensure that the average visitor has some exposure to the subject of slavery, but unless half of Williamsburg's presentation focuses on the lives of blacks, the institution will continue to present an unrepresentative picture of the 1780s community.[40]

And even if such attention were to be given to Afro-Americans, the living-history format would probably impede the presentation and discussion of certain subjects. As with current Williamsburg programs, music, religion, and other aspects of slave culture, as well as daily work routines, would remain easiest to show to visitors. A much different but equally important subject, slave whippings, could not be feasibly re-created. Other subjects, including slave auctions and the daily humiliations masters visited on slaves, would probably never be shown because they would be unpleasant for the staff members who re-created them and because they might alienate visitors. The Williamsburg experience suggests, therefore, that it is easiest for a living-history museum to improve its historical presentation and incorporate recent scholarship when change does not require fundamental alterations in the museum or in its image as a nonthreatening, entertaining destination for tourists.

Research that Outpaces Teaching: The Limitations of a Museum's Staff

A living-history museum seeking to present sound and compelling history must concern itself with more than its physical plant and its visitors' expectations. Its biggest challenge is to develop a staff capable of transmitting a sophisticated message to the public. Consequently, new museums, without the constraining history of an institution like Colonial Williamsburg, have still faced massive obstacles to successful living history. In most cases they have remained unable to gather the human resources necessary to complete this task. For this reason, Old World Wisconsin, one of the most impressive, ambitious, and interesting of recently founded living-history museums, only very imperfectly presents its chosen subject to the public. In 1976 the State Historical Society of Wisconsin established Old World Wisconsin in rural Eagle, which is in the southeast part of the state thirty-five miles from Milwaukee. The new museum started with an interesting concept: to show the development and ultimate assimilation of various immigrant populations into nineteenth-century Wisconsin.[41] To do this, the museum's staff located and restored the homes, barns, and outbuildings of Wisconsin's Norwegian, German, Belgian, Bohemian, and Finnish settlers.

The project rested on a prodigious amount of research.[42] Using documentary sources, archaeology, and analyses of material culture, the staff looked at individual families and specific communities as well as national cultures. Oral history captured reminiscences and descriptive accounts of lifestyles and farming methods. Staff historians returned to Europe, where they visited the settlers' original communities to learn how agricultural methods and construction techniques were modified in the new land.

Careful decisions were then made before furnishing each house. In planning for the Norwegian-American 1865 Anders Ellingsen Kvaale Farm, for example, curator E. Emilie Tari divided the available objects into three categories: those brought from Norway, those made by the immigrants in Wisconsin, and those purchased in Wisconsin. Before any artifact or reproduction was placed in the house, it was compared with probate inventories and considered in relationship to the three categories.[43] The process produced an understanding of quite subtle differences between the material culture of the various ethnic groups shown at Old World Wisconsin. The museum's scholars have also discovered striking yet previously unexplored variations among the ways members of different groups used the same tools and carried out the same agricultural processes.[44]

Living-history museums like Old World Wisconsin, which carry out such extensive preparatory research, have made a notable contribution to scholarly understandings of the past. The process of re-creating a historical setting and historical lifestyles causes museum-based historians to ask questions that might otherwise remain unasked. The need to fill every part of the site with accurate furnishings and then to interpret it correctly requires staff members to be comprehensive in their research strategy and to gather new information. When such research is pursued imaginatively and placed in broader context, it can show specific individuals embedded in a particular region at a given time.

Armed with such detailed information on concrete historical settings and moments, Old World Wisconsin has successfully argued that small variations in different groups' material culture suggest large differences in attitudes and culture. The scholarship generated at Old World Wisconsin is consequently beginning to reshape historians' understanding of rural life in the agrarian Midwest.

There are limitations to the degree to which this sophisticated historical knowledge can be transferred to the public, however. The main problem is the nature of the museum's work force. The "interpreters," who demonstrate historical processes at Old World Wisconsin and speak with the visitors, are the main vehicle for teaching at the site. In fact, personal engagement is one of the appeals of living history—most visitors are more comfortable and find it more enjoyable to watch activities and talk with museum staff members than to read labels or examine objects.

But this teaching method puts a heavy burden on the living-history museum's interpreters. In contrast to gallery exhibits, where curators and scholars present their knowledge directly through the displays and labels, researchers at label-free living-history museums transmit their information and ideas indirectly through the interpreters. Old World Wisconsin, which is open only seasonally, does not offer its interpreters year-round employment; many stay for just a single season.[45] In that time, they can learn only a modest amount of the information the researchers have gathered and cannot develop a complete range of teaching techniques for presenting what they know to the public. Unless they are already skilled teachers and historians, they can interpret the museum's historical message only superficially. The unfortunate result is that even serious visitors to Old World Wisconsin are not likely to detect the subtle differences between the cultures presented at the various farms. For example, a recent graduate-student visitor complained that the costumed interpreters failed to add any depth or detail to the information presented in the museum's orientation slide program.[46]

Staff Training and Program Maintenance

Even if a living-history museum can acquire a less-transient staff, it must devote substantial resources to training if it wishes to present a consistent and sophisticated historical message. How much of the historians' vision of the past gets conveyed to the public is determined by how well the interpreters are trained. A half-million visitors come yearly to Old Sturbridge Village in central Massachusetts, but much of its research department's work is directed at an audience of fewer than two hundred: the interpreters who re-create life in an 1830s New England town.[47]

Those responsible for research and training at Old Sturbridge Village must divide their time between adding new information to the museum's interpretation and maintaining the existing level of interpretation. Despite relatively low staff turnover, twenty to thirty new interpreters (about 15 percent of the interpretive staff) are hired each year. These new staff members go through at least eight days of introductory training. But only after they have participated in a winter's round of seminars, focus groups, lectures, and individual projects does their historical knowledge and teaching skill begin to approach that of the staff members they replaced.

By examining training from the point of view of a particular exhibit, one sees the extensive effort required for a living-history museum merely to maintain itself. In 1979, Old Sturbridge Village revised its Fitch House exhibit. To interpret more accurately the lives of a cosmopolitan center-village printer's family influenced by economic changes and new urban fashions, the house was refurnished and reinterpreted. A team of researchers, museum educators, curators, and interpretation specialists prepared three training notebooks, each with more than seventy-five pages of material for the house's interpreters to use. They then introduced the interpreters to the new content and teaching methods during a five-day training workshop.[48]

If the Fitch House project were a gallery installation, the work would have been complete at this point. The new content would be on the walls for visitors to see, read, and absorb; it would require minimal upkeep. The Fitch House has required much more extensive maintenance, however. The house's lead interpreter must not only train about a half-dozen new interpreters for the exhibit each year but must monitor the existing interpreters to make sure they have not forgotten anything. In an environment in which so much is passed on verbally and is repeated so many times over the course of a day, it is easy for information to change subtly and unconsciously over time. After a staff member has repeated an incorrect detail or interpretation fifty times, it sounds like the truth. To prevent such alterations, periodic training updates are scheduled for the Fitch House staff. Moreover, new programs and new information must be added periodically to keep the staff members interested in and excited by a subject that they first learned about and began to communicate to visitors close to a decade earlier.

Unfortunately, it is hard to set up a structure and training process that vigilantly maintains standards once a new living-history exhibit is installed. Researchers and curators must give most of their attention to new projects once the current exhibit is finished. Moreover, their training as scholars and connoisseurs produces a natural tendency to be more interested in other aspects of their jobs than ongoing staff training. Interpretation department staff members who actually work teaching the public also tend to focus on new projects at the expense of old. The result can be a gradual decline in the quality of presentation in an exhibit.

Old Sturbridge Village's Richardson Parsonage experienced such a slump during the past decade. A major refurnishing, research, and interpretive training effort in 1975 created an exhibit showing the lives of a minister's family. Daily thematic tours on such topics as reform, transportation, and education presented the new content in a way different from any of the museum's other exhibits. The attention given the new exhibit and the sense of innovation helped create an unusually committed staff that worked together to present exciting historical interpretation.[49]

Interpretation department administrators, curators, and researchers soon turned their attention to other exhibits, however. New information was only infrequently passed on to the parsonage interpreters. Because the exhibit was no longer a top priority, new staff members were added to the house carelessly, including some who were unreceptive to the unique thematic tour approach. A few of the reproduction furnishings became shabby, while others were overprotected and underused. A lead interpreter eventually was selected to supervise the staff and maintain the exhibit, but she also was asked to manage a second, even larger house exhibit and participate in planning special events, so she had insufficient time to revitalize the parsonage. Many of the house's interpreters consequently began to feel unappreciated and at odds with one another. The content of the conversations with visitors may have remained the same, but the spirit was no longer there. What had been innovative and exciting in 1975 now seemed stale and mundane.

Because Old Sturbridge Village did not adequately maintain the new installation in Richardson Parsonage, it has taken considerable effort over the past four years to turn the situation around. Some overdue physical changes and extensive staff training efforts have begun to improve the quality of the visitor's experience.

Time Travelers Who Romanticize the Past

Even the best trainers in living-history museums have only limited influence on what the public finally sees, since the history presented is also influenced by the particular sorts of people who work there. The costumed interpreters at living-history museums are a diverse group that includes students taking time off from their studies, budding museum professionals developing job skills they can use to advance within the field, retirees seeking part-time income and diversion, craftspeople practicing their chosen trade, people hoping a museum will offer them more interesting employment than conventional work places, and those committed to using the museum to educate the general public. But the most distinctive and influential interpreters may be the living-history buffs, who work in these museums primarily because they enjoy the sense of time travel, of experiencing another time period.

The skills and seriousness of the members of this group vary widely. Some of them are, in Jay Anderson's phrase, "weekend warriors"—the estimated fifty thousand military reenactors—who then decide to seek either part- or full-time employment in a living-history museum. Others were introduced to the concept of living history by participating in the fantasy re-creations of groups like the Society for Creative Anachronism. Still others start with a scholarly interest in a particular time period that then develops into a desire to experience that era.[50]

Especially at some of the "purer" living-history sites and those that emphasize role playing, this group of committed living historians is a dominant factor. Their desire to experience the past often gives them an admirable dedication to authenticity in the details of material culture. They make sure to wear their costumes accurately, use correct tools, and even learn proper dialects and phraseology. They are frequently more important than the museum's curators, researchers, or administrators in transmitting concern for accurately re-creating the details of the past to the rest of the costumed staff.[51]

But the buffs, with their almost-religious belief in living-history re-creation, can also have an undesirable effect on the historical interpretations presented at a museum. As Jay Anderson discovered, many of them enjoy the experience of being part of another era because they seek to escape modern society, at least temporarily. He found that many of them "prefer the past to the present" and "often say they were born in the wrong century." [52] Some of them consequently romanticize the past and see it as better than the present—somehow simpler, purer, nobler, or more enjoyable. Even as they study and discuss the gritty details of past experience, they seek to turn their backs on contemporary America. Although the living-history buffs play a useful role by arguing to the public that history is not a simple story of inevitable progress, they too often make this point by idealizing the past and misinterpreting the present, particularly if their institutions do not have a solid scholarly base and strong leadership.

Living-history museums unconsciously encourage buffs to romanticize the past and visitors to misread it by being unclear about what one learns from re-creating historical processes. Living-history re-creation has produced new information and new insights, but its limits too often are ignored. The best and most careful uses of re-creation as research have been narrowly defined and labeled as "experimental archaeology." [53] For example, the only way to

Experimental archaeology at Old Sturbridge Village's pottery. (Old Sturbridge Village. Photograph by Robert S. Arnold.)

learn how fast certain historical vehicles could travel is to try them. By using historical tools, scholars can discover the relative difficulty of various processes and the time it took to complete a given task. Other experiments can show which tools were more effective or more durable.

Much of this experimental archaeology has taken place in England, Denmark, and other European countries, but Americans have tried similar experiments. At Old Sturbridge Village, for example, documentary research and archaeological excavation supervised by Director of Research John Worrell uncovered information on nineteenth-century potter Hervey Brooks's kiln and other aspects of his pottery operation. But such traditional research neither revealed the kiln's effectiveness nor showed how its operation shaped Brooks's economic role or relations. When a reproduction kiln was built and then used, it produced new information that could be learned in no other way.[54]

Interpreters' participation in such research improves their morale and makes them better historians and teachers, as long as experiments remain limited to historical processes. But the most ambitious American experimental archaeology project mistakenly also tried to uncover past values and attitudes. Colonial Pennsylvania Plantation, a small living-history museum founded in 1972, sought to re-create an early-eighteenth-century Quaker farm fifteen miles from Philadelphia. Led by folklorist and living-history advocate Jay Anderson, the plantation saw itself "as a laboratory in which serious investigators" would test "their understanding of a colonial farm by seeking to re-create its original environment."[55] Archaeologists worked alongside architectural historians, who shared the grounds with costumed "interpreter-researchers."[56]

Colonial Pennsylvania Plantation's emphasis on living history as research was exhilarating to staff members. They felt themselves to be on the cutting edge of the new social history and worked with an intense seriousness. The experiments produced additional information about colonial agriculture, raised new questions to investigate through more traditional research methods, and yet taught staff members how little they knew and how much would never be learned. Visitors also felt the institution's intensity and appreciated the focus on historical methodology. They began to think of historical study not as memorization of unchanging facts but as an open-ended process in which new information inevitably produces reinterpretation.[57]

Colonial Pennsylvania Plantation's successes were tarnished by its leaders' failure to define clearly what could be learned from experimentation. The staff was encouraged to think it was learning to feel what it was really like to live in the early 1700s, yet it is impossible to experience that era's consciousness. Analysis of primary source documents is more helpful at uncovering such attitudes than any attempt to relive the past.

At Colonial Pennsylvania Plantation, some important differences between past and present were ignored in the attempt to give staff and visitors an emotional experience. As one interpreter-researcher realized at the time, when she did a process, she "did not have the solid familiarity that comes only from doing a thing many, many, times." Moreover, she was relating to modern visitors while doing the historical activities.[58] Furthermore, the staff could never re-create the social structure, religious beliefs, and family relationships in an eighteenth-century community. Such problems not only confused staff members who wanted to experience the past but produced staff dissension and staff exhaustion. For those staff members who were not discouraged, Colonial Pennsylvania Plantation merely provided a setting to play out fantasies of both history and social life.[59]

To Role-Play or Not to Role-Play?

An institution that overcame all the logistical and personnel obstacles that living-history museums face would still have to use teaching methods that can easily produce an inaccurate representation of the past. No living-history teaching technique has proved to be without serious problems. Museum professionals long have debated the relative merits of the two main teaching approaches: third-person interpretation and first-person interpretation, also known as role playing or character presentation. Although most sites mix role playing with third-person interpretation, some museums are vigorous proponents of one or the other technique.

The initial living history experiments in the early twentieth century used the third-person approach. Staff members appeared in period costumes and re-created historical processes, but they always spoke about the past from the viewpoint of the present. Over time, a different interpretive style, first-person interpretation, developed. Its roots were partly in the theatre, but it also emerged naturally, and sometimes unwittingly, from the conversations staff members had with visitors, especially in craft shops. Visitors entering a blacksmith shop, for example, might ask the interpreter if he were the blacksmith. He would frequently answer yes and then go on to discuss what *he* was doing and how long it took *him* to make a hook or learn his trade. Was the blacksmith speaking as a twentieth-century museum staff member or as a historical character? The distinction did not always matter, since the answers to many questions would have been the same in either case.

Some museums built upon staff members' tendency to answer questions in the first person and encouraged interpreters to play the roles of historical characters. Such role playing often was introduced without considering the consequences. For example, a museum representing a seventy-five-year period might embrace role playing without appreciating that experience, social and economic situations, and attitudes would vary dramatically during that period.

In effect, such museums, some of which still persist in this approach, presented their chosen era as undifferentiated and unchanging.

Other museums gave more serious thought to the implications of first-person interpretation. Plimoth Plantation in Plymouth, Massachusetts, took the lead in developing, implementing, and disseminating the theory and practice of first-person interpretation. Plimoth was incorporated in 1947 for the purpose of "the creation, construction, and maintenance of a Pilgrim Village as a Memorial to the Pilgrim Fathers." Because none of the early settlers' original buildings survived, the museum village needed to be composed entirely of reproductions. For the museum's early leaders, Harry Hornblower II, a local history and archaeology buff, and his father, Ralph, this was not entirely a disadvantage. They were able to use an isolated location three miles from the actual settlement to build a nearly full-scale replica of the insubstantial community that was virtually the entire European presence in the region as of 1627.[60]

In the late 1960s and the 1970s, two recently arrived leaders, archaeologist James Deetz and historian David Freeman, revised the museum's programs and inspired the staff. They rooted Plimoth Plantation's presentation in such recently published scholarly works as John Demos's *A Little Commonwealth: Family Life in Plymouth Colony* (1970) and George D. Langdon, Jr.'s *Pilgrim Colony: A History of New Plymouth, 1620–1691* (1966).[61] For interpreters at Plimoth Plantation, the early 1970s were an exciting time when the museum seemed to be at the center of scholarship in its field and was developing a reputation among museum professionals for innovative programming. The interpreters diligently sought to represent the religious, political, social, and working lives of the Pilgrims. Some gradually began to speak as if they were the Pilgrims and not modern commentators. They experimented with portraying specific (historically documented) residents of 1627 Plymouth, as well as generic or composite characters. This first-person interpretation represented a grass-roots movement among the staff rather than an official institutionwide policy, and some interpreters maintained their twentieth-century third-person perspective. Yet the role players felt their efforts grew from and reflected the experimental, innovative tone set by Deetz and Freeman.[62]

The Plimoth Plantation interpreters' experiments with first-person interpretation were not always successful. Some staff members effectively created a sense of another time, while others merely confused visitors or appeared confrontational by refusing to answer anachronistic questions that referred to the world after 1627. Nevertheless, the staff's attempts to speak with modern visitors from the perspective of the seventeenth century prodded the institution to define research questions that would make the role playing more accurate and more effective. For example, the administration decided the staff should speak in the dialects of the actual residents of 1627 Plymouth, but the reconstruction of such forgotten language patterns was a major undertaking. Martyn Wakelin, a linguistics scholar at the University of London, worked several years to identify four primary dialects used in London in the 1600s, and by 1985 he had identified fourteen more. This linguistic information was compared with data about the origins of the Pilgrim settlers in various districts in England to determine which dialects were appropriate for specific staff members to use in their conversations with visitors.

In 1978 the Plimoth Plantation administration decided to rely solely on first-person interpretation and to require each staff member to play the role of an individual who actually lived in the community in 1627. The museum tried to get visitors to see themselves as anthropologists investigating an unfamiliar community. The staff members were no longer "interpreters" but "cultural informants" and the visitors became the "interpreters."[63] Unfortunately, some visitors did not relish their new role and found the staff members' peculiar speech patterns and unwillingness to acknowledge anything after 1627 threatening and offputting.

Over time, however, the museum's staff developed strategies to make visitors more comfortable in the unusual environment. For example, in the early years of Plimoth role playing, interpreters sometimes alienated camera-carrying visitors by feigning ignorance of photography and refusing to pose, but they gradually learned how to respond to visitors' perceived need for souvenir pictures. One skilled interpreter, when asked by visitors if they could take his picture, sincerely replied that "I'm so sorry, I don't have one to give you." But while visitors laughed at his joke, the interpreter straightened up into a pose, indicating with body language that they could indeed photograph him. Another interpreter responded to a would-be photographer that "if you know how to do that, you certainly may." He then pointed at the camera and remarked that "they say if you press that little button, it will take your image. I've never seen it happen but they all say it is true." The visitor got so caught up in the role-playing game that he then earnestly explained the concept of photography, seemingly forgetting that the interpreter was merely a twentieth-century person dressed in a seventeenth-century costume.[64]

By 1980, Plimoth Plantation's administration and staff were trumpeting the first-person approach as the best way to teach in a living-history museum. "The shift from third-person past to first-person present," wrote Deetz, "goes a long way toward making the interpretation convincing to the visitor. After all, if the visitor is given to believe that the houses are the way they were, why shouldn't the interpreters also fit into this plan?" Rather than have the staff members demonstrate activities for the public, Deetz wanted them, in effect, to live in the re-created community and to engage in particular productive activities only when needed.[65]

First-person interpretation at Plimoth Plantation nicely captures the sense of another world in which the residents are going about their daily tasks and activities. The staff members stand straight in multiple layers of wool and linen, look visitors in the eye, smile and laugh in a relaxed manner, and then speak in a slow, deliberate style that almost seems to be a different language. Visitors are startled at first. But they gradually become more comfortable and more polite and careful. They often respectfully ask, "May I speak with you, sir?" and then proceed to raise detailed questions about the Pilgrims lives' and attitudes. As one visitor was overheard to say to a couple entering, "If you listen to them long enough, you start talking like them—and then, you're into it." [66]

But even at its best—as at Plimoth and Indiana's Conner Prairie—first-person interpretation poses problems. Staff members not only must be taught the historical content of the site and appropriate teaching methods but also must receive thorough training in period speech patterns and theatrical techniques in order to play adequately the part of a historical character. The institution may need to undertake extensive research on subjects, such as period language, which are necessary to staff members' effective role playing but may not teach visitors much more than that people in the past spoke differently.

Moreover, first-person interpretation can actually mislead visitors about the past and about historical research. The interpreters can never say, "I don't know," to a question that their historical character could have readily answered, even if historians are completely unsure of the answer. A visitor to Plimoth, for example, could ask a female character if her children always obey her commands or if she always agrees with the life-course decisions they make. The staff member would need to answer, even though historians have only scanty information about the domestic attitudes of Plymouth's residents. When a living-history museum attempts to re-create a less fully documented community, the problem is magnified. As Deetz himself has admitted, "the possibility of any such simulation being true to what it is attempting to re-create is exceedingly slim. There are just too many variables that are beyond control. If Myles Standish were to reappear in modern Plimoth Plantation, it is certain that he would not quite know where he was." [67]

Sites that use third-person interpretation are in a better position to explain how they differ from the historical reality they ostensibly represent. They can also more easily teach visitors about the nature of historical research and historical knowledge by explaining what is not known about a given subject. Among the most valuable statements a visitor can hear in a living-history museum are "Historians do not know for sure what the answer to that question is" and "Historians disagree in their interpretation of that subject."

First-person interpreters not only must pretend to know more than the modern historian, they also must feign ignorance of subjects well known to the contemporary scholar and teacher. At Plimoth, the staff cannot discuss what happened to the community and its culture after 1627. To be authentic, the role player should not even demonstrate a good understanding of the historical forces shaping the community if the character represented, like most people, had only a limited awareness of the meaning of an era's social changes. But the role player is inevitably tempted to help visitors analyze their museum experience by subtly incorporating clues on how to compare the past with the present or by giving special attention to the most historically meaningful aspects of the culture. In so doing, the role player may become a more effective teacher but a less accurate character.

Third-person interpreters have an easier time placing the culture they depict into historical perspective and helping visitors to analyze it. They can elaborate on the meaning of particular historical developments and can show visitors more explicitly how to compare the past with the present. As one third-person interpreter, an Old Sturbridge Village blacksmith recently noted, "We can show visitors what it was like to make a weld in the old days, and we can relate it to the modern-day electric weld. We can forge a nail, a process that takes from one to three minutes, and compare that process with modern machines which spew nails out with great rapidity." [68]

But third-person interpretation has its limitations as well. Museums that rely on it give visitors less of a sense of being in another world than do sites like Plimoth Plantation. Third-person interpretation cannot draw visitors as easily into the past and pique their curiosity about unfamiliar subjects. Third-person interpreters are also unable to use a historical persona as a cover for raising controversial or difficult subjects, such as the religious bigotry of the Pilgrims or their attitudes towards death. Moreover, as James Deetz has noted, it can be "confusing to hear a person dressed in 18th-century costume speaking in modern colloquial idiom about what 'they' did in the past." [69] In fact, dressing the staff in costumes can be a pointless gimmick to make a site seem quaint. The costumes may only serve to give uninformed staff members an undeserved symbol of knowledge and authority. So one style may do a better job of teaching visitors an understanding of historical change and historians' methods, while the more theatrical approach probably is more successful at stimulating interest in the past.

Neither first-person nor third-person interpretation is best for every site, historical subject, or situation. Total role playing is better suited to Plimoth Plantation than to an institution where many untouchable antiques are on display, where the community's residents are poorly documented, or where visitors must be asked to imagine important aspects of the community that cannot be shown. In fact, for many sites the best approach is to mix third- and first-person interpretation and choose the right one for the particular situation, even though this can lead to visitor confusion.

Ultimately, even though museum professionals dwell on the distinction between living-history museums using third- and first-person interpretation, the more important cleavage in the field remains between those living-history museums that base their interpretation on careful research and training and those whose administrations and staffs make up a version of the past to please the public. In this latter category are institutions with administrations so ignorant of the nature of historical research that they blindly rely on a few outdated secondary works by antiquarians or casually copy what they have seen in other living-history museums, even if the historical period and geographical setting is entirely different. Whether such museums use first- or third-person interpretation is immaterial.

Should History Live?

Living-history museums must continually remind staff members and visitors that they do not actually represent the past; they are merely *models* of past communities where staff members present *interpretations* of history. Yet living-history museums constantly claim they are "re-creating the past" and that modern Americans can "relive" or "experience" history by visiting them.

The use of such promotional phrases is probably unavoidable, as is visitor confusion between reality and illusion when they are in living-history museums. Visitors ask interpreters, "Is that object real?" "Are you really a weaver?" "Is this building real?" and "Are you actually doing that work?" thereby showing concern for reality in museum presentation and confusion over it.

Even museum professionals cannot easily define reality at living-history museums. For example, which object presents a more authentic picture of the past at a living-history museum seeking to depict an 1830s store, an original object that no longer looks like it did when it sat new on the store's shelf or a reproduction? What does *real* mean at Old World Wisconsin or Old Sturbridge Village, where antique buildings have been relocated from various towns in the region to suggest settlement patterns that were typical, not actual? Is Colonial Williamsburg more real or less so because it depicts an actual community but mixes in modern amenities and reproduced buildings?

Ultimately, the distinction between reality and illusion at living-history museums is probably insignificant.[70] It is best to think about living-history museums not as time machines but as akin to theatrical productions in which the sets are more complete and accurate than in most plays and the goal is to use the setting and the cast of characters to teach about the past.

Despite all the difficulties of presenting the past through the medium of living-history, there are considerable advantages to teaching history using a living-history museum. Compared with the classroom, books, films, or gallery exhibits, the living-history setting provides more ways to reach the public and stimulate interest in history. Their real power is their multisensory approach. As John Kouwenhoven has noted, there are limitations to language and all thoughts are not best transmitted through words. "Just as there are sight-thoughts," Kouwenhoven reminds us, "there are also feel-thoughts, smell-thoughts, taste-thoughts, and sound-thoughts."[71] Living-history museums can present texture, color, odor, and sound. By engaging visitors' senses, living-history museums can then broaden the imagination. And although such museums require skilled interpreters if they are to discourage misinterpretation and to show visitors how to learn from the sensory impressions around them, interpreters have a real advantage over other history teachers since they have such interesting and varied teaching aids and instructional materials.

Living-history museums have focused increasingly on the history of people rather than on material culture. Even though many museum professionals may be oriented towards analyzing objects, most members of the public prefer to focus on human behavior and the personalities of individual people. And even though museum professionals may savor the well-crafted exhibit label, most Americans prefer to watch and talk with historical interpreters than read labels. So living-history museums will likely remain popular. By capitalizing on the public's preference to make the study of history an active rather than passive pursuit, living-history museums can turn museum visitors into investigators of the past.

NOTES

1. Jay Anderson, *The Living History Sourcebook* (Nashville, Tenn.: American Association for State and Local History, 1985), 7–128. Anderson's selections are idiosyncratic but collectively are fairly representative. In this and the next paragraph, we quantify the information Anderson presents.

2. Michael Wallace, "Visiting the Past: History Museums in the United States," in Susan Porter Benson et al., eds., *Presenting the Past: Essays on History and the Public* (Philadelphia: Temple University Press, 1986), p. 158.

3. There is no comprehensive history of living-history museums. Michael Wallace's provocative "Visiting the Past: History Museums in the United States" is the best brief history of American history museums and devotes much of its attention to living-history museums, especially Colonial Williamsburg and Greenfield Village. Charles Hosmer, Jr.'s more detailed study, *Preservation Comes of Age: From Williamsburg to the National Trust, 1926–1949* (Charlottesville: University of Virginia Press, 1981), treats living-history museums as preservation projects and is also strongest on Williamsburg and Greenfield Village. The first section of Jay Anderson's *Time Machines: The World of Living History* (Nashville, Tenn.: American Association for State and Local History, 1984), 17–81, looks more specifically at the history of living-history museums. Its strengths, as well as its limitations, are perceptively analyzed in David Glassberg's

"Living in the Past," *American Quarterly* 38 (Summer 1986), 305–10, which pinpoints key themes that would need to be examined in a full study of living history. See also Edward Alexander, *Museums in Motion: An Introduction to the History and Functions of Museums* (Nashville, Tenn.: American Association for State and Local History, 1979), and Candace Matelic, "Through the Historical Looking Glass," *Museum News* 58 (March–April 1980), 35–45.

4. Wallace, "Visiting the Past," 140–41.

5. Anderson, *Time Machines*, 25–27; Charles Hosmer, Jr., *Presence of the Past: The Preservation Movement in the United States before Williamsburg* (New York: G.P. Putnam's Sons, 1965), 213–16.

6. On Pennsbury Manor's establishment as a historic-house museum, see Hosmer, *Preservation Comes of Age*, 444–50.

7. Goodwin quoted in Anderson, *Time Machines*, 30; Rockefeller's statements appear in Anderson, *Time Machines*, 30, and David Lowenthal, *The Past is a Foreign Country* (Cambridge: Cambridge University Press, 1986), 326. Details of the Williamsburg restoration process are in Hosmer, *Preservation Comes of Age*, 11–73.

8. On the origins of these outdoor history museums, see Hosmer, *Preservation Comes of Age*, 97–132, 363–65.

9. For a review of Colonial Williamsburg's craft demonstrations, see John Cotter, "Exhibit Review: Colonial Williamsburg," *Technology and Culture* 11 (July 1970), 417–27.

10. Visit by author, February 1986.

11. Cary Carson, "Living Museums of Everyman's History," *Harvard Magazine* 83 (July–August 1981), 22. This article is the best starting point for understanding the effects of the new social history on living-history museums.

12. Andrew Baker and Warren Leon, "Old Sturbridge Village Introduces Social Conflict into its Interpretive Story," *History News* 41 (March 1986), 7.

13. Elizabeth Fox-Genovese and Eugene Genovese, "The Political Crisis of Social History: A Marxian Perspective," *Journal of Social History* 10 (Winter 1976), 205–20; Tony Judt, "A Clown in Regal Purple: Social History and the Historians," *History Workshop Journal* 7 (Spring 1979), 68, 71; Thomas Schlereth, "It Wasn't That Simple," *Museum News* 56 (January–February 1978), 36–39; Thomas Schlereth, "Causing Conflict, Doing Violence," *Museum News* 63 (October 1984), 45–52; Thomas Schlereth, "The History Behind, Within, and Outside the History Museum," *Curator* 23 (December 1980), 261.

14. John Patterson, "Conner Prairie Refocuses its Interpretive Message to Include Controversial Subjects," *History News* 41 (March 1986), 12–15; Baker and Leon, "Sturbridge Introduces Conflict," 7–11. For a description and evaluation of several museums' programs on conflict, see Kate Stover, "Interpretation of Historical Conflict in Living History Museums," M.A. thesis, John F. Kennedy University, 1988.

15. Darwin Kelsey, "Outdoor Museums and Historical Agriculture," *Agricultural History* 46 (January 1972), 105–6; Darwin Kelsey, "Harvests of History," *Historic Preservation* 28 (July–September 1976), 22; Marion Clawson, "Living Historical Farms: A Proposal for Action," *Agricultural History* 39 (April 1965), 110–11.

16. Schlebecker promoted the concept of living history farms in *The Past in Action:*

Living History Farms (Washington: Smithsonian Institution, 1967) and *Living Historical Farms: A Walk Into the Past* (Washington: Smithsonian Institution, 1968). With Gale Peterson, he charted the movement's progress in *Living Historical Farms Handbook* (Washington: Smithsonian Institution Press, 1972).

17. On Freeman Farm, see Kelsey, "Outdoor Museums," passim.

18. The symposium proceedings appeared as a special issue of *Agricultural History* 46 (January 1972) and were reprinted in Darwin Kelsey, ed., *Farming in the New Nation: Interpreting American Agriculture, 1790–1840* (Washington: Agricultural History Society, 1972).

19. Living History Farms later added a fourth time period by re-creating an 1870s rural town center. Anderson, *Time Machines*, 52, 54–56.

20. The leading figures in the movement became the first ALHFAM officers: Murray was the first president, Kelsey was vice-president, and Schlebecker was secretary-treasurer. "A Chronicle of the Association for Living Historical Farms and Agricultural Museums," *ALHFAM Bulletin* 5 (March 1976), 9–10.

21. David Percy, *Living Historical Farms: The Working Museums* (Accokeek, Md.: Accokeek Foundation, 1981), 1, 45.

22. John Schlebecker, "Social Functions of Living Historical Farms in the United States," *Museum* 143 (1984), 34.

23. The Firestone Farm project is described in a special issue of *Henry Ford Museum and Greenfield Village Herald* 14, no. 2 (1985).

24. Schlebecker, "Social Functions," 33–34. Some museum professionals have emphasized the practical importance to the modern world of living historical farms' preservation of rare genetic material and low-technology agriculture. See, for example, Richard Roosenberg, "Historical Farming and the Developing World: Our Past Can Serve Again," *ALHFAM Annual: Proceedings of the Annual Meeting, 1983* (1985), 32–36; and William Reid, "The Role of Living Historical Farms in the Preservation of Rare Breeds," *Countryside* 70 (May–July 1986), 63–64.

25. Dale Jones, "Bringing History to Life through Theatre," paper presented to the Association for Living Historical Farms and Agricultural Museums Annual Conference, June 1987.

26. On Williamsburg's cultural influence, see Warren Susman, ed., *Culture and Commitment, 1929–1945* (New York: George Braziller, 1973), 6–8; *Teaching History at Colonial Williamsburg* (Williamsburg: Colonial Williamsburg Foundation, 1985), 15; Carl Feiss, "Preservation of Historic Areas in the United States," *Historic Preservation* 16 (1964), 145.

27. David Lowenthal, "The American Way of History," *Columbia University Forum* 9 (Summer 1966), 31; Ada Louise Huxtable, "Lively Original Versus Dead Copy," *New York Times*, May 9, 1965; Walter Muir Whitehill, " 'Promoted to Glory . . .': The Origin of Preservation in the United States," in Albert Rains et al., eds., *With Heritage So Rich* (New York: Random House, 1966), 43.

28. Zora Martin Felton, "Colonial Williamsburg: A Black Perspective," in Susan K. Nichols et al., eds., *Museum Education Anthology, 1973–1983: A Decade of Roundtable Reports* (Washington: Museum Education Roundtable, 1984), 85.

29. *Colonial Williamsburg: Official Guidebook and Map* (Williamsburg, Va.: Colonial Williamsburg Foundation, 1972), v.

30. Visits by the authors and colleagues, July 1985, June 1986, February 1987. Williamsburg's current exhibits and programs are described and their rationale explained in *Teaching History at Colonial Williamsburg*.

31. For an overview of recent physical changes at Williamsburg and the limitations of those changes, see Michael Olmert, "The New No-Frills Williamsburg," *Historic Preservation* 37 (October 1985), 27–33.

32. "Colonial Williamsburg Featuring 1987 Package Plans," Colonial Williamsburg, 1987.

33. Thomas Henegar, letter to the editor, *Historic Preservation* 38 (May–June 1980), 5.

34. Hosmer, *Preservation Comes of Age*, 38–44.

35. Colonial Williamsburg's *Official Guidebook and Map* describes the current Williamsburg landscape and the various restaurants and visitor amenities.

36. Rex Ellis, "Black Programs Comes of Age, *The Colonial Williamsburg Interpreter* 7 (May 1986), 1; Shomer Zwelling, "Social History Hits the Street: Williamsburg Characters Come to Life," *History News* 35 (January 1980), 10–12; Rex Ellis, "We've Learned a Great Deal Since the Summer of '79," *Colonial Williamsburg News* 8 (July 1986), 5.

37. *Teaching History at Colonial Williamsburg*, 45, 49–50; Ellis, "Black Programs Come of Age," 2. When Zora Martin Felton returned to Williamsburg in 1984, she was pleased with the changes; see Felton, "An Afterword, 1984," in *Museum Education Anthology*, 85–86. For the current state of black history at Colonial Williamsburg, see also the special issue on the black experience of *The Colonial Williamsburg Interpreter* 9 (January 1988).

38. *Colonial Williamsburg*, 7–9 (1985–86); Ellis, "Black Programs Come of Age," 2. Dennis O'Toole, Colonial Williamsburg's vice-president for historic area programs and operations, acknowledged in 1984 that the programs then in place represented "only first steps, and small ones at that, toward the ultimate goal of fully integrating the story of Williamsburg's and tidewater Virginia's black residents into interpretation"; see Dennis O'Toole, untitled comments, in *Museum Education Anthology*, 86. Four years later, while heralding further progress, O'Toole still admitted that "we have yet to make the story of Williamsburg's eighteenth-century black majority one of the central threads of our interpretation of the town"; see Dennis O'Toole, "Interpreting the Black Experience at Colonial Williamsburg," *The Colonial Williamsburg Interpreter* 9 (January 1988), 1.

39. Ellis, "Black Programs Come of Age," 2.

40. Thad Tate's monograph *The Negro in Eighteenth-Century Williamsburg* (Williamsburg, Va.: Colonial Williamsburg, 1965) presents a clear picture of its subject, one still considerably different from that which the average visitor would paint after a visit to Williamsburg.

41. Mark H. Knipping and Richard J. Fapso, "The Anders Ellingsen Kvaale Farm: Early Norwegian Commercial Agriculture, Circa 1865," unpublished training report, Old World Wisconsin, 1978, 1.

42. See for example, Knipping and Fapso, "The Anders Ellingsen Kvaale Farm"; and Martin Perkins, "The Four Mile House: A Village Hotel in Transition," *ALHFAM Annual: Proceedings of the Annual Meeting, 1983* (1985), 32–36.

43. E. Emilie Tari, "Interior Furnishings Plan, Kvaale Farmhouse," unpublished training paper, Old World Wisconsin, 1979, 4–9.

44. Interview with E. Emilie Tari, curator at Old World Wisconsin, April 11, 1986.

45. Interview with Kathleen Ernst, assistant curator of interpretation at Old World Wisconsin, April 11, 1986.

46. Interview with Kate Stover, April 15, 1986.

47. The information on Old Sturbridge Village in this and the following paragraphs was gathered during the authors' work there.

48. The Fitch House project is described in Jack Larkin's "Facelift for Fitch House," *Rural Visitor* 19 (Fall 1979), 4–6, and assessed in D. Geoffrey Haywood and John W. Larkin, "Evaluating Visitor Experiences and Exhibit Effectiveness at Old Sturbridge Village," *Museum Studies Journal* 1 (Fall 1983), 42–51.

49. The Richardson Parsonage project is described in a special issue of the *Rural Visitor*, 15 (Summer 1975).

50. The third section (pp. 135–77) of Jay Anderson's *Time Machines* is the most complete study of military reenactors, fantasy re-creators, and other living-history buffs. *Living History Magazine* is directed at the buffs and reports on their activities.

51. Richard Handler found a similar tendency for interpreters to shape the public presentations at living-history museums, but in his case the staff members were much different from the living-history buffs in background and motivation; Richard Handler, " 'We Just Talk as We Please, More or Less': Individual Interpretation and Institutional Control at Outdoor Museums," paper presented to a conference on "Collections and Culture: Museums and the Development of American Life and Thought" at the Wilson Center, October 1987.

52. Anderson, *Time Machines*, 186.

53. A brief introduction to experimental archaeology is included in Anderson's *Time Machines*, 85–118. For an interesting extended study, see John Coles, *Experimental Archaeology* (London: Academic Press, 1979); see also John Worrell, "How Do You Test History in a Lab?" *Rural Visitor* 19 (Summer 1979), 4–6.

54. John Worrell, "Re-creating Ceramic Production and Tradition in a Living History Laboratory," in Sarah Peabody Turnbaugh, ed., *Domestic Potters of the Northeastern United States* (New York: Academic Press, 1986), 81–97.

55. David Callendar, Jr., "Reliving the Past: Experimental Archaeology in Pennsylvania," *Archaeology* 29 (July 1976), 174.

56. Anderson, *Time Machines*, 102.

57. Interview with Ross Fullum, April 10, 1986; Anderson, *Time Machines*, 104.

58. Jane Livingston Diary, Bishop's Mill Historical Institute Library, 1974, 1.

59. Several former staff members of Colonial Pennsylvania Plantation were interviewed, including Nicholas Westbrook (April 7, 1986), Jane Livingston (August 18, 1986), Ross Fullum (April 10, 1986), and Ernst M. Palmer (May 31, 1986).

60. For information on the institution's early years, see Hosmer, *Preservation Comes of Age*, 129–30, 350–51.

61. Interview with Lynn Travers, director of interpretation at Plimoth Plantation, July 25, 1986.

62. Ibid.

63. James Deetz, "The Link from Object to Person to Concept," in Zipporah W. Collins, ed., *Museums, Adults and the Humanities: A Guide to Educational Programming* (Washington, American Association of Museums, 1981), 32.

64. Visit to Plimoth Plantation, July 23, 1986.

65. James Deetz, "A Sense of Another World: History Museums and Cultural Change," *Museum News* 58 (May–June 1980), 43–45.

66. Visit to Plimoth Plantation, July 23, 1986.

67. Deetz, "Sense of Another World," 44.

68. Quoted in Nicholas Zook, "They're Keeping the Old Crafts Alive at Old Sturbridge Village," *Worcester Sunday Telegram*, May 3, 1987.

69. Deetz, "Sense of Another World," 44.

70. If one's goal is preservation of historic structures rather than education, it of course is important whether a building is a restoration or a reconstruction and whether it is on its original site or has been moved. Living-history museums have been attacked as an expensive and ineffective approach to historic preservation. Walter Muir Whitehill, for example, charged that museum villages "only incidentally . . . serve the cause of historic preservation" and that the substantial sums of money spent to reconstruct the Pilgrims' houses at Plimoth Plantation and comparable buildings at other living-history museums could have been used more fruitfully to preserve hundreds of genuine old buildings. See Walter Muir Whitehill, "The Right of Cities to Be Beautiful," in Albert Rains et al., eds., *With Heritage So Rich* (New York: Random House, 1966), 51–53.

71. John Kouwenhoven, "American Studies: Words or Things?" in Marshall Fishwick, ed., *American Studies in Transition* (Philadelphia: University of Pennsylvania Press, 1964), 33.

Historic Houses

4

John A. Herbst

Historic houses offer the most tangible expression of popular interest in local history. Launched in the 1850s with efforts to conserve two sites associated with George Washington—his wartime headquarters in the Hasbrouck House at Newburgh, New York, and his home at Mount Vernon, Virginia—the movement to preserve and restore historic houses has captured the attention and energies of countless Americans over the past century and a quarter. But the popular appeal of the historic house also presents problems for museum professionals who, increasingly, have established themselves as permanent residents there. In particular, the close interest and involvement of the public have forced public historians to be especially sensitive to both the needs of local caretakers and the interpretive demands of the houses' history. This essay examines the special challenges faced by volunteer boards and museum professionals who want historic houses to reflect the best historical scholarship. Even though issues of preservation and furnishing are important for historic houses, I focus here on interpretive issues, particularly the relationship between scholarship and stewardship. I look especially at the strategies used by a handful of the most forward-thinking historic-house staffs in their efforts to reinterpret the physical legacy in their charge.

Historic structures are as varied as they are numerous. They have come to represent everything from the stately residences of the rich and famous to the more modest homes of purely local figures. Mount Vernon is perhaps the quintessential example of a house museum preserved around the life and legend of a great American. The residence remains open seven days a week throughout the year and attracts more than one million visitors each year.[1] By contrast, the Log House in Upper St. Clair, Pennsylvania, the suburb of Pittsburgh where I reside, is opened by the township historical society only a few times during the year for community and school events. The Log House belonged to an early settler, and rather than paying homage to a nationally prominent individual, it is a local effort to preserve a preindustrial residence for antiquarian interests.

These two examples suggest a wide range of content for historic houses, but they also point to a common motivation for the past preserved and presented on site: an antiquarian, often romanticized infatuation with history or some small part of it. Indeed, the tendency of house museums to eulogize the past fits squarely with Michael Wallace's recent examination of history museums in general. Such institutions, he argues, have traditionally functioned as outlets for the patriotic and filiopietistic urges of status-conscious elites.[2] Edward P. Alexander has identified the same trends behind institutional efforts to preserve the past, emphasizing that "history museums too often follow the conventional anecdotal great man, great events approach to history instead of considering economic, social and cultural factors."[3]

The historic house, given its intrinsic focus on a single person or family, is particularly prone to this tendency to elevate the individual over his or her context. But one can point to at least a few examples that suggest at least some shifting in interpretation that introduces a larger social context to historic structures. An emphasis on industrial history, for example, is reflected in Eckley Miner's Village, a state-operated historic site located in the once booming anthracite coal region of northeastern Pennsylvania. Here, several houses from a typical coal-patch town have been restored and interpreted to reflect the lifestyles of more ordinary folk. Similarly, the Worker's World exhibit at the Hagley in Wilmington, Delaware, used a gallery exhibit to complement the owners' and foremen's houses preserved on site. Even more interesting are the few instances where fairly traditional historic houses and homes have extended interpretation to open other chapters in their particular history. Tours of President Martin Van Buren's retirement home, Lindenwald, in Kinderhook, New York, now consider the role of domestic servants in the household as a way to interpret nineteenth-century social structure and the influence of Irish immigration.[4]

There is hope, then, for a more balanced presentation of historic houses. Yet most individual house museums still fall prey to great-man interpretations rather than a broader sociohistorical analysis. Sonnenberg Gardens in Canandaigua, New York, for example, is the late-nineteenth and early-twentieth-century estate of Mary Clark Thompson, who spent a small part of the year there. Yet the elaborate gardens, arboretum, and greenhouses required an army of skilled gardeners, many of them residents. During tours of the grounds, however, the people who actually implemented the garden's design and cared for the property in the early twentieth century remain invisible. At least in 1985, tour guides stuck steadfastly to the story of largely absent estate owners in spite of questions about the workers.

In part, this resistance to broader interpretation can be traced to the way historical houses enter the public domain. The success and historical integrity of such institutions are affected directly by the path the property takes to museum ownership. Put simply, the beliefs of those who led the drive to preserve the house continue to shape policy even after the house has been turned into a working museum.

Most often, old homes are preserved as historic-house museums through the volunteer efforts of dedicated local citizens. Such grass-roots groups frequently face a monumental task taking many years. In rural McDuffie County in eastern Georgia, for example, the Wrightsboro Quaker Community Foundation spent two decades saving and restoring Rock House. When the foundation was organized in the 1960s to preserve the history of the small eighteenth-century Quaker neighborhood of Wrightsboro, some of the houses, including the Rock House, were vacant or abandoned. As with many similar preservation groups, one person played a decisive role. Pearl Baker, a nurse with a hobbyist's interest in history and genealogy, published a genealogical history of the Wrightsboro families and analyzed the Rock House's unusual architecture. After persuading the house's owners to donate it to the foundation, she organized its physical restoration and placed it in the National Register of Historic Places.

After Baker's death in 1977, another foundation member, Dorothy Jones, took over. Having obtained a county-sponsored minimum-wage Comprehensive Employment and Training Act position for the project, Jones devoted herself full time to raising funds and developing widespread local support. The project required Jones and her colleagues to go far beyond her local community. To help secure a $42,000 restoration grant from the Interior Department's Heritage Conservation Recreation Service, foundation members and local politicians met in Washington with Georgia-born President Jimmy Carter. Jones convinced Georgia Governor George Busbee to match the federal grant, should it be awarded. An additional $18,000 from the sparsely populated county's local government and $30,000 from businesses and individuals made it possible for restoration work to be completed. The restored Rock House was dedicated in 1981.[5]

It is not surprising if, after such herculean efforts, the proud local residents of McDuffie County want their historic house's interpretive content to bolster community morale and glorify its past. It is unlikely that the dedicated foundation members would willingly abandon control to paid museum professionals. In this case, however, Dorothy Jones had used the long years of restoration to train herself as a museum professional and to make contacts with others through professional-association meetings. But more commonly, founders of historic houses remain unaware of the broader field of history museums and may consequently have a quite narrow vision for the house or an incomplete understanding of its educational potential. Even when they are no longer on the scene, their successors may be hesitant to tamper with the initial vision out of respect for the founders' undeniably crucial achievements.

The challenge for museum professionals is to incorporate sound historical scholarship and current museum practices into a historic house's presentation without antagonizing its existing constituency. For example, the professionals may need to define a specific period of interpretation for a house museum that has a much longer social and architectural history. They should also investigate and document the life of the house to sort out fact from fiction. In the process, however, they may discover unexpected information and move the museum in a direction that runs counter to the motives of the board of trustees, the prejudices of volunteer guides, or the expectations of the visiting public. For various reasons, all these groups may be captive to a romantic vision of seemingly larger-than-life figures who lived in the house. Finally, the stewardship of a historic house may fall to a multipurpose organization whose agenda for a physical plant has to be as varied as its mission statement.

My vantage point in understanding historic-house museums comes in part from the five years I spent as the principal museum professional involved in establishing a new museum devoted to labor and working people's history, with headquarters in a historic home outside Paterson, New Jersey. During this time, I first worked as a trustee and volunteer with the fragile organization that sought to acquire the Botto House National Landmark. The structure was the home of Italian-American silk weavers and a weekly rally site for mass meetings in the Paterson silk strike of 1913, which was led by the Industrial Workers of the World.

Later I became the first paid director, with the task of implementing a museum on the site. I was then forced to deal with the varied motivations and perspectives of some of the key individuals who helped to incorporate the museum. The experience demonstrated both the undeniable grip of the founders' motives on the institution and the crucial role of museum professionals who seek to define period representation, strive for accurate site interpretation, reflect current scholarship, and reach out to involve new audiences—all without alienating original sources of support.

The Romance of a Grand Past

To remain fresh and relevant in a changing world, some house museums have been casting their interpretation toward a broad approach that moves beyond "great men, great events" history. The Hermitage, a museum in northern New Jersey, presents an interesting study of the problems involved in this transition and how difficult it is for institutions to pull away from the romance of a supposedly grand past.

The Hermitage is a state-owned site in Ho-Ho-Kus, New Jersey, which has been operated since 1972 by Friends of the Hermitage, a local volunteer group. This organization leases the property and administers it, a practice common among state systems of historic sites wishing to encourage local groups to support properties in their area. (The National Trust for Historic Preservation has a similar policy for some of its properties.) The organization assumed responsibility for a house with a rich nineteenth-century history shrouded in misty historical connections and legends relating to principal players in the American Revolution. The site, although not necessarily the house, was the scene of a romantic chapter in the American Revolution when the Prevost family owned the estate. In 1778, George Washington and his officers were guests of Theodosia Prevost for four days. Aaron Burr later courted Mrs. Prevost, by then a widow, and the couple were married at the estate on July 2, 1782.

The location of Mrs. Prevost's "neat and convenient house, completely furnished for a gentleman's family," could very well have been at the rear of the present building. The present-day house known as the Hermitage was begun around 1720 in the Dutch style with a "steep, medieval roof line." [6] It was small and unpretentious until purchased by the Rosencrantz family in 1807. In 1849, Dr. Elijah Rosencrantz II retained architect William H. Rantlett to remodel and expand the farmhouse. Rantlett was sensitive to the Revolutionary War connections of the property, connections that had devolved during the Rosencrantz tenure in the house, known then as Waldwic Cottage. The architect wrote that "Waldwic Cottage is one of the few remaining houses in the country which have been consecrated by historical events. It was once, in ante-Revolutionary times, the residence of a wealthy English family, and during the war was at different times the stopping-place or headquarters of Washington, and . . . the resort of the most accomplished officers in the American Army." [7]

It is the Rosencrantz house, a Gothic Revival villa, which the visitor sees today. The Rosencrantz family derived its considerable means and local prominence from management and involvement in local manufacturing. Although the Rosencrantz wealth derived from nineteenth-century industry, their property's associations with Washington, Burr, and Theodosia Prevost nostalgically recalled the preindustrial era. This eighteenth-century legacy provided the family with a country seat "consecrated" with romantic and noble antecedents.

The Hermitage came to the state of New Jersey through the last Rosencrantz, Mary Elizabeth, born in 1885. As the family fortune dwindled and relatives passed away, Mary Elizabeth clung tenaciously to the family home. For a time, in the years before 1931, she opened her parlor as a tearoom to attract visitors on Sunday automobile outings through the Washington associations. She connected various rooms with Washington and Theodosia, pointing out where the general had supposedly said farewell in 1778 and where Burr's courting of Mrs. Prevost had taken place.

Her genteel poverty grew ungenteel after 1931 when she closed the tearoom. Over the next forty years, she and a companion gradually retreated to a single room heated by a coal stove. Rosencrantz refused many offers to purchase the property, located in the growing suburbs of booming Bergen County near New York City. "She revered every inch of her home," a commentator wrote, "and she was determined to deliver it intact to posterity. She perceived herself as custodian of the past and caretaker for posterity." In 1970 she and her companion died five days apart. Her will bequeathed "to the State of New Jersey the historic Hermitage and all its furnishings and the land upon which it stands to be used as a museum and park." [8]

Rosencrantz had fallen victim to the illusions of her property's eighteenth-century associations. Her gift to the state contained almost nothing of the Revolutionary War period: practically nothing remained of the 1720 farmhouse, which may not have been the Prevost residence anyway. Instead, Mary Elizabeth Rosencrantz conveyed to the public domain a home that reflected very well an upper-middle-class lifestyle of the mid–nineteenth century. Rantlett's 1849 renovation had created a villa mirroring the Rosencrantz family's domestic escape from "the mechanized world of the Industrial Revolution" that built its fortune. [9]

This particular legacy became part of the challenge undertaken by Friends of the Hermitage, organized in 1971 to stop vandalism of the property and to win state-sponsored preservation. Attacking the problem of deterioration and arousing public interest, the volunteer group researched the history of the property and, in partnership with the state, contracted for various master plans.

In 1986, Friends of the Hermitage hired JoAnn Cotz, a cultural historian, and me to consult on the interpretation being developed for the property. The existing interpretation wavered somewhat ineffectually between a focus on the Revolutionary War visit of Washington and the Burr-Prevost courtship on the one hand and the Rosencrantz tenure on the other. We were retained to suggest how the many studies by architects, archaeologists, historians, anthropologists, and dedicated volunteer researchers could be integrated into a comprehensive framework. The board of trustees hoped such a framework would direct future research, restoration, interpretation, and development of the site.

We pointed out that although the site had historical associations running from the eighteenth to the twentieth centuries, the bulk of the house's history was squarely in the mid–nineteenth century, reflecting industrialization, the emergence of a middle class, and other developments in the economy, culture, and state and national politics. An emphasis on the national period in the American experience would draw upon the eighteenth-century past and point toward the unclear future conveyance of the property to the public in the twentieth century.

The report on interpretation found that the property's Gothic Revival architectural style and the glorification of the Revolutionary War legacy accurately reflected characteristics of the widespread romantic movement in the mid–nineteenth century. We recommended that eighteenth-century history be presented as "myths and legends only partially founded in fact . . . stories which were dear to the nineteenth-century family and to the last owner who spent the great portion of her life captive to its significance." [10]

Since reviewing the report, Friends of the Hermitage has worked to adopt the approach so that a master plan for future work and programming can be developed. Although the small paid staff and several board members favor the new approach, a number of volunteers still adhere to the misty Revolutionary connections first promoted by the Rosencrantzes. The group is still attempting to resolve the question of period and emphasis of interpretation.[11] The Hermitage house, therefore, presents a situation where the group in charge of the institution was unhappy about the lack of an interpretive focus. In spite of professional assistance, the motives of the founder (who left no descendants to represent her point of view) still prevent resolution of a critical problem.

A Shift of Time and Themes

In the early 1970s, the National Society of the Colonial Dames altered dramatically the interpretation of the Ximenez-Fatio House which it operated as a museum in St. Augustine, Florida. Before this transformation, the 1798 house, built by Andrés Ximenez, a wealthy Spanish citizen, had been used to interpret the last years of the Spanish occupation and thereby illustrated a crucial period in the history of "the oldest city in America."

Whereas Friends of the Hermitage struggled to revise its structure's interpretation, the Colonial Dames switched smoothly to a new approach: it authorized new research and then used the results to change the period being represented. Instead of rooting interpretation in the house's eighteenth-century origins— the lifestyle of a wealthy Spanish businessman—the society shifted the focus to the structure's nineteenth-century story: a house operated by a succession of well-born, down-on-their-luck businesswomen. This reconceptualization permitted the house to speak for a different period and with a broader range of historical voices. Historian William Seale, one of the consultants who worked on the project, noted that the effort had placed this chapter of the Colonial Dames "in the vanguard of a national movement toward a sharpened factual interpretation in house museums." [12]

Like the Hermitage in New Jersey, the Ximenez-Fatio house was shrouded in a romanticized and, in this case, imperial legacy. The Colonial Dames had acquired the property in 1939 from an heir of Louise Fatio, the last proprietor of the hotel. Over the years, the society kept the house, including the oldest kitchen in St. Augustine, in excellent condition, making necessary repairs and capital improvements. It rented part of the building to provide income and security and used the rest of the building for meeting rooms and eventually a museum. Not surprisingly, this early museum took the form of a large collection of Spanish antiques and reproductions, artifacts from the sunset of the Spanish presence in Florida.[13]

By the 1960s, however, this fairly standard interpretation was challenged by new research that suggested a more complex legacy for the property. In particular, the historical record was reexamined to determine all the past owners of the property. Adding to what was known about Andrés Ximenez and his business, this research yielded a wealth of information—and a significantly different historical perspective. After 1825, during Florida's period as a U.S. territory, the building was converted into a hotel owned by a succession of women. These four owners—Margaret Cook (1790–1879), Eliza C. Whitehurst (1786–1838), Sarah Petty Anderson (1782–1896), and Louise Fatio (1797–1875)—had similar backgrounds. All were gentlewomen who had fallen on hard times and turned to running a guest house as a socially acceptable occupation for women of their class. This history of ownership by a series of independent, strong-minded and capable women and the work associated with a hotel operation suggested women's history as a basic interpretive theme.

Along with revealing gender issues, new research opened yet another social-history topic: the economic function of the hotel and the region in the nineteenth century. Florida received its first wave of tourists in the 1820s. Documents showed that the guests at the Ximenez-Fatio House came to see the sights, recover from severe illnesses, or escape from harsh northern winters. Tourism offered a particularly appealing theme for modern museum visitors, many of whom were tourists themselves.

Armed with current research based on sound documentary evidence, the local Colonial Dames leadership set in motion a plan for refocusing the interpretation to reflect the building's operation as a hotel and to illuminate the themes of women's history and tourism. The enthusiasm of the members was kindled by their involvement as researchers and by the plans for new interior restoration and furnishings produced by first-rate historians.[14]

After auctioning much of the collection housed earlier in the Ximenez-Fatio House, the Colonial Dames outfitted the museum on the basis of such primary sources as house inventories. Clues to items needed for guest bedrooms were found in newspapers, which recorded guests' deaths and the personal effects they left behind. This enabled the museum to add authentic touches. Once restoration activities had produced a noticeable change, the Colonial Dames reduced admission fees to bring community residents and out-of-town visitors into the museum. Attendance improved along with the interpretation.[15]

How were these changes accomplished? Why did the Ximenez-Fatio House succeed in moving on when others do not? Unified leadership within the Colonial Dames–St. Augustine chapter proved invaluable. Like the Friends of the Hermitage in New Jersey, some Colonial Dames members were devoted to the museum's former approach, but the absence of a founder, descendant, or other major personality in the organization allowed the introduction of change without organizational power struggles. The leadership of the chapter provided a certain momentum for action, which kept the project moving. When objections surfaced, they came from community residents who vigorously promoted the Spanish era of the city and opposed weakening that aspect of the house's history. Here the historical record was a good bulwark against criticism flowing from promotional quarters. The consultants' involvement was used to full advantage as outside unbiased experts. Learning about how tourists vacationed in the nineteenth century has proved a successful link to local history for today's visitor, and this strong interpretive theme helped the Colonial Dames make the change.[16] Embracing a broader approach to its history has made the St. Augustine chapter of the Colonial Dames one of the best known and most admired in the national organization, and the state organization periodically backs up its pride in the Ximenez-Fatio House Museum with special financial support.

Confronting Stereotypes and Controversial Subjects

The efforts of the Colonial Dames with the Ximenez-Fatio House emphasize the importance of creative research in revising standard interpretations. Sometimes, though, better historical presentations depend on the sensitivity of the museum's staff to the social and political concerns of the larger community. The Mission Houses Museum in Honolulu, Hawaii, went off site to improve and extend routine historic-house interpretation. It chose to deal directly with stereotypes, misinformation, and social conflict in order to show some of the major forces which shaped modern Hawaii.

The museum's parent organization was founded in 1851 as the Hawaiian Mission Children's Society, created by the children of New England Calvinist missionaries who had come to Hawaii during the previous thirty years. Beginning with the native Hawaiian royalty, the missionaries converted the kingdom to Christianity, introduced a written language, began schools and health care, codified laws, and helped the small kingdom deal with the mercantile interests of competing Western nations.

The missionaries played a controversial role in Hawaiian society. They were accused of destroying a native culture, meddling in the politics of an independent nation, and controlling the economy to their own advantage. A number of children and grandchildren of the original mission families acquired land through marriage to Hawaiian royalty and entered into business pursuits that dominated the economic activities of the islands. At least two of the so-called Big Four companies, Castle and Cooke and Alexander and Baldwin, which monopolized the islands until World War II, were launched by prominent missionary families. These leadership positions in the islands' economy, politics, and society made the missionary forebears a target for criticism.[17]

The Hawaiian Mission Children's Society reflected the wealth and control exercised by many of the missionary descendants. And over time it evolved into a historical organization emphasizing the often interconnected genealogical ties of the missionary descendants. By 1910 its four thousand members sought more deliberately to memorialize the sacrifices and contributions of the missionaries. The society was well on its way, in other words, to using history for the purpose of self-aggrandizement.[18]

After 1910 the society acquired three buildings in Honolulu. The first, the Frame House, was built in the 1830s and served as a multifamily home for missionaries. The second building was home from 1820 to 1900 to Levi and Maria Patton Chamberlain, representative members of the mission community. The third house, the Printing Office, was where the important work of printing the Bible in Hawaiian took place, as did the publication of laws, schoolbooks, and other material which had a lasting effect on the Hawaiian Islands.

Until 1970 the museum, based in the three buildings, opened only occasionally, serving as a quiet memorial to the early mission families and as a centerpiece for a genealogical club that documented and verified ties to the earlier group. During the 1970s, a more formal museum structure emerged, with regular visitor hours. Finally, in 1979, a reinterpretation began, carried out in part through the introduction and rearrangement of period furnishings and interpretive displays.

During the interval, however, vast changes had occurred which significantly affected the Mission Houses Museum's potential audience. The Big Four's economic monopoly had been broken after World War II, and so, too, had the political sway of the old business and social elite. The 1960s brought about a renewed study and appreciation of a vanishing Hawaiian culture so damaged by the missionaries, who had opposed such native arts as hula and surfing and who attempted to change dress customs and abolish native religions. By the late 1970s, many residents of the islands felt as though the missionaries had done more than anyone to destroy native self-esteem and encourage the disappearance of a race.

Yet the missionaries' deeds, motives, and efforts were more complex. They had become stereotyped on the basis of impressionistic research and attitudes generated by the position of some of their descendants. It was the museum staff's task to break through these to provide a more accurate historical view.

In 1985, funds provided by the Hawaiian Committee for the Humanities supported the Mission Houses Museum's project, called Missionaries in Hawaii. Six public programs held throughout the islands used role playing, audience participation, and discussion to explain the lives of the missionaries and other Hawaiian residents of the 1820s. The role players portrayed native Hawaiians, seminary students, sea captains' families, and merchants, as well as members of the Congregational Mission. Eleven hundred people of various ancestries attended.

The project served as a catalyst for an ongoing reinterpretation of the Mission Houses Museum, one that has affected not only interpretive techniques and content but also the composition of the guides. Today, Saturday visitors to the museum are rewarded with first-person interpretation by white and Hawaiian guides who assume the role of nineteenth-century characters, actual or composite. These include male and female missionaries, Hawaiian students associated with missions, an antagonistic chief, a Hawaiian minister, a sailor, and a sea captain's wife. These characters also conduct meetings that capture the flavor of mission activities in the Honolulu of 1831. One of the topics, "A Plea for Baptism," features the character of Hannah Homes, *hapahaoli* (half-white) daughter of a merchant, making her defense on readiness to enter the church. This role-playing exercise helps the visitor to understand the nature of the missionaries' brand of religion and the new society of mixed races which was to become such a feature of modern Hawaii.

Other components of the museum honestly address the social tensions that resulted from missionary settlement activities in the islands. A program titled "Is Eating Dog Flesh a Sin?" reflects the cultural clashes between Hawaiians and Americans in an area where the Bible failed to provide a clear answer. In "Should a Christian Dance?" the character of the Reverend Hiram Bingham sermonizes on the evils of dancing. This program deals directly with the regret in the islands today over the missionaries' suppression of native customs, in this case the hula.

As with the Colonial Dames' historic house in St. Augustine, the Mission Houses Museum has moved to broaden aspects of its region's history and, as a hereditary membership society, to validate other historical experiences in its locality. "Tales of Kamehameha" is a role-playing program which has native and foreign characters sharing traditional Hawaiian storytelling concerning the legends, tales, and history of King Kamehameha and the unification of the islands. In general, the new programs move beyond the conventional historic-house subject of domestic lifestyles to interpret broadly the missionaries' interaction with and influence on native cultures.

The Mission House Museum's creative programming was the key to ensuring a positive response to its new historical content. The sermons, role playing, and interesting and unusual characters were enormously popular with visitors. By linking revised content to appealing teaching methods, the museum staff presented its governing board with a popular and artistic success. The staff could argue convincingly that the new interpretation was not only more accurate historically but served to build, enlighten, and captivate the museum's audience. The staff made sure that the Mission Children's Society, the museum's governing board, had a good grasp of the new programs' effects on the community. The society has consequently supported and been pleased with the changes. The result has improved the image of the society.

The innovative role-playing programs have also proved rewarding for staff by humanizing the lives of the historical characters whose deeds and homes had previously been so memoralized and sanctified that they had become one-dimensional. New scholarship on the missionaries and the groups they interacted with has provided new directions for interim restoration and furnishings.[19]

In the case of the Mission Houses Museum, a decision to address conflict and controversial attitudes has been healthy for the institution and has opened the museum's doors to a broader segment of the population. In short, the museum has confronted the ambiguities its houses embody rather than avoiding them. It has taken a major role in reexamining the turbulent forces which brought about the Hawaii of today.

The Homes of the Famous

Sometimes new-social-history scholarship and a broader recasting of a historic house's interpretive story do not seem the way to satisfy or expand a house's audience. Although changes at both the Ximenez-Fatio House in St. Augustine and the Mission Houses Museum produced more visitors and resonance with current concerns of area residents, the governing boards of some other historic houses would consider these two museums to be interesting anomalies. At many historic houses, a great-man approach to history seems so natural and inevitable that alternatives are dismissed as irrelevant. The governing boards of the homes of nationally known individuals, such as presidents, noted authors, and generals, correctly assume that most visitors arrive expecting and wanting a history of the great man. But that does not mean the historical interpretation of such houses should remain static or that it is impossible to expand their content.

The Woodrow Wilson House, a property of the National Trust for Historic Preservation, in Washington, D.C., undertook a major reinterpretation to enrich the museum's content and enliven its teaching methods. With funds from the National Endowment for the Humanities, the Wilson House staff assembled a team of historians, museum educators, a film specialist, and an architect. The project team concluded that the house's collections and period rooms could illuminate more than the life of one famous individual. They selected as the house's theme "Woodrow Wilson: The Washington Years, 1913–1924" and encouraged the staff and docents to discuss the broad social history of that era. The house became a vehicle for showing the effects on upper-middle-class lifestyles of changing home technology, social reform, and World War I. The team wrote a detailed outline of the period, prepared a lengthy bibliography, and produced a model training manual. These written materials—in effect, a curriculum for the house—identified events and issues to discuss with visitors.[20]

The reinterpretation project also changed the ways in which the docents interact with the public. New participatory tours encourage visitors to assess the material culture in each room. For example, when visitors are in the bedroom, the guides may ask them to find clues to Wilson's personality. Or visitors may be asked to compare the main stairs with the back stairs. The guides bring along newspaper articles, literary sources, and photographs for analysis. Such teaching strategies attempt to empower visitors to be their own historians and seek to develop skills that can be used in visits to other historic houses.[21]

The Wilson House's approach represents a considerable advance over most historic houses, but it is not easy to implement. The volunteers need considerable training, but problems of turnover and recruitment make it hard to maintain an adequate pool of well-trained guides. So the house's interpretation is sometimes more successful on paper than in practice.

The Historic House as Multi-Purpose Building

As historical organizations evolve into more professional institutions, a more intellectually honest period representation and interpretation can conflict with other functions of an organization which has to operate within a historic house. Operating organizations are often uncertain of their mission and the role they play with regard to stewardship of a historic house.

The Passaic County Historical Society faced this problem of facility and historic representation at Lambert Castle in northern New Jersey. The mansion, which sits atop Garret Mountain above the nineteenth-century industrial center of Paterson, was built in 1892 by Catholina Lambert, a prominent silk manufacturer. Lambert erected what has been referred to as a "savage face" in sandstone to house an extensive art collection he had amassed. An English immigrant, Lambert was a self-made man whose relations with his employees were notoriously bad. He was one of the most visible hard-liners during the general silk strike of 1913, which involved the Industrial Workers of the World.

In 1922 the property was sold to the county of Passaic, which subsequently tore down half the castle. The remaining wing stands in a county-operated park in a location particularly accessible and inviting to park users. In 1927 the Passaic County Historical Society, which had been founded two years earlier by a fairly typical group of prominent citizens, antiquarian collectors, and history buffs, began operating a museum on the first floor.

When the society hired its first professionally trained director in 1982, fifty years of county history collecting had filled formerly glorious rooms with wooden and glass cases containing the usual range of historical-society materials. In one cabinet of curiosities, visitors saw a china chocolate set "used by the Empress Josephine," a three-dimensional foundry sign, an unrealistic tin model of John P. Holland's first submarine (tested in Paterson), and assorted marbles, fans, and candle molds.

As the new director, Catherine Keene, attempted to set future directions for the society, the question of interpreting the castle as Lambert's home arose. Many of the more than ten thousand yearly visitors to the museum came because of the house's striking location and imposing appearance. They expected to learn about the person who built such an edifice. But the professional staff lacked furniture and other objects from Lambert's tenure in the castle. With only some impressive dining-room pieces, a substantial gravity clock, and smaller items remaining, the absence of artifacts made the building itself the real Lambert artifact.

The staff could not focus its presentation entirely on Lambert anyway. Although visitors were confused by the haphazard display of county memorabilia that did not have a clear interpretive goal, there was a real need for the Passaic County Historical Society to present other aspects of county history besides the story of Lambert and the Paterson silk industry. The staff faced a challenge of illuminating this broader community history in the society headquarters building while meeting the visitor's expectation of finding the castle interpreted as a historic home.[22]

The solution to the dilemma came from a jointly sponsored public program. In 1983 the Passaic County Historical Society entered into a consortium with the nearby Botto House National Landmark and the Paterson Museum to sponsor an exhibition on the silk industry in Paterson. The Botto House received funds in May 1983 from the National Endowment for the Humanities for an exhibit, "Life and Times in Silk City," which opened in April 1984. The exhibition was divided into three site components. "The Worker" at the Botto House used an Italian silk worker's home. "The Process" was presented in the renovated mill that served as the facility for the Paterson Museum. The castle interpreted the role of the elite in Silk City.

The Passaic County Historical Society used the influx of money, expertise, and creativity which the exhibition partnership generated to banish the haphazard display methods from the museum's public rooms. To prepare for its exhibit component on the silk elite, an interpretive strategy was developed to select some rooms that would lend themselves to period representation and identify others for contemporary exhibits that were not site specific.

The staff determined that the drawing, music, and dining rooms would be the most effective areas to interpret as period rooms. This decision was based on the rooms' physical conditions, the surviving evidence, and the story suggested by these rooms and their furnishings. The staff also decided that contemporary interpretive exhibits could best be presented in the mansion's large enclosed center court, an area that had served as Lambert's painting gallery. Its use as a gallery, therefore, was in keeping with Lambert's own intention.

During the yearlong run of "Life and Times in Silk City," the gallery held the exhibit on the lifestyle of those who owned the Paterson mills. Afterwards, the staff continued to use the space for changing exhibits on such topics as county folk art. The three period rooms which had received furnishings and decoration remain to interpret Lambert's residence in the house. Short of an additional or alternate facility, the professional staff feels it has utilized the structure to fulfill its mission in the broadest terms and struck a compromise between stewardship and interpretation which is effective for the institution and its constituencies.

A historic house, Thomas Schlereth has observed, contains "at least two histories: its existence as an actual residence and its past and present life as a house museum." Indeed, it is that dual component that has made the house museum a particular challenge for museum professionals and public historians. Sometimes the two histories coexist peacefully. More often, as these case studies demonstrate, efforts to convey broader social history are impeded, to varying degrees, by the museum's own assorted and accumulated furnishings: the desires and beliefs of its traditional constituency, the sometimes myopic vision of its founders or inheritors, and the restraints of its own local political and social environment.

Tensions between stewardship and interpretation, in short, are perhaps more common to historic houses than any other medium of public history. But these museums, as their popularity attests, offer one of the more exciting and accessible bridges between local history and the public. Although their traditional interpretation may be confined to a particular time and place, their stories, like biographies, present perspective on often impersonal chapters in American history. Museum professionals must work to tailor those individual histories so that the legacy of any particular house museum extends beyond the particular. The historic house's greatest asset is its personal history; its greatest potential lies in its ability to engage the public and sensitize it to the larger social context that has shaped that history and is in turn reflected in it.

Acknowledgments

I wish to acknowledge Curtis Miner for his helpful collaboration on this chapter, as well as suggestions made by Debra Pope, Lizabeth Cohen, Thomas Carroll, Ellen Rosenthal, JoAnn Cotz, and Glenn Grant which vastly improved this work. I want to thank the representatives of the historic houses with whom I spoke and most especially the editors of this volume for their careful shepherding and patience.

NOTES

1. Attendance figures, Mount Vernon Ladies' Association of the Union.

2. Michael Wallace, "Visiting the Past: History Museums in the United States," in Susan Porter Benson, Stephen Brier, and Roy Rosenzweig, eds., *Presenting the Past: Essays on History and the Public* (Philadelphia: Temple University Press, 1986), 137–61.

3. Edward P. Alexander, *Museums in Motion* (Nashville, Tenn.: American Association for State and Local History, 1979), 89.

4. Patricia West, " 'The New Social History' and Historic House Museums: The Lindenwald Example," *Museum Studies Journal* 2 (Fall 1986), 22–26.

5. Charles Phillips, "The Old Rock House Restored," *History News* 37 (April 1982), 6–11.

6. "The Hermitage," The Friends of the Hermitage, no date, 4.

7. Ibid., 4.

8. Ibid., 4.

9. Ibid., 5.

10. JoAnn Cotz and John A. Herbst, "Interpretive Plan for the Hermitage, Ho-Ho-Kus, New Jersey," 1986.

11. Interview with Florence Leon, director, Friends of the Hermitage, March 10, 1987.

12. William Seale, "The Ximenez-Fatio House in St. Augustine, FL," *Antiques Magazine* 131 (February 1987), 426–31.

13. The Ximenez tenure in the building initially saw its use as a kind of public house, with liquor, gambling, and cockfights as attractions for a clientele that was certainly male. This aspect of the property's history was not emphasized by the Colonial Dames.

14. Interview with Mrs. Charles Lockwood, Colonial Dames of America, July 20, 1987.

15. Interview with William Seale, August 26, 1986.

16. Upgrading of the site continues. The Colonial Dames purchased adjoining land once part of the original property in order to reconstruct the outbuildings of the kitchen complex, such as the laundry and chicken yard. The patio, a major feature of the house, will be landscaped to provide a more accurate historic setting.

17. "Missionaries in Hawaii," Hawaiian Mission Houses Museum, no date; Noel J. Kent provides a harsh critique of the missionary descendants' rise to economic and

political power in *Hawaii: Islands Under the Influence* (New York: Monthly Review Press, 1983).

18. *The Maile Wreath: Hawaiian Mission Children's Society, 1852–1970* (Honolulu: Hawaiian Mission Children's Society, 1969).

19. Interview with Debra Pope, director of the Mission Houses Museum, February 12, 1987. The Chamberlain House will have a new time period of interpretation. Moving the time period to 1850 will allow the museum to deal with the influences of mission children who over the years assumed economic and political leadership in the islands.

20. *Manual for Woodrow Wilson House Museum Guides*, vol. 2, *Interpretation* (Washington: Woodrow Wilson House, 1985).

21. Ibid.

22. Interview with Catherine Keene, director of the Passaic County Historical Society, March 10, 1987.

Pioneer Museums 5

David Lowenthal

North American pioneer museums are less a special type of museum than a unique set of ideas and values expressed in museum form. Their features and programs shade into those of outdoor and living-history museums generally and of farm and rural museums in particular. But their audience appeal and modes of display are their own. Their resonance for Americans cuts across other museum categories.

To understand that resonance calls for a brief prologue on what both pioneers and museums mean to Americans. In its sense of leading an advance, taking the first steps in some new enterprise, settling a new country, the term *pioneer* is not exclusively American. Since the early seventeenth century, it has been a term of approbation in Britain, designating those who led the way in scientific endeavors, for example. But the original and far commoner Old World usage stems from the medieval French term for a foot soldier who prepares the way for the main army by digging trenches and repairing roads. This pioneer was a common laborer doing the mundane work of an inferior and subordinate. The pioneer was also linguistically linked with the peon, a footman who held the horse of a noble or knight, and the pawn, an enslaved debtor.

None of these humble and pejorative connotations carried over into Anglo-America (though *peon* did into Mexico). From the start, *pioneer* here referred to those who went to settle a new country, paving the way for others. In this they resembled frontiersmen; but unlike the migratory frontiersman, the pioneer, having paved the way, then settled down into it. He was the harbinger of permanent change. The term was mainly one of laudation. Thus Pioneer Day in Utah commemorates the Mormons' 1847 arrival in Salt Lake City, and Pioneer Day in Idaho commemorates Britain's relinquishment of the Oregon territory in 1846.[1]

Though *pioneer* has special resonance for Americans, the activity of pioneering is by no means exclusive to North America; most New World cultures have engaged in it. And offshoots of European colonial enterprise in Australia and South Africa, likewise only sparsely inhabited and lightly impacted before European conquest, have had pioneering histories in some ways like our own. But nowhere else, not even among the Voortrekkers, has the pioneering experience had the same germinative effect on normative ways of being, nor entered so deeply into the national psyche.

As with pioneers, so with pioneer museums. Outdoor and rural-life museums are to be found throughout the world, but few outside North America explicitly address pioneer themes. Although pioneer museums are neither uniquely nor exclusively North American, they are characteristically so and highlight traits that differentiate American and Canadian museums and their visitors from those elsewhere.

Above all, pioneer museums are emphatically unlike traditional museums in their techniques, successes, and weaknesses. They are virtually antimuseum museums, museums for people who do not like museums and mostly avoid them. They are not repositories of high culture, they are not temples of hushed reverence, they are not places where children have to be kept in order, where things must not be touched, where custodians' main role seems to be protecting precious masterpieces—in fact, pioneer museums do not have masterpieces. If these stereotypes are a trifle outdated, they are still widely held to be true of museums generally.

Such stereotypes notably persist in Britain, despite recent revolutions in museumgoing and museum management. The image most frequently associated with the museum there is the cemetery. Their aura of monumental death stems from the late-nineteenth-century municipal museums that sought to instill moral thinking and behavior; built in the image of classical temples and Gothic churches, museums served the masses as intimidating reminders of ruling-class power and of their own ignorance.[2]

Today the British similarly value their beleaguered old museums, now "overtaken by an expansion of their interests and concerns quite unpredictable" at their founding. Having grown "piecemeal from the passions of private collectors . . . at a time when art and science were not widely separate endeavours," as a museum defender puts it, "in their haphazard way they have become valuable repositories of reference material that can never be matched by the sanitized and neutered new museums of America."[3]

Britons never let up on the sanitized recency of American history, the bumptious naivety of American reenactments, the purloined Old World heritage at San Simeon and the Cloisters and the Getty, the philistine indecencies of American museums. (It was such snobbery that evoked Donald Horne's tirade, *The Great Museum*, against the elitist anachronisms of European museums.)[4]

Traditionally, Americans preferred future prospects to past reminders; they disdained what was dead and gone. The notion of Earth's Holocaust, the ritual burning of the old and the outworn, reflected a "good riddance to bad rubbish" stance averse to museums. "It is said that our country has no past, no history, no monuments!" exclaims an American in an 1864 best seller on seeing the decayed dungeons of a British castle. "I am glad of it. Better her past should be a blank page than written over with such bloody hieroglyphics as these!"[5] Like many other Americans, Mark Twain rejected Italy as a "vast museum of magnificence and misery."[6] Among Europeans, by contrast, *museum* became a term of abuse only with Nietzsche and the turn-of-the-century Futurists.[7]

The classic expression of American museophobia was Hawthorne's 1856 tirade against the British Museum:

> It quite crushes a person to see so much at once; and I wandered from hall to hall with a weary and heavy heart, wishing . . . that the Elgin marbles and the frieze of the Parthenon were all burnt into lime, and that the granite Egyptian statues were hewn and squared into building blocks, and that the mummies had all turned to dust, two thousand years ago; and, in fine, that all the material relics of so many successive ages had disappeared with the generations that produced them. The present is burthened too much with the past. We have not time . . . to appreciate what is warm with life . . . ; yet we heap up all these old shells.[8]

The cult of fashion prevented people from seeing "for rubbish what is really rubbish; and under this head might be reckoned almost everything one sees at the British Museum. . . . Nine tenths of those who seem to be enraptured by these fragments, do not really care about them."[9]

Yet Hawthorne wavered about the museum as about much else in English tradition. If he found it so dispiriting, why did he keep coming back? For he haunted the place; indeed, he actually took rooms at 24 Great Russell Street just a few doors away. Many other nineteenth-century Americans publicly excoriated European museums while privately enjoying them, much as social realists of the 1930s used to exhort fellow Americans to eschew the fantasies of foreign museums for the realities of their fish farms and sewer systems.

Others avidly acquired European relics and copies to vivify a transatlantic past familiar to most Americans from books but seen by very few with their own eyes.[10] And still others, highly conscious of the need to preserve evidences of past and present American life for descendants whose lives would be utterly different, were at the same time busy establishing state and local collections of archives and, in some cases, of artifacts. To such early and mid-nineteenth-century Americans, museums were not burdensome legacies but vehicles of instruction essential to both scholarship and patriotism.

One such American was the pioneer conservationist George Perkins Marsh. Marsh is most famous for *Man and Nature*, his classic exposé of the unforeseen effects of resource exploitation and plea for restoring ecological balance.[11] Less well known is Marsh's advocacy of museums as educative forces, though he played a signal role in founding and sustaining the Smithsonian Institution.[12]

It was during the inception of the Smithsonian that Marsh turned his attention, in an 1847 address at Union College, to the importance of collecting artifacts of American life. Marsh's argument was avowedly populist, to use the current term. Collections of artifacts would give Americans what they could not get from books: the actual history of the people themselves rather than merely of their rulers. Needed for such a history were not archives, genealogies, and treaties, but ordinary things that reflected life as lived by most people: "[To] know what have been the fortunes of the mass, their opinions, their characters, their leading impulses, their ruling hopes and fears, their arts and industry and commerce, we must see them at their daily occupations in the field, the workshop and the market; . . . invade the privacy of their firesides and unveil the secrets of their domestic economy; we must live and suffer and toil with them . . . to determine both what and why they were [from] those sources from which alone the true history of a *people* can be learned." To be sure, "we cannot . . . preserve the natural features of the world in which our ancestors lived and labored, suffered and enjoyed." But many of the things they themselves made and used were still extant: "A complete collection of their agricultural and mechanical implements, and of the coarse furniture and domestic utensils of their humble habitations, would aid posterity very materially in forming a lively conception of their mode of life, and a just estimate of their characters." [13]

The present seemed to Marsh "an auspicious moment for collecting and treasuring up" materials conducive to such historical insights. Moreover, museums could present this story more vividly and memorably than the written word, for "the pictured tombs of Thebes are fraught with richer lore than ever flowed from the pen of Herodotus, and an hour of buried Pompeii is worth more than a lifetime devoted to the pages of Livy."

This is the first known proposal for a museum of American life. The attitudes and even the phraseology of Marsh's 1847 essay presage today's outdoor museums. The workaday things of ordinary folk; the material and the earthy; the vivid sense of life from seeing and handling artifacts; the environmental emphasis; the empathetic identification—it is all foreshadowed here.

So too is the image of progress implicit in modern outdoor museum display. "Observe the father of the family at his heavy toil in felling the woods, and breaking up their virgin earth," Marsh adjures his audience. "How rude his implements, how formidable the resistance of the primitive forest, how slow his conquest of an untamed soil. Compare his clumsy plow, his ill-forged axe and his heavy hoe, with the light, well-balanced and neatly-finished tools of his descendants." And the progress was social as well as material, for "with all this toil, [the pioneer] was compelled to be ever ready with loaded musket to repel the lurking savage; . . . such is the picture of the lives of your own fathers" in what are "the now smiling fields and verdant hills of our Eastern States." [14] In effect, Marsh sought what we would now call a pioneer museum. Let us see how we have since created what Marsh aimed at. [15]

Pioneer locales are relatively recent adjuncts to outdoor museums, those preserved and re-created historic areas that have for a century past exemplified bygone American epochs and ways of life. Up to the end of the nineteenth century, pioneer environments were seen as debilitating and corrupting, not virtuous or enlivening. To Lincoln's early biographers, New Salem was a handicap he had overcome, "a stagnant putrid pool," a "dunghill." Only after Turner panegyrized the frontier as the seedbed of democracy was New Salem reborn as the locale that had shaped Lincoln's character, and was itself reshaped in 1916–18 "to look like it did when Lincoln lived there." [16]

Pioneer structures and locales began to compete for tourist attention in the 1960s. At least fourteen of the eighty-four sites listed in the 1978 *Restored Village Directory* emblazon *pioneer* on their mastheads. [17] It is significant that the key word is more often *pioneer* than *frontier,* let alone *wilderness.* The distinction is crucial: the frontiersman was a nomad at home in the wilderness, which he left little altered; the pioneer was essentially a settler who detested wilderness. Visitors relate to restored and re-created scenes of pioneers pushing out beyond the frontier and transforming the wilderness. They may mourn the passing of the backwoodsman's untrammeled landscape, the cult of the loner and the machismo of the wide-open spaces immortalized by Hollywood and Marlboro—but these spaces are wide open only because they are good for nothing else. They are not part of our own history. It is rather with the transformed landscape of the pioneer that we identify.

Like the landscape they commemorate, re-created pioneer scenes embody a wide range of features: a Kentucky blockhouse, a log house in Missouri, a sod-roofed dugout in Nebraska. These are scattered down the centuries and across the continent from the Massachusetts forest of the 1620s to the Saskatchewan prairie of the 1920s, and westward to Walla Walla. But the pioneer museum heartland is the Great Plains.

Pioneer depictions are less similar as scenic features than as states of being. They are alike mainly in being remote from present-day circumstance; even those of fifty years ago convey an atmosphere utterly different from the present. More than most human landscapes, more even than the wilderness, the pioneer scene is gone for good. Few vestiges survive. It cannot be brought back and can be only feebly reconstituted.

A 1970s attempt to replicate Great Plains pioneer life, modeled on simulation at Plimoth Plantation, showed how hard it was realistically to relive even this quite recent pioneer past. Only four of thirteen participants at the Stuhr Museum of the Prairie Pioneer in Grand Island, Nebraska, remained five whole days on the nineteenth-century site, the others commuting daily between past and present; they had no farm animals, did no plowing or harvesting, and were well aware that they faced few of the threats endured by actual pioneers.[18]

Visitors flock to pioneer museums not to reenact their forebears' lives but to celebrate the differences from their own; to affirm their connection with a heritage, not to relive it. Pioneer museums return visitors to their roots—not roots in the remoter sense of Alex Haley and Old World origins, but the nearer American past. Pioneer museums are felt, and many deliberately seek to purvey, an American founding myth.

What enables them to portray that myth so effectively is that it is so recent. Pioneers in Europe are forgotten in prehistoric mists. Pioneers in America are close at hand, vividly recalled and particularized: they are not a horde of anonymous ancients, but Grandma Jessie and Great-Uncle Jake. In Marsh's day, they were mothers and fathers. Four generations on, New England's pioneers are further back, but pioneering in the northern Great Plains dates from the 1920s and 1930s, with some literally pioneering fathers still alive. But one generation back, or four or five, their identity and our close ties with them are indubitable. That makes pioneer museums profoundly absorbing to many visitors. And visitor experience shapes and confirms their special nature.

Besides emphasizing beginnings and roots, pioneer museums, like much pioneer literature, celebrate traits and attitudes felt to be admirably American as opposed to European and to Indian ones. Even if some pioneer museums now struggle to accommodate the cult for Native American ways and values, their main aim is to depict and applaud the pioneer transformation of America, to Indians' detriment if not exclusion and extirpation.

Certain presumed pioneer traits—self-reliance, manliness, faith in progress—recur again and again as museum themes. Each offers a reading of the past in supposed contrast with a more comfortable yet morally inferior present.

Pioneer self-reliance is shown to reflect remoteness from central support and authority. Life's stern necessities required the pioneer family to act on its own in a fashion inconceivable in highly organized modern society. Inner-directed, sure of his goals, the resolute pioneer that museums portray is a self-reliant individual. Few museum visitors would guess that pioneers were crucially dependent on supplies and markets, advice and culture, ultimately on military support from Washington or some territorial capital; far from being autonomous, they were wholly bound up with larger American institutions.[19]

Manliness may dismay modern feminists, but it packs them in at pioneer museums, just as it continues to sell Louis L'Amour. Even if L'Amour's women "walk beside men, not behind them," the men are powerful, omnicompetent, and unambiguously masculine, the women avowedly maternal.

Notwithstanding revisionist revelations about pioneer actualities, the pioneer museum accords each sex its distinct pioneer virtues.[20]

Finally, they stress pioneers' unfailing zest for life and confidence in achievement. The accompanying hardships and loneliness were endurable through faith that efforts would be rewarded, that nature tamed would be bountiful, that setbacks were temporary, and that the way on lay ever upward. And the pioneers' fortunes became those of all America, made strong and prosperous by their cumulative efforts.

Pioneer-village museums achieve their aims by emphasizing process, activity, participation, and identification. It is less the locale that matters than how it is transformed, what people did rather than the structures that sheltered them. "The structures are certainly important as 'containers'," explains the Stuhr Museum's educational director, "but the most important things are the lives of the people who lived and survived here."[21] Visitors come to Yorkton to find out "who were the people who turned the great lone land that was Saskatchewan into a mosaic of cultivated fields."[22] The antecedent locale is merely the point of departure; the main point now is to see how pioneering perfected it.

Thus authenticity of locale and material structure counts for little in pioneer museums; few care what it was precisely like before or even afterward, only how it was changed. Initially a peril and a challenge, the pioneer landscape became a promise betokening a future. Its portrayal must focus not on materials but on motivations. This is the opposite of the modern Western museum's characteristic "illusion of a relationship between things [in] place of a social relation."[23]

Pioneers transformed patches of wilderness into particular gardens; in many pioneer museums the pioneers are specific, the wilderness and the garden general ideas. Hence the Stuhr Museum does "not portray any real or particular town, . . . ours is a 'type'."[24] The concern with types in place of specifics suits present-day needs to select and skew past details. Unlike places such as Plimoth Plantation, where actual historical individuals are simulated, Conner Prairie Historic Village guides play the parts of people who *might* have lived in the settlement in 1836. The saga of the 1836 Christmas presentation there is a case in point.

Visitors had come to Conner Prairie in Noblesville, Indiana, year after year to enjoy an old-fashioned pioneer-community Christmas. In 1978, curatorial concern for authenticity all but eliminated Christmas and confined seasonal activities to butchering a hog. When dismayed visitors stayed away, the drop in receipts forced curators to "adjust" settlers' biographies to permit Christmas talk and activity. Thus the upstate–New York origins of a Methodist family were shifted toward the Hudson Valley "to get enough Dutch influence to have come across St. Nicholas," and converting the doctor's wife from Presbyterian to Episcopalian left room for more Christmas greens to slip into their house.[25] It was easier to tamper with these prototypical historical "realities" than change the public's concept of Christmas.

That is why pioneer villages are among the least authentic of historic reconstructions. And relics of pioneer days that do claim authenticity are often displayed in totally incongruous settings, like Lincoln's "birthplace" cabin lost within its huge classical temple.[26]

Along with process goes an emphasis on activity. Pioneer museums portray pioneer forebears as perpetually industrious—even their leisure was strenuous folk dancing. Blacksmithing, sheep shearing, wool dyeing, spinning, grain flailing, winnowing, weaving, shingle making, sawmilling, cooperage, cabinetmaking, log squaring are ceaseless at most pioneer villages. The Idaho Museum and Pioneer Village Historical Society caught this flavor in 1980 with demonstrations of flint knapping and wheat weaving, an operating model railway, Boise Little Theater actors in period costumes, a performance of *Bertha Goes West* by the Boise Puppetry Guild, and souvenir handbills pouring out of an 1851 press.[27] "Activity is the more humanizing influence," as the Stuhr Museum puts it—not looking at static objects. Because "most of the machines have been restored and still operate," Harold Warp Pioneer Village in Minden, Nebraska, boasts that "you'll feel you are there, living, working, and WATCHING AMERICA GROW."[28]

The visitor feels he is there not simply by watching but by participating in some pioneering craft. Teaching one another to tan hides, make beef jerky, fashion musket balls, and load and fire weapons, visitors at Pioneer Arizona "produce the feel of life in the barren land that was territorial Arizona."[29] Active involvement is central to the whole outdoor museum approach, to be sure. "Why should we bother to restore old buildings to display historical objects," as they say at Old Economy, "when we can much more easily and less expensively provide a total experience . . . involving all the senses?"[30]

Process, activity, and participation not only make history come alive, they encourage the visitor to imagine himself back in the past. "You'll feel you are there," says Harold Warp; "you can almost imagine yourself in the past," Yorkton assures us, "as you view a trapper's cabin [or] a Ukrainian home." Some museum-induced identification with the past transcends empathy. "The problems of the people in 1880 are still very much the same problems of the people in 1980," according to the Stuhr Museum—farm prices and energy. Whatever the accuracy of this assertion, the supposed similitude is vital: "It is important that visitors know that the problems" were the same then as now.[31]

Yet such identity conflicts with the primary appeal of pioneer museum villages as seminal beginnings of progress. Old-timers there enjoy nostalgic memories; youngsters "marvel at the stamina of their forebears," as Harold Warp puts it. Indeed, they ought to contrast their own with the pioneers' lives; that was the whole point of the pioneer experience, "going out to suffer . . . — to die—that others might live—and by living build." [32] Visitors are encouraged to identify not with the pioneer past but with the future that past projects: their own present.

These nostalgic regrets in no way conflict, however, with the credo of progress. Much as they enjoy the pioneering muscle and strength of purpose that transformed the wilderness, few visitors would exchange their own comforts for such a life. It is a pioneer-museum message that we owe our present prosperity to these herculean labors. That prosperity has perhaps not increased happiness, but even if the fruits of progress taste less good than expected, few would relinquish them. Thus the visitor to pioneer museums both admires the laborious past and sees how much better off he himself is, because his present emerges out of that past. In few historical museums today is progress from past to present so deliberately traced.

Spared the perplexities of authenticity, pioneer museums suffer grave confusion between portrayals of means and ends, foresight and hindsight, differences between past and present perceptions. For example, wilderness was a locus of savagery and squalor for most pioneers, but pioneer museums tend to portray it as a realm of felt virtue and grandeur.

Since subduing the wilderness is what pioneering was for, it is natural to feature this activity as necessary and desirable. But in common with romantic fiction and film, pioneer museums also show pioneering attitudes at odds with that activity—and with historical reality. They envisage the pioneer alone in nature where the air was clean, the water pure, the flora and fauna inexhaustible (however profligate he might be)—an environment far superior to today's. Against that wilderness the pioneer is depicted as pitting his strength, sharpening his powers of observation, and gaining an intimate knowledge of nature. Seen in retrospect, the pioneer landscape becomes at once a natural paradise and a perfect setting for mastering nature.[33]

This bears little relation to pioneers' own views of their lot. We now ascribe spiritual sustenance to an environment they found gloomy and lonely, and bent every effort to replace with order and artifice. Some frontiersmen enjoyed untouched nature, but most pioneers viewed the wilderness as an intensely repugnant "enemy" to "vanquish." The New England wilderness was "howling," "dismal," "terrible," the prairie barren, endless, locust-ridden; pioneers everywhere celebrated the extirpation of wild and savage nature.[34]

The rifle and the axe seemed to Frederick Jackson Turner appropriate pioneer symbols, for "they meant a training in aggressive courage, in domination, in directness of action, in destructiveness." [35] Pioneer museums in our conservation-minded era paradoxically celebrate pioneer activities utterly wasteful of nature's goods. Pioneer zest and strength reflected their certitude that woods, swamps, and wildlife were largely nuisances.

The immortal tale of George Washington's hatchet highlights ambivalence towards pioneer destructiveness—an ambivalence that ever since Cooper's *Leatherstocking Tales* has made Americans feel at once proud and ashamed of conquering the wilderness.[36] How appropriate to give a hatchet, essential for civilizing the wilderness, to the Father of His Country on his own birthday! "Do you want destruction of the wilderness reconciled with admiration of the wilderness? Shame at its destruction reconciled to a vision of a virtuous people? Tell the cherry-tree story."[37] Or, as moderns may prefer, go to a pioneer museum and wield one yourself.

What do these pioneer museums imply about the role of museums in American life generally? They illustrate how museums reflect wider cultural images and aspirations. Just as earlier American museums modeled their displays on department stores,[38] and British museums compete with historic houses for tourist trade, so pioneer and other outdoor museums coexist with local state fairs, shopping malls, and summer camps. And pioneer museums are hard pressed to match the vivid immediacy of media images of pioneer life.

American museums today reflect changing public demands more swiftly and wholeheartedly than museums elsewhere. Both democratic faith and economic survival dictate the supremacy of popular taste; entertainment merges with instruction to a degree unacceptable in staider societies; seemliness and dignity exert fewer constraints. Nowhere but the United States would museums have engaged marketing firms to assess first-person interpretive techniques or inaugurated them with a showmanship so unsuited to Old World museum precincts. If Bateman's *Boy Who Breathed on the Glass in the British Museum* is the archetype of museum experience in Britain,[39] in the United States it is the drunkard wandering the lanes of Colonial Williamsburg. The Old World museum still is yoked with the library, the archive, the cloistered sanctuary; the New World museum is teamed not only with pedagogy but entertainment, the marketplace, and the political forum.

The original purpose of museums was to reveal how the present had acquired and put in order the past, the exotic, and the distant; "today they demonstrate the ephemerality of all systems," suggests John Berger.[40] Museums themselves are increasingly ephemeral; in Britain new ones come into being every ten days, old ones perishing at an uncertain rate. Shifting their goals in response to public demand, American museums are highly ephemeral in character.

Less lumbered by possessions and less object-oriented than their European counterparts, American museums focus more readily on process and activity—pioneer museums especially. Yet by the same token they may vanish as quickly as they have come. Even more ephemeral than most museums, they owe meaning and appeal to that moment when the living memories they portray are just passing away with the grandchildren of folk who heard them from the actual pioneers themselves. At a similar remove from American Revolutionary origins, in the late nineteenth century personal recollections likewise gave way to commemorative monuments and written chronicles.[41] As Clanchy has shown for late medieval England, Nora and Zonabend for France, and Pina-Cabral for rural Portugal,[42] transitions from memory to written record occur in various ways and tempos in different cultures; but no sense of heritage is long static.

Museums in transition serve sometimes as way stations for residual traditions, sometimes as foci for preserving or reviving national or ethnic sentiment, sometimes as counterweights to calamitous loss or distressing "progress." When pioneer museums cease to draw crowds of visitors, only a few will survive to collect, display, and enact their no longer fashionable messages, as old-fashioned holdouts against swiftly changing museum tastes that in America swallow up agencies devoted to cherishing even the special American past.

NOTES

1. Mitford M. Mathews, ed., *A Dictionary of Americanisms on Historical Principles* (Chicago: University of Chicago Press, 1951), 1250.

2. Nicholas Merriman, "Museums, Material Culture and a Sense of the Past," paper at a symposium on Museum Studies and Material Culture, University of Leicester, England, March 1987; idem, "Attitudes to the Past and the Use of Heritage in Britain," seminar on Uses of the Past, University College London, November 27, 1987.

3. Brian Sewell, "A Case of Arts for Oblivion," *The Times* (London), April 2, 1988, 8. See Great Britain, National Audit Office, *Management of the Collections of the English National Museums* (London: H.M.S.O., 1988).

4. G. Donald Horne, *The Great Museum: The Re-presentation of History* (London: Pluto Press, 1984).

5. Emma D. E. N. Southworth, *Self-raised; or, From the Depths* (1864) (New York, 1884), 433–34.

6. Mark Twain, *The Innocents Abroad, or the New Pilgrim's Progress* (1889) (New York: New American Library/Signet, 1966), 182–85.

7. David Lowenthal, *The Past Is a Foreign Country* (Cambridge and New York: Cambridge University Press, 1985), 365, 378–82.

8. Nathaniel Hawthorne, *The English Notebooks*, ed. Randall Stewart (New York: Modern Language Association of America, 1941), journal entry March 27, 1856, p. 294.

9. Hawthorne, *English Notebooks*, September 29, 1855, p. 242.

10. Lowenthal, *Past Is a Foreign Country*, 115–17; Neil Harris, *The Artist in American Society: The Formative Years, 1790–1860* (New York: George Braziller, 1966), 124–44.

11. George Perkins Marsh, *Man and Nature* (1864), ed. David Lowenthal (Cambridge, Mass.: Harvard University Press, 1965).

12. George Perkins Marsh, Speech on the Bill for Establishing the Smithsonian Institution, Delivered in the House of Representatives of the United States, April 22, 1846 (Washington, 1846); David Lowenthal, *George Perkins Marsh: Versatile Vermonter* (New York: Columbia University Press, 1958), 80–93.

13. George Perkins Marsh, *The American Historical School: A Discourse Delivered before the Literary Societies of Union College* (Troy, N.Y., 1847), 8–10, 26; Lowenthal, *George Perkins Marsh*, 101–3.

14. Marsh, *American Historical School*, 11, 25–26.

15. What follows incorporates a revision of parts of my article "The Pioneer Landscape: An American Dream," *Great Plains Quarterly* 2 (Winter 1982), 5–19.

16. Richard S. Taylor, "How New Salem Became an Outdoor Museum," *Historic Illinois* 2 (June 1979), 1–3.

17. *Restored Village Directory*, 5th ed. (New York: Quadrant Press, 1978).

18. Roger Welsch, "Very Didactic Simulation: Workshops in the Plains Pioneer Experience at the Stuhr Museum," *History Teacher* 3 (1974), 356–64.

19. Merle Curti et al., *The Making of an American Community: A Case Study of Democracy in a Frontier County* (Stanford, Calif.: Stanford University Press, 1959). See also Gilbert C. Fite, "Prairie Farmer: A View after Three Centuries," *Agricultural History* 50 (1976), 275–89.

20. Nicholas J. Karolides, *The Pioneer in the American Novel, 1900–1950* (Norman: University of Oklahoma Press, 1967), 260; on L'Amour, Lowenthal, *Past Is a Foreign Country*, 354. See Annette Kolodny, *The Lay of the Land: Metaphor as Experience and History in American Life and Letters* (Chapel Hill: University of North Carolina Press, 1975); idem, *The Land before Her: Fantasy and Experience of the American Frontiers, 1630–1860* (Chapel Hill: University of North Carolina Press, 1984).

21. Warren Rodgers to the author, November 19, 1980.

22. Yorkton Museum brochure (Saskatchewan Western Development Museum), circa 1980.

23. Susan Stewart, *On Longing: Narratives of the Miniature, the Gigantic, the Souvenir, the Collection* (Baltimore: Johns Hopkins University Press, 1984), 165. See also James Clifford, "Objects and Selves—an Afterword," in *Objects and Others: Essays on Museums and Material Culture*, ed. George W. Stocking, Jr. (Madison: University of Wisconsin Press, 1985), 236–46, ref. on p. 239.

24. Rodgers, November 19, 1980.

25. Robert Ronsheim, "Christmas at Conner Prairie: Reinterpreting a Pioneer Holiday," *History News* 36, no. 12 (1981), 14–17. Subsequently, visitors were encouraged to discuss the changing views of Christmas; see John Patterson, "Conner Prairie Refocuses Its Interpretive Message to Include Controversial Subjects," *History News* 41, no. 2 (March 1986), 12–15.

26. Lowenthal, *Past Is a Foreign Country*, 273–76.

27. *The Mountain Light* 19 (Fall 1980), 4.

28. Rodgers, November 19, 1980; Harold Warp Pioneer Village (Minden, Neb.) brochure, 1980.

29. Shaaron Cosner, "Melting Pot at Pioneer," *Americana* 8, no. 3 (1980), 68–73.

30. "Old Economy as a Museum," Old Economy, Pa., typescript, circa 1980.

31. Rodgers, November 19, 1980.

32. Courtney Ryley Cooper, *The Last Frontier* (1923), quoted in Karolides, *Pioneer in the American Novel*, 250.

33. For example, S. Lyman Tyler, "Americana Collections Reflect Our Continuing Fascination with the Frontier and the West," *Western Historical Quarterly* 8 (1977), 443–54.

34. Roderick Nash, *Wilderness and the American Mind* (New Haven: Yale University Press, 1967); Peter N. Carroll, *Puritanism and the American Wilderness: The Intellectual Significance of the American Frontier, 1629–1700* (New York: Columbia University Press, 1969).

35. Frederick Jackson Turner, "Pioneer Ideals and the State University" (1910), in *The Frontier in American History* (New York: Henry Holt, 1927), 269–70.

36. Nash, *Wilderness and the American Mind*, 76–77.

37. James Oliver Robertson, *American Myth, American Reality* (New York: Hill and Wang, 1980), 14.

38. Neil Harris, "Museums, Merchandising, and Popular Taste: The Struggle for Influence," in *Material Culture and the Study of American Life*, ed. Ian M. G. Quimby (New York: W. W. Norton for the Winterthur Museum, 1978), 140–74.

39. H. M. Bateman, *The Boy Who Breathed on the Glass in the British Museum, A Criticism of Life* (London: H. Pordes, 1964).

40. John Berger, *New Scientist*, July 16, 1987, 65–66.

41. Michael Kammen, *A Season of Youth: The American Revolution and the Historical Imagination* (New York: Knopf, 1973), 21, 163.

42. Michael T. Clanchy, *From Memory to Written Record: England, 1066–1307* (Cambridge, Mass.: Harvard University Press, 1979); Pierre Nora, "Entre mémoire et histoire: la problématique des lieux," in *Les Lieux de mémoire: 1. La République*, ed. Pierre Nora (Paris: Gallimard, 1984), xv–xlii; Françoise Zonabend, *The Enduring Memory: Time and History in a French Village* (Manchester: Manchester University Press, 1984); João de Pina-Cabral, "Paved Roads and Enchanted Mooresses: The Perception of the Past among the Peasant Population of the Alto Minho," *Man*, n.s. 22 (1987), 715–35.

From Battle Ground to Pleasure Ground: Gettysburg as a Historic Site

6

John S. Patterson

On Monday, July 6, 1863, three days after the end of the Battle of Gettysburg, Northern newspapers furnished readers with vivid accounts of the climactic moments of the engagement. Viewed through the language of reports from the field, Gettysburg was a sublime and inspiring landscape—the verbal equivalent of a grand romantic painting. Virtually overnight, the small Pennsylvania town became famous. Monday's papers also made it clear that, in its grim way, the engagement had fueled national pride by inviting comparison with the greatest battles of nineteenth-century Europe or classical antiquity. A headline in the *Philadelphia Inquirer* announced that Gettysburg had eclipsed Waterloo, while a *New York Times* correspondent insisted that "there never was better fighting since Thermopyalae [*sic*] than was done yesterday by our infantry and artillery." To a *New York Herald* reporter, on the other hand, it was the poetry of John Milton that came to mind: "The way shell and grape and cannister [*sic*] flew about, and their deafening roar[,] was suggestive of the chained thunderbolts and hailed globe in Milton's description of the great aerial contest between the opposing angels."

The fighting was scarcely over, but the mythologizing process that would turn the bloody battleground into one of the nation's most precious shrines—and a powerful magnet for tourists—was already well under way. This chapter will consider some of the activities on the field in the aftermath of the battle and then look briefly at three later phases in the development of Gettysburg from a battleground to a pleasure ground: an era of Northern reunions and monumentation that ran from the late 1870s until about 1895, when control of the battlefield park passed from the Gettysburg Battle-field Memorial Association to the federal government; a period of War Department control and national reunions that lasted from 1895 into the 1930s, a decade that witnessed both the transfer of the park holdings from the War Department to the National Park Service and the last great veterans reunion on the field; and a post–World

War II era in which, as the Civil War vanished from living memory, new battles were fought at Gettysburg over the boundaries, commercialization, and twentieth-century meanings of the "hallowed ground."

While Unionists far from Gettysburg were celebrating an anxiously hoped-for victory, residents of the Pennsylvania community where the battle had been fought were acutely aware that they were in a disaster area. During the three-day struggle, some 170,000 soldiers had gathered around a town with a population of just under 2,500. When the fighting ended, thousands of bodies were strewn over farmers' fields or hastily buried in shallow graves; more than 20,000 wounded men lay in makeshift hospitals in schools, churches, houses, and barns, and the swollen carcasses of several thousand dead horses were rotting in the July heat. Townspeople who had fled to the countryside returned to their homes through scenes of unforgettable horror. On the Monday after the battle, while distant newspaper readers were savoring accounts that emphasized the dramatic spectacle of the engagement, Lydia Zeigler, daughter of the steward of Gettysburg's Lutheran Theological Seminary, was walking home from her refuge with friends beyond the southern end of the field:

Pen cannot described [sic] the awful sights which met our gaze on that day. The dying and the dead were all around us—men and beasts. We could count as high as twenty dead horses lying side by side. Imagine, if you can, the stench of one dead animal lying in the hot July sun for days. Here they were by the hundreds. All day long we ministered to the wants of the suffering, and it was night when we reached home, or what had been home, only to find the house filled with wounded soldiers. Oh, what a home-coming! Everything we owned was gone— not a bed to lie on, and not a change of clothing. Many things had been destroyed, and the rest had been converted to hospital purposes.[1]

The glorious victory had left behind a blasted landscape and a community in desperate need of outside assistance.

By the second week in July, as the armies moved south to continue their struggle, Gettysburg was experiencing its first massive influx of civilian visitors. Many came as helpers. There were doctors and nurses and the volunteer bearers of supplies, agents of the Sanitary Commission or the Christian Commission who (along with the townspeople) had to take on much of the burden of caring for the wounded of both armies. In addition to civilians who brought more or less systematic medical assistance, the already overburdened resources of the town were further taxed by the arrival of relatives of men who had been reported killed, wounded, or missing. Grieving family members swarmed over the field, desperately searching for their loved ones, and in the process they frequently added to the health hazards of the community. A Lancaster newspaper later reported the case of a woman who had ordered the opening of nineteen graves on the field before finally discovering the remains of her husband in the twentieth![2]

In addition to visitors who brought assistance, reporters, photographers (including Alexander Gardner, Timothy O'Sullivan, and Matthew Brady), and at least one historian (John Bachelder, who spent the next thirty years recording—and marketing—the Gettysburg story) came to record the scene. Then there were visitors who for one reason or another were unable to resist the urge to see the field for themselves. A few of the nonhelpers may be classified as out-and-out scavengers (the image of one such grave robber, "a battlefield vulture" according to the caption of the picture, was captured by a photographer after he was arrested while stripping the pockets of a dead soldier) and many others (to the consternation of the Quartermaster Corps officer charged with securing government property) were determined to gather souvenirs among the battlefield debris. These visitors were denounced by critics for indulging "idle curiosity," but they were not without defenders. Michael Jacobs, a professor at Pennsylvania College, generously credited them with a kind of impulsive patriotism, a desire to assure themselves "of the certainty and the magnitude of the victory."[3] In any event, though the town was ill equipped to receive them and the pleasures of their travel were of an exceptionally lugubrious sort, they may be considered the battlefield's first tourists.

A Lebanon, Pennsylvania, newspaper editor who set out for Gettysburg on July 8 left a fascinating account of his excursion and of the people and scenes he encountered along the way. After futile efforts to find an easier route, he took a train to Carlisle and set out to "foot it" to the scene of the battle: "The road was lined with travelers on foot, on horseback, and in every imaginable kind of vehicles." Heavy rains had left the creeks swollen and forced the travelers to take lengthy detours. "The roads were rivers, and the fields lakes. . . . When not up to the knees, and sometimes body, in water we were stuck fast in the mud and sand at almost every step. Such a forlorn set of creatures as we were, and there were hundreds in the same predicament, the sun never shone upon in that section." After spending the night in a barn ("where probably fifty others had already lodged"), they reached Gettysburg the next morning. The editor and his party had tramped forty-eight miles since leaving Carlisle. When he finally reached his destination, the Lebanon journalist quickly confirmed the impressions already recorded by other reporters and found that a few hours on the field more than satisfied his curiosity:

Upon entering town, in every direction could be seen the marks of strife upon the buildings made by cannon and musket balls. The streets were a perfect Babel, filled with vehicles of every description—Government teams, ambulances, wagons bringing hospital stores, carriages, horsemen, officers riding backwards and forward at full speed, and thousands of wounded Union soldiers were walking along the streets, or lying on the pavements, along the houses, fences, curbstones, and Court House and churches and many other buildings were filled with the more severely wounded. We passed on to the Cemetery and from thence took a stroll over a part of the scene of battle on Friday. The destruction of property within its range, and which extends for miles is almost complete, and the desolation is sickening. Hundreds of horses still remain where they fell, and the ground was literally covered with the material of armies. Unexploded shells, broken ones, balls of every kind, horse accoutrements, knapsacks, cartridge boxes, muskets, broken and unbroken, riddled and burnt buildings,—in short, it was a field of battle, which we have neither the inclination nor time to describe.—Suffice it to say that we soon had our fill of it.[4]

Most visitors who came for a glimpse of the awesome and horrifying scenes on the battlefield in the summer of 1863, like the Lebanon editor, quickly went on their way. Soon after the battle, however, two remarkable long-term projects began to take shape at Gettysburg. The outlines of the early history of the Soldiers' National Cemetery are relatively familiar (largely because the project touches one of the most famous episodes in the career of Abraham Lincoln), while the story of the Gettysburg Battle-field Memorial Association is much less well known. Both, however, played essential roles in the transformation of the bloody battleground into a peaceful shrine and tourist center.

By the last week of July, David Wills, a local lawyer appointed by Pennsylvania Governor Andrew Curtin to assist the state's soldiers and their families in the aftermath of the engagement, was negotiating for battlefield land on which to create a Soldiers' National Cemetery. The new seventeen-acre burial ground that took shape in the months after the battle (by March 1864 the bodies of more than thirty-five hundred Union soldiers had been gathered in it) was technically not our first national cemetery. Created through the voluntary cooperation of the states represented in the Union army at Gettysburg, it was nearly a decade before it was even brought into the existing national cemetery system. Nevertheless, as many 1863 commentators noted, the Soldiers' National Cemetery involved cooperative commemoration on an unprecedented scale. The November 1863 consecration ceremonies attracted a crowd of fifteen to twenty thousand people (once again severely straining the resources of the community), and the attention of the nation was fixed upon "The American Necropolis," as *The New York Herald* termed it.

Eventually, notwithstanding his modest assertion that "the world will little note nor long remember what we say here," the brief address Abraham Lincoln delivered on that day would become a central part of our popular mythology. While the president's "few appropriate remarks" have probably inspired more adulation and analysis than any other speech in U.S. history, it seems worth recalling that they were also a fitting contribution to a commemorative project that, taken as a whole, provided a unified expression of mid-nineteenth-century American patriotic nationalism. Just as Lincoln's two-minute statement of American democratic ideals was balanced by Edward Everett's two-hour formal oration (with its ennobling classical allusions) so, too, when the cemetery was complete, the low, simple, semicircular ranks of graves with the names of individual soldiers cut into their surface would be grouped around an elaborate central monument that had been carved in Italy.

In the fall of 1863, the consecration services for the Soldiers' National Cemetery took place on the scarred fields of a still-uncompleted burial ground. In time, however, the brilliant plan devised by William Saunders, a landscape gardener on leave from the recently created Department of Agriculture, would help make the cemetery a sacred shrine in which classical and vernacular elements were brilliantly joined in a setting that emphasized natural renewal, *"simple grandeur,"* and (as Saunders put it in the report explaining his cemetery design) "a pleasing landscape and pleasure ground effect." [5]

In mid-August, soon after negotiations for land for the cemetery had been concluded, the second major project, the Gettysburg Battle-field Memorial Association, began to command public attention. This organization was the brainchild of David McConaughy, an imaginative Republican lawyer from Gettysburg whose name deserves a prominent place on the roster of early historic preservationists. In a public letter addressed to community leaders on August 14, McConaughy introduced his battlefield-preservation idea in language that, for the most part, would not sound out of place in a late-twentieth-century National Park Service master plan: "Immediately after the Battles of Gettysburg the thought occurred to me, that, there could be no more fitting and expressive memorial of the heroic valor and signal triumphs of our Army on the 1st, 2d, & 3 days of July, 1863, than the Battle field itself, with its natural and artificial defences preserved and perpetuated in the exact form and condition they presented during the Battles." [6]

By April 1864 the Gettysburg Battle-field Memorial Association (GBMA) had been chartered by the state, and in the following month one local newspaper reported that it already owned seventy acres of battlefield land and had received donations from all over the state, including about four thousand dollars from Philadelphia alone. The list of early donors included Jay Cooke and Thaddeus Stevens (once a Gettysburg resident), and the newspaper predicted a bright future for the organization: "Under its auspices it will not be long until historic shafts and memorial columns, works of art and taste, will rise upon these grounds to commemorate to all time the great deeds of valor and of patriotism, which render this Battle-field ever venerable." [7]

Over the next fifteen years, McConaughy devoted impressive (if gradually diminishing) amounts of time and energy to the GBMA. To win outside support, he encouraged the distribution and sale of canes cut from trees on the battlefield; he corresponded with popular historians, such as B. J. Lossing, author of the *Pictorial Field-book of the American Revolution*, through whom he offered the New-York Historical Society part of a scarred tree trunk from Wolfe's Hill; he served a term in the Pennsylvania Senate and labored to win appropriations for the GBMA; he worked with John Bachelder, the artist-historian-promoter, to encourage battlefield reunions, such as an 1869 gathering that brought high-ranking Union officers to the new Springs Hotel, from the veranda of which they ventured forth to identify positions their troops had occupied during the battle; and he sent Henry Wadsworth Longfellow and John Greenleaf Whittier suggestions for a battle-related poem that they might find useful in their "literary laboratory." (Whittier, in fact, promptly took McConaughy's advice; "The Hive at Gettysburg," first published in the *Independent* on December 2, 1869, translates into verse the Gettysburg lawyer's account of a shattered drum that had become a bee hive on a battlefield farm).[8]

Notwithstanding McConaughy's multifaceted campaign to promote preservation and to make the field an attractive place to visit, Gettysburg's development was uneven during the fifteen years after the battle. There were many visitors, of course, and there were a number of important organized activities. On the Fourth of July in 1865, shortly after the end of the war, the cornerstone was laid for the monument in the Soldiers' National Cemetery, and four years later ceremonies were held for the almost-completed monument. But these large gatherings and formal activities were quite widely separated in time and limited in scope. Moreover, with the exception of the 1869 officers reunion, they centered on the Soldiers' National Cemetery, which, starting in the late 1860s, was also the scene of substantial (though still largely local) Decoration Day gatherings.

In some respects, McConaughy's temperament may have limited the pace of Gettysburg's development. A fiery and contentious man, he was a decidedly controversial figure. Both the beginning and the end of his involvement with the GBMA involved bitter disputes. In 1864, when Governor Curtin asked David Wills about the proposed memorial association, Wills fired off a scathing letter denouncing the project. To some extent, Wills's criticism reflects his suspicions of McConaughy's motives and the animosities generated by a still-smoldering dispute between the two Adams County lawyers. Beyond the personal antagonism the letter discloses, however, many of Wills's objections to the preservation scheme also provide powerful (if inadvertent) reminders of the remarkably forward-looking dimensions of McConaughy's ideas about historic preservation. Wills observed, for instance, that "the earthen breastworks between Culp's Hill & Cemetery Hill & the redoubts on Cemetery Hill have already been very much defaced. They were made, first by piling up rails and then throwing up earth on top. The farmers have in most instances dug out their rails and the effects of the rains have settled the earth very much." On the other hand, he argued, "Little Round Top is a steep, barren hill of rocks and stones & the stone defences on it will never be disturbed." There were, he insisted, rocks enough "to meet the demands of the community for all purposes for centuries." In Wills's eyes, then, the project was "in part visionary and impracticable and in part entirely useless" and his letter to Governor Curtin underscores the difficulty he had in conceiving of the importance—or even the possibility—of preserving the battlefield. Sixteen years later, when new leaders captured control of the association, the notion of maintaining and marking the lines of battle no longer seemed visionary, but McConaughy was by now perceived as an impediment to the success of the undertaking. In July 1880 the new directors appointed a committee to "demand all books, Documents and papers . . . belonging to the organization," and four years later they were still wrangling with McConaughy over records.[9]

Personal disputes may have slowed Gettysburg's development in the fifteen years after the war, but there were other more important factors limiting large-scale visitation. While the battlefield was relatively accessible from the major Northern population centers (and not yet a powerful attraction for Southerners), it was by no means an easy trip; in the 1860s it took about eight hours to get from Philadelphia to Gettysburg on the regularly scheduled trains. G. G. Benedict of Burlington, Vermont, probably captured the feelings of many veterans when he informed McConaughy in 1864 that "I do not think it would pay to have a local committee of the Battlefield Association in this place. I believe I am the only man here who was present at the battle, though many are scattered about in different parts of the State. Still we are so distant and so few comparatively will ever have an opportunity to visit the ground that I fear much cannot be expected in the way of co-operation with the association." [10] Nine years later, a Philadelphia newspaper expressed similar concerns in response to a proposal to put a statue of General George G. Meade at Gettysburg: "If the statue is erected on the field of battle, but one out of a thousand people would ever see it, all of whom, if it were put in a populous city, and where the great, busy mass of men could have access to it at all times, would turn to it for study and historic improvements." [11]

Although the 1869 reunion at the Springs Hotel briefly captured national attention, other efforts to bring groups of veterans back to the field fared far less well. In 1875 the town eagerly anticipated a Fourth of July visit from a group of Pennsylvania veterans; afterwards even the town's Republican newspaper conceded that "the promised military 're-union' was a fizzle and didn't amount to much, being made up of a dozen or two representatives of the several regiments." [12] Three years earlier a more ambitious undertaking had also ended in disappointment. The summer encampment of the Pennsylvania Grand Army of the Republic (GAR) was scheduled at Gettysburg during the ninth anniversary of the battle. A campsite for several thousand men was prepared, extra supplies of food were ordered, a reduction in the railroad fare was announced, and it was even reported that President Grant and Generals Meade, Sheridan, and Burnside would attend. As it turned out, none of the well-known military heroes appeared; in fact, few veterans of any sort showed up. When the affair was over, the *Gettysburg Star and Sentinel* sadly noted that "not over 200 men were in attendance, altogether, and most of these were scattered about in hotels, with scarcely a corporal's guard in camp." [13]

By the late 1870's, however, the situation was changing. In 1877, John Vanderslice, a GAR activist, delivered a Decoration Day oration in which he pointedly reminded veterans "how rapidly our ranks are thinning out, how soon our beloved order shall live only in history . . . how soon the last veteran shall be mustered out." [14] In the following year he took the lead in arranging a successful Pennsylvania GAR reunion at Gettysburg, and in 1880 he helped engineer the takeover of the GBMA board. Between 1880 and 1895, the battlefield park was expanded dramatically as Gettysburg enjoyed an era of Northern reunions and regimental monumentation. By 1893, Karl Baedeker's *The United States* was informing tourists that "over $1,000,000 has been expended on the grounds and monuments. The battlefield is probably better marked, both topographically and by art, than any other battlefield in the world." [15]

Now every summer brought substantial numbers of veterans to Gettysburg for outings that quickly developed a comfortable and familiar pattern. The men, sometimes accompanied by their families, arrived on special trains, the trip having become faster after completion of the Gettysburg and Harrisburg Railroad in 1884. At the station they were greeted by bands and local dignitaries, and then they either headed for hotels and rooming houses or marched through town, under arches of evergreens decorated with military emblems, to their campsite on east Cemetery Hill. During their visit they could greet old friends, tour the field, and search for relics (an increasingly unrewarding pastime); they could attend long campfire meetings with group singing and comic or patriotic recitations (in 1880, for instance, Vanderslice regaled his comrades with a recitation of "Barbara Fritchie"); they could listen to seemingly endless speeches that rehearsed the heroic deeds of the past or reminded the veterans of their continuing importance and entitlements ("It cannot be said of our republic that it has been ungrateful to its defenders," declared one speaker in 1893. "We have given $100,000,000 a year to the soldiers of our wars; and let no man be chosen to rule over us who will take a dollar from the pension of a worthy veteran."); or they could enjoy concerts by post bands, such as the Marietta Hawks, who serenaded the camp in 1887 while showing off their colorful uniforms: "a cream colored shirt, blue pants, white belts, red tie and red badge, with a bullion fringe." There were, to be sure, less wholesome distractions. The *Gettysburg Star and Sentinel* complained that the quiet decorum of summer Sundays was sometimes marred by "the unseemly cries of numerous curbstone merchants." The paper noted with disgust that "even the monkey and fat woman show was on hand." For the most part, however, the pursuits of the Grand Army men seem to have been wholesome and their behavior exemplary.[16]

The reunions offered attractive opportunities to combine patriotism and pleasure, to enjoy a vacation that would also provide a reassuring sense of social order, a strong feeling of comradeship, and a renewed pride in past accomplishments. The battlefield itself was now a peaceful rural spot (an 1885 guidebook actually described a picnic ground near Little Round Top as "this Paradise"[17]), a tranquil oasis in a late-nineteenth-century era of turbulent and often unsettling change. As the years passed, time softened the visible marks of battle and the landscape provided a pleasing sense of the rejuvenating powers of nature. Still, the changes could be bewildering. In an 1880s edition of *Gettysburg: What to See and How to See It*, Bachelder warned that such radical changes had been made on the field that "even the veteran who fought over it . . . will be confused at the sight of unfamiliar paths and avenues; with the multitudes of monuments which dot the landscape; with the smooth lawns and luxuriant growth of foliage and flowers, where once the scant grass hardly covered the sterile soil." [18]

It was also inescapably true that the ranks of the "boys" who had fought at Gettysburg in 1863 would grow thinner each year. After the veterans were gone, who would tell their story? How would future generations understand the importance of what they had done? Such questions gave particular urgency to the work of marking the lines of battle and putting monuments on the field. These were tasks many veterans took increasingly seriously. In the 1880s the GBMA drew up elaborate regulations governing the placement of markers, and by the mid-1890s several hundred regimental monuments, generally paid for by state appropriations that were often supplemented by contributions from the veterans themselves, had taken up positions along the lines of battle.

Identifying a regiment's position was a complex job that could easily set off heated skirmishes among the veterans. The most elaborate but by no means the only dispute concerning the placement of a regimental monument involved the Seventy-second Pennsylvania, which after a long court battle won the right to put its monument on the front line, where, it insisted, the monument should be. Although monuments varied widely in size, material, and cost, many of them (like that of the Seventy-second Pennsylvania) offered heroic representations of enlisted men; and most of the pieces reflected, at least to some degree, the individualized conceptions of men who were active in the Northern regimental associations (often led by former officers) as modified by the design conventions of the monument companies that produced them.

South along Cemetery Ridge, ca. 1885. (Gettysburg National Military Park)

South along Cemetery Ridge from Zeigler's Grove tower, ca. 1900. (Gettysburg National Military Park)

The veterans who returned to Gettysburg to dedicate the monuments might be growing old ("With the youngest of us life is at its noon," one speaker declared in 1889, "but many of us stand where the shadows are lengthening."), but the bronze and granite soldiers scattered around the field would remain forever young and vigilant, symbolic guardians of the Union on the *very spots* the soldiers had consecrated with their blood.[19]

In 1895, a short discussion of "Art on the Battlefield" in the *Century* provided both a critique of the existing statuary at Gettysburg and a signal that "the hallowed ground" was entering a new phase of development. To the *Century*'s critic, it seemed that "for the most part that beautiful field—the chosen valley of the nation's salvation—has become for lack of coordination in plan and good taste in execution an unsightly collection of tombstones." Insisting that "the heroes of the civil war are worthy of the best that History and Art can give them," the critic argued that to do the job right it was necessary to consult "the best landscape architects" and "a competent board of sculptors." To tell their story effectively, monuments "must be few" in number, so "the unit of celebration . . . should be the corps. The sense of historical perspective is lost by allowing each regiment to determine the proportion and character of the memorial."[20] The *Century* critic spoke in language that would become thoroughly familiar in the twentieth century: in the past, the survivors of geographically based Northern regiments of volunteers had tried to tell their own story in individualized monuments; in the future, most new monuments would celebrate generals or states or abstract ideas, and much of the (increasingly centralized) planning for the development of the battlefield park would be given over to professional artists and experts.

It was also in 1895 that the holdings of the GBMA—some six hundred acres of land, more than three hundred monuments, and seventeen miles of roadway—at last passed into the control of the federal government. By the time of the transfer, the historian of the memorial association proudly noted, "every one of the 313 volunteer regiments and batteries of the Federal army, except the three of West Virginia, has its position upon the field marked by a monument or memorial, and several of the regiments have second positions also marked."[21] Now, however, the era of regimental monumentation, preoccupation with the Northern lines of battle, and virtually exclusive control of the grounds by old Unionists was over. For the next thirty-eight years, the battlefield was administered by the Department of War, operating for much of that time through the Gettysburg Battlefield Commission, made up of Civil War veterans and composed with a careful eye to ensuring representation for former Confederates. At last the battlefield was literally a *national* possession, to be maintained, developed, and marked with funds appropriated by Congress.

One small incident that took place in October 1895 provides a revealing glimpse of the shifts in attitudes and relationships that were now taking place on "the hallowed ground." Major William M. Robbins, Confederate veteran and member of the carefully balanced three-man Gettysburg Battlefield Commission, noted in his journal that he had driven out to be "a silent participant" at the dedication of the Thirty-second Massachusetts monument, "as seemed to be my *official* duty as a Commissioner. I joined in singing the patriotic songs. The veterans present were quite as friendly to me as if we had fought on the same side in the Civil War and I felt quite at my ease among them." Later he rode over the field with some of the Yankees, and they confessed that a minister with their group "had said to some of them (aside) 'What does that rebel mean by making himself so free and familiar among us today?' and one of the old vets. replied to him, 'Well, I guess he thinks the war is over.'—We all had a good laugh together over the lingering prejudice of the preacher, the only man there who felt so." [22]

With the battlefield now under the control of the War Department, it seemed appropriate—indeed, necessary—to document the Southern story on the field. Accordingly, in the late 1890s the commission began to acquire ground that had been occupied by Confederate troops during the battle; in doing so, it was aided by an 1896 Supreme Court decision, *United States* v. *Gettysburg Electric Railway Company,* upholding the power of the government to condemn land for the purpose of historic preservation. While the issues that had divided the North and South faded (the separate-but-equal doctrine sanctioned in *Plessy* v. *Ferguson,* probably the most widely known Supreme Court decision of 1896, provides one measure of late-nineteenth-century eagerness to find a formula to resolve divisions between *white* Americans), the park's area continued to expand. By 1931, two years before jurisdiction of the battlefield was transferred from the War Department to the National Park Service, a *National Geographic* article observed that "there is pride in every American heart that this battle field is now a military park" and noted that the government owned 2,530 acres of land at Gettysburg. [23]

During the War Department years, the commission promoted the development of a balanced and militarily detailed interpretation of the events of July 1863 by erecting hundreds of battlefield markers to indicate troop movements in an objective and nonjudgmental way. The commissioners also took an obvious (and protective) pride in the increasing number of carefully maintained roads that wound along the lines of battle and made old field positions accessible to aging veterans, or younger visitors, as they toured the park in buggies or automobiles. After 1915, the uniformed guides who led tourists over the field at standardized rates were first required by the commission to earn a license by passing a written examination on the battle. [24]

Although the pace of monumentation decreased substantially in the early years of the twentieth century (perhaps the most notable Northern additions were a monument to the U.S. Regulars, erected in 1909, and the Pennsylvania monument, dedicated in 1910), the commission actively encouraged Southern states to put monuments of their own on the field. This was slow work, but eventually the pieces did begin to appear: Virginia's imposing statue of Robert E. Lee rising over a group of his men was set into place in 1917, Gutzon Borglum's North Carolina group arrived in 1929, Alabama's monument was dedicated in 1933, and after World War II other former Confederate States continued to add monuments to the park.[25]

While men who had actually fought at Gettysburg were increasingly outnumbered by their grandchildren, two twentieth-century reunions helped fix the battlefield in the American imagination not simply as the site of a single Civil War engagement but as a national symbol of reunion, progress, and peace. In July 1913, nearly 55,000 Civil War veterans (16 percent of them former Confederates) gathered for an outing largely paid for by state and federal governments. Their average age was seventy-two, and they came from almost every state in the Union to be housed in eight-man tents and fed by U.S. Army cooks while they swapped stories, posed for photographers, and listened to round after round of speeches. The chairman of the Pennsylvania Commission set the tone in his opening remarks. "It matters little to you or me now, my Comrades, what the causes were that provoked the War of the States in the Sixties," Colonel J. M. Schoonmaker declared. What *did* matter was that the survivors on both sides had been "mercifully spared" to see their children "sweep San Juan Hill, sink the Spanish fleets in Santiago and Manila Bays, and thundering at the gates of Pekin, establish our country a power second to none on earth." The speech making lasted four days (longer than the battle!) and reached a fitting climax in a Fourth of July address by Woodrow Wilson, recently inaugurated as the first Southern-born president since the war.[26]

When the reunion was over, editorial writers throughout the country noted that it had been, as the *New York Times* said, "proof of a Great Reconciliation." However, the *Times* found another significance in the gathering; it also seemed to point up advances in "practical efficiency in the use of scientific knowledge." Comparing the sanitary and hygienic environment provided for the old boys in blue and gray with the conditions encountered fifteen years earlier by young soldiers in the Spanish-American War, the paper concluded that "the army Surgeon is taking his proper place at last, and the army Commissary is no longer obliged to see the grafting politician and the thieving contractor . . . engage in the profitable distribution of poison. We have, therefore progressed in more than harmony between North and South." [27]

Some of the veterans involved in the 1913 reunion had mounted an unsuccessful effort to win government support for a peace memorial at Gettysburg. Twenty-five years later, the Peace Light Memorial became an organizing

Dedication of the Peace Light Memorial, July 3, 1938. (Gettysburg National Military Park)

symbol of the last great reunion on the battlefield. By 1938 the roster of surviving Civil War veterans was dwindling rapidly. The average age of the 1,845 men who were able to make the trip (this time 26 percent of them were former Confederate soldiers) was well over ninety. Elaborate arrangements again were made to protect their health and ensure their pleasure. Each veteran was permitted to bring an attendant, and in addition to the various adult officials who directed the affair, Boy Scout couriers stood by to assist (and learn from) the living links with a distant struggle.[28]

On July 3, a crowd estimated by the *New York Times* at 150,000 gathered for the highlight of the reunion: the unveiling of the Peace Light Memorial, ignition of its eternal flame, and a speech by President Franklin D. Roosevelt. The spectacle of aged former adversaries meeting for a friendly farewell around a monument that called for "Peace Eternal in a Nation United" was an appealing one. The old warriors were also impressed by a "monster military parade" (as the *Philadelphia Inquirer* called it) and an elaborate display of the tools of modern warfare during the reunion ("If we had anything like this," a veteran was heard to say, "there would have been no Civil War."). Still, in a sense, these activities provide ominous foreshadowings of troubles that lay ahead. Even the symbolism of the Peace Light Memorial seems less than completely reassuring when it is considered closely. In the decade of the Great Depression, only seven states had actually agreed to contribute funds for the monument. Moreover, after serving up a front-page headline about the lighting of the peace flame, the *New York Times* noted in a small story two days later that the "eternal" light would be turned on only at night![29]

During World War II, travel to Gettysburg slowed to a trickle. In December 1945, however, the installation of parking meters in the downtown area provided a signal that the community was preparing for new waves of automotive activity. Another indication of the primary form postwar visitation would take surfaced in 1947 when the Reading Railroad, following the example set five years earlier by the Western Maryland, announced that it intended to discontinue passenger service because it was losing thirty-six thousand dollars a year on its Gettysburg run. Cars long had played a vital part in tourist activity at Gettysburg, of course; as early as 1918 the Battlefield Commission had noted that most visitors were arriving in automobiles. Now, in the aftermath of World War II, automobile travel quickly returned to prewar levels and then moved on to outdistance anything that had gone before. Expansion of the Pennsylvania Turnpike in the late 1940s—initially opposed by some Gettysburg residents who feared it would reduce tourist traffic by diverting cars from Lincoln Highway, which ran through town—and the launching of the federal Interstate Highway System in the mid-1950s gave visitors from distant places increasingly easy access to the area.[30]

Early in 1961 the National Park Service released figures showing that during the previous year more than 1.3 million people had visited the park. Since then, visitation has fluctuated considerably, rising to more than 2 million by the time of the battle's centennial in 1963, declining to near the 1 million mark at the time of an oil crisis or an "incident" such as that at Three Mile Island in 1979. Though the specific numbers are elusive (twentieth-century tourists arriving at a park without restricted entry points are at least as hard to count precisely as nineteenth-century battle casualties), in the late 1980s, Gettysburg National Military Park was attracting about 1.5 million visitors each year. Still one of the nation's most precious shrines, Gettysburg has also become a mass tourist attraction. A mid-1970s Pennsylvania Department of Community Affairs report estimated 1973 tourist expenditures in the Gettysburg area to be between $15.1 and $20.8 million, and a 1987 study conducted by officers from the U.S. Army War College contended that annual direct tourist spending in the area had risen to more than $40 million.[31]

The tourist appeal of mid-twentieth-century Gettysburg was undoubtedly enhanced by Dwight D. Eisenhower, who purchased a farm near the town in the 1950s. The presence of the World War II hero, who occasionally led famous guests over the field, brought Gettysburg fresh, if geographically remote, military associations even as the Civil War was at last passing beyond living memory. In 1956, the year of Albert Woolson's death, a bronze statue of the last Union veteran was added to the line of monuments along Cemetery Ridge. Though Woolson had not joined the army until 1864 and had no real link with the Battle of Gettysburg, his metallic presence on the field provided a permanent reminder of the extent to which "the hallowed ground" had come to memorialize more than the events of July 1863. Gettysburg was associated with some of the nation's most celebrated military accomplishments and commanders, and the beauty of the park landscape seemed to show that the scars of even our bloodiest conflicts could be healed, that out of warfare could come reunion and regeneration.[32]

However, it would be inaccurate to suggest that post–World War II Gettysburg was an altogether tranquil place. The emergence of a multimillion-dollar tourist industry around the battlefield involved an ongoing series of clashes that often have been labeled "the second Battle of Gettysburg." Complaints that the scene of the great battle was being exploited by greedy speculators who sought easy profit from the sacrifices of the nation's heroes were nothing new, of course. Such criticism had been heard since the battered armies of Meade and Lee marched away in the summer of 1863. In the 1950s, however, it intensified in volume and intensity. "Hucksters Cash In on Relics Where Our Fathers Fought," lamented the headline in a story by Jack Daum that appeared in the *Washington Times-Herald* in July 1952. According to Daum, "tourists entering Gettysburg are repeatedly propositioned by professional guides, peddlers and expensively 'free' side shows featuring Civil War relics." He was especially offended by the fact that "less than 300 yards from the spot where Abraham Lincoln delivered his immortal address, tourists are urged to buy 'souvenir' beer openers, 'Gettysburg powder puffs' and lurid ash trays with the inscription, 'Put your damn ashes here.'" Daum's portrait was probably somewhat overdrawn. When a friend sent him a clipping of the article, along with a sympathetic note suggesting that "it is just one of those unfortunate things beyond your control," J. Walter Coleman, superintendent of Gettysburg National Military Park, said he regretted that the *Washington Times-Herald* reporter had offered a distorted view of the situation and added that "it is unfortunate that he did not present a better discussion of a very real problem." [33]

However exaggerated Daum's account, there could be little doubt that major new battles over development were taking shape on "the hallowed ground." In 1959, for example, a long article in the *Harrisburg Patriot-News* outlined the key positions under assault as "Commercialism Launches 2nd Battle of Gettysburg"; another newspaper report described the new battles as "Custard's Last Stand"; and the *Wall Street Journal* characterized the issues involved in the "Second Gettysburg Battle" as "An Expanding Town vs. Historians." Behind the particular complaints about increasing commercialization lay several basic facts: Gettysburg was attracting more and more people, virtually all of whom had been born well after the 1860s. Moreover, quite a few of these younger tourists brought with them little knowledge of the battle or the events surrounding the creation of Soldiers' National Cemetery. There were visitors, no doubt, for whom a trip to the battlefield was still a pilgrimage to sacred ground. For many other travelers, however, Gettysburg was probably not the central item on their itinerary but was, rather, one stopping point, a place to pause for a brief lesson in history and patriotism, on an extended vacation.[34]

In any event, there could be little doubt that the growing number of visitors did offer significant opportunities (as well as challenges) for the community. In 1954 a number of area businessmen joined forces to encourage tourism and improve coordination between steadily expanding travel-related activities by establishing the Gettysburg Travel Council. The new organization was dedicated to the proposition that "the 'travel dollar' is the most lucrative business a town can have, because it is new money, money earned elsewhere and deposited in the vacationing area." The council's first president was an aggressive young businessman, Leroy Smith, whose career exemplified the entrepreneurial opportunities afforded by the tourist industry. A flamboyant figure cut from the classic cloth of the American self-made man, Smith had started his career by peddling magazines door to door in Chicago and Evanston, Illinois. Later, during World War II, he served for four and a half years as a U.S. Army Air Corps officer. Smith arrived in Gettysburg not long after the war, bringing with him limited financial resources but apparently boundless

Aerial view of Gettysburg during ceremonies honoring the 100th anniversary of the battle, July 1963. (Gettysburg National Military Park)

energy and ambition. By the time of his death in November 1987, he had built an elaborate network of businesses that dominated the Gettysburg area tourist scene and that, in fact, had started to stretch well beyond Pennsylvania. In addition to purchasing and reshaping some older Gettysburg attractions—the Lincoln Room Museum in the large brick house on the square once owned by David Wills (a building Smith eventually turned over to Gettysburg College) and the house where Jennie Wade was shot and killed during the battle—he went on to develop or acquire control of many of the town's most prominent newer tourist attractions.[35]

In fact, it is only necessary to name some of Smith's principal undertakings, filling out the list with a few phrases culled from the brochures that promote the various exhibits, to indicate the broad contours of private tourism-related activities at Gettysburg during the past three decades:

—The buses operated by Gettysburg Battlefield Tours offer a two hour trip over the field ("you can have one of the most rewarding and exciting experiences of your life" while riding in "our air conditioned coaches" and listening to the story of the battle "with Dramatized Living stereo Sound").

—The Gettysburg Battle Theatre and Cafeteria features, in addition to "Home Cooking," "25,000 Hand-Painted Miniatures," "Quadraphonic Sound and Moving Maps [that] bring to life every major event of the decisive three-day Battle—in a manner everyone can understand."

—The Soldier's National Museum features "the most beautiful Dioramas ever created of the Civil War" and "*all* major events of the Civil War."

—The Hall of Presidents and First Ladies furnishes an opportunity for visitors who may be satiated with Civil War exhibits to see "Our Presidents (including Ronald Reagan) in exact life-size, meticulous in every detail, reproduced in wax."

—Old Gettysburg Village offers an assortment of (recently erected) "quaint shops."

—The Heritage Motor Lodge ("4 Restaurants within 500 ft. of Motel") and the Holiday Inn ("In the center of everything") provide rest for weary travelers.

Two package plans made available through the Gettysburg Tour Center offer tourists "a wonderful way to make your visit to Gettysburg more enjoyable, convenient and economical" while reducing the listed admission prices to the various exhibits (including a few outside the organizations controlled by Smith) for visitors who purchase tickets to either five or ten attractions at once. Although the attractions obviously differ in specific subject matter and mode of presentation, taken as a whole they offer a revealing glimpse of late-twentieth-century Gettysburg. The brochures' liberal doses of superlatives and repeated promises of savings, convenience, comfort, easy intelligibility, and abundant shopping and dining opportunities disclose a twentieth-century "pleasure ground" that seems far removed from the landscape William Saunders, the brilliant landscape architect who devised the plan for Soldiers' National Cemetery, envisioned when he used the phrase in connection with his design for the cemetery grounds in 1863.

Although Leroy Smith undoubtedly assembled the most extensive post–World War II roster of privately operated attractions for visitors to Gettysburg, the single most visible (and controversial) tourist facility to emerge in these years was Thomas Ottenstein's National Gettysburg Battlefield Tower. In the summer of 1974, after a bitter and protracted legal struggle—a battle that finally pitted Ottenstein against Pennsylvania Governor Milton Shapp, who attempted unsuccessfully to invoke an environmental-protection amendment to the Pennsylvania Constitution to block construction of the tower—the 307-foot-high tower's elevators opened to the public. To the tower's developer, it was a monument to the free-enterprise system and a marvel of modern technical and interpretive design, including high-speed elevators, earth-tone carpeting recommended by experts as a way to combat acrophobia, and a twelve-minute sound presentation laden with human-interest stories and assembled by a team of historical consultants and media experts. To many students of the Civil War, historians, and environmentalists, however, the structure was an appalling intrusion on one of the nation's most precious shrines.[36]

The tower, its "ruled hyperbolic paraboloid sheet of bolted steel pipes connected to the center shaft with radial members" stretching so far into the sky that it is all too easily visible from afar, dwarfs the monuments and markers so lovingly (if sometimes argumentatively) placed on the field by veterans of the battle in earlier years. In a sense, the National Gettysburg Battlefield Tower—which, like such other privately operated tourist attractions as the Soldier's National Museum and the National Civil War Wax Museum, obviously has found it useful to identify itself prominently as a "national" exhibit—can be taken as a highly visible emblem of private commercial development at Gettysburg. In any event, it is clear that by the time plans for the tower were announced in 1970, the basic elements of the touristic landscape of late-twentieth-century Gettysburg were already thoroughly established. In that year, the Yellow Pages of the Gettysburg telephone directory carried listings for about a dozen museums and nearly forty motels; a decade and a half later, the directory listings told an essentially similar story. The 1985 Yellow Pages identified twelve museums (plus separate entries for an "Amusement Place" and several "Tourist Attractions"), forty-one motels, and twelve campgrounds.[37]

Over the years, museums and restaurants come and go, of course, but during the so-called Second Battle of Gettysburg, which has now continued for more than thirty years, the battle lines have become pretty well established. When one tourist operation falls, another is soon ready to take its place. The Prince of Peace Museum (where one could go to " 'Spend your finest hour' as the life of Christ unfolds before you in 3 dimensions") has now vanished,

Gettysburg, 1988. (Gettysburg National Military Park)

and the space it once occupied is filled by the Colt Heritage Museum of Fine Firearms. In the fall of 1987, the orange roof of Howard Johnson's restaurant, a familiar sight along Steinwehr Avenue for thirty years, fell to the wrecker's ball. HoJo's demise caused some local residents to feel a momentary twinge of nostalgia. "It was really the first restaurant out there," recalled the establishment's opening day hostess, who had fond memories of serving Richard Dreyfuss, Lucille Ball, and the Yale Glee Club. Nevertheless, by the spring of 1988 a new Friendly's outlet was ready to move into line alongside the more-experienced veterans among Gettysburg franchises. Their distinctive logos proudly displayed like the battle flags of Civil War military units, museums and restaurants have taken up strong positions on the west side of Steinwehr Avenue. Moving north from the Gettysburg Battle Theatre and Cafeteria, with its "Home Cooking," visitors encounter Kentucky Fried Chicken, Hardee's, McDonald's, Friendly's, the Lincoln Train Museum, the National Civil War Wax Museum, and Elby's.[38]

Across the street from this formidable array of privately operated franchises and museums, much of the southeastern end of Steinwehr Avenue belongs to the more pastoral public domain, now totaling more than thirty-five hundred acres, maintained by the National Park Service. Recognizing its role as the heir of the remarkable vision of historic preservation (and patriotic commemoration) initially articulated by David McConaughy's Gettysburg Battle-field Memorial Association in the days after the great battle, the Park Service, in its 1982 General Management Plan, directly borrows the language of the 1864 Articles of Incorporation of the GBMA to explain that the purpose of the park is "to hold and preserve the battlegrounds of Gettysburg . . . with the natural and artificial defenses, as they were at the time of said battle, and by such perpetuation, and such memorial structures as a generous and patriotic people may aid to erect, to commemorate the heroic deeds, the struggles, and the triumphs of their brave defenders." [39] In the latter half of the twentieth century, the task of holding and preserving—and interpreting—the famous battleground has posed formidable challenges for its custodians.

At the end of World War II, the Park Service offices were located in rooms on the second floor of the Post Office building in downtown Gettysburg. Though extensive internal Park Service discussion of the need for a substantial museum and interpretive center had begun as early as 1942, it was twenty years later, a year before the Gettysburg centennial, that the Visitor Center was finally completed. In addition to providing space for the park administration and a modest museum display area, the new structure was designed to house Paul Philippoteaux's huge cyclorama depicting the climactic moments of the battle, a painting that had been purchased by the government in the early 1940s and since then, according to a Park Service report, had been housed in a "silo-like structure" that "is unsightly, poorly ventilated and lighted, has no heat, and does not permit adequate interpretation." [40]

The new Park Service facility, situated near a grove of trees not far from the scene of Pickett's charge, was designed by Richard Neutra, a prominent Los Angeles architect. At the beginning of the project, addressing a dinner meeting in Gettysburg in 1959, Neutra offered a fascinating and revealing view of his conception of the Visitor Center. "This building will last forever," he declared. "Many honored guests will come here and many distinguished speaker[s] will speak. Their speeches must be brief because the building itself is most important and comes first. This building will be a shrine for many nations and the free world." Neutra's somewhat grandiose remarks bear an ambiguous relationship to the completed structure, which rather resembles an outsize oil storage tank, but the architect's insistence on the preeminent importance of the *building* certainly does disclose a basic tension between his view of the center and the notion of the importance of preserving "the battlegrounds of Gettysburg . . . as they were at the time of said battle." [41]

Actually, from the beginning of discussions about the best site for the Visitor Center, there had been some Park Service officials who opposed locating the building on a prominent and undeveloped part of the field. In October 1942 the acting regional director sent a memorandum to the superintendent at Gettysburg explaining that he favored a site "at the northeast corner of Hancock Avenue and the road leading to Meade's Headquarters," since the land was already owned by the government, the spot would offer an appropriate battlefield vista for visitors who had just seen the cyclorama, the ground was undeveloped and suitable for economical construction, and it was "most strategically located with regard to interpretation, public contact, and administrative control." A few days later, Frederick Tilberg, a Park Service historian at Gettysburg, responded vigorously to these arguments. Considering the size of the museum that would be needed to house the cyclorama, Tilberg insisted, "its location near the Angle would be an objectionable intrusion upon historic ground. The Angle and Meade's Headquarters, and the entire surrounding area, should be preserved in their wartime character. A structure of this size near the Angle would not be in agreement with our desire to prevent private citizens from building houses on what is essentially important battle ground." [42]

In 1942, when the nation's resources were fully committed to the task of winning a twentieth-century war, construction of a facility to help Gettysburg visitors understand the great nineteenth-century struggle still lay some distance in the future. For the time being, unresolved questions about the building's location could be buried in the files. The issues involved, however, would not disappear. Twenty years later, when Neutra's Visitor Center was finally completed, it took up a fairly prominent battlefield position, though one that was somewhat less exposed than that proposed in 1942. In any event, completion of the Visitor Center emphatically marked the arrival of the Park Service *on* the field, not simply to preserve and mark it, but to *explain* it to large numbers of visitors at a single site. Within a few years, increasing sophistication about historic preservation would make the location of the center something of an embarrassment.[43] Though it could hardly be described as gaudy, the building *was* a substantial intrusion on the historic scene. In this sense it was not wholly dissimilar to the commercial exhibits springing up along Steinwehr Avenue to the west or to the National Tower, which, in the 1970s, rose to the east.

In August 1971, acquisition by the Park Service of the Gettysburg National Museum, another of the privately operated attractions that had made effective use of the "national" label, in this case since the early 1920s, marked a further stage in the agency's effort to furnish visitor services on the field. Located directly across the street from the national cemetery, the museum had an "Electric Map" that offered an orientation program for tourists and housed a substantial collection of artifacts, as well as trinkets of the kind that had offended the *Washington Times-Herald* reporter so much when he visited Gettysburg in the early 1950s. Designating the recently acquired museum as the Visitor Center and renaming Neutra's 1962 building the Cyclorama Center, the Park Service, since the mid-1970s and within the limitations of its budget (even in seasons of peak visitation, both buildings are regularly closed by 6 P.M.), has attempted to strengthen and develop interpretive programs that now include short ranger-guided walks, costumed programs related to Civil War and Gettysburg campaign themes, and longer walking tours of particular portions of the battlefield.[44]

Its $2,350,000 purchase price made the Gettysburg National Museum the most costly post–World War II addition to the government's holdings, but persistent and hard-fought skirmishes over other real estate in the vicinity testify to the continuing efforts of the Park Service to protect the most significant portions of the battlefield from alterations that would disrupt the historic scene. Though construction of the National Tower and the commercial action along the Steinwehr Avenue battle line have provided highly visible examples of modern development in the area, the struggles between progress and preservation at Gettysburg have not been altogether one-sided. In addition to purchasing a number of farms that seemed ripe for future residential or commercial development, the Park Service has captured and sought to restore to its nineteenth-century appearance land occupied by a variety of private businesses ranging from snack bars to service stations, from motels to souvenir stands. Perhaps the most dramatic single acquisition was the mid-1970s purchase of Fantasyland Storybook Gardens, a twentieth-century pleasure ground that, according to a 1974 advertisement, featured "Exciting rides, great shows, thrilling attractions on 35 fun-filled acres." Shortly before Fantasyland opened in 1959, its originator, A. Kenneth Dick, insisted in a letter to the *New York Times* that the government already owned enough land at Gettysburg. His park, Dick insisted, was a tasteful venture that would give the community the kind of economic development it needed and would offer children "who are too small to understand the Civil War . . . something to do and see." [45]

Now Fantasyland is gone, its grounds purchased more than a decade ago by the Park Service for $1,491,410. But the long Second Battle of Gettysburg still rages. In the mid-1980s after the Gettysburg Battlefield Preservation Association, a nonprofit group that supports National Park Service preservation efforts, purchased a farm in order to turn it over to the government, local concern about additional erosion of the tax base stalled the transfer. The incident finally provided the impetus for a detailed Park Service study of the boundaries of the park with the hope that the result might make it possible to set a congressionally established permanent park boundary.[46]

Beyond the specific issues of which parcels of land should or should not be included within the park lie broader questions that long have been matters of concern at Gettysburg and in the nation. How should the claims of the past be balanced against the needs of the present? How can a community maintain an appropriate balance between historic preservation and economic development? How are passionate local concerns to be weighed against broad, if more remote, national interests? What constitutes a proper relationship between government regulation and individual freedom? What meanings about the bloody battle can we glean from the bucolic park landscape of the present? What powerful stories are still hidden deep in the stones and fields? (Walking on the fields, one does remember tales from the past. When J. T. Trowbridge visited Gettysburg in 1865, he encountered Mr. Culp, who told him that when the battle was over, his "meadow, below Cemetery Hill,—a lot of near twenty acres,—was so thickly strown with Rebel dead that . . . he 'could have walked across it without putting foot upon the ground.' "[47]) When *is* one old enough to learn and understand the stories? A century and a quarter after the three-day struggle at Gettysburg, which left behind more than fifty thousand casualties, a battered Pennsylvania countryside, and some extraordinary heroic legends, "the hallowed ground" of the nation's most elaborately monumented Civil War battlefield remains one of our most precious shrines *and* a twentieth-century pleasure ground that continues to be a source of intense, complex, and fascinating controversy.

Notes

1. Lydia Catherine Zeigler Clare, "A Girl's Story of the Great Battle," 3. These mimeographed recollections (written about 1900) are in the Civil War Collection, Gettysburg College Library.

2. *Lancaster Daily Express*, November 16, 1863.

3. Michael Jacobs, "Later Rambles Over the Field of Gettysburg," *United States Service Magazine* 1 (1864), 66–67; Earl J. Coates, "A Quartermaster's Battle of

Gettysburg," *North-South Trader* 5 (1977), 17–21; on photography in the aftermath of the battle, see William A. Frassanito, *Gettysburg: A Journey in Time* (New York: Charles Scribner's Sons, 1975).

4. *Lebanon Advertiser*, July 15, 1863. I am grateful to Jim Barrett, a former student, for bringing this fascinating account to my attention.

5. *Revised Report of the Select Committee Relative to the Soldiers' National Cemetery* . . . (Harrisburg, Pa.: Singerly & Myers, 1865), 148, 147. For additional information about the cemetery project (and a more detailed listing of studies of the cemetery), see John S. Patterson, "A Patriotic Landscape: Gettysburg, 1863–1913," *Prospects* 7 (1982), 315–33; for a recent study of Lincoln and the Gettysburg Address, see Philip B. Kunhardt, Jr., *A New Birth of Freedom: Lincoln at Gettysburg* (Boston and Toronto: Little, Brown and Co., 1983).

6. D. McConaughy to Rev. Dr. C. P. Krauth & Others, August 14, 1863, in the McConaughy Papers, Civil War Collection, Gettysburg College Library. In his useful overview of Gettysburg's history from 1863 to the early 1980s, *Gettysburg: The Story Behind the Scenery* (Las Vegas, Nev.: KC Publications, 1983), William C. Davis provides a sensible brief discussion of McConaughy's role in the early development of the park (see especially pp. 10–17); for another useful brief review of the history of the development of Gettysburg National Military Park, starting with McConaughy's activities after the battle, see Kathleen Georg Harrison, "A Fitting and Expressive Memorial," *Gettysburg Compiler* (Gettysburg, Pa.: Times & News Publishing Co., 1988), 28–34.

7. *Adams Sentinel*, May 17, 1864.

8. McConaughy discusses the shipment of canes from the battlefield in a letter to Henry Carey Baird, May 3, 1864, in the Edward Carey Gardiner Collection, Historical Society of Pennsylvania. The following items are in the McConaughy Papers, Civil War Collection, Gettysburg College Library: Benson J. Lossing to D. McConaughy, August 22, 1863; a copy of the printed invitation to the 1869 reunion on stationery with an artist's rendering of the Springs Hotel; McConaughy's copies of letters to Longfellow and Whittier, dated September 13 and 14, 1869.

9. In the aftermath of the battle, McConaughy and Wills became involved in a bitter dispute involving the burial of the Union dead. Acting with characteristic speed, McConaughy, who was president of the board of directors of Evergreen Cemetery, reached verbal agreements with two landowners on Cemetery Hill to purchase ground to expand the local cemetery so that it could include the remains of large numbers of soldiers who had been killed in the battle. He was furious when Wills, acting as the agent for the Pennsylvania governor, later sought to undermine the arrangement in order to secure land for Soldiers' National Cemetery. The dispute raged on for about two weeks in late July and early August 1863, and it was resolved only through the intervention of a group of local leaders who were determined to avoid allowing the argument to prevent selection of the best possible site for the new burial ground. Davis mentions the quarrel in *Gettysburg: The Story Behind the Scenery*, 10; for a more extended discussion, see Kathleen R. Georg, " 'This Grand National Enterprise': The Origins of Gettysburg's Soldiers' National Cemetery and Gettysburg Battlefield Memorial Association," unpublished paper, Gettysburg National Military Park (GNMP), revised November 1982. Wills's denunciation of McConaughy's proposed memorial

association is in a letter to Governor A. G. Curtin, March 21, 1864, Pennsylvania State Archives, RG 19, Adjutant General, General Correspondence, Box 21 (January–June 1864). For the views of the association's directors on McConaughy in the 1880s, see "Minutes of the Gettysburg Battle-field Memorial Association, 1872–1895," on file in the GNMP, 77, 79, 107.

10. G. G. Benedict to McConaughy, March 12, 1864, in the McConaughy Papers, Civil War Collection, Gettysburg College Library.

11. Clipping from the *Philadelphia Press* of a dispatch from Harrisburg dated March 14 [1873]. Newspaper Clipping File, GNMP.

12. *Gettysburg Star and Sentinel*, July 8, 1875.

13. *Gettysburg Star and Sentinel*, July 11, 1872.

14. *Gettysburg Star and Sentinel*, June 7, 14, 1877.

15. Karl Baedeker, *The United States* (New York: Da Capo Press, 1971), 236. This edition is a reprint of the original 1893 edition.

16. *Gettysburg Star and Sentinel*, July 25, 1878; July 22, 1880; July 19, 1887; William F. Fox, ed., *New York at Gettysburg* (Albany, N.Y.: J.B. Lyon Co., 1900), 1:237.

17. William Ralston Balch, *The Battle of Gettysburg: An Historical Account* (Harrisburg, Pa.: Gettysburg and Harrisburg Railroad, 1885), 127.

18. John B. Bachelder, *Gettysburg: What to See and How to See It*, 9th ed. (Boston, 1889), 21.

19. John P. Nicholson, ed., *Pennsylvania at Gettysburg* (Harrisburg, Pa.: Wm. Stanley Ray, 1904), 1:546, 412–13 (for a brief statement about the location controversy at the dedication of the Seventy-second Pennsylvania monument).

20. "Art on the Battlefield," *Century* 50 (1895), 796.

21. Figures on the transfer of the holdings of the GBMA to the War Department are taken from John M. Vanderslice, *Gettysburg: A History of the Gettysburg Battle-field Memorial Association* (Philadelphia: Gettysburg Battle-field Memorial Association, 1897), 255–56; Vanderslice notes the extent of the regimental monumentation on p. 262.

22. William M. Robbins, Journal entry for October 25, 1895. Robbins Journals, GNMP.

23. "The Most Famous Battle Field in America," *National Geographic* 60 (1931), 75.

24. The commissioners noted in 1913 that "many complaints come to the Commission from tourists at the absence of a control of the Guides over the Battlefield and their charges, in many cases." See *Annual Report of the Gettysburg National Military Park Commission, 1913*, 16. In their annual report for 1916 (p. 9), the commissioners noted that the first examinations had been given during the previous year.

25. "The Location of the Monuments, Markers and Tablets on the Battlefield of Gettysburg" (revised 1976 by the Office of Planning and Resource Preservation, GNMP).

26. *Fiftieth Anniversary of the Battle of Gettysburg: Report of the Pennsylvania Commission* (Harrisburg, Pa., 1913). Colonel Schoonmaker's remarks are on pp. 95–96, and Wilson's speech is on pp. 174–76. In their tributes to reunion, a number of speakers left unmistakable clues about its *terms*. The GAR commander, for example,

twice emphasized that the war was between men of the same race (p. 103), and the governor of Indiana spoke of the struggle as "a war to the death between men of the Anglo-Saxon race" (p. 117).

27. *New York Times*, July 7, 1913.

28. The 1913 Peace Memorial proposal is noted in *Fiftieth Anniversary*, 166, 167, 173. On the seventy-fifth anniversary reunion, see Paul L. Roy, *The Last Reunion of the Blue and the Gray* (Gettysburg, Pa.: Paul L. Roy, 1950); Patricia S. Dougherty, "A Nation's Fond Farewell: The Last Reunion of the Blue and Gray," *Pennsylvania* 5 (1986), 28–33; Anna Jane Moyer, "Tenting Tonight, Boys! The Last Reunion of the Blue and Gray," *Gettysburg Compiler* (Gettysburg, Pa.: Times & News Publishing Co., 1988), 35–40. Harry Stokes reviews the history of the Peace Memorial at Gettysburg in "Gettysburg's 'Peace Jubilee': Fiftieth Anniversary Rededication of the Eternal Light Peace Memorial," *Gettysburg Compiler*, 41–47.

29. *New York Times*, July 4 and 5, 1938; *Philadelphia Inquirer*, July 3, 1938; Davis, *Gettysburg: The Story Behind the Scenery*, 40, notes the serious undertones of the military activities.

30. The activities and developments mentioned in this paragraph were all reported in the *Gettysburg Times*: December 8, 1945 (parking meters); December 31, 1942 and March 28, 1947 (railroad service); May 6, 1947 (opposition to the Pennsylvania Turnpike extension).

31. For pre-1960 visitation figures, see the *Gettysburg Times*, October 3, 1953, and January 1, 1958; the 1960 visitation figure is reported in the *Gettysburg Times*, January 2, 1961. For a discussion of more recent visitation trends and figures for 1972–81 (never below a million a year), see "General Management Plan for the Gettysburg National Military Park and Gettysburg National Cemetery" (GNMP, December 1982), 37; in "A Fitting and Expressive Memorial," *Gettysburg Compiler* 34, National Park Service historian Kathleen Georg Harrison estimates annual current visitation at 1.5 million. Estimates of the economic effects of tourism at Gettysburg are offered in Stephen S. Fehr, "A Study of the Economic Impact of the Gettysburg National Military Park and Tourism on the Gettysburg Area" (Pennsylvania Department of Community Affairs, 1975), xiv, 137–41, and George L. Youngblood, Jerry Bussell, Jesse T. Stacks III, and Gerald R. Wilson, Jr., "The Economic Impact of Tourism Generated by the Gettysburg National Military Park on the Economy of Gettysburg" (a special study sponsored by Gettysburg National Military Park and supported by Shippensburg University's master's degree program, 1987), 64, 70.

32. For a profile of Woolson, see the *Gettysburg Times*, May 7, 1953; the dedication of the Woolson statue is noted in the *Gettysburg Times*, September 7, 1956; Bruce Catton provides a moving statement about the meaning of the death of the last Union veteran in "Muffled Roll for Grand Army," *Life* 41 (August 20, 1956), 19–25. The *Gettysburg Times* reported Eisenhower's decision to buy a farm in the area on November 20, 1950.

33. Jack Daum, "Hucksters Cash In on Relics Where Our Fathers Fought," *Washington Times-Herald*, July 5, 1952; note from Phil H., Superintendent George Washington Birthplace National Monument, to [J.] Walter [Coleman], July 7, 1952, and reply from Coleman, July 14, 1952. GNMP Vertical File, 501–3.

34. Hans Knight, "Commercialism Launches 2nd Battle of Gettysburg," *Harris-*

burg Patriot-News, April 5, 1959; Robert D. Novak, "Second Gettysburg Battle: An Expanding Town vs. Historians," *Wall Street Journal*, January 8, 1959; "Custard's Last Stand," clipping from unnamed newspaper in Gettysburg Newspaper Cuttings, 1958–1961, GNMP.

35. *Gettysburg Times*, January 21, 1955. For brief descriptions of Leroy Smith and his various activities, see the *Harrisburg Patriot-News*, December 23, 1984; *Gettysburg Times*, August 8, 1983, November 27, 1987, November 30, 1987.

36. *National Tower at Gettysburg: The Exclusive Story* (Harrisburg, Pa.: National Gettysburg Battlefield Tower, 1978). This booklet provides details on the tower's development and technical specifications as seen by the developer. For two informative newspaper stories about the tower that were published while the controversy was in full heat, see Bill Richards, "Tower Power," *Washington Post*, October 28, 1973, and Ben A. Franklin, "Gettysburg Tower Opens 'For the People' and Profit," *New York Times*, July 28, 1974.

37. The technical specifications of the tower are described in *National Tower at Gettysburg*, 9. I consulted the Yellow Pages of the 1970 and 1985 Gettysburg telephone directories at, respectively, the Adams County Historical Society and the reference room of Heindel Library at Penn State–Harrisburg.

38. T. W. Burger, "One 'Ho-Jo' to go: Restaurant Demolished," *Gettysburg Times*, December 4, 1987.

39. "General Management Plan For Gettysburg National Military Park and Gettysburg National Cemetery," December 1982, 3.

40. The assessment of the condition of the cyclorama is in Frederick Tilberg's "Museum Prospectus" (November 27, 1956), 1, in GNMP Visitor Prospectus File 11–45, 1941–1960s.

41. *Gettysburg Times*, December 18, 1959.

42. Memorandum from Fred T. Johnson, Acting Regional Director, NPS, to Superintendent, GNMP, October 14, 1942; Memorandum for the Superintendent, GNMP, from Frederick Tilberg, October 19, 1942, GNMP Visitor Prospectus File 11–45, 1941–1960s.

43. It is interesting to note that a draft version of the GNMP General Management Plan, completed in January 1977, commented that the Cyclorama Center, as it was by that time named, "due to its location on the 3rd Day Battlefield—the area of Pickett's Charge—and its obvious color—white—is a gross intrusion" (p. 15); the January 1977 Draft Plan went on to support the creation of a new Visitor Center, to be located on the field of the first day's battle (p. D-7). The General Management Plan finally approved and published in December 1982, on the other hand, did not include the critical comment about the location of the Cyclorama Center. Responding to criticism of the proposal for a new Visitor Center, and recognizing that such a center was unlikely to be built in the near future, the plan instead emphasized the need to focus "on making what improvements are possible without moving the park's visitor center" (p. 50).

44. *Gettysburg Times*, August 19, 1971. For my own assessment of the "Electric Map" and the Gettysburg landscape in the mid-1970s, see "Zapped at the Map: The Battlefield at Gettysburg," *Journal of Popular Culture* 7 (1974), 825–37.

45. A. Kenneth Dick, letter to the editor, *New York Times*, June 14, 1959; 1974 brochure published by the Gettysburg Travel Council.

46. The sale price for Fantasyland is taken from the *Gettysburg Times*, February 14, 1976. For a useful brief report on the controversy sparked by the proposed Gettysburg Battlefield Preservation Association gift of the thirty-one-acre Zephaniah Taney farm to the Gettysburg National Military Park, see Jerry L. Gleason, "Gettysburg park growth stirs debate," *Harrisburg Patriot-News*, May 25, 1986. The boundary study, still under way, possesses particular significance since the park has essentially reached the acreage limits set when the federal government took control of the battlefield park holdings in 1895. The Park Service has sought broad community involvement in the project, and in its preliminary reports on the boundary study it seems to have made an effort to present its future acquisition hopes in extremely careful language. "When private land is purchased by the federal government, it is removed from property tax roles [*sic*] thus reducing local tax revenues," warns a March 1988 "Boundary Study Update." "This boundary concept attempts to be particularly sensitive to this issue by limiting the amount of land which would be purchased to only that which is necessary for meeting conservation and management objectives, approximately 250 acres" (p. 15).

47. For J. T. Trowbridge's account of his visit to the battlefield, see "The Field of Gettysburg," *Atlantic* 16 (1865), 624.

Mickey Mouse History: Portraying the Past at Disney World

7

Michael Wallace

> Industry has lost credibility with the public, the government has lost
> credibility, but people still have faith in Mickey Mouse and Donald Duck.
> —Marty Sklar, vice-president, WED Enterprises, Inc.

Walt Disney never got a Ph.D., but he was, nevertheless, a passionate historian. At Disneyland in California and Disney World in Florida, the past is powerfully evoked for visitors through the use of music, movies, robots, and the latest in special effects. As more than thirty-three million people visited these attractions in 1987, one might fairly say that Walt Disney has taught people more history, in a more memorable way, than they ever learned in school, to say nothing of history museums.

But a closer inspection of the theme parks raises questions as to who should properly get credit for their creation. There are, it turns out, *two* Walt Disneys. First there was the familiar mustachioed fellow we all know, the man we might call Original Walt. It was Original Walt who built the Magic Kingdom in Disneyland in the 1950s. Later, the Magic Kingdom was cloned and transported to Disney World in Florida. Today both kingdoms remain essentially intact, frozen in time, their presentations of Main Street, Frontierland, Adventureland, and the Hall of Presidents reflecting Original Walt's 1950s-style approach to history.

Original Walt died in 1966, despite persistent rumors that he had himself frozen and may yet be back. But in a way he *did* live on. As WED (Walter Elias Disney) Enterprises, Inc., he was reincarnated as a corporation.

In the 1970s, this Corporate Walt, claiming it was carrying out Original Walt's wishes, forged an alliance with other corporations (the crème de la crème of U.S. multinationals). Together they built EPCOT (Experimental Prototype Community of Tomorrow) in Disney World next door to the Magic Kingdom. EPCOT, too, is saturated with history, but of a remarkably different kind from Original Walt's 1950s version. It is these two historical perspectives, side by side in Orlando, that I want to explore and juxtapose.

Scrutinizing the Disney parks, in addition to being intrinsically interesting, affords some insights into the growing world of commercialized history. Nowadays it often seems as if the past gets presented to popular audiences more by commercial operators pursuing profit than by museums bent on education. Vacationers can now motor to dozens of historic theme parks: Knotts Berry Farm, Busch Gardens, Six Flags Over Texas, Dodge City, Railroads USA, Indian Village, and Safari World are only a few of the places that are blurring the line between entertainment center and actual museum. It well behooves museum professionals to assess these competitors for public attention. What effect, if any, does corporate sponsorship have on the historical information presented? What is audience response to (and effect on) mass-marketed history? Tracking the transformation of Original Walt into Corporate Walt provides a case study which begins to provide answers to these questions.

Main Street and Its Enemies

In the early 1950s, Walt Disney set out to build an amusement park that was clean, wholesome, and altogether different from the seedy carnivals he remembered from his youth. Against great odds (bankers frowned on the project and he had to borrow on his insurance policy to do the initial planning), he brought Disneyland into being in 1955. At the heart of the project, right along with his fantasy characters, Disney placed a series of history-flavored entertainments.

This was new for Walt. Aside from the spectacularly successful *Davy Crockett: King of the Wild Frontier*, a few costume dramas, such as *Rob Roy, the Highland Rogue* and *Song of the South* (whose idyllic depiction of master-slave relationships drew NAACP fire), Walt had shied away from history. Perhaps his turnaround was influenced by the crowds flocking to John D. Rockefeller, Jr.'s Colonial Williamsburg and Henry Ford's Greenfield Village as 1950s Americans took to the highways in search of their roots. Certainly his technique resembled that used at Williamsburg: he transported visitors back in time.

The minute you stroll through the turnstiles into the Magic Kingdom you "turn back the clock," as your guidebook tells you, "to the turn-of-the-century." [1] Your first steps take you to Main Street, the heart of a small American town. It's a happy street, clean and tidy, filled with prancing Disney characters. It has a toylike quality, perhaps because it's built five-eighths true size ("people like to think their world is somehow more grown up than Papa's was"). [2] It's like playing in a walk-in dollhouse that is simultaneously a shop-

Walt Disney's inspiration for Main Street in the Magic Kingdom: Marceline, Missouri, ca. 1905. (State Historical Society of Missouri, Columbia)

per's paradise equipped with dozens of little olde-time shoppes with corporate logos tastefully affixed.

But Main Street, ostensibly, is grounded in historic reality. It was fashioned, we are told, out of Disney's recollections of his turn-of-the-century boyhood in Marceline, Missouri, a small town one hundred miles northeast of Kansas City. The intent, Walt said, was to "bring back happy memories for those who remember the carefree times it recreates." [3] This is puzzling to those familiar with Disney's own story, which was rather grimmer.

Disney's father, Elias, a hardscrabble small operator, drifted back and forth between country and city in an unsuccessful attempt to establish himself and his family. After failing at citrus growing in Florida, he moved to Chicago, where he worked as a carpenter on the Columbian Exposition of 1893 and then established a hand-to-mouth small contracting business. Walt was born in 1901, just before the business failed and the family moved again, this time to a forty-eight-acre farm near Marceline on which Elias entered into the precarious and indebted life of the American small farmer. (Perhaps the then pervasive agrarian resentment of bankers was a source of the elder Disney's socialism; he voted consistently for Eugene Debs and subscribed to the *Appeal to Reason*). Walt was set to hard farm labor (drudgery which his two elder brothers escaped by running off) and a diet of stern patriarchal beatings. In 1910, Elias failed again. Forced to sell the farm and auction the livestock, he moved to Kansas City, Missouri, bought a newspaper route, and set Walt and his remaining brother, Roy, to work as newsboys; Roy ran away the following year. After living meanly in Missouri a few more years, Elias drifted back to Chicago, where he became chief of construction and maintenance in a jelly factory and put Walt to work washing bottles. Finally, in 1919, Walt made his own break. He spent the early 1920s in Kansas City as a commercial artist, hustling hard to stay alive and ahead of the bill collectors. In 1923 he moved to Hollywood, where his career began to click. [4]

The confectionery quality of Magic Kingdom's Main Street thus bears little resemblance to Disney's real childhood home. And indeed a Disney official history confesses that, "historically speaking, this Main Street was quite unlike the real Main Streets of yesteryear. Here, everything would always remain fresh and new. And the rows of old-time shops and the traffic vehicles and all the other elements would function together in harmony and unison unlike anything grandfather ever experienced." [5]

Original Walt's approach to the past was thus not to reproduce it, but to *improve* it. A Disney imagineer (as the designers style themselves) explains how the process works: "What we create is a 'Disney Realism,' sort of Utopian in nature, where we carefully program out all the negative, unwanted elements and program in the positive elements." [6] (This vacuum-cleaning of the past is reminiscent of Walt's film work, in which he transformed Grimm's Gothic horror tales into cute and cheery cartoons.) As another Disney planner puts it: "This is what the real Main Street should have been like." [7]

The Disney people don't consider this retrospective tidying up an abuse of the past; they freely and disarmingly admit its falsification, pointing out that this is, after all, just entertainment. But they also insist they are bringing out deeper truths. John Hench, a leading member of the organization, expanded on this in an interview, explaining that Disney sought to recapture the *essence* of a period. "You take a certain style, and take out the contradictions that have crept in there through people that never understood it or by accident or by some kind of emergency that happened once and found itself being repeated —you leave those things out, purify the style, and it comes back to its old form again." [8] Like the French architect Viollet-le-Duc, who in the 1860s and 1870s, strove to restore churches to imagined Gothic purity, Original Walt aimed to strip away the accretions of time. In the case of Main Street, Hench explains, he was striving to re-create the Victorian era, "which is probably one of the great optimistic periods of the world, where we thought progress was great and we all knew where we were going. [Main Street] reflects that prosperity, that enthusiasm." [9]

The decades before and after the turn of the century had their decidedly prosperous moments. But they also included depressions, strikes on the railroads, warfare in the minefields, squalor in the immigrant communities, lynching, imperial wars, and the emergence of mass protests by populists and socialists. *This* history has been whited out, presumably because it would have distressed and repelled visitors. As Hench noted, "Walt wanted to reassure people." [10]

Walt's approach, though it had its roots in Hollywood, was emblematic of larger developments in 1950s America. The dominant culture, seemingly determined to come up with a happy past to match its own contented present, contracted a selective amnesia. Leading academic historians downplayed past conflicts and painted optimistic, even uplifting pictures of the American past. Colonial Williamsburg's recollection of olden times conspicuously excised the presence of black slaves, 50 percent of its eighteenth-century inhabitants. Greenfield Village, another conflict-free small town, overlooked such realities of rural life as foreclosures and farmers' movements. Walt's Main Street, therefore, can perhaps best be understood as part of a larger trend. As a stage set that cultivated nostalgia for a fabricated past, it contributed its bit toward fashioning an image—now deeply etched into popular memory—of the Gay Nineties as a world without classes, conflict, or crime, a world of continuous consumption, a supermarket of fun. At the same time, it fastened this image on the future. Just as Colonial Williamsburg provided the model for thousands of "colonial" suburbs, Disneyland's Main Street became a model for the developing American shopping mall and ye olde entertainment centers beginning to festoon the American landscape. On the face of it, Eisenhower-era citizens could assume that America's present had evolved gently, naturally, and inevitably out of its past.

There *are* places in Disneyland that recall the bumpier patches of the good old days. At Frontierland and Adventureland, contradictions are not deleted but dwelt upon. Here we go on rides that travel to the distant and benighted places which once threatened civilization. In the Wild West, Darkest Africa, and the Caribbean, we are in the domain of dangerous opponents: Indians, pygmy headhunters, pirates. But there is no real danger in these realms. As Hench explains: "What we do here is to throw a challenge at you—not a real menace, but a pseudo-menace, a theatricalized menace—and we allow you to win." [11]

Scary but harmless images are a stock in trade of amusement parks. But it is striking that Disney's pseudo-menaces are all historical ones—the ghosts of once vigorous but now defeated enemies of Main Street—transformed into fun-filled characters. On the ride up the Congo River, your affable host regales you with such witticisms as "These natives have one thing in mind; they just want to get ahead." The robot pirates are agreeably wicked, and the robot women seem to enjoy being ravished. In Frontierland you can hole up in an old fort and shoot Indians, with a barrage of canned gunfire as an accompaniment (this was Walt's favorite part of the park).

For all the whizzing bullets, the experience of reliving ancient passions is a soothing one. For one thing, as Hench comments shrewdly, these are "old-fashioned weapons. They're part of the safe past. Nobody worries about the past." [12] For another, cowboys and Indians is a well-established and conventional game, and historical conflict is thus shuttled into a regressive world of childhood fantasy. Frontierland and Adventureland brush up against some realities of the past, but in the end they serve as ritual reassurance of Main Street's triumph over its opponents.

Abe and Audioanimatronics

The Magic Kingdom includes a direct portrayal of American history at the Hall of Presidents. The hall has a peculiar history of its own. Designed in 1957–58, it was put on the shelf because Disney imagineers lacked the technology to produce it. Breakthroughs in audioanimatronics (robot building) came in the early 1960s, and at the 1964 World's Fair, Disney tried out the new engineering. In collaboration with the state of Illinois, he built the Visit With Mr. Lincoln pavilion, starring an artificial Abe. In the 1970s the original Hall of Presidents show was dusted off, and the Lincoln robot became its centerpiece.

The Hall of Presidents is housed at Liberty Square in a mockup of an eighteenth-century Philadelphia mansion. Visitors wait for the next show in the rotunda, where paintings of the Founding Fathers establish respectful atmospherics. Then they are ushered into a theater (and told that no eating is allowed—"to maintain the dignity of the presentation"). A film begins. It shows the Founding Fathers making the Constitution. We learn that the new document was soon challenged by the Whiskey Rebels, a churlish mob, and that George Washington crushed them. Then slaveholders, an aristocratic mob, threatened it again. Andrew Jackson threatened to hang them from the nearest tree. Finally the Confederates launched the greatest challenge to date, and Lincoln took up the burden of defense. The movie implies that internal disorder remains the chief threat to America's survival.

The film ends. With great fanfare the screen goes up, revealing a stage full of robot presidents. All of them, from Washington to Reagan, are in motion, nodding or solemnly (if somewhat arthritically) gesticulating. They are done up with scrupulous attention to detail. George Washington's chair is a precise reproduction of the one in which he sat at the 1787 Constitutional Convention. Their costumes are authentic down to the last stitch. Wig makers in Guatemala reproduced their hair strand for strand. (The attention to detail, characteristic of Hollywood costume dramas, again reminds us of Disney's cinematic roots.)

A sepulchral voice-over calls the roll of these men "who have defended the Constitution." The audience is hushed, perhaps in awe at the solemnity of the occasion, perhaps in amazement at the spectacle of thirty-odd robots twitching about on stage. When the roll call gets to FDR and the more recent presidents, there is a whisper here and there. But when it gets to Nixon, chortles and guffaws break out. The contrast between the official history and living memories is too great (Nixon as defender of the Constitution?), and the spell snaps under the strain. I asked later if this was simply a bad day for Mr. Nixon and was told that, no, the crowd always rumbles when RN takes his bow.

The Nixon disturbance is symptomatic of a larger problem with the Hall of Presidents. By the 1970s, for all its technical sophistication, its ideology was old-fashioned, less believable than it was in the heyday of McCarthyism. The Disney people deny any dissatisfaction with it, but in retrospect we can see that in the 1960s they began exploring alternatives to the nationalistic approach. The transition to the eventual solution (EPCOT) was provided by another Disney 1964 World's Fair exhibit, the Carousel of Progress, created in collaboration with General Electric.

Progress Is Our Most Important Product

At the Carousel of Progress, Disney takes visitors on a ride through time. After they settle down in the Carousel's small theater, the curtain rises on a robot middle-class family at home in 1900. Mom, Dad, and the kids are chatting about housework. They have the latest in labor-saving devices—gas lights, telephones, iceboxes—and *think* that life couldn't be any easier, but *we* see that poor Mom is still subject to all kinds of drudgery. Luckily, as Dad reads in the paper, some smart fellers down at General Electric are cooking up new gadgets. At this point the theater begins to revolve around the stage (accompanied by a cheery ditty whose refrain is "Now is the best time, now is the best time, now is the best time of your life") until it reaches a new stage, this one set with 1920-style robots. Mom and Dad enthuse about their new machines—percolators, refrigerators, electric irons—but note that those research people at General Electric are still at it. And on we go to 1940, and finally to 1960. Things have really progressed now. Dad is cooking dinner (though somewhat clumsily) and Mom is celebrating passage of a bond issue (on which she had time to work, thanks to her GE dishwasher and dryer). At ride's end, a hearty voice-over concludes that we live in "the best time" ("one of the reasons is that electricity has improved our lives"), and that things will get even better ("each new year and each new day will bring a better way of life"). Finally we are shuttled toward the Kitchen of Tomorrow to see what General Electric has dreamed up for us next.

The Carousel of Progress is more than simply an extended commercial break. It is a paean to progress, defined as the availability of emancipatory consumer goods. This was new for Disney. He had tended to political rather than commercial themes. But it was an old line of argument for industrial corporations. Even the pseudo-feminist claim that household commodities liberated women had been advanced by advertisers since the 1920s and had been a staple at the 1939 World's Fair. I would like to suggest that the Disney-GE collaboration represents an important merging of several longstanding traditions of American culture.

Consider, first, the roots of Disney's Magic Kingdom shows. They descend, in part, from the patriotic dioramas, tableaux vivant, and waxworks of the nineteenth century. Disney upgraded the technology—viewers were hauled *into* the dioramas and robots replaced live actors or wax representations—but the red, white, and blue spirit remained much the same.

In the 1950s, Disney married this tradition to the amusement park, a form that beer magnates, real-estate developers, and transportation kings had fashioned for the urban working classes in the 1880s and 1890s, and whose culmination was Coney Island. Disney's park was a cleaned-up version directed at a middle-class "family" audience. He quite consciously stripped away the honky-tonk legacies of the carnival. It might be said that Disneyland represented another skirmish in a centuries-old struggle by the middle classes against popular culture's dangerous tendency to turn the world upside down. By customary right, medieval carnivals—Twelfth Night, the Ship of Fools, Bartholomew Fair—allowed the dispossessed to ridicule the high and mighty and even (symbolically) to seize power for a day. Disney's park erased any lingering traces of rituals of revolt and substituted highly organized, commodified fun. In this the Magic Kingdom shows were like Rockefeller, Jr.'s Williamsburg and Ford's Greenfield Village, which eliminated from history what their sponsors found inconvenient and unwelcome. But the essence of the form, selective reconstruction of the past, goes way back: to late nineteenth-century Scandinavian open-air museums and (in spirit) to such eighteenth-century aristocratic productions as Marie Antoinette's play peasant village (complete with marble-walled dairy), French *folies*, such as Parc Monceau, and the great landscape parks of the English gentry, which excised all signs of daily peasant activity and eradicated any sense of time other than the artificially constructed "natural."

In the 1960s, Disney took the Magic Kingdom approach and merged it with a favorite form of the entrepreneurial bourgeoisie: the industrial exposition. These expositions, of course, go back to London's 1851 Crystal Palace (and New York City's 1853 copy). They afforded places to show off, and sell, new inventions. They were also sites of ideological production, of boasting about how technology and business would transform the future.

From the perspective of its sponsors, the exposition form had long been riven by an annoying inner tension between commercial exhortation and crowd-pleasing carnival elements. The 1893 Columbian Exposition had huge buildings devoted to transportation, manufacture, and electricity presented in historical perspective; it also had seedier entertainment pavilions, located outside the White City, including "a real Dahomey village of genuine savages."[13]

The 1939 World's Fair overcame this dichotomy to a degree by subordinating celebration of production to fascination with consumption. Rather than the traditional presentation of awesome machinery, the fair showcased consumer goods: companies displayed their commodities in dazzling and fun-filled surroundings. General Motors's Futurama shuttled visitors along in comfortable moving chairs; AT&T fostered audience interaction with a talking machine; and General Electric offered a House of Magic ("The packed audiences," it was noted, "came away thrilled, mystified, and soundly sold on the company."). Another GE show contrasted the lives of Mrs. Drudge and Mrs. Modern, anticipating the Carousel of Progress's argument of gender emancipation through household appliances. For all this, the fair's first year was a financial failure, partly because of the high admission price, partly because of the heaviness of the social message.

The financial and corporate sponsors presented the World of Tomorrow as the product of a rejuvenated capitalism, a decade of depression and state intervention behind it. Entrepreneurs and technocrats would promote a rich future of mass plenty if given the opportunity—and public funds. At Futurama, as Walter Lippmann noted, General Motors "spent a small fortune to convince the American public that if it wishes to enjoy the full benefit of private enterprise in motor manufacturing, it will have to rebuild its cities and its highways by public enterprise." [14] The agitprop turned many off, critics and visitors skirted the educational and cultural theme exhibits, and even the *New York Times* called the fair a laboratory for "tomorrow's propaganda." In its second year, the fair brought back sideshows and hootchy-kootchy girls.

Twenty-five years later, the 1964 Disney-GE collaboration put sanitized entertainment at the service of business boosterism and pointed the way to EPCOT, which would brilliantly and successfully merge *all* these techniques and traditions, retaining the advantages and shedding the liabilities of fairs, waxworks, museums, and carnivals. One of the keys to the breakthrough was the Disney ability, adroitly displayed at the Carousel, to construct highly selective versions of the past.

Free Enterprise Forever

Walt's original vision of EPCOT had nothing to do with history. The Experimental Prototype Community of Tomorrow was to be a laboratory city in which twenty thousand people would live. Disney dreamed of "a planned, controlled community, a showcase for American industry and research," a permanent testing ground for new ideas in urban planning. Under its gigantic bubble dome, American know-how, ingenuity, and enterprise would overcome the ills of urban life. ("In EPCOT there will be no slum areas because we won't let them develop."[15])

This extraordinary project might seem quite a jump from an amusement park, but the overheated reaction Disneyland evoked may have been instrumental in EPCOT's creation. Walt had been praised extravagantly as an urban planner. James Rouse, master builder of new towns and historical shopping malls modeled on Main Street (Boston's Faneuil Hall, Baltimore's Harbor Place, New York's South Street Seaport) told a 1963 Harvard conference that Disneyland was the "greatest piece of urban design in the United States today." [16] Architectural critic Peter Blake called the Anaheim park the only significant new town built in the United States since World War II—"staggeringly successful"—and suggested, only half-humorously, turning Manhattan over to Disney to fix up.[17]

All this went to Walt's head and he flowered into a utopian capitalist. This was partly a family legacy: as Michael Harrington has perceptively noted, Disney's father had been an admirer of Edward Bellamy's "warmhearted, futuristic authoritarianism." [18] Partly, perhaps, Walt had been inspired by the 1939 World's Fair's Democracity, a scale model of a perfectly planned "World of Tomorrow"—a "vast, Utopian stage set" housed inside the great globe of the Perisphere. Whatever its roots, the hothouse atmosphere of the Kennedy-

Johnson years speeded the process. Gigantic projects of social reconstruction seemed plausible in those boom years and though Walt was a Goldwater Republican (and an early financial supporter of Ronald Reagan) he too dreamed of creating a Great Society.

Like Johnson, Disney acted boldly. By 1965 he had bought up, secretly, forty square miles (*twice* the size of Manhattan) in central Florida. The state, anticipating mammoth tourist revenues, granted him virtually feudal powers. Democracy for the residents of the Community of Tomorrow would have been a nuisance. ("There will be no landowners and therefore no voting control.") [19] To ensure that EPCOT ran smoothly, Walt would be king.

But in 1966, in the midst of planning the new society, Walt died. WED Enterprises considered going ahead with his prototype city, but the company was nervous; it could see lawsuits in its future from disgruntled and disfranchised residents. So it scrapped the notion of a living city and went with a safer version, an extension of Disney's collaboration with General Electric. WED proposed to some of the biggest corporations in the United States a joint project: construction of a permanent world's fair. There the companies, with the help of Disney imagineers, would display evolving technologies and promote their visions of the future. EPCOT was thus transformed from utopian community to sound business proposition.

By targeting grown-up Mouseketeers instead of their offspring, WED got itself out of an impending crisis, a looming baby bust that promised to shrivel its traditional prime market of five- to nine-year-olds. (A similar marketing strategy recently dictated scrapping Dick Van Dyke movies for PG films like *Splash*: preteens no longer flocked to traditional Disney fare, and the studio was forced to respond to this cultural shift.) The participating companies would also profit: they could advertise new product lines and drape themselves in the mantle of Disney respectability, no small matter in the anticorporate atmosphere of the 1970s.

The corporate giants agreed. Kraft declared that sponsorship of a land pavilion was "the most effective way we can enhance our corporate identity." General Electric explained that "the Disney organization is absolutely superb in interpreting our company dramatically, memorably, and favorably to the public." Kodak observed, somewhat baldly, that "you might entrance a teenager today, but tomorrow he's going to invest his money in Kodak stock." General Motors took a broader view, noting not only that EPCOT would give them the chance "to make contact with millions of motorists" but that "it will be a good opportunity to point out how technological progress has contributed to the world and the free enterprise system." [20]

In the end, major multinationals, notably those who had been most successful at the 1939 fair, signed on to tell Americans what life would be like in the twenty-first century. At EPCOT, Exxon explains energy and AT&T

does communications. Transportation is presented by General Motors, the land by Kraft, the home by GE, imagination by Kodak. Each corporation has a high-tech pavilion, the heart of which is a ride. Seated passengers are conveyed through tunnels which open out into drive-through dioramas: stage sets crammed with robots, videos, and holograms. Supplementing each ride are exhibits, films, and hands-on demonstrations. The pavilions are grouped into an area of the park called Future World.

Nation-states were also invited to EPCOT. England, France, Germany, Italy, Japan, China, Mexico, Canada—usually in conjunction with national businesses (Japan Airlines, British Railways, Labatt Beer)—exhibit their wares and promote travel to their shores. Disney imagineers helped them design terrains that portray the "essence" of their culture. Presiding over this World of Nations is the host pavilion, the American Adventure (presented jointly by American Express and Coca-Cola), devoted entirely to presenting the history of the United States.

In 1982, EPCOT opened. It billed itself as "a community of ideas and nations and a testing ground where free enterprise can explore and demonstrate and showcase new ideas that relate to man's hopes and dreams." In its first year, more than twenty-two million people visited. More businesses and countries signed on. By 1984, total investment had reached $1.75 billion and was still climbing.

Tomorrow's Yesterdays

An amazing amount of Future World is devoted to remembering things past. Virtually all the rides are time travels. Passengers settle themselves into moving vehicles which carry them from the dim past to an imagined future. Voice-over narrators, like those on TV commercials, explain the passing views and propound an interpretation of historical development.

Each multinational historian has its own style. GM's tends toward the relentlessly cheery; the past was endlessly droll, even wacky and zany. AT&T's is more portentous: "Who are we? Where are we going?" it asks in sepulchral tones as we climb aboard our time machines, and it informs us that the answer must be sought in the "Dawn of Recorded Time." But it is the similarities that compel attention.

There is a discernible corporate vision of history. At first blush it appears merely that of the Carousel of Progress writ large: history is a record of the invention of commodities which allow man to master his environment. But EPCOT goes beyond this. The temporal dimensions are far grander: from the cavemen to outer space. And, significantly, each corporation admits there have been problems in the past.

Each journey begins in prehistoric times. GM's history of transportation has robot Neanderthals "stumbling around" by footpower. Exxon's history of energy commences with robot dinosaurs (reminiscent of those in *Fantasia*) battling one another in a primeval swamp as fossil fuels cook beneath their feet. AT&T's history of communication starts with cavemen attacking mammoths and painting on walls.

Then man climbs out of primitive times. GM's man does this in an unrelievedly hearty way. As we ride along (accompanied by a background ditty proclaiming that "it's fun to be free, to go anywhere, with never a care"), we watch man slowly produce improved forms of transportation—canoes, horse-drawn vehicles—until we reach that favorite corporate period, the Renaissance. Here GM's robot Leonardo turns from culture to engineering: he is shown tinkering with a flying machine while a scowling robot Mona Lisa model taps her foot. Then it's on to the Era of Inventions and a cornucopia of improvements—bicycles, horseless carriages, trains, airplanes—that bring us to the present.

AT&T's trajectory is similar. It tracks the slow progress of communications. Egyptians invent scrolls (a robot pharoah gives dictation to a robot secretary), Greeks give birth to theatre (robots declaim on stage), and monks illuminate manuscripts (one is shown cutely snoring at his desk). When AT&T hits the Renaissance, it tilts (unlike GM) toward the cultural dimension, featuring a robot Michelangelo, on its back, laboring at the Sistine ceiling. Then AT&T's man also enters the jet stream of progress, and inventions tumble out on what seems a self-sustaining basis.

But when the rides reach the near past, there is a sudden departure from triumphalism. Each corporation acknowledges some blemishes on the record. To be sure, many were inconsequential: one General Motors diorama jovially depicts the first traffic jam (which it blames on a horse). Other problems were serious. Kraft reminds us graphically of Dust Bowl days. Exxon reminds us that an energy crisis emerged. The past was *not* the best of all possible pasts.

The corporate histories are less than clear about *why* problems emerged. Some seem facts of nature: dinosaur days bequeathed us limited quantities of fossil fuel. But people are responsible for others. Kraft tells us that "we" (or, occasionally, "technological man") made mistakes. "We" abused the environment. "We" polluted the air. There is a hint that "unplanned development" had something to do with it (a practice, presumably, in which multinationals do not engage).

Luckily, we are given to understand, people (or, more precisely, corporations) are working on these problems. The adjacent exhibits expand on this, and we shall return to them.

Each ride then breaks through the troubled recent past into the future. The future is always set in outer space. The narrative tapes and ditties shut off, *Close Encounters of the Third Kind* music comes on, laser beams flash, and we are launched into awesome starry expanses in which space stations and satellites hover. In the future, problems have been eliminated, presumably by the corporations, whose logos are visible everywhere (as in the movie *2001*). Life in space looks remarkably like life on sitcom TV. Mom back on Earth communicates (via AT&T's network) with Sis up on the space station, and they chat about homework and boyfriends. There's a sense of serene ordinariness about the future, which is not accidental. Hench believes "nobody worries about the future, because that's going to be up in space, in the space colonies." [21] And Marty Sklar, WED vice-president, says: "We admit to being optimistic over man's future. You can call EPCOT our answer to the gloomy future predictions of the Club of Rome." [22]

Subsidiary exhibits explain the basis for this optimism—corporate problem solvers are at work. Kraft, in full environmentalist regalia, talks about the need for symbiosis with the land, shows films about replanting forests and reoxygenating rivers, and explains the artificial farms of the future. AT&T appropriates Buckminster Fuller's environmentalist imagery—its geodesic-dome pavilion is called Spaceship Earth—and shows how AT&T's network will overcome communications bottlenecks on Earth and in outer space. Exxon tells us it is working away at solar power (the roof of its pavilion is bejeweled with photoelectric panels). Solar, sadly, still seems far from practicable. So, Exxon explains, until the big breakthroughs come, we must rely on oil (videos sing the romance of offshore rigs and ecologically correct pipelines) and coal (films prove that strip mining can be beautiful). Exxon also wants us to keep the nuclear option open, and visitors can play at running a nuclear plant. But the company is not heavy handed about plumping for oil or atoms. All options must be kept open and in competition, including geothermal and biomass. Let the best one win.

GM, another corporate environmentalist, also believes in open options. In its Engine of the Future show, films project cartoon characters onto large overhead screens. Each promotes a different energy-conscious design. On the left, GM's own persona, a jolly cowboy, pitches for an improved internal-combustion engine. Then alternatives are presented: an Archie Bunker sort favors coal, a yuppie lady pushes solar, even the omnipresent Leonardo has a better idea. All these notions are shot down for one reason or another. Finally, on the extreme right, we meet a character who looks like a cross between mad scientist and Japanese dwarf and sounds like Peter Lorre. He is working, fanatically, on a totally pollution-free and inexpensive water engine that uses hydrogen. In the grand finale, this crackpot blows everything up, and flames sweep across all the screens. Then cowboy Tex gets the floor back, applauds the others, says they have a ways to go before they beat out the "good ole reliable internal combustion engine" but assures them General Motors wants them all in competition so that the consumer will benefit in the end. (Consumers are indeed never far from GM's mind; the last exhibit is a showroom of current-model GM cars. GM is the most vulgar self-promoter—a hucksterism perhaps related to declining car sales?—but even the suavest of the multinationals have their tacky moments.)

EPCOT's sensitivity to social and environmental problems is rooted in the 1970s corporate world's awareness of its image problems. Business wanted, with the aid of Disney publicists, to refurbish itself in the public mind. EPCOT designers knew Magic Kingdom boosterism would not suffice, so the imagineers admitted to problems in the past but rejected corporate responsibility for them. More imaginatively still, they presented business as the cutting edge of the ecology movement. America's problems, Corporate Walt says, are technical ones; responsible corporations are the Mr. Goodwrenches who can fix them. A Kraft VP summarized the strategy: "Hopefully [visitors to our pavilion will] be aware that major organizations are working at new ways of controlling the land—without disrupting the ecology—to ensure an adequate food supply. To our benefit will be the message that here is Kraft with that kind of concern." [23]

This is a difficult message to sell. Exxon the champion of alternative energy? General Motors the promoter of mass transit? Kraft and agribusiness the practitioners of symbiosis with the land? AT&T the savior of Spaceship Earth? As in the case of the Nixon robot, the discrepancy between claim and reality invites ridicule. Corporate Walt, a skillful communicator, tries to bridge the gap, not only through bald assertion but in more indirect ways as well.

As in the Magic Kingdom sets, a whiteout approach is at work: silence blankets the sorry environmental record of the corporations. (This doesn't fool people who know better, but it doesn't enlighten those—particularly children—who don't.)

Another technique is EPCOT's bravura display of technological mastery and management capacity, which seems intent on inducing awe at the capabilities of the corporations, as machines in Greek temples once impressed the populace with the power of the gods. Imagine, the place implies, what business could do if let loose on America's ills (and never mind it created many of them in the first place, or that the cost of attaining EPCOT-level efficiency, a billion dollars per hundred acres, seems a mite high). EPCOT thus forms a chapter in capital's long-standing attempt to control social space as it controls production space; it echoes company-town experiments from Lowell to Pullman (all of which failed, but hope springs eternal).

But the most subtle and perhaps most powerful of the methods at work is the historical analysis that permeates the entire operation. Future World implies that capitalist development is natural and inevitable. It does so by riding visitors, literally on rails, from a bowdlerized presentation of the past to an impoverished vision of the future. The progression goes like this: history was made by inventors and businessmen; the corporations are the legatees of such a past (their slogan might be: "From Leonardo to Exxon"); this pedigree entitles them to run tomorrow. Citizens can sit back and consume.

Disney did not invent this approach; it had respectable academic roots in modernization theory. This analysis, fashionable during the 1950s and 1960s, updated the Victorian belief in a march of progress from savagery to civilization, substituting a trajectory from traditional to modern society, with the latter-day terminus understood to be contemporary America. It is worth noting that EPCOT's popularization of modernization theory, reactionary though it is, was the product of a relatively liberal corporate culture. Had EPCOT been designed in the tooth-and-claw world of the 1980s, it would probably have argued that the driving force of history was profit maximization, an approach that might make the actual version seem positively benign.

Corporate Walt's history is bad history. All historical interpretations are necessarily selective in their facts, but here the silences are profoundly distorting. Consider, for example, that in all EPCOT's depictions of the past as a continuous expansion of man's possibilities through technology, there is not a word about war. Nothing about the critical impetus it provided through the ages to scientific development. Nor about the phenomenal destruction such development wrought. And nothing about the contemporary possibilities of planetary extermination. Perhaps the imagineers stuck their heads in the sand on this one because they wanted us to think only the most positive thoughts. But the Magic Kingdom's justification for ostrichism ("this is only an entertainment park") doesn't wash here; EPCOT is explicitly devoted to enhancing understanding. Perhaps, as in Fantasyland, they think the wish is parent to the fact. Or perhaps the silences are related to the fact that many corporations are producing armaments as well as toasters and that if they and Reagan have their way, the outer-space dioramas of the future will have to be reconstructed to include killer satellites.

Corporate Walt's history, like modernization theory, is unidirectional. There were never any forks on the path of progress, never any sharp political struggles over which way to go. EPCOT visitors would never guess that millions of Americans once objected to motoring down the capitalist road. The implication, moreover, is that there are no alternatives now. If there have been problems, they have been the price of progress; the only solution is full speed ahead on the corporate space shuttle; minor course corrections can be left to the pilot. Corporate Walt and the multinationals have produced a past that leads ineluctably toward *their* kind of future.

Corporate Walt's history is a top-down version. Popular political movements don't exist in this past. Rendering ordinary people invisible as makers of history hardly encourages visitors to believe they can make their own future.

(And EPCOT's influence goes far beyond visitors: its sponsors have launched a massive outreach program to the nation's classrooms; they are mass-marketing lesson plans and videos on land, energy, and communications.)

Corporate desire to fudge the past, combined with Disney's ability to spruce it up, promotes a sense of history as a pleasantly nostalgic memory, now so completely transcended by the modern corporate order as to be irrelevant to contemporary life. This diminishes our capacity to make sense of our world through understanding how it came to be. The Disney version of history thus creates a way of not seeing and perhaps a way of not acting.

Good historical analysis informs people about the matrix of constraints and possibilities they have inherited from the past and enhances their capacity for effective social action in the present. EPCOT's Future World does the opposite: it dulls historical sensibility and invites acquiescence to what is. It should, consequently, be regarded not as a historical, but as a historicidal enterprise.

Warts and All

EPCOT's American Adventure—American Express's & Coca-Cola's direct exploration of U.S. history—is intriguingly different from the high-tech pavilions; it also marks a startling departure from Original Walt's 1950s approach to the subject.

Like the Hall of Presidents, American Adventure is housed in a simulated Georgian mansion staffed by costumed hosts and hostesses. Again there is an inspirational antechamber, with quotes by authors ranging from Herman Melville to Ayn Rand. But here there are no films, no rides. The model is closer to a TV variety show, with the presentation emceed by Ben Franklin and Mark Twain robots. The American Adventure consists of a series of turns by computer-operated robot ensembles, alternately raised and lowered by a 350,000-pound apparatus below the floorboards. The technology, as usual, is stunning. The robots are the latest in lifelike humanoids. The Franklin robot actually walks up stairs. The research into details (the size of Revolutionary War cannonballs, Alexander Graham Bell's diction) is as scrupulous as ever. And this dazzling technology, when set in motion, proceeds to tell, in twenty-nine minutes flat, the entire history of the United States.

At first the show seems merely a spiffed up Hall of Presidents. It begins with an inspirational reading of the Pilgrims-to-Revolution period (robot rebel soldiers chat at Valley Forge, while a George Washington robot sits dolefully on a robot horse). But with independence won, and westward movement under way, the show departs dramatically from the expected. Emcee Twain tells us that "a whole bunch of folks found out 'we the people' didn't yet mean *all* the people," and a Frederick Douglass robot is hoisted up on stage. As he poles (somewhat improbably) down the Mississippi, Douglass speaks of the noise of chains and the crack of the whip and of his hope that "antislavery will unlock the slave prison." A subdued Civil War sequence follows, using Brady photographs to stress costs rather than glory.

The Civil War over, a new wave of immigrants pours in. This, Twain tells us, heralds "a new dawn to the American Adventure." But as we resign ourselves to melting-pot platitudes, a clap of thunder introduces a Chief Joseph robot. He notes that the new dawn means a final sunset for his people, who are being shot down like animals. He gives his famous "I will fight no more forever" speech, reminding us (as Twain says) of "our long painful journey to the frontiers of human liberty."

Then it's on to the 1876 Centennial. But before launching into a Carousel of Progress–type paean to inventions, a Susan B. Anthony robot surfaces. In ringing voice she says: "We ask justice, we ask equality be guaranteed to us and our daughters forever," and adds, quoting Edison (with whom she most improbably shares the stage), that "discontent is the first necessity of progress."

Edison, Carnegie, and the roll call of inventions then have their moment, but after hearing about zippers, trolley cars, vacuum cleaners, and airplanes, a robot naturalist John Muir reminds us that all this growth posed a threat to America the Beautiful and urges a robot Teddy Roosevelt to build national parks. Next come World War I—"ready or not, we were thrust into the role of world leader"—and Lindbergh's flight. But then comes the Crash of 1929, which "tarnished the golden dreams of millions," and we are into the Great Depression era. Here the set is a weatherbeaten southern post office–cum–gas station. Two black and two white robots sit on the front porch (there is a lot of implausible retrospective integration in the show). They strum "Brother, can you spare a dime," chuckle about former millionaires in New York, and listen to FDR on the radio talking about "fear itself." (There is also a momentary descent into tacky self-promotion: the shack is plastered with contemporary Coca-Cola and American Express ads.) Then Will Rogers plumps for military preparedness, FDR announces Pearl Harbor, and we are into World War II, which consists entirely of a stage set featuring Rosie the Riveter fixing a submarine.

The postwar material plays it safer. History becomes popular culture. A series of filmic images of personalities are projected—like *People* magazine covers—which then float up into clouds, to the accompaniment of ethereal music about America spreading its golden wings and flying high. It's an eclectic and distinctly integrated assortment, including Jackie Robinson, Marilyn Monroe, Jonas Salk, Satchmo, Elvis, Einstein, Walt Disney, Norman Rockwell, John Wayne, Lucy, Billie Jean King, JFK (giving his ask-not speech), Martin Luther King (giving his "I have a dream" speech), Muhammad Ali,

Arnold Palmer, the U.S. Olympic hockey team, and the men on the moon. We end with a blaze of traditional Disney patriotism, with Ben and Mark perched atop the Statue of Liberty foreseeing a long run for the American Adventure.

American Adventure is thus a dramatic departure from the Hall of Presidents (and the spirit of Future World). American history is no longer just about great white men; indeed it seems to be largely about blacks, women, Indians, and ecologists. The show doesn't celebrate law and order; it recalls the words of critics. In some ways, the American adventure represents an extraordinary step forward.

How do we account for it? One answer is the effects, by the mid-1970s, of the black, women's, antiwar, and environmentalist movements that had heightened popular consciousness. After a generation of protest, 1950s celebrations would no longer do for public historical presentations; even Colonial Williamsburg had to restore blacks to its streets. As a Disney briefing pamphlet for hosts says: "We couldn't ignore certain major issues that questioned our nation's stand on human liberty and justice." [24] An American Adventure executive insisted that "the warts-and-all perspective is appreciated by most visitors because our country is not perfect and they know it." [25] In the last analysis, I believe, shifts in popular opinion forced the Disney people to update their ideology.

The writers, though not academics, were also influenced by the new social historians who reconstructed U.S. history in the 1960s and 1970s. Dr. Alan Yarnell, a UCLA historian who was consulted on the project, insisted that "the Jesse Lemisch approach—history from the bottom up" replace the great-white-men verities. The corporate sponsors went along with this approach. The heavy intervention of businessmen into Future World scripting was missing here, perhaps because it was an area of lesser political concern. Amex and Coke simply assumed from the Disney track record that nothing embarrassing would emerge from the design process.

In the end, they were right. Despite the trappings of the new social history, American Adventure remains Disney history. The imagineers imposed a theme of "Dreamers and Doers" on the show: the past had to be portrayed in an upbeat manner. So Susan B. Anthony, Chief Joseph, and Frederick Douglass notwithstanding, American history is still a saga of progress. The dissatisfactions of blacks, women, and ecologists are presented as having been opportunities in disguise. As Disney literature puts it: "Inevitably, Americans have overcome the tragedies of their controversies, which ultimately led to a better way of life." [26] In American Adventure, social contradictions are transcended as easily as are natural ones at Future World. The agents of change, moreover, were individual speakers and writers, not collective social movements. The spokespersons of the discontented knocked, and the door was opened.

Some controversial aspects of U.S. history remain completely unacknowledged, most notably the history of labor. While the show embraces individuals associated in the public mind with the struggle for civil rights and civil liberties (that is, the individual rights of particular groups), it finds itself unable to deal with a movement long founded on principles of collective rights and collective action, namely unions. This reluctance, perhaps, is also rooted in the ongoing challenge labor represents to the capitalist *system* as well as to the particular corporations bankrolling the exhibits.

The silences get louder the closer the show gets to the present. There are no 1960s ghetto uprisings, no campus protests, no feminist or ecology movements, no Watergate. Most notoriously, there is nothing about Vietnam. One of the designers explained that "I searched for a long time for a photograph of an anti-war demonstration that would be optimistic, but I never found one." (A picture of a helicopter was recently added, a distinctly minimalist response to complaints.)

Though willing to accept that the past was made by the discontented, the show disconnects the present from that tradition. It abandons the narrative line on reaching the postwar period—King is there, but as an icon, not a spokesman for a movement—and it implies our problems are things of the past. At show's end, Mark and Ben counsel us to worry only about the perils of plenty, the problem of how to use leisure time, and how each individual can fulfill his or her dreams. But because the show refuses to acknowledge the social constraints on individual actors—sexism and racism, poverty and unemployment remain obstinate components of contemporary U.S. culture—it peters out into complacent boosterism. Forced to confront a changed American popular historical consciousness and to incorporate the work of radical scholars, it opts for damage control. It defuses the danger inherent in the intrusion of real history by redeploying it within a vision of an imperfect but still inevitable progress.

Education and Entertainment

Does Corporate Walt's history have an impact? How does it affect the millions of people who visit? There is little direct evidence one way or the other. Only a few hundred have written letters, the largest single response coming from Vietnam veterans complaining about the obliteration of their experiences. But what do such cavils mean when set beside Disney World's status as the biggest single tourist destination in the entire world? What accounts for this stupendous success?

Demographic statistics provide an avenue to an answer. The class spectrum of EPCOT visitors is dramatically narrow. They come from groups doing best in terms of pay and personal power on the job: the median income is

$35,700, and fully three-quarters are professionals or managers. (Professional and technical personnel account for 48 percent of attendees, managers and administrators for 26 percent.) This is not a working-class attraction (craftsmen, 4 percent; operatives, 4 percent; sales, 8 percent; service, 2 percent; laborers, 2 percent). Nor do blacks (3 percent) or Hispanics (2 percent) come in large numbers. (To a degree these demographics simply reflect the cost of getting there: only 22 percent of visitors come from Florida; 71 percent are from elsewhere in the United States, chiefly the Northeast and the Midwest.)

A process of class self-affirmation seems to be at work. Certainly Disney World seems intent on providing reassurance to this class, on presenting it with its own pedigree. EPCOT's seventies-style liberal corporatism seems tailor made for professionals and technocrats. It is calibrated to their concerns —nothing on labor, heavy on ecology, clean, well-managed, emphasis on individual solutions, good restaurants—and it provides just the right kind of past for their hipper sensibilities. Perhaps, therefore, professionals and managers (many of whom, after all, function as subalterns of capital) flock there because it ratifies their world. Perhaps they don't *want* to know about reality, past or present, and prefer comforting (and plausible) stereotypes.

Yet many in this class are at least potentially antagonistic to the multinationals. Their members have spearheaded the ecology movement. It was their growing sophistication that made it impossible for Disney to recycle 1950s approaches, either in films or theme parks (approaches now dismissed by a younger generation as Mickey Mouse). We must be suspicious of blaming messages on the receiving public, even such an affluent one as this.

Would accurate history bore or repel them? Perhaps not. Audiences often respond favorably where conventional wisdom says they won't. (A dramatic and relevant comparison might be with the spectacularly successful *Roots*, which for all its Hollywood devices and elisions was a striking departure from *Gone with the Wind*.) Do Disney's sitcoms in space work because people want reassurance, or because that's all they're being given? Are visitors getting what they want, or what corporate publicists want them to want?

There is no simple answer to these questions. Some of EPCOT's consumers may be inclined to adopt the comfortable and convenient ideologies purveyed there. Others have no vested interest in or are profoundly disserved by doing so. Regardless of predisposition, however, EPCOT's casual subordination of truth to entertainment impairs visitors' ability to distinguish between reality and plausible fiction.

The consequences for museum curators are serious. Most museum visitors are probably alumni of Disney's parks (or of those established by competitors). Their prior encounters (I would suspect) have helped shape their expectations, both of form and content. This is not all bad. There are a host of imaginative techniques the imagineers have invented to attract consumers;

some of them (the more affordable ones) might well be deployed by heretofore staid institutions. But museums might also consider taking up the cudgels against the misinformation purveyors (which include Hollywood movies, TV docudramas, and mass-market fiction as well as theme parks). An occasional exhibit devoted to decoding and critiquing the messages promulgated by such cultural institutions might be an enlightening and enlivening use of museum resources.

More broadly still, I think the country at large needs to reflect upon the consequences of the corporate commodification of history. George Kennan once noted that "when an individual is unable to face his own past and feels compelled to build his view of himself on a total denial of it and on the creation of myths to put in its place, this is normally regarded as a sign of extreme neurosis." A similar diagnosis, he argued, was warranted for a society "that is incapable of seeing itself realistically and can live only by the systematic distortion or repression of its memories about itself and its early behavior." [27] Kennan was referring to the Soviet Union. But the United States suffers from a similar malady. The past is too important to be left to the private sector. If we wish to restore our social health, we had better get beyond Mickey Mouse history.

Acknowledgments

I would like to thank, for their splendid advice, counsel, and encouragement: Jean-Christophe Agnew, Jeanie Attie, Paul Berman, Ted Burrows, Jeanne Chase, Hope Cooke, Peter Dimock, Liz Fee, Brooks MacNamara, Ruth Misheloff, Bob Padgug, Roy Rosenzweig, Danny Walkowitz, Jon Wiener, the Summer 1984 members of the Cummington Community of the Arts, and the staff at Walt Disney World. An earlier version of this essay appeared in *Radical History Review* 32 (March 1985), 33–57.

NOTES

1. *Walt Disney World: A Pictorial Souvenir* (Walt Disney Productions, 1977), 6.

2. Disney quoted in Richard Schickel, *The Disney Version: The Life, Times, Art and Commerce of Walt Disney* (New York: Simon and Schuster, 1968), 316

3. *Walt Disney World: A Pictorial Souvenir*, 6. For an insightful analysis of Main Street, see Richard V. Francaviglia, "Main Street USA: A Comparison/Contrast of Streetscapes in Disneyland and Walt Disney World," in the special issue of the *Journal of Popular Culture* on theme parks [15, no. 1 (Summer 1981), 141–56]; other useful essays in that issue include David M. Johnson, "Disney World as Structure and Symbol: Recreation of an American Experience," (157–65); Margaret J. King, "Disneyland and Walt Disney World: Traditional Values in Futuristic Form," (116–40); and Margaret J. King, "The New American Muse: Notes on the Amusement/Theme Park," (56–62).

4. For biographical information see Richard Schickel's excellent study *The Disney Version* and Michael Harrington, "To the Disney Station," *Harper's* 258 (January 1979), 35–39.

5. *The Disney Theme Show: From Disneyland to Walt Disney World, A Pocket History of the First Twenty Years* (Walt Disney Productions, 1976), 1:12.

6. Ibid., 1:31.

7. Ibid., 1:12.

8. Charlie Haas, "Disneyland is Good for You," *New West*, 3 (December 4, 1978), 18.

9. Ibid.

10. Ibid.

11. Haas, "Disneyland," 16.

12. Ibid.

13. Elting E. Morison, "What Went Wrong with Disney's World's Fair," *American Heritage* 35, no. 1 (December 1983), 72.

14. Quoted in Warren I. Susman, "The People's Fair: Cultural Contradictions of a Consumer Society," reprinted in Warren I. Susman, *Culture as History: The Transformation of American Society in the Twentieth Century* (New York: Pantheon, 1985), 225.

15. Quoted in Harrington, "To the Disney Station," 38.

16. *Disney Theme Show*, 1:15.

17. Peter Blake, "Mickey Mouse for Mayor!" *New York Magazine* (April 1972), 41–42.

18. Harrington, "To the Disney Station," 39.

19. Disney quoted in Harrington, "To the Disney Station," 38.

20. Quotes from Earl C. Gottschalk, Jr., "Less Mickey Mouse," *Wall Street Journal*, January 26, 1979, 27; "A Disneyland of Corporate Promotion," *Business Week* (March 26, 1979), 114; and Harrington, "To the Disney Station," 86. Florida's Governor Reubin Askew was similarly taken with the plan: "This isn't just another undertaking of a private corporation", he enthused. "This is a stimulation and a recommitment to the entire system of private enterprise—without which whatever economy we may have in the industrialized West couldn't be what it is today." *Walt Disney Productions Annual Report 1978*, 6.

21. Haas, "Disneyland," 19.

22. Gottschalk, "Less Mickey Mouse," 27.

23. "Disneyland of Corporate Promotion," 114.

24. Epcot Center, *The American Adventure* (Walt Disney Productions, 1982), 5.

25. Letter from Frank R. Stansberry, March 21, 1984.

26. *The American Adventure*, 5.

27. George F. Kennan, "Two Letters," *The New Yorker* 60 (September 24, 1984), 56.

Part Two

The New History and the New Museum

Speaking of Women: Museums' Representations of Women's History

8

Barbara Melosh

Even during the Reagan era with its hostility toward feminism, public displays of all sorts, from advertising to weddings to museum exhibits, attested to the wide ripples of the women's movement. This essay considers museum exhibits as part of a public discourse, a language that is at once vehicle and agent of social change. In this discourse, all voices are not equal. This essay examines the language of exhibits and the special ritualistic and sanctifying voice of museums. I consider exhibits as texts whose selections and omissions reveal much about professionalism and patronage in the shaping of popular historical understanding. I argue that the presentation of women's history in museums illuminates the museum's role in the larger process of unraveling and rebuilding a cultural center, a process of incorporation and accommodation that constantly renews and fortifies dominant ideology. Exhibits in women's history both facilitate and contain the reconsideration of women's lives that feminists demand; indirectly, they show us how far we have come and how far we have yet to go.[1]

The resurgence of the women's movement in the 1970s brought new visibility to women's lives and inspired a renewed search for women's history. In this quest museums have been both leaders and followers. On the one hand, curators have long recognized the importance of material culture as a record of ordinary lives and as often-neglected evidence for the history of invention, diffusion, and consumption. Museum collections and exhibitions are repositories of a kind of historical evidence newly validated when university-based scholars reinvented social history in the 1960s. Once confined to the record of bygone manners and customs, a collection of engaging curiosities with little meaning for the larger movements of national life, social history shed its previous marginality by arguing for the significance of ordinary lives and by undertaking a revision of the historical canon itself. In this ambitious new agenda, history "from the bottom up" not only would add ordinary lives to the record but would challenge periodization and interpretive paradigms based solely on a history of politics and great men. As historians influenced by the women's movement sought to extend the methods of social history to the materials of women's past, they had few monographs or university courses to guide them but could find abundant evidence of women's lives in museums that had preserved the objects women made and used. And yet historians in museums were seldom innovators in this revision of the received wisdom of the past; more often, they borrowed selectively from scholarly work initiated elsewhere.

This tendency to borrow and interpret rather than to present original findings has led many observers and some curators themselves to think of museum exhibits as a kind of trickle-down from "real" historical work done elsewhere. But exhibits are never simply passive mirrors of scholarly work. Even when they are based on scholarship conducted elsewhere, they are not translations but highly selective adaptations. What have historians in museums selected from the scholarship of women's history, and how do we account for their choices? Most broadly, a survey of museum exhibits raises questions about voice and audience. How do curators talk about history? To whom and for whom do they speak?

My questions are informed by my personal and intellectual interests in issues of professionalism and history and by my employment in both a museum and a university. As a person with a foot in each world, I am intrigued by the possibilities and resources of the museum for reaching a larger audience for historical work, aware of how much museums and universities have in common, and bemused and frustrated by the gaps and silences that often separate historians working in museums from those based in universities. I reject the assumption of some historians and curators who see an essentially separate role for universities and museums, with museums relegated to the implicitly lesser task of popularizing history for a public assumed to have little interest in the arcane work of scholarship.

If exhibits share important commonalities with classroom teaching or written scholarship as tools of public education and historical work, curators nonetheless work with a distinctly different medium. Museum displays offer possibilities that are at once more constricted and more expansive than those available to the scholar trafficking in the conventional printed medium of articles and books. The writer of an exhibit labors under a severe economy of language: because visitors must take in the message from a tiring standing position, even the largest exhibit must limit its written text. The planning and presentation of exhibits raise useful questions about how best to speak to an audience of generalists. At a time when university-based historians are increasingly troubled by their separation from this audience, the work of historical museums offers suggestive testimony about the possibilities of creative synthesis and of finding a language that distills without diluting historical interpretation.[2]

If curators have to spend words carefully, they have an embarrassment of other riches. Historians who rely primarily on words to convey ideas may well envy the curator's and designer's resources of color, line, arrangement, sound, light, images, and objects. The museum has the advantage of engaging its audience with the visual enticements of video, film, and photography. In addition to the allure and immediacy of these media, they may also render exhibits more accessible because they provide a visual experience that is familiar to viewers from an electronic and image-saturated culture. This essay emphasizes the importance of visual presentation as part of the "text" of an exhibit, for the design of a display is no passive vehicle but an active element that may enhance, reinforce, modify, or even subvert the message of the labels.

I have chosen to review exhibits that are explicitly presented as women's history, for such displays allow us the most direct look at how curators try to shape and revise popular historical understanding in this field. My selection entails some significant omissions. For one, I have limited my discussion of an emerging use of women's history in larger synthetic exhibitions that include sex as a significant category of social history, considered along with race and class. Living museums and historic houses appear only briefly in my essay, although such sites offer special opportunities for interpretation of women's history because of their focus on community and domestic life. Finally, the selection of exhibits discussed below is of necessity somewhat arbitrary in another way, limited by scheduling and geographical proximity.

Recovering Women's Pasts

Historians of women have participated in the fruitful interdisciplinary ferment of women's studies, benefiting from the methods and traditions of other fields as they have sought to reimagine their own. Drawing on a tradition whose organizing ideas would denaturalize human culture, feminist anthropologists have supplied a number of powerful ideas about women's place. Gayle Rubin's "Traffic in Women" argued for a linguistic marker to separate biological woman from the social construction of womanhood; in a usage that many have adopted, she reserved *sex* to describe what was irreducibly biological and *gender* to describe the cultural elaborations added to the bare minimum of biological difference.[3] In *Woman, Culture and Society*, Michelle Z. Rosaldo and Louise Lamphere presented a collection of articles that set out a bold revision of human culture and history: they proclaimed that women's subordination was universal but rebutted the biological explanation that such widespread evidence suggested. Women were everywhere secondary, they declared, but across different societies women performed every imaginable task of human society and culture.

In the same anthology, Sherry Ortner proposed a rewriting of French anthropologist Claude Lévi-Strauss. Adapting his theory of the universal categories of nature and culture, she argued that in each society's ideological map, women represented nature and men stood for culture. In Lévi-Strauss's scheme, every society valued culture—the invented, human order—over untamed or "raw" nature. Ortner argued that because women bore children and nursed them, they had come to be associated with nature, both feared and revered, and the subject of constant efforts of ritual and technological control. Rosaldo proposed a similar universal bifurcation of social institutions. Everywhere work was divided into public and domestic or private realms, and everywhere men claimed the public functions—whatever that culture considered most crucial and self-defining—while women were associated with the lesser tasks of the private or domestic, usually child rearing and the work arranged around it.[4]

The public-private paradigm translated feminist politics into a conceptual revision that suggested new research strategies. It challenged the boundaries of scholarly discourse by arguing that the study of women was both legitimate in its own right and essential for understanding society as a whole. It broadened the range of scholarly investigation with its version of the ideology of 1960s social movements: if the personal was political, it was also historical. A new feminist anthropology reinforced the tradition of social history that sought (as in the *Annales* school) to render social life as a totality.

As scholars unearthed evidence of women's historical experience, new conceptual and strategic questions emerged. Historians have struggled to find a language to convey women's complex and contradictory relationship to the rest of social life. Women stand both inside and outside their own culture; they are both subject and other in history. Women are everywhere integrated at the most intimate levels of private life, half of every class and ethnic group, yet everywhere separate, inhabiting a social sphere defined by gender within their own groups and sharing with other women a common exclusion from the most privileged realms of public life. Other historians have proposed a reorientation of this question to ask not how women fit into history but rather how the discipline of history must be reimagined to take account of female experience.[5]

As I have examined representations of women's history in museums, I judge them implicitly against my own working definitions. A fully realized history of women, I would argue, must convey women's simultaneous participation in and alienation from a dominant culture that defines them as other. It must consider difference and inequality among women, for class, race, ethnicity, sexual orientation, marital status, and age are also inseparable parts of women's experiences and consciousness. It must capture a sense of female agency even as it depicts the limitations that bound women's ability to act.

How have historians in museums used and contributed to this ongoing revision? Museum exhibitions have been most successful in recovering and interpreting women's participation in public life. Historians in museums are asking, "Where were the women?" and even in exhibits not fundamentally reoriented by this question, women's presence is recently acknowledged. Historians in museums have been slower to address the issues of private life. In its infrequent exploration of the domestic sphere, women's history in museums forms a curious reverse image to the published scholarship of women's history. As Hilda Smith has documented, articles, books, and dissertations concentrate on the private; investigations of family, domesticity, and women's relationships with one another heavily outweigh research in education, politics, or work.[6] Tellingly, despite this burgeoning literature, exhibits rarely offer critical examinations of domesticity, family, or sexuality. I examine a few exhibits that do tackle some of these subjects and then consider the significant silences that remain. The conclusion suggests some promising directions for further work and speculates about the future of women's history in museums.

Public Life: Work and Politics

Several of these presentations illustrate the contributions and limitations of what Gerda Lerner has called compensatory history, a revision of the record that adds women without fundamentally reordering the categories or questions of historical analysis. Though this approach to women's history by definition makes no conceptual leaps in the understanding of the past, its recovery of female accomplishments is both intellectually and politically empowering. Compensatory history challenges the selectivity and male bias of traditional historical accounts, and its record of women's achievements celebrates female agency. Its use of traditional historical categories, less inspiring to scholars rethinking historical method, may be an asset in public presentations: compensatory history uses already recognized markers of achievement to guide its audience through the less-familiar territory of women's lives.

Though not an exhibit, Marion Tinling's *Women Remembered: A Guide to Landmarks of Women's History in the United States* merits attention for its remapping of the landscape of historical memorials.[7] Organized by region, this guide is a massive work—more than seven hundred pages—that directs travelers to the many material reminders of women's past, including historical sites, markers, buildings, monuments, and place-names. Actually seeing sites such as these would not in itself tell one much about women's history, and yet their inclusion is valuable; such entries restore the historical meaning of memorial sites, a significance that often becomes blurred or lost to later generations. Well written, well organized, and well indexed, the guide is a pleasure to page through.

Entries of familiar areas produced a few disappointments about the selection and description of sites. The decision to exclude monuments to generic womanhood—the nurse, the pioneer woman, and the like—increases the bias toward "famous" women already embodied in the monuments themselves. A more serious flaw is the failure to provide any feminist gloss on the interpretations available at the historical sites that are included. For example, Tinling commends the participation of female benefactors in the reconstruction of the Tryon Palace and Gardens in New Bern, North Carolina, a place that provides a tour full of historical misinformation and punctuated by 1950s-style sexist humor about the "ladies." Still, whether as tourists or simply armchair travelers, those interested in women's history will find many rewards in this informative compendium.

When curators began to incorporate deliberate investigations of women's history into museums and historical sites, many turned first to the narrative of women's paid labor. In some ways the choice is surprising: in classrooms, often the first (and sometimes the only) deviation from an orthodox historical narrative was a discussion of women's political lives: the winning of suffrage and women's prominence in a variety of reform movements. But by the 1970s, women's work was on the agenda, a prominent topic in public discussion, feminist political efforts, and historical inquiry. Popular culture continues to contain newly favorable portrayals of working women, especially those in elite jobs: once stigmatized as "mannish," the career woman now more often represents the enviable possibility of "having it all"—profession, power, glamor, and family.

The National Women's Hall of Fame perhaps reflects the recent cultural fascination with the career woman. Like *Women Remembered*, it uses a familiar form to highlight women's contributions to public life. Located in Seneca Falls, New York, birthplace of the women's movement, the hall celebrates female accomplishment in a straightforward biographical presentation of women of achievement. The project was conceived in 1968 when a committee of women raised $166,000 to buy the building and establish a museum. The Hall of Fame opened in 1979. Periodically, the National Honors Committee elects new women to the hall in a intricate procedure that combines popular participation and expert review. A committee of women's historians makes up the ballot by considering nominations from the general public (visitors are invited to leave their suggestions in a box at the exhibit), then forwards the slate to the National Honors Committee, twenty-five male and female experts in the fields represented in the hall. Recent honorees, inducted in 1986, are geneticist Barbara McClintock, writer Harriet Beecher Stowe, and women's-rights advocate Lucy Stone.

The very existence of the hall and its private financing offer testimony to the active support for women's history outside the usual avenues of foundation, public, or university auspices. At the same time, its entirely traditional approach seems dated in the company of the growing number of more innovative and ambitious exhibits. Its recent struggle for funds suggests as well the precarious status of such isolated independent efforts.

"Black Women: Achievements Against the Odds" might be seen as a kind of transitional exhibit, poised midway between compensatory history and a more analytical and revisionist social history. Developed at the Smithsonian's Anacostia Neighborhood Museum (ANM) in 1974, the exhibit was modified and redesigned for circulation by the Smithsonian Institution Traveling Exhibition Service (SITES).[8]

The exhibit melds a message of black pride and feminist consciousness. An opening label, a quotation from Margaret Walker, signals the exhibit's celebration of female agency: black women's history is "born not only of their enslavement, long years of servitude, and suffering, but also of their hopes, aspirations, and initiatives." Dozens of biographical sketches honor individual women's contributions in literature, art, reform, the healing arts (dentistry, pharmacy, medicine, and nursing), law, business and industry, government, education, sports, entertainment.

In documenting these achievements, the exhibit offers powerful evidence of the double barriers of race and sex. Entertainers' biographies document the relentless racial typing of black performers: Thelma Butterfly McQueen played the scatter-brained Prissy in *Gone With the Wind* while aspiring to Shakespearean roles; Hattie McDaniel won an Oscar for her performance as Mammy in *GWTW* and then went on to play a black maid in the title role of *Beulah*. Other biographies show how black women confronted the barriers of sex in their own communities. Educator Lucy Ellen Moten (1851–1933) had to convince one board of education that her good looks would not compromise her performance on the job, and to promise that she would eschew theatre, dancing, and cards. Rebecca Lee, the first black female doctor, graduated from New England Female Medical School in 1864; Howard University's black medical school did not graduate a woman until 1877. Through these vivid individual biographies, the exhibit creates a pantheon of black heroines whose stories tell much about the oppression of racism and sexism even as they document the resilience of these extraordinary women.

"Black Women" self-consciously resists some common popular and historical assumptions about its subject; but in the process, the exhibit misses the interpretive opportunities of its own rich material. Louise Hutchinson, curator of the original show at ANM, explained that the featured women were deliberately selected for their accomplishments in traditional male fields in an effort to balance a history that honored black women mostly as loyal mothers, wives, sisters, and daughters. The rigorous focus on these women's public lives celebrates female agency but does little to explore the historical and social conditions that shape its expression. Instead, the presentation abstracts biography from a larger history, emphasizing instead the exceptional personal qualities of successful black women. Ironically, "Black Women" denies its own organizing insight: that black women, however diverse and individual in their achievements, are indeed a group bound by the double burden of racism and sexism. Instead, the show ultimately participates in one of the powerful shaping myths of American culture, the belief that individuals can make their own lives after all, even when the deck is stacked against them.

A group biography that sought to generalize from these women's experiences would deepen the historical interpretation of this exhibit—a choice that would also condition its optimism with a more troubling message. Upward mobility of individuals both affirms and threatens groups excluded from the privileges of the dominant culture: such ambivalence is a fundamental dimension of the experience of success in America. To investigate the conditions of making it as a black woman would mean confronting the divisions of class and color within the black community. The labels suggest those divisions: some of the achievers were born into slavery, some were children of sharecroppers or tenant farmers, others grew up in middle-class families. How did these different class positions weight the odds? Reflecting contemporary politics of black culture, the exhibit remains silent on the division of color. But in the ugly history of racism, color has often been destiny: light-skinned blacks were the first to gain niches of acceptance in white society and Afro-Americans themselves have sometimes taken on the dominant culture's value of lightness. How did these women experience standards of beauty that were doubly alienated, defined by men and by whites? To its credit, the show refuses a facile history of progress: the portraits of living women explicitly convey the message that the struggle for equality is not over. But the topical organization displaces a needed historical assessment of change and persistence in black women's lives.

In omitting private life from the biographies, the exhibit enforces a strict historical equality. If we were to view comparable profiles of famous men, we would probably not ask whether they were husbands or fathers. Nonetheless, the omission seems contradictory. The exhibit singles out sex as a significant category and then excises a critical, perhaps determining, element in accounting for achievements against the odds. In the nineteenth and early twentieth centuries, white women who succeeded in public roles were much less likely to marry than others, and those who did marry seldom had children. Is this true for black women? If not, what sustained them in bearing the load of work, family, and community responsibilities? Finally, "Black Women" joins the virtually universal conspiracy of silence about women who choose other women for emotional and sexual relationships.

"Black Women" is nonetheless a considerable achievement for its wide research and strong presentation; it is also a model of resourceful distribution. It has shown twice at ANM, a small, informal museum removed from the bustling central mall and downtown area. The museum is off the beaten track for most out-of-town visitors but very accessible to the residents of Anacostia, its predominantly black southeastern District of Columbia neighborhood.[9] The exhibit was redesigned on easily mounted panels for travel and has been shown in more than one hundred locations. SITES also distributes the exhibit as a set of twenty posters available for sale at two hundred dollars, along with black-and-white glossies for publicity and a handbook that gives tips on public-affairs programming. In yet another incarnation, "Black Women" is available as a three-year calendar that uses photographs and sketches from the exhibit. This combination of flexible exhibiting methods and energetic distribution makes "Black Women" unusually accessible, overcoming the problems of cost and logistics that restrict the circulation of many exhibits.

" 'Send Us a Lady Physician': Women Doctors in America, 1835–1920" offers a less-sanguine reading of women's struggles for a place in public life.[10] Ruth Abram, the show's producer, became interested in the subject of women in medicine when she discovered that her great-aunt Sarah Alice Cohen was a physician who graduated in 1879 from the Women's Medical College of Pennsylvania. Abram developed an independent organization for promotion of history, Paraphrase; raised her own funds for the exhibition; and organized a board of consultants that included curators and university-based historians of women. The exhibit combines original research with close reading of scholarly work, especially Mary Roth Walsh's *Doctors Wanted: No Women Need Apply.*[11] In this account, history is not progress but, rather, a cautionary tale. Fighting public disapproval and the opposition of most male doctors, nineteenth-century women eventually gained a precarious foothold for their sex. But success proved fragile: after 1920, the number and proportion of female physicians fell into sharp decline.

Gay Victorian piano music draws the visitor into an entrance framed by a nineteenth-century gazebo with ivy entwined on white lattice. This path leads to a circle of portraits representing the class of 1879, and radial displays then follow the twenty members down their postgraduate paths into private practice, missionary work, or hospital positions. Another section explores the domestic lives of these women, many of whom married and bore children as they remained professionally active. Surrounding the gazebo and its associated displays, a timeline outlines women's position in medical education and practice. This section features the conventional account of prominent female physicians, such as Elizabeth Blackwell and Ann Preston, describing their struggle to gain entrance to the male bastions of medicine. Audio components, not working during my visit, are designed to play a continuous accompanying narration. Above the main story, an associated timeline matches women's medical history with larger national and international events.

An innovative final section evokes medical diagnosis as a metaphor for historical interpretation. X-ray light boxes present the various historical explanations offered for the eclipse of female physicians after 1920, including decreased demand for female doctors as Victorian mores changed; a retreat of women themselves from the field; a renewed insistence on the primacy of motherhood; closing of women's medical colleges as a new generation of women mistakenly believed these separate institutes were obsolete; and the decline of the women's movement. The final label uses the past to warn against complacent confidence in women's progress: though women are represented in medicine in increasing numbers and proportions, they have not yet achieved equality, and what has been gained might again be lost.

The exhibit design, unfortunately, is often jarringly at odds with this lucid and challenging text. The gazebo and piano music create the impression of a Disney set piece. Like most traveling exhibitions, " 'Send Us a Lady Physician' " includes only a small number of artifacts. Rather than accepting this limitation, the producers chose to surround the actual period objects with a clutter of stylized Victoriana. Flanking the gazebo, two medium-size areas attempt to re-create the ambience or look of the nineteenth century by impressionistic renderings of domestic space: for example, a unit of open shelves and cubbyholes is stuffed with dolls, toys, and dry goods, apparently to represent some of the material surroundings of affluent households. These visual elements reproduce a reductive and stereotyped view of Victorian gentility.

At moments the design seems to satirize its own stereotypes. In one corner, for example, an ornate silver tea set stands next to an anatomical model and photographs of a cadaver dissection, an amusing juxtaposition of elements that uses spatial choices to dramatize the contrast between expectations for female gentility and the realities of medical work. This vignette suggests the possibilities of an extended application: the design could capitalize on the contrasts between drawing room and surgical amphitheater, Victorian mansion and urban tenement.

Instead, the stagy design has a disorienting and alienating effect as the visitor is constantly confronted with the artifice of an invented past. The visual language of the exhibit drastically undermines the text. The words of this exhibit challenge visitors to rethink the facile assumptions of a history of progress, to become actively engaged in a more complex rendering of the past. The design imitates the inducements of theme-park history, inviting visitors to become spectators and consumers. In its coy rendition of elite Victorian culture, presumably the background of most nineteenth-century female physicians, the exhibit misses an opportunity to explore how these women used the resources of their class to overcome the restrictions of their sex. And we lose sight of female doctors themselves in an exhibit that does little to evoke the actual settings of medical work.

"Perfect in Her Place: Women At Work in Industrial America" is a heartening example of an exhibit that uses recent historical scholarship with intelligence and imagination; it is also another example, albeit more subtly problematic, of an exhibit whose visual presentation partially subverts its text.[12] "Perfect in Her Place" weighs the opportunities and constraints of women's paid work. As American industry burgeoned in a situation of acute labor shortage, women gained new access to employment. But work was no straightforward leap to emancipation, for most women were relegated to low-paying and less-skilled jobs. "Perfect in Her Place" demonstrates the resilience of ideology, showing how employers and male workers invoked nineteenth-century sentimental notions of womanhood to proclaim women's special fitness for menial, exacting, and repetitive tasks. The exhibit documents a range of women's jobs, mostly in manufacturing, and uses contemporary pieties about women's fragility as ironic contrast to the realities of women's work, often dirty, arduous, and unsafe. The text and accompanying catalog are attentive to divisions of race, class, and ethnicity among women, revealing intricate hierarchies within a sex-segregated work force. Eschewing the evasive language of many exhibits, "Perfect" acknowledges economic and sexual exploitation; it documents conflicts among women and between men and women.

This sophisticated and coherent argument, though, is somewhat undermined by the accompanying visual presentation. In its original installation at the National Museum of American History (1981), the exhibit included machines, patent models, work implements, and the products of women's industrial labor. Though "Perfect" rejects the technological determinism and history of progress that pervade many presentations, those paradigms seem to drift in against the primary intention of the exhibit, as if they were ghosts in the machines themselves. The repetitive format shows machines or tools in front of graphics that show women operating the technology on display. The graphics, many from *Scientific American*, are visually appealing and legible, good illustrations of machine design. Unfortunately, though, in a visual presentation whose primary elements are machines and technical drawings, the text's focus on working women blurs. The graphics also belie the critical perspective of the labels. The text informs readers about the hazards and injustices of work, but the illustrations are paeans to technological progress. In this best of all possible pictorial worlds, intricate machines are attended by well-dressed, healthy-looking young women. In many, the machines and their operators are pictured in splendid isolation, removed from the factory floor and the supervisor's discipline. Occasional photographs present an instructive contrast: the camera records women bending over their tasks in crowded, cluttered workrooms under the watchful eyes of supervisors. Finally, "Perfect" offers an example of how the museum setting itself may shape and contain a critical message. Gleaming machines enclosed in neat cases, artful lighting, carpeted floor, and harmonious pastels all further remove the viewer from the less-manicured world of working women.

Women's political history finds a voice in two exhibits, each in its own way the product of the women's movement. Before the revival of the women's movement, the very limited attention given to women in conventional historical accounts was almost exclusively focused on the fight for suffrage. Some early work in the new wave of women's history proposed important and provocative interpretations of suffrage, understood as part of the larger sweep of the women's movement.[13] As the field grew, some scholars mined organizational sources to recover women's participation in political movements and to recast the history of reform with that new evidence.[14] Although little of the later literature has yet appeared in the broader interpretations of American history presented in museums, the history of the women's movement itself is chronicled at two very different sites. The first, the National Woman's Party (NWP) headquarters in Washington, D.C., recounts a chapter in the history of feminism recently rediscovered by women's historians. Sponsored by the remnants of the NWP, the exhibit has the characteristic narrowness of internal institutional history, even as it is also inspiring and praiseworthy for preserving a history that is manifestly not represented elsewhere for public audiences. The second example, the Women's Rights National Historic Site at Seneca Falls, New York, represents a new departure for the National Park Service (NPS). The development of this site, opened in July 1982, demonstrates the far-reaching influence of the new social history, at least for a brief moment in the Carter years.

Women have seldom had the economic and social resources or the historical self-consciousness to create monuments to women's-rights organizations. The Sewall-Belmont House, headquarters for the National Woman's Party since 1929, is a notable exception. Donated in 1929 by Alva Belmont, the genteel elegance of the furniture and architecture attests to the elite background of many NWP members. Still extant, the NWP has successfully fended off several efforts to claim this prime real estate overlooking the Supreme Court and the Capitol. Threatened with demolition first for a parking lot (1958) and then to accommodate the Senate's expanded quarters (1972), the house has since been named a national historic landmark and thus has gained a modicum of security.

The National Woman's Party was the successor of Alice Paul's Congressional Union, established in 1913 when the National American Woman Suffrage Association rejected Paul's militant strategies. Renamed the National Woman's Party in 1917, the group held itself apart from the Progressive coalitions of the 1920s and 1930s, divided from social reformers by an uncompromising commitment to equal rights that rejected prevailing views of female dependence or women's special needs as mothers. Instead, the NWP worked tirelessly for the Equal Rights Amendment (ERA), written by Alice Paul and first proposed as a constitutional amendment in 1923.[15]

The NWP's appeal for landmark status called for "an historic shrine which would commemorate the women's movement," a phase which reveals much about the approach taken there. Under a beautiful stained-glass fan window, the Hall of Statues pays tribute to the leaders of the women's movement. Busts of Susan B. Anthony and Elizabeth Cady Stanton stand side by side on the left, facing Lucretia Mott and Alva Belmont (NWP patron and president) on the right. Portraits commemorate militant suffragists of the Congressional Union who were jailed in 1917 when they refused to remove their picket from the White House gates. A portrait of Inez Milholland Boissevain on a white horse eulogizes the NWP's embodiment of sacrifice for the cause. Exhausted from campaigning for suffrage through seven states, Boissevain collapsed and "died for the freedom of women." At the end of the hall, a marble and ivory statue of Joan of Arc completes the iconography of female leadership.[16]

The architecture and furnishings are both artifacts of the women's-rights movement and testimony to the material conditions that enabled their work. The Chairman's Room, for many years Alice Paul's workroom, is furnished with Susan B. Anthony's desk and a chair used by Elizabeth Cady Stanton, embodying the hard work and staunch commitment of feminist foremothers. Oil paintings of NWP members and an elegantly appointed formal dining room indicate the class background of many NWP members.

This museum challenges the canon of historical greats but shares the conventional definition of history as politics and public life. Its presentation reclaims a significant chapter of women's self-organization, and it affirms feminist struggles by celebrating heroines who resisted the limits of patriarchal society. The NWP also provides a kind of compensatory history by commemorating women who were unusually outspoken or accomplished in traditionally male arenas.

But in the end the exhibit suffers the common myopia of institutional self-portraits. Its political history is one-dimensional. The Sewall-Belmont House tour offers only a vague sense of the divisions in the suffrage movement from which the NWP emerged. The party's commitment to the Equal Rights Amendment is presented in isolation, with little explanation of the conflicting strategies and historical significance of twentieth-century feminism. Oddly, even in the face of the defeat of ERA ratification, the visitor will find little here to challenge a complacent belief that the women's-rights movement is virtually over, its major objectives achieved. We get only glimpses of the internal life of the NWP, its conflicts and decisions, the relationship between national and local organizations, the texture of daily life in the headquarters itself. The presentation embodies a curious irony: it celebrates the militant history of the NWP frozen in a mythic past, distant from the confusions, struggles, and aspirations of the contemporary women's movement.

The Women's Rights National Historic Site is an important new departure, a significant commitment of public funds to women's history. Still under development, this site owes its existence to the National Park Service's mandate to expand in the Carter years, and to the energy and vision of Judy Hart, now supervisor of the site. In 1978 she was working in land acquisition for the National Park Service, responsible for recommending potential new sites. Perusing *The National Parks: Index*, Hart noted the eloquent silence about women's history and a cursory footnote explaining that there was no separate category for black history, since interpretation of Afro-American lives was incorporated into existing sites. She recommended two sites for development: a historic black church in Boston, and Seneca Falls, New York, birthplace of the women's movement.[17] Enabling legislation for site development was approved by Congress in December 1980. For 1982, the year the park was to open, a budget of $120,000 was cut in half at the last minute; nonetheless, Hart hired seven people, leased a building for the visitors' center, and commissioned historian Judith Wellman, a scholar of the 1848 Seneca Falls women's-rights convention, to do the introductory exhibit. In July, actor Alan Alda cut the ribbon on the Women's Rights Historic Park, and historian Gerda Lerner gave the keynote speech at an accompanying conference on women's history.

At the visitors' center, a good exhibit and slide show narrate the history of the 1848 Seneca Falls convention, where women excluded from public proceedings of the antislavery movement met to consider their conditions as women and to articulate the demands of a new women's-rights movement. A tour includes the restored Elizabeth Cady Stanton house and Wesleyan Chapel, where the convention was held (now a laundry; the park plans to restore it). The Park Service also owns the McClintock House in nearby Waterloo, where the Declaration of Sentiments was written.

The Stanton house holds only tantalizing glimpses of the domestic life of Elizabeth Cady Stanton. The uses of each room and even the exact configuration of the house at different times are not certain. Stanton's wallpaper patterns have been reproduced from surviving samples, and a few original furnishings remain—Stanton's desk, a love seat, her piano. Facing these limitations of artifacts and evidence, the Park Service has resisted a common strategy of filling out original pieces with others "of the period." Instead, the interpretive program uses the house tour to tell visitors more about Stanton's life and thought; ideas take precedence over objects.

This relatively new site is actively developing its programs and audience. Hart has worked to involve women's historians as one constituency of the park, calling on scholarly expertise to develop programs and organizing two academic conferences. In accordance with the public mission of the Park Service, interpretation is directed at a broader audience, intended to be accessible to visitors with a seventh-grade education. Through outreach programs to local schools, the park's staff encourages a local constituency and strives to fill a gap in the curriculum by providing instructional materials on women's history.

The limited data available suggest that the park has gradually broadened its audience. About seventeen thousand visitors a year come to the site, the usual attendance for parks in locations like Seneca Falls. Park Ranger Margaret McFadden noted that in the first years of operation, female visitors and those already knowledgeable about women's history dominated; in 1986, men were better represented, comprising about 40 percent of all park users. Local and regional visitors, most common in the early years, are now balanced with a strong national constituency; in 1986, 46 percent were from outside the immediate area. Minority visitors are notably underrepresented at less than 1 percent of all visitors in 1986, perhaps because the park is distant from ethnically diverse urban centers.[18]

Private Life: Domesticity and Housework

The vigor and energy of these explorations of women's public history have not yet been matched by an equivalent effort to interpret private life, even though museums are rich repositories of the material culture of domesticity. Butter molds, apple corers, churns, earthenware and china, quilts, corsets, historic houses themselves leave abundant testimony of the conditions and character of women's lives. This significant silence echoes with the suppressed politics of the women's movement, even as the absence of an important discussion reveals the limitations of the museum's characteristic voice.

In the 1970s, some of the most innovative and controversial historical research on women focused on the nineteenth century and the emergence of an industrial order that separated home and work, accompanied by a cultural ideology that emphasized sexual difference and separation. Many historians explored women's domain, the private or domestic sphere, probing the history of domesticity, marriage, childbirth, sexuality, female friendship.

Carroll Smith-Rosenberg's influential work provided a new way of seeing women's separation from much of public life. At the Second Berkshire Conference on Women's History in 1973, Smith-Rosenberg electrified a large audience with readings of nineteenth-century women's letters, documents of the intense emotional relationships these women shared. Published in the first issue of *Signs* in 1975, "The Female World of Love and Ritual" has been repeatedly invoked by women's historians.[19] Many used Smith-Rosenberg's work to elaborate an idea of women's culture, a term that signaled emphasis on female agency and autonomy even within the constraints of women's subordination.

Women's culture was no academic coinage. Minted in the 1970s women's movement, it expressed a buoyant affirmation of womanhood against a dominant ideology that devalued women. Devoted to women's concerns and mostly comprised of women, feminist organizations stood in sharp relief against a culture dominated by heterosexual institutions and associations. In consciousness-raising groups, feminists claimed a separate space from which to articulate a critique of sexism; and here women subjected marriage, sexuality, housework, mothering, and a host of heretofore private issues to political scrutiny. Women affirmed female friendship, rejecting an insistent heterosexual ideology that implicitly devalued such bonds. In the charged experience of shared politics, many women acknowledged a newly tenuous sense of the boundaries between friendship and sexual intimacy, and for some those boundaries dissolved. Though only a few women advocated rigorous separation from men and heterosexual institutions, many feminists enthusiastically patronized women-only music festivals, concerts, dances, bars or restaurants that allowed a temporary immersion into a separatist world. This cultural ferment, its assertion of a woman-centered perspective, created new conditions for reading historical evidence.

Notwithstanding its unruly origins, the idea of women's culture has recently been turned to more conservative uses. As a few feminist critics had warned, the celebration of women's separate world might be read as legitimization of women's secondary status in the public world.[20] In one startling recent example, Sears, Roebuck used it as a defense against charges of sex discrimination pressed by the Equal Employment Opportunity Commission. Sears used the expert testimony of historian Rosalind Rosenberg to argue that women had different values from men and did not want more lucrative commission sales jobs.[21]

Removed from the context of the women's movement, the idea of women's culture has sometimes lost its original edge to slide into sentimentality, offering a nostalgic vision of the world we have lost now that women are striving to take their places in public life. Ironically, it may be precisely this denaturing of the idea of women's culture that will render it more palatable for wider public consumption.

"The Light of the Home" at the Margaret Woodbury Strong Museum in Rochester, New York, builds its theme and narrative on the scholarly literature of nineteenth-century separate spheres.[22] Opening in 1982 as one of the museum's inaugural exhibits, "Light" demonstrates the exciting possibilities of scholarship interpreted through material culture and the exhibit medium. It is telling in another way, too, for the exhibit notably excludes representations of sexual conflict, political ideology, or female homosociality.

Cutout figures of American middle-class women beckon the visitor into the hall, where dim lighting focuses attention on the profusion of objects in the cases. The exhibit narrative follows the chronology of female life cycles, with a series of cases representing childhood and adolescence, courtship and marriage, motherhood, religion and death. In other sections, leisure, beauty, home decoration, housework, and health care come to life through objects. In the postmodern mode, the exhibit borrows selective details of line and style to evoke Victorian aesthetics—a suggestion of vaulted church windows above the case on Victorian weddings; stenciling to set off the section on motherhood; segments of dark paneling; and throughout, backgrounds in the deep colors favored in Victorian style.

The exhibit is most successful in its close integration of object and text. The visitor is immersed in the visual environment of Victorian America, surrounded by the elaborate design, intricate patterning, and sentimental imagery characteristic of late-nineteenth-century material culture. The text augments sensitive visual arrangement to encourage visitors to "read" objects as evidence for social experience. A label near an ornate card receiver explains the ritual of calling; the text beneath a formidable set of hoops and corsets offers information on the damage that fashion wrought on women's bodies. Two other devices actively solicit visitors' involvement with the material world of the Victorians. Touch stations offer Braille labels and replicas or duplicates of objects with legible textures or shapes. Such devices not only make an exhibition more accessible to blind visitors, they also enhance the museum experience for the sighted. In one corner, visitors look at the floor plan of a large Victorian house; the label asks visitors to think about how the design reveals the hierarchies and activities of the household.

The shortcomings of "The Light of the Home" reflect both a broader problem with nineteenth-century women's history and the special pitfalls of exhibition. The major conceptual flaw is a failure to distinguish adequately between experience and ideology of Victorian womanhood. The opening label states the issues by indicating the intricate relationship of social life and ideal visions, but neither text nor visual representation offers a consistent interpretation of that relationship. Through most of the exhibit, ideology and experience blur. Objects representing the domestic ideal, such as sentimental paintings and images on advertising cards, are not distinguished from objects that provide evidence of everyday life, such as pessaries, nursing bottles, or housecleaning equipment. Admittedly, such a distinction is not always easy or useful, as one example in the exhibit dramatizes: children's toys with religious motifs both attested to Victorian ideology and made piety a part of a child's daily experience. But without more of an effort to engage this difficult conceptual issue, the exhibit becomes confusing and the ideology disembodied.

Adding to the problem is a vagueness about both class and agency that makes the ideology of domesticity seem all pervasive and irresistible. Beyond the laudable specification of the middle-class locus of this ideology, the exhibit does not say who belonged to the middle class or how it was located within a larger class structure. Yet the objects and subjects selected offer some strong opportunities for such a presentation; for example, the section on housework might have focused more on domestic service and its role in maintaining Victorian middle-class life. And ironically, the exhibit succeeds so well in re-creating the ambience of Victorian bourgeois culture that it is difficult to imagine how anyone ever escaped its reach. The vital political movements that drew their moral force and their female constituencies from domestic ideology are unfortunately absent from this exhibit. It mentions dress reform but gives little hint of women's importance in antislavery agitation and temperance. And the exhibit does not mention the nineteenth-century women's movement itself, though Susan B. Anthony's house stands just a few blocks away from the museum.

In contrast, "Impact: Technology in the Kitchen" brings a refreshing critical edge to its exploration of one aspect of women's domestic lives. Drawing closely on recent revisionist histories of housework, "Impact" debunks the widespread belief in liberation through technology.[23] The exhibit opened in 1985 at the Brattleboro Museum and Art Center in Brattleboro, Vermont, and then traveled to two other locations in 1986–87.[24] I saw it at the Museum of Our National Heritage in Lexington, Massachusetts.

The opening label informs the visitor that the time women spend in housework has not changed significantly despite the multiplication of labor-saving devices. Through a series of five settings, from the low-tech kitchen of 1830–1860 to "High Tech at Home, 1970–1985," the exhibit displays the transformation of kitchens through electrification, plumbing, changes in food marketing and processing, and a plethora of new tools and equipment. Four interspersed segments develop histories of particular technologies in more detail, dealing with laundry, cutting and mixing tools, food containers, and floor-cleaning methods.

The well-written text probes the relationship of work and technology. The labels remind visitors that the home is part of its larger technological and social matrix: household technology relies on local water and gas lines, electrical systems, and other technologies that in turn take shape from political choices and economic interests. The text conveys historian Ruth Schwartz Cowan's striking argument about the shifting division of labor, from the preindustrial household, where food preparation involved concerted effort from more than one member of the household—men chopped wood while women tended fires and cooked, for example—to mid-twentieth-century kitchens designed for efficient operation by a lone woman. The exhibit repeatedly exhorts the visitor to weigh the often marginal improvements of technology against the environmental costs and to consider the irony of labor-saving devices that ultimately created "more work for mother."

In a few places this powerful and usually persuasive argument seems overstated. For example, "From Knife to Cuisinart" observes that "chopping is still chopping, and still requires human effort" and concludes that food processors provide only marginal improvements over "a good sharp knife." Readily rebutted by anyone who has chopped with both knife and food processor, this kind of argument reflects an undercurrent of Luddism that runs through the exhibit. There are only sporadic efforts to distinguish between more- and less-useful technologies, and there is a whiff of moralism and asceticism in the sweeping critique of consumption. Still, the exhibit succeeds admirably in conveying the nuanced argument about how new technologies erase their own labor-saving potential by abetting a relentless escalation of standards.

The design of "Impact" expresses the politics of the text with an appropriate aesthetic of spareness and visual unity. Glistening white walls, clean lines, and careful lighting reinforce the text's critique of consumption. The visual unity and coherence provided by the five kitchen settings dramatizes the accretion of gadgets as the simple lines of wood and minimalist equipment yield to a jarring proliferation of manufactured clutter. But this intention may be lost on some audiences because of the distinctly minority status of the exhibit's anticonsumerist aesthetic.

"Impact" illustrates another dilemma of exhibit writers and designers trying to convey a complex message even as they seek unity and coherence of presentation. The virtues of the simple and elegant design are also its limitations, for while the text explains the division of labor and the larger technological setting, the visual presentation focuses attention on the technology of the kitchen shown in isolation. The message of the exhibit would have been more powerful with some visual components to reinforce the major interpretive themes. For example, the influence of technology beyond the individual household might easily have been suggested by photomurals seen through kitchen windows, indicating the preindustrial setting of the early kitchen and then showing its modification with electrical lines, gas lights, and other images evocative of urban or suburban settings. Graphics of kitchen layouts and photographs of family members doing (or simply observing) domestic chores would have strengthened the argument about the shifting division of labor.

Nonetheless, "Impact" is a very important exhibit, for it stands virtually alone in its willingness to engage the issue of domestic conflict, or even to seriously consider the household as a workplace. Looking at "Impact" helps bring into focus the very different assumptions embodied in the usual representations of domesticity. The typical historic-house tour, for example, relies subtly on nostalgic associations of home. Tours characteristically begin in the ceremonial front rooms, take visitors upstairs to family bedrooms and sitting rooms, and end in the kitchen. At the hearth, visitors often are invited to sample freshly made cookies, or corn bread with hand-churned butter. Costumed docents demonstrate domestic duties but rarely identify themselves as enacting the roles of the servants or slaves who usually did such work. Such presentations convey the hard work of domestic labor, but this message is overlaid with a nostalgia for craft as visitors savor homemade baked goods or watch candle dipping. In implicit contrast to the embattled contemporary household, the kitchen scene at the historic house evokes a mythic family free of conflict and unfettered by women's aspirations for a life beyond the domestic sphere.

Museums have both the scholarly resources and the collections to make sweeping improvements in their representations of domesticity. Outdoor museums and historic houses are obvious sites for such integration, and some reports document thoughtful and sophisticated revisions based on scholarship in women's history. Christina Simmons, for example, observed well-informed enactments at Conner Prairie, a living history museum in Indiana, where staff members responded knowledgeably (and stayed in character) when she inquired about abortifacients and contraception.[25] In another promising example, Patricia West has described a new interpretive program at the Martin Van Buren Historic Site; in that most traditional of shrines, a presidential house, visitors glimpse a broader social history in a tour that discusses the role of domestic servants who lived and worked there.[26] Innovations like these show how historical interpretation opens up once freed from the confines of sentimental views of family.

Public and Private: "Virginia Women"

Few if any other exhibits have attempted to set out a sustained narrative of women's history that encompasses both public and private life. Thus " 'A Share of Honour': Virginia Women, 1600–1945" deserves special attention, for it undertakes the ambitious task of rendering three hundred years of women's experience. Organized by an independent group of twenty-five women with the support of the governor's wife, Lynda Johnson Robb, the project was financed by the Virginia Foundation for the Humanities and Public Programs. The original show in Richmond opened in November 1984; a traveling version circulated during 1985–87.

I saw the traveling exhibit at George Mason University in Fairfax, Virginia. Well-designed panels presented an appealing mixture of graphics, historical photographs, artifacts in small cases, and photographs of objects used in the original exhibit. The installation in a medium-sized gallery lent an accessible and intimate atmosphere to the exhibit. When I saw it, visitors seemed unusually attentive to the text. Animated conversations went on among companions and sprang up among visitors who had come to the exhibit alone.

"Our story is not always one of progress," one of the first lines of the text declares, even as it also signals an intention to acknowledge female agency in a "portrait of what women did achieve despite many obstacles." This exhibit presents an intelligent and lucid assessment of women's status as it was defined by colonial and industrial society. The text avoids the pitfalls of sources biased toward white middle-class women's lives by specifically addressing questions of evidence and by using the history of Indian and black women to reorient the narrative. Many visitors will be startled, for example, by the presentation of early European settlement, which focuses on the many women who came to Virginia as indentured servants or slaves.

The narrative confronts another enduring truism—women's history as history of progress—by emphasizing the gains and losses of changing historical conditions. For example, the exhibit portrays the new opportunities of colonial society for some women, then depicts the nineteenth century as a time of constricting possibility as women's secondary status became codified in law and legitimated in an ideology of female domesticity. This rich interpretation of the nineteenth century reflects the strong scholarship of historian Suzanne Lebsock, who worked on the project.[27] Throughout, provocative juxtapositions of visual material reinforce the text, encouraging the visitor to consider the many determinants of women's condition and the significant divisions of class and race among women. The use of state history, engaging anecdote, and biographical example lend immediacy and specificity to the more general account.

As the narrative moves into the years after the Civil War, it loses some of the clarity and interpretive focus that distinguish the opening sections. This diffuseness reflects, in part, the more fragmented scholarship for twentieth-century women's history. It may also reflect the political considerations of presenting recent history. In any case, the optimistic history of progress presented in this part stands in contrast to the more subtle assessments of the rest of the exhibit.

The accompanying catalog, written by Lebsock, succeeds admirably in addressing a general audience without sacrificing historical sophistication. Thoughtful, witty, and engaging, Lebsock's writing draws readers into the intricate work of reconstructing the past through partial and often ambiguous evidence.[28]

The Common Wealth of Women, the film that circulates with the exhibit, distorts the message of the show in a presentist history of progress. Cutting back and forth from contemporary interviews and historical narrative, the film scans the past in search of role models for today's women, a superficial idea of historical meaning that leads to a flat and anachronistic interpretation. For example, in an early scene, two contemporary farm women affirm the value of staying out of the paid labor force to care for children; then the film moves to a narrative of a preindustrial society that valued women's economic contributions. This segue dramatizes the exhibit's interpretation of the relative advantages of preindustrial life for women, but its overall effect is nostalgic and its rhetoric simplistic. By proposing the preindustrial economy as a kind of lost ideal, it evades the reality of the dependency and vulnerability of non-wage-earning women in a fundamentally different economy and society.

Unintentionally, the film is itself a documentary of a narrowly construed 1980s feminism and a testament to the durability of an American ideology of success. The historical narrative is bent to the service of a single assertion endlessly reiterated: as one embarrassingly stagy interviewee puts it early in the film, "Women can do anything!" The film serves up an intriguing double message here: it praises women's traditional virtues of "compassion, cooperation, service and nurture" even as it urges women to claim their places in a public life where such qualities are of dubious utility, if not an outright liability.

The film offers a positive message of female agency—"you can take charge of your life and you can make changes," another interviewee asserts—but this rhetoric of the self-made woman leaps facilely over the social and economic conditions that limit women's possibilities. With a single exception the featured women are securely middle-class; the sole working-class woman, once employed in an oyster-shucking plant, gets a nursing degree and a better job. Similarly, the persistent burden of the double day—women's unpaid work at home added to her wage-earning labor—is represented only in a few remarks by a black professional woman who is the divorced mother of two children. The prescription for success is education and unwavering will; never mind that education often does not translate into better economic possibilities for women and that marriage remains the most powerful determinant of a woman's economic status. The film concludes that "women must reassess the way they view themselves," as if insecurity and lack of self-assertion are to blame for women's unequal share of "the common wealth." The jarring discontinuity between film and exhibit perhaps demonstrates one of the liabilities of public programming by committee.

Women's History and Museums

This review of women's history in exhibits captures museums at a revealing transitional moment. This essay and others have documented the pervasive influence of social history—and, directly and indirectly, the influence of social movements—on museum presentations. These exhibits embody a sensitivity to gender and recognition of female aspiration that illustrate the wide response to at least some feminist claims. At the same time, a pattern of significant omissions reveals a kind of selectivity that amounts to censorship. No Orwellian Ministry of Culture looms over curators; nor do directors and boards commonly issue fiats about what is allowed and what is forbidden. Nevertheless, though few curators would wish to acknowledge it openly, most of us operate under a tacit, perhaps sometimes even unconscious, sense of limits on what can be said. Seldom couched in explicitly political terms, not necessarily ideological in their intentions, these restrictions are nonetheless political in their effects. They find expression in what one might call the language of the museum, the characteristic discourse and modes of representation associated with exhibits.

We can begin to chart the lexicon of the museum by noting first what is not said. The elisions in public representations of women's history fall into two broad categories: subjects that concern women's bodies and subjects that deal with sexual conflict. Both subjects have been extensively explored in the scholarly literature of women's history, within the women's movement, and in print and electronic journalism, making their absence in museums especially glaring.

The medical history of obstetrics and gynecology offers an opportunity for exhibits to explore the intersection of women's biology and social history, and again museum collections hold many objects that lend themselves to the exploration of this subject, including forceps, gynecological instruments, uterine models, and drugs. Exhibits occasionally do include a few instruments, but omission and euphemism reign. For example, at the National Museum of American History, which does provide an unusual if brief section on childbirth, visitors read that babies are born through birth canals, not vaginas.[29] An instructive contrast is Judy Chicago's "Birth Project." Many museums have refused to exhibit Chicago's work, offended by her explicit representations of female genitalia (an artistic choice that also has stirred controversy among feminists). A maverick artist, Chicago might seem an unlikely source of scholarly work on women's history. Yet her "Birth Project" opens with a densely worded history of childbirth well informed by recent scholarship.[30]

Mechanical contraception and legal abortion have wrought revolutionary changes in women's lives in the twentieth century. Control over reproduction improved women's health, facilitated a widening participation in public life, and allowed women more control over their domestic lives. But in the museum's representation of women's history, the history of contraception is conspicuously absent. The subject lends itself readily to representation through the visual evidence of pamphlets, advertisements, patent medicines, and the devices themselves; when museums leave behind the lingering conventions of Victorian delicacy, they will have a wealth of resources to collect and exhibit.[31]

Needless to say, sexuality in all its variants is excised from the museum.

Heterosexuality is at least implied in displays of valentines, wedding gowns, cradles, and family portraits; in contrast, homosexuality is uniformly suppressed. So far, its only public representations have been sponsored by lesbians themselves. One example is Judith Schwartz's book and slide show on Heterodoxy, a group of independent-minded women who congregated in Greenwich Village in the 1910s, 1920s, and 1930s. The Lesbian Herstory Archives is an important collection of papers, books, and photographs.[32]

As Thomas Schlereth has observed, conflict and violence are systematically underrepresented in historical museums, yet they have often played a significant role in American life.[33] In women's history, scholars have taken up the history of divorce, prostitution, domestic violence, and class and racial conflict among women, but it is a rare exhibit that acknowledges these subjects.[34] In part, these issues present a problem for the visual medium of the museum, for they are issues suppressed in the self-presentation of family life and therefore leave fewer traces in the record of material culture. Divorces are not customarily marked with public ceremonies, and therefore there are few material counterparts to the wedding gowns, bouquets, matchbooks, and invitations that attend a marriage. Similarly, family photograph albums edit out unhappy or violent passages in the life of a household. Images of racial and class conflict are more abundant, but they pose another kind of problem. Curators must consider how to frame and present such images so that they will not reinforce the very prejudices they embody.

The museum's characteristic discourse also submerges conflict in the convention of the obligatory happy ending. Like ceremonial time capsules, museums serve as repositories of a highly selective public memory; their representations of national life often rely heavily on images of nostalgia or accomplishment. The agenda of a more critical social history, including women's history, has made only partial inroads against this celebratory view. Under the alchemy of the museum's language, even bad news becomes good news in the "social problems" formula. Exhibits acknowledge past failures to live up to democratic ideals, celebrate the efforts of individuals from disadvantaged groups to overcome obstacles and earn admission to the mainstream, and affirm that "the system" works after all.[35]

Museum directors need not conspire to perpetuate this well-worn formulation, for members of aspiring groups themselves often keep the faith. Feminist scholars and curators are drawn to inspiriting images to celebrate and sustain women's struggles, as illustrated in such exhibits as the Women's Hall of Fame and "Black Women: Achievements Against the Odds." Those who have struggled to win access to museums recognize their sanctifying effects and their power as arbiters of public memory; no wonder, then, that even self-consciously critical exhibitors might wish to claim the museum's voice of affirmation for women. Still, if we would be honest historians, we must escape the tyranny of the happy ending.

An implicit code of civility powerfully shapes the content and tone of exhibits. I borrow the term *civility* from William Chafe's study of the civil-rights movement in Greensboro.[36] Chafe perceptively analyzes how liberal whites controlled and contained the agenda of civil rights: they would support moderate reform if black leaders would defer to whites, accept gradualism, and request rather than demand their rights. Through this code of civility, Greensboro whites set the limits of acceptable dissent. Museums share an unwritten code of civility that also serves to limit discourse and suppress conflict. Most museum directors practice active damage control, striving to avoid any material that might upset or offend their constituencies.

When taken to its limit, this kind of self-censorship leads directly to the blandness of prime-time television, whose commercial sponsorship enforces a virtual blackout of many subjects or treatments. It calls for a network-influenced idea of balance, maddeningly invoked only when any critical viewpoint surfaces and, as in television reporting, crudely interpreted as equal time for two sides, even though complex issues often have more than two sides and even when the evidence clearly weighs more heavily in support of one position than another.

The language of the museum remains timid in part because of the museum's special relationship to its audience. Tax-supported museums use public resources and occupy public space; in law, most museums are trusteeships, charged with the care of collections and bound by specific responsibilities to their donors and their larger publics. Museum audiences have free access to visiting exhibits, but not to the means of producing them. The restrictions of access—it takes money and various kinds of expert knowledge to produce an exhibit—have led some museum curators and directors to assume a certain paternalism, a sense that they must speak not only *to* but *for* a wider audience. The result has been that intellectual freedom is interpreted more narrowly in the museum than in the university, to the detriment of its historical work.

The paternalistic interpretation of a museum's public role also shapes a characteristic voice that one might call "museumspeak." Constrained to represent a diverse and amorphous public, curators often resort to a bland synthetic mode. The syntax of museumspeak often begs the question of historical agency through the passive voice or abstract grammatical subjects, such as "society" or "the people." The concealed authorship of most exhibits compounds the problem. Though a few museums have begun to credit exhibits to specific curators, consultants, designers, and the like, most maintain the convention of unsigned exhibits.[37] The voice of the museum thus becomes disembodied, an authoritative narrative voice that denies interpretation.

Sponsorship, whether from public money, corporations, or private donors, inevitably influences how museums speak and what they talk about. Though most museums try to control direct interference by specific policies or judicious selection of potential patrons, the patron exerts a fundamental influence simply in the very act of granting or withholding funds. Tax-supported projects are not free of the constraints of sponsorship, but with public funds the sponsor's influence is indirect and mediated. Frequently, state, federal, or municipal financing supports the general program budget rather than supporting specific projects directly.

As museums encounter more pressure to raise money from private sources, the patron's influence is magnified and museums are thrown back on donors who often have a very direct stake in the content of exhibitions. Corporate or professional organizations fall into two patterns of museum patronage. Some choose to support exhibits that deal with subjects close to their own work, such as the American Society of Anesthesiologists, which financed "Pain and Its Relief." Others, especially large corporate donors, have philanthropic foundations separated from their general operations and are not necessarily concerned with a narrow definition of relevant subject matter. Such donors often are attracted to exhibits that lend the luster of prestigious "high" culture; any number of corporate-financed art exhibits might serve as examples. Women's history—indeed any kind of social history—does not fit naturally into either agenda and likely will suffer if museum directors allow their priorities to be set by what outside sponsors are willing to finance.

A range of strategies provides the best hedge against shifting winds of money, fashion, and politics. Within museums, women's historians should work to integrate a serious consideration of gender into every exhibit, an important intellectual goal in its own right and a way to keep women's history from being marginalized as a special interest. We have to consider how to use limited resources and energy, weighing the strengths and limitations of different forms of exhibition. Not surprisingly, the strongest critical and interpretive exhibits reviewed here—"Perfect," "Impact," and " 'Lady Physician' "—were temporary exhibits, a form that often gives the curator more license to experiment and interpret, to speak in a more individual voice. Historians in museums can also support independent efforts, such as " 'Lady Physician,' " thus helping to broaden access to the medium of the exhibit and nurturing perspectives that are not fettered by the bureaucratic imperatives of established museums. We need to strengthen the ties between the museum and other arenas of historical work. Feminists outside museums have been active participants in shaping this new wave of work; their continued support will be crucial to preserving and extending it.

Finally, even as feminists work to represent women's history in museums, we should resist being cast only as gadflies, the gender consciences of our institutions. Instead, we need to convey the more far-reaching theoretical agenda of women's history, its struggle to reimagine the discipline of historical work. This critical historical perspective can help to move museums and their audiences beyond the idea of history as a ritual of nationalism. Historians in museums have a special responsibility to close the gap between scholarly and popular conceptions of the past, to convey a more complex sense of history as a flexible and time-bound medium, explicitly interpretive and partial in its constructions of the past. Representing women will not in itself accomplish this large task. But if museums are prepared to engage the concerns of women's history in the synthetic mode of the exhibit, we may be able to lead, not just follow, in the reshaping of a critical social history.

Acknowledgments

I am grateful to the Smithsonian Institution for supporting travel expenses through the Research Opportunities Fund and for granting research time for the preparation of this article. I am pleased to acknowledge the close readings and very helpful suggestions of Warren Leon, Dolores Root, Roy Rosenzweig, Christina Simmons, and Patricia West.

In citing exhibitions, I have followed the practice of individual museums. Some institutions acknowledge the work of individual curators, designers, and the like; most do not, instead presenting exhibitions as the collective product of the museum.

NOTES

1. In an earlier article, Christina Simmons and I surveyed a range of exhibits done between 1964 and 1984 and detected a gradual evolution, from unself-conscious presentations of women's lives to interpretive exhibits attentive to the questions and scholarship of women's history. See our co-authored "Exhibiting Women's History," in Susan Porter Benson, Stephen Brier, and Roy Rosenzweig, eds., *Presenting the Past: Essays on History and the Public* (Philadelphia: Temple University Press, 1986), 203–21.

My discussions of the Sewall-Belmont House and "Black Women: Achievements Against the Odds" rely heavily on material in "Exhibiting Women's History," used with the permission of Christina Simmons and Temple University Press.

2. For a recent example of historians' concerns about audience, see Thomas Bender, "Wholes and Parts: The Need for Synthesis in American History," *Journal of American History* 73, no. 1 (June 1986), 120–36, and further discussion in David Thelen, Nell Irvin Painter, Richard Wightman Fox, Roy Rosenzweig, and Thomas Bender, "A Round Table: Synthesis in American History," *Journal of American History* 74, no. 1 (June 1987), 107–30.

3. Gayle Rubin, "Traffic in Women," in Rayna R. Reiter, ed., *Toward an Anthropology of Women* (New York and London: Monthly Review Press, 1975), 157–58.

4. Michelle Zimbalist Rosaldo and Louise Lamphere, eds., *Woman, Culture and Society*, (Stanford, Calif.: Stanford University Press, 1974); see especially Rosaldo's "Woman, Culture, and Society: A Theoretical Overview," 17–42, and Sherry B. Ortner, "Is Female to Male as Nature Is to Culture?" 67–88. This provocative thesis

immediately became the focus of debate among feminist scholars. Just after its publication, at the Second Berkshire Conference on the History of Women, Natalie Davis argued in her keynote speech that the idea of public and private was itself a historical construction, not a universal, and called for a historical explanation of the emergence of this set of cultural categories. Anthropologists subjected both sections of the thesis to a thoroughgoing critique. Some contested the idea of universal female subordination; for an early example, see Karen Sacks, *Sisters and Wives: The Past and Future of Sexual Equality* (Westport, Conn.: Greenwood Press, 1979). Others disposed of the public-private nature-culture dichotomy; see, for example, Carol McCormack and Marilyn Strathern, eds., *Nature, Culture, and Gender* (Cambridge: Cambridge University Press, 1980). But whatever their ultimate limitations, these ideas have had a powerful and fruitful influence on the interpretive frameworks of women's history. The public-private paradigm continues to inform much research, teaching, and writing in women's history; it is a testament to its vigor that, thirteen years later, the idea is still being rebutted. In 1987 the seventh Berkshire Conference on the History of Women invited participants to consider the fluid boundaries of public and private, the ways in which women's experience challenges the ideology of separate domains.

5. A full discussion of the current debates about the methods and aims of women's history is beyond the scope of this essay. Perhaps the most influential historian of women has been Gerda Lerner, who has captured a wide audience both inside and outside the university: see, for example, her essays on women's history in *The Majority Finds Its Past: Placing Women in History* (New York: Oxford University Press, 1979) and *Women and History* (New York: Oxford University Press, 1986). Lerner has remained a strong advocate of women's history as a distinct field, arguing that an integrated synthesis is premature given the massive research yet to be accomplished.

For a recent example of the argument about separation versus integration, see Joan Scott, "Rewriting History," in Margaret Randolph Higonnet, Jane Jenson, Sonya Michel, and Margaret Collins Weitz, eds., *Behind the Lines: Gender and the Two World Wars* (New Haven, Conn.: Yale University Press, 1987), 21–30. See also the debate that has swirled around Scott's recent argument that linguistic representation is the key to historical understanding of gender: Joan W. Scott, "On Language, Gender, and Working-Class History," *International Labor and Working-Class History* 31 (Spring 1987), 1–13, and in the same issue, responses from Bryan Palmer (14–23), Christine Stansell (24–29), and Anson Rabinbach (30–36). And see also Scott, "A Reply to Criticism," *ILWCH* 32 (Fall 1987), 39–45.

6. Hilda L. Smith, " 'Female Bonds and the Family': Continuing Doubts," *Organization of American Historians Newsletter*, 15, no. 5 (February 1987), 13–14; Hilda L. Smith, "Female Bonds and the Family: Recent Directions in Women's History," in Paula A. Treichler, Cheris Kramarae, and Beth Stafford, eds., *For Alma Mater: Theory and Practice in Feminist Scholarship* (Urbana: University of Illinois Press, 1985), 272–91. Smith criticizes what she sees as the scholarly neglect of women's public lives, and in this perspective the museums' concentration on work and politics might be seen as a positive counterbalance.

Gerda Lerner's more recent survey of women's-history research appeared as this article was going to press. See her overview and research agenda, "Priorities and Challenges in Women's History Research," *American Historical Association Newsletter, Perspectives* 26, no. 4 (April 1988), 17–20. Lerner's examination of recent dissertations in women's history suggests that a shift may be under way; biography, labor and work, and education were the three most common subjects of dissertations completed between 1981 and 1987 (p. 19).

7. Marion Tinling, *Women Remembered: A Guide to Landmarks of Women's History in the United States* (Westport, Conn.: Greenwood Press, 1986).

8. "Black Women" has enjoyed high demand and an unusually long run; SITES plans to continue the exhibit until 1990, when it will be considered for another extension.

9. I saw "Achievements Against the Odds" when ANM occupied rented quarters on Martin Luther King Jr. Avenue SE; in April 1987 the museum moved to its current location at 1901 Fort Place SE, also part of the Anacostia neighborhood.

10. And see the accompanying publication: Ruth Abram, ed., *"Send Us a Lady Physician"* (New York: W. W. Norton, 1985).

11. Mary Walsh, *Doctors Wanted: No Women Need Apply: Sexual Barriers in the Medical Profession, 1835–1975* (New Haven, Conn.: Yale University Press, 1977).

12. "Perfect in Her Place: Women at Work in Industrial America," exhibit at the National Museum of American History, Smithsonian Institution, Fall 1981–Spring 1982. Under the auspices of Smithsonian Traveling Exhibition Service, "Perfect" has been traveling since 1982. See also Deborah Warner, *Perfect in Her Place* (Washington, D.C., 1981), the accompanying catalog.

13. See, for example, Eleanor Flexner, *Century of Struggle: The Woman's Rights Movement in the United States* (Cambridge, Mass.: Harvard University Press, 1959); Aileen S. Kraditor, *Ideas of the Woman Suffrage Movement* (New York: Columbia University Press, 1965); William O'Neill, *Everyone Was Brave: A History of Feminism in America* (Chicago: Quadrangle, 1971); Ellen C. DuBois, *Feminism and Suffrage: The Emergence of an Independent Woman's Movement* (Ithaca, N.Y.: Cornell University Press, 1965). "We the People," a bicentennial exhibit at the National Museum of American History, included women's suffrage and the campaign for the Equal Rights Amendment in its account of the broadening of political participation over the course of American history.

14. For example, Ruth Bordin's *Woman and Temperance: The Quest for Power and Liberty, 1873–1900* (Philadelphia: Temple University Press, 1981) rejected the prevailing view of Prohibition as the last gasp of small-town Protestantism to argue that it was a gender-conscious and sometimes feminist movement.

New research on a wide range of women's reform activities has led to a sweeping reassessment of the Progressive movement and, to some extent, the New Deal. "Women and the Progressive Era," a March 1988 conference jointly sponsored by the National Museum of American History (Smithsonian Institution) and the American Historical Association, illustrated the vigor and breadth of such investigations; conference proceedings are forthcoming.

15. For recent histories of the National Woman's Party, see Susan D. Becker, *The Origins of the Equal Rights Amendment* (Westport, Conn.: Greenwood Press, 1981), and Nancy F. Cott's broader interpretation of the NWP in *The Grounding of American*

Feminism (New Haven, Conn.: Yale University Press, 1987). Cott's provocative work offers a broad and synthetic view of the politics and social history of the twentieth-century women's movement.

16. Edith Mayo's work has alerted me to the fuller context of these images. In a paper presented at "Women in the Progressive Era" (see note 14 above), she provided examples of the recurrent motif of the herald used in suffrage imagery and noted many explicit references to Joan of Arc. Leading suffrage parades on a white horse, the young Boissevain illustrates the NWP's deliberate and dramaturgical use of such imagery; her early death lent new intensity to the NWP's appropriation of this heroic iconography.

17. Currently, the best-known and most-visited National Park Service site dealing with black history is the birthplace of Martin Luther King, Jr. in Atlanta, Georgia. The Maggie Lena Walker Historic Site in Richmond, Virginia, interprets the life of Walker (1869–1919), daughter of a former slave and the first American woman to become a bank president. Whitman Mission in Waiilatpu, Washington, incorporates women's history into its interpretation of a Protestant mission established in 1836, a settlement that included the first two white women to make the journey overland to the West. The Clara Barton Historic Site in Glen Echo, Maryland, commemorates the famous Civil War nurse and founder of the American Red Cross.

Women's history is still represented in only a small percentage of NPS sites. The American Historical Association is working in cooperation with NPS to identify and recommend more sites for development; Page Putnam Miller heads the project at the AHA, 400 A Street SE, Washington, DC 20003.

18. Information on attendance comes from interviews with Director Judy Hart and Park Ranger Margaret McFadden, who also provided me with written analyses of visitation for 1986. Though National Park Service regulations discourage questionnaire or interview surveys, head counts do provide a rough sense of the audience for the Women's Rights National Historic Site.

19. Carroll Smith-Rosenberg, "The Female World of Love and Ritual," *Signs* 1, no. 1 (1975), 1–29.

20. For a very useful exchange on the relationship of women's culture and feminist politics, see Estelle Freedman, "Separatism as Strategy: Female Institution Building and American Feminism, 1870–1930," *Feminist Studies* 5, no. 3 (Fall 1979), 512–29, and Ellen C. DuBois, Mari Jo Buhle, Temma Kaplan, Gerda Lerner, and Carroll Smith-Rosenberg, "Politics and Culture in Women's History: A Symposium," *Feminist Studies* 6, no. 1 (Spring 1980), 26–64.

21. See Ruth Milkman, "Women's History and the Sears Case," *Feminist Studies* 12, no. 2 (Summer 1986), 375–400, and Alice Kessler-Harris, "Equal Employment Opportunity Commission v. Sears, Roebuck and Company: A Personal Account," *Radical History Review* 35 (April 1986), 57–79.

22. "The Light of the Home," organizer, Mary-Ellen Perry; historian, Harvey Green; designer, Keith Murphy. The accompanying publication is Harvey Green, *The Light of the Home: An Intimate View of the Lives of Women of Victorian America* (New York: Pantheon, 1983).

23. Ruth Schwartz Cowan, *More Work for Mother: The Ironies of Household Technology from the Open Hearth to the Microwave* (New York: Basic Books, 1983), and

Susan Strasser, *Never Done: A History of American Housework* (New York: Pantheon, 1982).

24. "Impact: Technology in the Kitchen, 1830–1985," curator, Martha Coons; exhibition designer, Sarah Buie; project director, Dolores Root; research assistant, Christine Dzierzeski; graphics, Claudia Cassidy, Christine Dzierzeski, Debbie Lazar; fabrication, Tony Farnum, John Winney.

25. Melosh and Simmons, "Exhibiting Women's History," 210–11.

26. Patricia West, " 'The New Social History' and Historic House Museums: The Lindenwald Example," *Museum Studies Journal* 2, no. 2 (Fall 1986), 22–26. For a broad and provocative history of historic houses, see West's "Clio at Home: Historic House Museums and the History of Women," M.A. thesis, State University of New York at Albany, 1988.

27. See Suzanne Lebsock, *The Free Women of Petersburg: Status and Culture in a Southern Town* (New York: Norton, 1984).

28. Exhibit produced by the Virginia Women's Cultural History Project, opened in November 1984 in Richmond, Virginia; traveled 1985–87. *"A Share of Honour": Virginia Women, 1600–1945* (Richmond, Va.: The Project, 1984); essay by Suzanne Lebsock, checklist and catalog entries by Kym S. Rice.

29. "Pain and Its Relief," National Museum of American History, Smithsonian Institution, 1983–88.

30. I saw installations of "The Birth Project" in Madison, Wisconsin, and Washington, D.C. The historical section, written by historian Barbara Baldwin, is titled "Childbirth in America." See also Judy Chicago, *The Birth Project* (Garden City, N.Y.: Doubleday and Co., 1975).

31. The only representation of this subject that I have yet seen in the United States is a display of the Pill in "Milestones: 50 Years of Goods and Services" (Cooper-Hewitt Museum, Smithsonian Institution, New York), a small temporary exhibit that uncritically acclaimed the march of American consumer products. (The two-paragraph label, couched mostly in the revealing passive voice, credits the sexual revolution to the Pill and mentions women only once.) See the accompanying catalog, *I'll Buy That! 50 Small Wonders and Big Deals That Revolutionized the Lives of Consumers*, by the editors of *Consumer Reports* (Mount Vernon, N.Y.: Consumers Union, 1986.

32. The Lesbian Herstory Archives is run by Deborah Edel, Joan Nestle, and Judith Schwartz, P.O. Box 1258, New York, NY 10001. See Judith Schwartz, *Radical Feminists of Heterodoxy: Greenwich Village 1912–40* (Lebanon, N.H.: New Victoria, 1982). For a good discussion and very useful source list, see Lisa Duggan, "History's Gay Ghetto: The Contradictions of Growth in Lesbian and Gay History," in Benson, Brier, and Rosenzweig, *Presenting the Past*, 281–90.

33. Thomas Schlereth, "Causing Conflict, Doing Violence," *Museum News* 63, no. 1 (October 1984), 45–52.

34. A laudable exception is "Perfect in Her Place," which includes a prostitute's fan among its artifacts of women's work.

35. Of course this formula is not novel to museum exhibits; Frances FitzGerald dissects its powerful influence on a generation of history textbooks in *America Revised: History Textbooks in the Twentieth Century* (Boston: Little, Brown, 1979).

36. William Chafe, *Civility and Civil Rights: Greensboro, North Carolina, and the Black Struggle for Freedom* (New York: Oxford University Press, 1980).

37. Examples of museums that do list credits are the Margaret Woodbury Strong Museum in Rochester, New York, and the Brattleboro Museum and Arts Center in Brattleboro, Vermont.

Afro-Americans and Museums: Towards a Policy of Inclusion

9

James Oliver Horton and Spencer R. Crew

In 1974, Zora Martin Felton, director of education at the Smithsonian Institution's Anacostia Neighborhood Museum, visited Colonial Williamsburg. Although impressed by the careful preservation of Virginia's colonial capital, Felton was disturbed by the absence of black history. Afro-Americans constituted almost half the colonial inhabitants of Williamsburg, but they existed only as background shadows in the preserved version of the town's eighteenth-century past. Felton found blacks overrepresented among Williamburg's cafeteria workers but conspicuously absent from its interpretive staff.[1]

A year later, Thomas Greenfield, an instructor at Virginia Union University, noticed a similar situation at Thomas Jefferson's historic plantation home, Monticello. Even the docents' language denied the troublesome existence of slaves, euphemistically called servants when a reference was absolutely unavoidable. Greenfield also noted that the site interpreters used the passive voice when referring to Monticello's blacks, focusing attention away from the majority of the plantation's residents. Docents switched to the active voice, however, when they pictured Jefferson's actions. They might explain that "Mr. Jefferson designed these doors" but use a passive "The doors were installed originally in 1809" when referring to the activities of slaves. As surely as Jefferson designed the doors, black slaves built and installed them, yet interpreters' language highlighted the master's actions but buried the slaves' contributions.[2]

Such selective presentations of the past are not unique to Colonial Williamsburg and Monticello. In the 1980s the contributions and experiences of black people still are often excluded from the public presentation of our nation's history. Yet the renaissance in black history in the 1960s has made the historic reality of the Afro-American experience more difficult to ignore totally. Since then, museums, historic sites, and historic-theme presentations have wrestled with the decisions of how, or sometimes whether, to integrate their exhibitions. Often they have found the answer in the inclusion of one or two "exceptional blacks." But this concentration on exceptional blacks ignores the lesser-known but no less significant makers of Afro-American and American history and perpetuates the mythology of America as an egalitarian and racially homogeneous society.

Unfortunately, many museums have minimized the experience of Afro-Americans and their centrality to American history. Too often the burgeoning scholarship in black history has not found its way into the public presentations that have shaped the historical consciousness of millions of Americans. This essay considers this apparent gap between recent scholarship in Afro-American and social history and the public exhibition of American history. It is concerned with the origins of this gap in institutional unwillingness to recognize the importance of Afro-American history to a realistic understanding of American culture. It also focuses on other factors that limit a more complete presentation of America's past, such as institutional staff size and composition, types of collections, local politics, and budgetary constraints.

In order to understand institutional responses to recent Afro-American historical scholarship, we sent questionnaires to 104 museums selected from lists provided by the American Association of Museums and the African American Museums Association. We sampled publically and privately sponsored museums of different regional focuses and of various sizes. Some of these institutions concentrated exclusively on black history, while others had a more general American-history focus. Our return rate was high (more than 50 percent), with many of the respondents providing additional information about their programs and exhibition plans. Follow-up telephone calls and site visits supplemented the questionnaires.

The questionnaire responses highlighted the multiplicity of institutional settings. Museums and public history displays on Afro-American history were located in every region of the country and used a variety of methods to engage visitors. Most of these organizations used traditional exhibition methods, which featured artifacts and labels to convey information on national, regional, state, or local history topics. The Chicago Historical Society, the Valentine Museum in Richmond, Virginia, and the Atwater Kent Museum in Philadelphia exemplified this approach. Within this more traditional group, there were specialized institutions focusing on particular aspects of American life. Afro-American museums like the DuSable Museum in Chicago and the National Afro-American Museum and Cultural Center in Wilberforce, Ohio, represented 15 percent of the museums responding to our questionnaire. The Jazz Museum in New Orleans and the Museum of the Confederacy in Richmond represented different types of specialized museums. Living-history presentations, such as the programs at Williamsburg in Virginia, Freetown Village at Indianapolis in Indiana, and Old Sturbridge Village in Massachusetts offered another style of historical exploration. In these settings, visitors are transported back in time to observe life in a specific era in American history.

Until recently, most historical institutions focused on a very narrow segment of history. They concentrated on major military campaigns, historic events, famous historical figures, or highly crafted historical artifacts. With few exceptions, they had little interest in the everyday life or the material culture of common folk. This tradition reflected the notion that only the extraordinary was worthy of preservation; the battlefield, the homes of the wealthy and politically influential. As this tradition has changed in historical scholarship, it has affected and is changing the nation's museums.

Early Afro-American Exhibitions

Black people long have realized the importance of preserving their history and have expended much effort over generations to that end. Meager resources made such preservation difficult, and racial prejudice limited access to better-financed and more widely recognized exhibition facilities. In 1851, black Bostonians launched a campaign to establish a permanent marker in memory of Crispus Attucks, the first black American killed in the Revolutionary era. Although it took nearly two generations of agitation, the city of Boston finally dedicated the statue in 1888.[3]

Throughout the nineteenth century, Afro-Americans recorded their contributions to the society and proudly extolled their heritage as willing patriots. They told their story in the pages of numerous publications and through the preservation of significant historical sites. Even before the Civil War a national convention of blacks established a library and reading room in New York to make Afro-American history accessible. Similar efforts followed in Cincinnati and Detroit.[4]

After the Civil War, blacks established several historical societies. But as Jeffrey C. Stewart and Fath Davis Ruffins suggest, these societies, "preferred to gather materials about Negro influence in Europe than to uncover evidence about American slavery." The museum established at Hampton Institute in 1868, for example, concentrated on the history of blacks abroad, particularly under the influence of William Shappard, who was fascinated with Africa. This focus on African antecedents to Afro-American culture, offered an alternative to Booker T. Washington's accommodationist philosophy, which stressed the American roots of blacks. It reflected instead the sentiment of African nationalists, such as Bishop Henry McNeal Turner, who advocated Afro-Americans' migration to the land of their origins.[5]

A few black scholars, including Harvard-trained historian W. E. B. Du Bois, worked to preserve the music and folklore of the plain people of Afro-

American society. Organizations like the Boston Society for the Collection of Negro Folklore, founded in the last decade of the nineteenth century, brought together a small dedicated group of early folklorists who gathered and preserved the artifacts of poor rural black people.

Despite this effort, the scarcity of funds and the influence of traditional museum practice encouraged black preservationists to focus on the lives and activities of black notables. At the death of Frederick Douglass, the great orator, abolitionist, and statesman, his home in Anacostia was preserved as the "black Mount Vernon." During the next few generations, the homes and birthplaces of educator Booker T. Washington and scientist George Washington Carver were preserved and filled with artifacts significant to the memory of their central figures.[6]

Concurrently, a new generation of black historians struggled to disseminate Afro-American history among scholars and the general public. Most notably, Carter G. Woodson, Harvard Ph.D., founded the Association for the Study of Negro Life and History and the *Journal of Negro History* in 1915. During the next four decades, Woodson, his journal, his organization, and his annual Negro History Week celebrations were the most influential sources of public presentations of Afro-American history. Several new manuscript collections, particularly Arthur Schomburg's collection of documents and manuscripts purchased by the Harlem branch of the New York Public Library, and the Moorland collection, established in 1914 at Howard University, provided primary material for scholarly research.[7]

In many Afro-American schools the story of blacks in American history was regularly taught, and Negro History Week festivities became an important part of the school year in segregated institutions of the 1930s and 1940s. Woodson directed *The Negro History Bulletin*, begun in 1937, specifically at public-school teachers and their students to encourage more consciousness and pride of race. As black children of this era grew to maturity, they carried with them an appreciation for the significance of their history and provided a ready constituency for a burgeoning Afro-American history movement. Yet most white Americans remained ignorant of these efforts.[8]

The few museums devoted to Afro-American culture and history were also invisible to whites. Several black universities, for example, provided exhibit space for historical and artistic presentations. In 1929, Howard University created a traveling exhibit of student works and established a permanent art collection and gallery the next year. Atlanta University opened an art gallery in its Trevor Arnett Library in the early 1930s and over the next few decades gathered an impressive array of Afro-American art and art objects.[9] About the same time, Tuskegee Institute in Alabama opened the George Washington Carver Museum. The initial collection, gathered in 1938, featured Carver's paintings, but it gradually expanded to include a variety of African and Afro-American art.[10]

The commitment of scarce resources to the collection and presentation of Afro-American art and history demonstrated the importance these institutions placed on preserving black American culture. Unlike prestigious white institutions, which received regular donations from wealthy alumni, black schools had no substantial endowments to support their operations. At best, black colleges depended on meager public funds or on limited and unpredictable grants from philanthropic agencies. Under these conditions, their support of museum activities, even on a limited basis, was impressive. Since most American museums shunned Afro-American art and history, black college officials realized that only through their efforts would students gain exposure to the historical achievements of their race.

In the 1950s, several museums expanded their holdings. Howard University, for example, added a collection of African art objects donated by the estate of black scholar and writer Alain Locke. A few other institutions also began to present black history, literature, music, and art. In Boston, Elma Lewis organized her school for the arts, and in San Francisco the Negro Historical and Cultural Association opened.[11]

The Civil-Rights Era

As the civil-rights movement exploded in the pages of newspapers and on television, the popular and scholarly study of racial prejudice grew rapidly. A few predominantly white colleges and universities instituted a course or two in the "new" field of Negro history. Oberlin College was one of the first to institute such a course: "The Negro in American History" in 1957. During the 1960s, partly as a response to student demand, some of the more progressive colleges and universities established not only individual courses in Afro-American history but entire programs dedicated to interdisciplinary study of the black American experience. The institution of such programs at Harvard, Yale, Columbia, Cornell and other nationally respected schools lent academic legitimacy to the study of things Afro-American.[12]

Outside the academy, black communities debated the significance of studying and presenting black history as a distinct field of American history. The civil-rights movement gave activists a sense of empowerment, and they demanded that a range of institutions, including museums, respond sensitively to their needs. Blacks recognized urban museums as important repositories of culture and history and insisted that they provide programs and exhibitions, relevant to Afro-American life, that honestly conveyed Afro-American contributions. They also sought representation on museum staffs and governing boards.

As demands for more black control over cultural institutions affecting black communities mounted through the 1960s, museums found it increasingly difficult to remain detached. Slowly and with difficulty, they began to employ practices, exhibit programs, and educational activities; adopt research methods; and establish outreach efforts in response to community pressure. The Smithsonian was one of the first major institutions to respond. In 1965, S. Dillon Ripley, its secretary, initiated meetings with a community group in Washington, D.C., Greater Anacostia Peoples, Inc., to discuss creation of a Smithsonian black-history museum in an old movie theater located in the heart of the black community of Anacostia.[13]

Opened in July of 1967, as the nation's first experimental neighborhood museum, the Anacostia offered programming and exhibitions that touched upon themes of local importance. Such exhibits as "Out of Africa" and "The Rat: Man's Invited Affliction" attracted numerous first-time museum visitors, as did the educational programs of films, music, and drama. The Anacostia Museum's success made it a model for community oriented museums.[14]

Even so, most museums were more cautious in responding to the flood of information produced by Afro-American historians and to the demands of the black community. Those institutions that actively sought to take up the challenge often faced controversy. In 1968 the Metropolitan Museum of Art in New York City undertook what museum director Thomas Hoving described as "a broad and very deep and continuing re-examination of all of our policies, our philosophies, our aims, and their day-to-day practice."[15] As a result, the museum hired minority youth during the summer as a means of introducing them to the museum and met with community groups to discuss future Metropolitan exhibitions and programs. From these meetings came "Harlem on My Mind," an extremely controversial multimedia exhibit exploring Harlem's sixty-eight-year black history decade by decade.[16]

Hoving and the museum staff saw the exhibition as more than an educational public display. They hoped it would have significant social effects and symbolize the Met's good-faith effort to respond to community interests and needs. Although the exhibition was not a total success—reaction to the show was mixed—the Metropolitan Museum distinguished itself from most other institutions which ignored demands for historical racial equity.

Militants and Museums

By the late 1960s there were a few cooperative efforts between museum professionals and community members. In November 1969 the Neighborhood Museum Seminar held at MUSE, a neighborhood museum operated in Brooklyn's Bedford-Stuyvesant district, focused attention on the differing internal and external visions of museums. Billed as a conference on the role of the museum in the community, the seminar gathered representatives from foundations, museums, communities, and government agencies, who discussed racism, cultural identity and minority mistrust of public institutions. No solutions emerged, but the conference pointed out the need for museums to reexamine their role in a changing society and to increase contact with local communities. If museums hoped to maintain their importance as cultural institutions, they had to involve the local community in the process of planning, policy-making, and program administration. This was no easy task. Professionals would have to surrender some control to nonprofessionals or remain open to charges of promoting white cultural dominance and ignoring minority contributions to American society and culture.[17]

Still, few museums responded. Finally, community protest turned confrontational. In 1970 the activist New York Art Strike and Art Workers Coalition interrupted the annual business meeting of the American Association of Museums (AAM) in New York. Declaring that the meeting must deal with the pressing issues of "war, racism, sexism and repression," the coalition accused museum professionals of complicity with the forces of social and economic oppression in American society. They argued that museums must reflect community values, not the special interests of the business and the social elite. An ad hoc AAM committee discussed the coalition's grievances and proposed that the museum community create a national workshop to examine museum responsibilities with regard to racism, sexism, repression, and war. Further, the committee urged that museums establish internships for women, blacks, Mexicans, American Indians, Puerto Ricans, and other oppressed people and institute policies which would "attend to the problems of racism, sexism and repression by implementing programs which further their solution." [18]

These resolutions demanded a new dedication on the part of the museum community towards greater social awareness in employment practices, educational programming, and exhibitions. Although many museum people did not agree with the coalition's tactics, the association took several specific steps to remedy racism in the museum world. With a grant received from the Department of Housing and Urban Development, for example, the AAM created a committee on urban museums, which developed guidelines for museums seeking to fulfill their responsibilities to the public. In addition, AAM meetings devoted sessions to minorities in museums, neighborhood centers, community involvement, and improved minority hiring. Similarly, more of the articles in *Museum News*, the journal of the AAM, considered the role of the museum in the midst of major social, racial, and political upheavals in society.[19]

Individual institutions facing demands for greater social responsibility used exhibits to examine important social issues. In 1971 the Museum of the City of New York mounted "Drug Scene in New York," an exhibit on drug abuse. Featuring life-size photographs of drug victims, drugs, and drug paraphernalia, the show provided a brief history and analysis of drug abuse in New York City. It also explained the effects and consequences of drug abuse, the methods of treatment, and the citywide effects of drugs. This unconventional exhibit increased the museum's attendance 400 percent and drew a diverse audience, including addicts seeking to overcome their affliction. The exhibit guides, themselves former addicts, provided information on treatment and facilitated contact with addiction control centers.[20]

A year later the National Museum of American History of the Smithsonian Institution opened "The Right To Vote." Organized for the 1972 presidential election, the exhibit chronicled the historical broadening of the American electorate. The exhibit displayed flags, clothing, posters, and other materials from the Selma, Alabama, voting-rights campaign and the Voting Rights Act of 1965. This exhibit reflected curator Edith P. Mayo's long-standing commitment to collecting and exhibiting contemporary materials.

In 1976 the Philadelphia Museum of Art, reflecting the museum director's call for more extensive outreach efforts, created its own contemporary multi-ethnic and multiracial show, "Rites of Passage." Through a series of small exhibitions, it examined five cultural groups and their influence upon Philadelphia. The Museum of Art staff worked closely with members of the Chinese, Jewish, Italian, Puerto Rican, and Afro-American communities. Each group selected the particular aspect of its culture it wanted highlighted in exhibition sites scattered throughout the city. This project was highly successful in enhancing the relations between the institution and the community. It extended the resources of the museum to the community and helped to stimulate community support for and interest in the museum.[21]

Urban museums were those most likely to feel increasing community pressure. Some attempted to broaden the appeal of their collections and exhibitions, but most did not. Community groups maintained pressure on local officials, but it seemed unlikely that minorities would ever exercise sufficient influence to bring about a major reorientation of white-controlled museums. In order to attract large black audiences, to reveal the major contributions of Afro-Americans, and to teach an appreciation for the rich multiracial history and culture of our nation, many believed that blacks had to control their own museums. Consequently, black-run institutions struggled into existence during the 1970s. These Afro-American museums followed the earlier examples of the San Francisco African-American Historical and Cultural Society (1955), the DuSable Museum in Chicago (1961), and the Afro-American Museum of Detroit (1965). In them, local residents found a comfortable environment which focused on their heritage.[22]

The Bicentennial and Black Museums

The American Revolution Bicentennial stimulated the creation of these black-run museums and allowed Afro-Americans more voice in the public presentation of their history and culture. Several cities used bicentennial funds to foster the establishment of Afro-American museums. Leading black residents of Philadelphia had insisted for many years that the city needed an institution focusing on the considerable local contributions of Afro-Americans. Their arguments fell on deaf ears until extensive lobbying and political pressure convinced conservative Mayor Frank Rizzo and the city council to appropriate two and a half million dollars for the construction of a black museum in the heart of Philadelphia's historic Independence Square district.[23]

Philadelphia's Afro-American Historical and Cultural Museum, which opened in 1976, was designed by a black architect and was the first such institution in the United States to receive official city support—a considerable achievement given the conservative nature of the city administration. Mayor Rizzo had received little black political support in his election, and he had not offered official encouragement to the city's Afro-American community. The project's success stemmed from the financial importance of historically oriented tourism to Philadelphia's economy, the black community's tenacity, and growing recognition (even by conservative public officials) of the legitimacy of presenting and preserving the Afro-American past. Such other museums as the California Afro-American Museum in Los Angeles (1977), the Great Plains Black Museum in Omaha, Nebraska (1976), and the National Afro-American Museum and Cultural Center in Wilberforce, Ohio (1972), also benefited from community pressure.[24]

Such pressure often took years to have an effect. Boston's Museum of Afro American History began in the mid-1960s with a committed group of volunteers concerned with the preservation of black history and culture. By 1970 the group was able to purchase the African Meeting House, the church home of the first black independent congregation in the city. Built by black workers in 1806, the structure symbolized the rich history of Boston's nineteenth-century black community, since it had provided a forum for both antislavery and civil-rights protest. Under the leadership of museum director Byron Rushing, the church received National Historic Landmark designation and funds from the National Park Service.[25]

Reconstructed after a 1970s fire that severely damaged it, the African Meeting House became the center for a major historic area on Beacon Hill, site of the city's largest nineteenth-century settlement of Afro-Americans. Official government recognition gave the Afro-American Museum of Boston a more stable financial base than most of its counterparts around the country. Like Philadelphia's Afro-American Historical and Cultural Museum, which received public support, Boston's museum seemed reasonably secure, at least in the short run. Most other black-museum projects were less stable financially, struggling along from year to year and sometimes from month to month.

In Brooklyn, New York, the Weeksville Society works continuously at generating funds for its operation. Dedicated to restoring the nineteenth-century black settlement of Weeksville, the society conducts archaeological digs, restores structures, and creates exhibitions at the site. Operating funds for the society come from contributions made by local residents, foundations, and members of the business community. Though Weeksville has been in existence since 1971, the society has not been able to create an endowment. Without a regular source of funds, Weeksville's programming and existence depend upon constant fund raising.

As the number of African American museums increased, so did the need to exchange information among these institutions. In 1978, after a series of seminars at the annual meetings of the Association for the Study of Afro-American Life and History, the African American Museums Association (AAMA) was born. The association brought together black museums and museum professionals who provided a clearinghouse for information on museum education, collecting, and conservation, as well as employment opportunities and information on Afro-American museum activities around the nation.[26]

The AAMA also sponsored a regular forum for general discussion among museum professionals at its annual conferences. These meetings examined improved methods of collecting, exhibiting, and interpreting Afro-American material culture in black museums and in traditional museum settings. The African American Museums Association also held regular sessions at AAM meetings, ensuring a broader influence on all museums that might exhibit black history and culture.

The African American Museums Association not only served existing institutions but also encouraged the creation of institutions focused on black history and culture. There are now well over one hundred such museums around the country. The association increased the pressure on traditional museums and historic sites to improve their representation of Afro-Americans in their exhibitions and public presentations. To their credit, several museums accepted the challenge, seeking new ways to include black history.

Black History in American Museums Today

Almost all (more than 75 percent) museums responding to our questionnaire reported that their exhibits had been affected by recent interpretations in both Afro-American history and social history, especially regional and local studies. In addition, several museums are contributing to historical scholarship through the research and writing of staff members. The Historic New Orleans Collection, for example, incorporated several of its collections into publications dealing with the multiracial character of Louisiana history. One of its publications, *Evidence of the Past*, a brief regional study of "free persons of color" in the nineteenth century, is used as a textbook supplement in state public schools.[27]

The North Carolina Museum of History disseminates historical information on black Carolinians from their collection through its journal *Tar Heel Junior Historian*. Museum educators also provide teachers with material to help interest students in historical research. Printed information sheets drawing on nineteenth-century fugitive-slave advertisements and other primary documents are furnished to students, who are then asked to answer questions on slavery and undertake small historical projects.[28]

Whereas some professional staffs are producing scholarship, others, particularly those at smaller museums, are so pressed with the daily institutional duties that research and writing are all but impossible. Some reported that they have trouble keeping current with the rapidly changing literature. Several respondents explained they lacked funds to maintain an adequate institutional library and depended upon limited and sometimes inaccessible public facilities. These problems are especially acute for small Afro-American museums. Their difficulties in keeping current with scholarship and carrying out new research are particularly significant, since these institutions report the largest percentages of minority visitors. Seventy-six percent of the visitors to Afro-American museums are minorities, as compared with less than 30 percent of visitors to other museums.[29]

For small museums without a specific collection focused on Afro-Americans, these problems pose particular complications. Several such museums expressed an interest in expanding their holdings and exhibitions in black history, but they needed financial and scholarly assistance. One respondent suggested that since his museum could not subscribe to more than a few publications, a list of the most useful Afro-American history journals would be helpful. Such comments suggest the need for closer collaboration between academic historians or larger museums and small, struggling institutions.[30]

The influence of Afro-American scholarship on museum exhibitions is difficult to judge. It ranged broadly from the inclusion of one black display during Black History Month, to a small permanent black exhibit, to a major effort to integrate black history into exhibitions. Larger, wealthier institutions were likely to have included some black materials in their exhibits, but size and level of support did not guarantee meaningful inclusion.

Until recently, for example, the Chicago Historical Society developed its exhibitions around objects already in its possession. These collections consisted primarily of artifacts acquired before 1950 and included little, if any, black material culture. Consequently, exhibits sponsored by the society largely ignored Afro-American activities in Chicago despite the size of the city's black population. It has only been during the last few years with exhibitions like "Making Music Chicago Style (1985)" that it has increased its efforts to collect black materials and to broaden the scope of its exhibitions. For many institutions like the Chicago Historical Society, the general integration of black history into institutional holdings and presentations is a slow process requiring a fundamental shift in collection and exhibition policies.

Several museums in the South have made efforts towards this end. By the mid-1970s, the Museum of the Confederacy in Richmond, Virginia, had incorporated aspects of the slave experience and the importance of slave labor to the Confederate war effort into its permanent exhibition. There is, however, little treatment of the slave community, free blacks, or of black people as Southerners during the period—a glaring omission given the importance of the free Afro-American community in Civil War Richmond.

Recently the Museum of the Confederacy has moved to broaden its treatment of blacks. In 1990 it will open an exhibition exploring Afro-American life in the Old South. The show will explore family, community, and cultural values of rural and urban black Southerners. In one of the most intensive efforts to date, the museum staff has identified artifacts and documents from collections scattered across the South. The museum also has engaged outside consultants in history and material culture to aid in the interpretation and design of the exhibit. A historical symposium and public lecture series, films, a catalog, and educational packets will accompany the exhibition, enhancing its public educational value.

The exhibition and educational programming planned at the Museum of the Confederacy is an important step, but the temporary nature of the exhibit may be problematic. A temporary exhibit may not have a long-term effect on museum exhibition policy. The museum must be careful that outside consultants, especially an outside curator, do not work in isolation, thus depriving the permanent staff of the benefits of direct participation in project research and interpretation. Knowledge gained through active involvement of permanent institutional staff will pay dividends in future exhibitions and educational activities.

An alternative approach is under way in the same city at the Valentine Museum, a local-history museum. Under the direction of Frank Jewell and Greg Kimball, the museum has set out a long-range plan that includes specific exhibits focusing on blacks, women, and Jews. Exhibits on post–World War II race relations in Richmond (including civil-rights activism) and a special project on Jackson Ward (a historically black district) highlight the museum's commitment.

The Valentine has established connections in the local and regional black community in a variety of innovative ways. In the fall of 1987 it announced a minority internship program to bring black students into the institution. This has been a learning experience for students and staff. Students are immersed in the museum world, often for the first time, and museum professionals benefit from a perspective not generally available to the institution.

During the same period, the Valentine engaged Marie Tyler-McGraw, formerly of the Afro-American Communities Project at the National Museum of American History, to aid in the creation of "In Bondage and Freedom." This exhibit on Richmond blacks during the decades before the Civil War opened in February 1988. As it took shape, there was substantial coordination with members of the Richmond black community. Staff members believe that relations formed between the Valentine and the local community helped to generate significant increases in the number of blacks visiting the museum after the opening of "In Bondage and Freedom." Our interviews confirmed this belief. Minority visitors with whom we spoke had learned about the exhibit through their church or some other community source.

The Valentine's experience exemplified what was true for most of the institutions we studied. Long-range planning, community coordination, the inclusion of scholars with knowledge of social and Afro-American history, and a determined staff effort supported at top administrative levels were crucial elements in broadening museum presentations.

The Greensboro Historical Museum in central North Carolina also has moved to expand its exhibition policy to include additional Afro-American programming. Started in 1924, the museum is housed in a church building. It is city-financed and has a local and regional collection focus. The museum added a curator of education, Gayle Fripp, to assist in exhibit development and interpretation. Under her guidance, the museum established a committee to advise on research and exhibit development. A permanent exhibit composed mainly of photographs focusing on the black community resulted. This exhibition increased both black interest in the institution and the number of black visitors. Fripp is convinced that the involvement of community members was crucial to this change.

Most museums in our survey reported that minorities constituted a substantial percentage of their visitors (30 percent) and that almost half (47 percent) of these minority visitors were Afro-Americans. Not surprisingly, museums near black communities reported the highest rate of black visitorship. Reflecting their growing awareness of their importance in American historical scholarship and the increasing likelihood of their story's inclusion in exhibits, minorities are visiting museums in larger numbers than before.[31]

More than three-quarters of museums reported an increase in minority attendance in the past decade. Small institutions, many of which focused specifically on blacks, experienced the largest increase and the highest level of minority visitorship. Significantly, those museums which added minorities to their staffs in the last ten years tended to have the largest increase in both the size of their minority visitorship and the establishment of temporary or permanent exhibits focusing on minorities or the incorporation of minorities in existent exhibitions.

What to Do?

Our survey suggests two approaches to incorporating the black experience into museum exhibitions. First, museum collections must be expanded. This solution is costly but relatively straightforward and is one that traditional museum techniques are equipped to handle. By establishing contacts in the black community, important items can be located. Such contacts evolve most naturally through museum-community steering committees or advisory groups. Hiring black museum professionals facilitates this process but requires a financial commitment by the museum. Hence, any practical approach to this staffing issue may require a governmental and a corporate commitment to the public-education function of museums. If museums are expected to broaden their educational service beyond the elite few to the public at large, their efforts will require substantial financial support.[32]

The second approach calls for museums to make better use of existing collections. Here too the counsel of an Afro-American studies specialist is invaluable. Often exhibits can be developed from existing collections if museum staff members understand the relationship between their artifacts and black history. A collection of mining equipment at the Colorado State Historical Society, for example, might very well form a base for an exhibit on blacks in the region's silver mines, even if the equipment is not specifically traceable to black miners. The Henry Ford Museum in Dearborn, Michigan, might do an exhibit on blacks in the auto industry, using production-line equipment as a general backdrop. In both cases, black-specific artifacts could be added, but the exhibit need not be based solely on such items. Several museums have adopted this technique of creating exhibits and thereby have enhanced their ability to create Afro-American displays.[33]

The National Museum of American History exhibit "Field to Factory: Afro-American Migration 1915–1940" used generic artifacts where black-owned objects could not be located. Photographic research and interviews of migrants substantiated the accuracy of the objects used. The exhibition generated public interest and information that allowed the staff to identify numerous black-owned objects in the hands of private individuals. Thus does exhibit creation become the impetus for collection diversification.

Living history offers another technique for illustrating Afro-American culture and incorporating the black experience into traditional historical presentations. Much of what is important about black history is the perspective and commentary it offers on the American experience, which can be effectively captured and conveyed to the public through historical drama. The imaginative use of theatrical programs suggests exciting possibilities for expanding traditional history exhibitions. Currently, living history is used in a variety of museum settings: traditional museums, house museums, historic sites, and historic districts.

Employing techniques developed at Colonial Williamsburg, the National Museum of American History used living history in 1983. Two actors, one black and one white, dramatized a dispute between a slave master and a slave set against the background of a pre–Civil War plantation. This public presentation brought a plantation-house exhibit to life and educated the viewing audience on important aspects of nineteenth-century Southern race relations. Museum patrons were ambivalent about watching a drama of interracial conflict. Nor were they entirely comfortable with a black man, even an actor playing a role, adopting the actions and the speech of a slave. Clearly, there are important complications involved in the use of living history, especially in the reenactment of human conflict. This issue of conflict in history is one with which museums and public presentations have not been comfortable but one which is too important to avoid.[34]

When Zora Martin Felton returned to Colonial Williamsburg in 1984, she found that it had changed. At the urging of a special committee, Williamsburg had created a living-history project which allowed visitors to learn about the complexity of life in the village from actors playing the roles of colonial residents. The program was initially launched with one white actor in 1978. The following year, six more characters were added, including three slaves. At first, visitors found the slave presentation confusing. They had difficulty distinguishing between the actors as real people and the characters they portrayed. This was especially a problem when some white visitors encountered black actors in character. One black actor playing the role of a slave was so convincing that a visitor reported to local authorities that blacks were being held in captivity at the site.[35]

This problem was solved when black actors provided a brief introduction preceding their performance or when black interpreters explained the historical context and answered questions. One particularly engaging portrayal is that of Belinda, a slave scullery maid who ran her laundry with pride and efficiency. This performance implicitly touched sensitive issues that any portrayal of a slave must consider. Belinda is portrayed as a person of dignity. Visitors obviously appreciated and learned from these theatrical presentations. Post-performance interviews indicated that the portrayals offered them insights into the complexity of black life in Colonial Williamsburg and enabled visitors to better understand the meaning and significance of race in colonial times.[36]

These changes made Williamsburg more hospitable to Afro-Americans and painted a more realistic picture of the colonial South. This new orientation did not come easily, however. It was prompted by outside political pressure from the black community and black museum professionals, combined with the commitment of individual members of the institution's administration. In the late 1970s, Dennis O'Toole came to the village as deputy director of museum programs, and Shomer Zwelling arrived as research historian. In 1979 they, in turn, recruited Rex Ellis from Hampton University. With the support of the administration, Ellis, now assistant director for African-American interpretation, and Dylan Pritchett, now black program supervisor, organized a tour focusing on black life in Williamsburg, educational programs for public schools, and a growing list of black characters.[37]

Old Sturbridge Village in Sturbridge, Massachusetts, also employed living history to incorporate Afro-American history and racial conflict into its re-creation of a nineteenth-century New England town. In 1985, for example, it re-created a public meeting during which Abigail Kelley, the fiery abolitionist, brought the visitor face to face with the nineteenth century's most explosive issue: slavery. Exchanges in the meeting illustrated the variety of opinions that would have been found in an antebellum New England town. Thus, although black actors were not initially included in the dramatization and although no black sites were re-created in the village, the historical importance of race and its centrality in nineteenth-century American life was presented in a striking way.

Unlike Old Sturbridge Village, Freetown Village in Indianapolis, Indiana, is not a historical place but a theatrical troupe. Dressed in late-nineteenth-century costume, they conduct hands-on craft workshops in candle making, butter churning, ice cream making, and printing. At various times during the year, special events, such as the traditional Juneteenth celebrations of emancipation, a nineteenth-century black wedding ceremony, or political gatherings, are featured. The troupe has become a favorite of church and school groups and performs regularly at the Indiana State Museum. Ophelia Wellington, founding director of the company, stresses the positive accomplishments of Indiana blacks in 1870. The intention is to illustrate the optimistic expectations of many black communities during the post–Civil War era. Conflict is not ignored, however; slavery and racial injustice in the late nineteenth century also are topics of discussion.

Living history will become more important as additional museums take up the challenge of Afro-American and social history. For institutions with limited funds and limited ability to collect the material culture needed for a full incorporation of Afro-American life, living history allows the use of the few artifacts available in a more educational and dramatic manner.

The innovation evident at some historic sites seems to have had little effect at Monticello. It remains much as it was when Thomas Greenfield visited in the mid-1970s. Docents continue to use the passive voice when referring to the activities of slaves, called servants on all but one occasion during our visit in the spring of 1987. There is still the illusion that anything of importance at Monticello centered on Jefferson. Only if visitors toured, unescorted, the tunnels beneath the main house did they come upon a small photograph exhibit telling of an archaeological project to restore the slave quarters and study the social and cultural lives of the great plantation's residential majority. This was the only evidence of the influence of recent scholarship at this historic site.

Monticello visitors might never know that those referred to as cooks, farm workers, or even skilled craftsmen were in reality plantation slaves. Our informal visitor survey showed that tourists did not associate slaves with such titles and that although most of the adults understood that Jefferson held slaves (only two of the twelve children knew this), slaveholding was seen as incidental to his life and that of the plantation. Unfortunately, the tour encouraged such views and did more to glorify Jefferson than to educate the public about life at Monticello.

A similar situation exists at Ash Lawn, the plantation estate of James Monroe. The active voice was used for Monroe and his family, while slave activities were indicated in the passive voice and only once in the seven times that slaves were mentioned were they actually referred to as slaves. The re-creation of the slave quarters at Ash Lawn was the most disturbing aspect of the restoration. To the rear of the main house were several small, neat, cottages, each with its own fireplace, glass windows, and assorted furnishings. One visitor commented that they resembled comfortable summer cottages. When the docent was asked about the typicality of such attractive dwellings as quarters for slaves, he replied, erroneously, that they were typical for the time and the region.

Ash Lawn thus glorifies its patriarch and romanticizes the slave era, confirming what many Americans would like to believe: that slavery was, in the final analysis, a paternalistic and largely benign institution. Not only is this picture unhistorical, it is unfair to both black and white Americans attempting to understand and come to terms with their history. Most disturbing about the distortions at Ash Lawn is the aura of scholarship surrounding them. Visitors are led to believe that the plantation restoration and historical commentary of docents is based on reliable research. The inaccuracies presented are therefore doubly damaging because of the authenticity of the setting and the authoritativeness of the presentation. The Ash Lawn story is inspirational and flattering to Monroe and to the American self-image, but it is largely inaccurate.

The mythologizing of the past is even more of a problem for historical presentations at theme parks because they influence so many more people. Visitors may have lower expectations that such history will be authoritative, but the impression received in these presentations shape the public vision. At Disney's Experimental Prototype Community of Tomorrow (EPCOT) near Orlando, Florida, the presentation of American history takes a distinctly optimistic tone. EPCOT sets out what can only be described as an American historical fantasy. A multimillion-dollar multimedia light and sound spectacle does much to raise the spirit but little to enrich the public historical knowledge. In the American Adventure, an animatronic figure of black abolitionist Frederick Douglass appeared, floating down an unnamed river (presumably the Mississippi) on a raft, audibly wishing for the end of slavery. The former slave is dressed in a white suit, and in an uncharacteristically conciliatory tone he tells the audience that the best hope for abolition rests with the publication of Harriet Beecher Stowe's antislavery novel *Uncle Tom's Cabin*. At another point, black scientist George Washington Carver is exhibited as a statuesque tribute to American creativity.[38]

That the exhibit does not completely ignore blacks is noteworthy, but the sanitized presentation of a heroic black figure here and there does not convey the black experience, nor does it illustrate the unique importance of race to the development of America. The sole reference to ordinary black people was the depiction of a group of southerners gathered on the front porch of a country store during the Great Depression of the 1930s. The two black characters are stereotypically portrayed, one strumming a banjo and the other laughing in a style reminiscent of Afro-Americans pictured in Disney's 1940s film classic *Song of the South*. Although the presentation seems to change periodically, the problem remains that Disney's America has a happy history in which both whites and blacks are optimistic. The inhumanity of human slavery or racism cannot easily be included.

Even though most understand that Disney is not in the business of scholarly presentation, the power of the message is overwhelming. Historians, for all their research in the last generation, cannot compete with the inspirational majesty of the Disney historical fantasy. Recent scholarship may have encouraged EPCOT's creators to include selected blacks in Disney's vision of America. This vision, however, will not allow the inclusion of the entirety of the black experience. The visitor is inspired but ill informed.

There are similar problems in the presentation of Africa at Busch Gardens in Tampa, Florida. There is no pretense of historical presentation in this mainly zoological park, and we included it in this article only because of its "focus" on Africa. Until recently the park was billed as "The Dark Continent." At shops displaying African wares, there were a number of interesting and informative labels explaining the role of crafts and craftsmen in African religion and culture. Should the visitor overlook these, however, there was almost nothing that illustrated African people and culture. There was an attempt to present national culture in the music-and-dance "Festival of Nations." Yet in a theme park focusing on Africa, it was striking that only the cultures of Europe, Israel, and Mexico were presented; no African Nations were included in the festival. Only twice were black Africans visible to visitors. Blacks made up a small marching band which toured the park, and one black man costumed in "native" dress emerged from an undergrowth-lined shore to startle visitors aboard the passing *African Queen*. The implication is clear: Africa is a land of exotic animals; the important cultures and people are found elsewhere. Although Busch Gardens does not claim to present scholarly history, it does reinforce stereotypes which affect the public historical consciousness.

Even in these theme parks there is evidence of the influence of recent historical scholarship. EPCOT has its few black images, Busch Gardens has its craft labels. All the museums answering our questionnaires indicated a desire to broaden their exhibitions and collections to include material on blacks, yet most had not done so. It is impossible to know whether institutions use limited funds as an excuse for not attempting to expand their holdings. Informal interviews with the staffs at those museums that did not answer our questionnaires were instructive. Some staff members hinted that the politics of including black exhibits at institutions dependent on financial support from white conservative communities is tricky at best. Others told of museum administrations unsympathetic to the idea of a multiracial exhibition policy. By and large, however, it was difficult to expose the attitudes which maintain racial homogeneity in most of the nation's museums. Yet these attitudes persist. Two of the museums that reported having blacks on their staffs, it was discovered, employed those blacks as custodians. Clearly the degree of commitment to meaningful change varies from one institution to another.

In its 1984 report *Museum for a New Century*, the American Association of Museums recommended that museums take strong steps to address the underrepresentation of blacks on professional staffs and in leadership and policy-making positions. Our survey findings support the assertion that museums which hire black professionals are more likely to integrate a multiracial perspective into their presentations and their collections. These museums are also more likely to attract black visitors. Our survey indicates that if institutions committed themselves to the inclusion of black exhibits, the effect could be felt quickly. More than half the institutions surveyed modified a portion of their exhibits at least twice a year. This schedule should allow rapid incorporation of black themes into exhibitions.

The more popular presentations of history in theme parks could be improved dramatically by the inclusion of more recent historical interpretations. The public is very likely to find a focus on people and culture entertaining. The larger problem for those seeking to tell an inspirational American story is how to deal with the historical conflict and contradiction sure to arise from the integration of history. This can be dealt with, however, by building into the story the truth of the ongoing struggle to achieve the American ideal—not a totally happy history, but a hopeful one nonetheless.

In museums, broadening the historical vision of America will provide a more accurate picture of our national past and will bring a new population into the institution, revitalizing these centers of public learning. There is no simple process for accomplishing this. There are financial problems, yes, but, more important, there are problems of resistance to change, especially change which demands a new attitude toward the place of race in the traditional halls of historic preservation. Committed, knowledgeable, and imaginative individuals, both inside and outside the museum, are the most important part of the equation. Much remains to be done.

Although a generation of progress in historical scholarship and exhibit innovation has had an effect, most museums remain bound by traditional collection and exhibition practices. As one respondent put it, "we remain the captives of generations of institutional policies derived from the habit of viewing museums as private preserves of a wealthy white society." Even as the end of the twentieth century approaches, "any other tradition is considered suspect."

Despite this truth, as our study indicates, there are committed individuals working towards meaningful change. Their efforts promise to convey a deeper sense of the complexity of American history and the diversity of the American experience.[39]

NOTES

1. Zora Martin, "Colonial Williamsburg—A Black Perspective," in Susan K. Nichols, ed., *Museum Education Anthology, 1973–1983: Perspectives on Informal Learning A Decade of Roundtable Reports* (Washington, D.C., 1984), 83–85.

2. Thomas A. Greenfield, "Race and Passive Voice at Monticello," *Crisis* 82, no. 4 (1975), 146–47.

3. See James Oliver Horton and Lois E. Horton, *Black Bostonians: Family Life and Community Struggle in the Antebellum North* (New York: Holmes and Meier Publishers, 1979), 118.

4. For example, see William C. Nell, *The Colored Patriots of the American Revolution* (Boston: R. F. Wallcut, 1855). See also Nell's earlier *Services of Colored Americans in the Wars of 1776 and 1812* (Boston, 1851); William Wells Brown, *The Black Man, His Antecedents, His Genius and His Achievements* (New York: T. Hamilton, 1863).

5. Jeffrey C. Stewart and Fath Davis Ruffins, "A Faithful Witness: Afro-American Public History in Historical Perspective, 1828–1984," in Susan Porter Benson, Stephen Brier, and Roy Rosenzweig, eds., *Presenting the Past: Essays on History and the Public* (Philadelphia: Temple University Press, 1986), 307–36; Harold G. Cureau, "The Art Gallery, Museum: Their Availability as Educational Resources in the Historically Negro College," *Journal of Negro Education* 42, no. 4 (1973), 452–61.

6. Jean A. McRae and Joyce E. Latham, "Bicentennial Outlook: The Enriching Black Presence," *Historic Preservation* 27, no. 3 (1975), 10–15.

7. The Moorland Collection was reorganized in 1930 as the Moorland Spingarn collection; see Stewart and Ruffins, "A Faithful Witness."

8. The influence of this educational effort on Afro-American children of the period

and as they grew to maturity during the 1940s and 1950s has not been studied. Perhaps this early education informed the reaction of the black adult community of the 1960s, which was very supportive of its children's efforts to establish black-studies programs in integrated public schools and colleges. It may also have provided an appreciative audience for museums, which in the 1970s and 1980s were starting to focus more attention on the black experience.

9. Cureau, 458–59.

10. Cureau, 459–60.

11. Cureau, 457.

12. James Oliver Horton, "Black Education at Oberlin College: A Controversial Commitment," *The Journal of Negro Education* 54, no. 4 (1985), 477–99. In 1968, Yale University sponsored a major conference on black studies; see Armstead L. Robinson et al., eds., *Black Studies in the University* (New York: Bantam Books, 1969).

13. "Keepers of the Story: Black Museums Preserve and Honor the Afro-American Culture Heritage," *Ebony* 36 (February 1981), 84–86, 88, 90.

14. Caryl March, "A Neighborhood Museum That Works," *Museum News* (October 1968), 11–16.

15. Thomas Hoving, "Branch Out," *Museum News* (September 1968), 16.

16. Ruth Berenson, "Harlem On Everybody's Mind," *National Review*, February 11, 1969, p. 125. This exhibition sought to illustrate the cultural achievements of Harlem residents as they struggled to overcome poverty and its attendant problems. It drew considerable criticism from those who believed that it had no place in an art museum, since it had "not a work of art (unless you include documentary photographs of doubtful quality) in the whole show." The introduction to the show's catalog, which had been written by public high school student Candice Van Ellison, was grammatically flawed and incomplete. Most serious were the charges that the show was anti-Semitic and insulting to the Irish and to Puerto Ricans. New York Mayor John Lindsay, who was a friend of Hoving, claimed the show displayed an "error in judgment." The show also was attacked by some blacks, who dismissed it as showing only the "white man's image" of Harlem.

17. Bernard Friedberg, "Museums Collaborative: A Broker for Cooperation," *Museum News* (April 1974), 20–24; Emily Dennis, "Seminar on Neighborhood Museums," *Museum News* (January 1970), 13–19.

18. David Katzive, "Up Against the Waldorf-Astoria," *Museum News* (September 1970), 12–17.

19. "Development of Urban Museum Centers," *Museum News* (September 1971), 37.

20. Joseph Veach Noble "Drug Scene in New York," *Museum News* (November 1971), 11–15.

21. Penny Bach, "Rites of Passage: A City Celebrates Its Variety," *Museum News* (September–October 1976), 36–42.

22. "Keepers of the Story."

23. "Afro-American Historical and Cultural Museum," handout, July 24, 1985; "New Directions," Afro-American Historical and Cultural Museum brochure, undated.

24. "Boston's African Meeting House: Symbol of Black Hope Since 1806," *History News* (December 1976), 241–42.; Byron Rushing, "Afro-Americana: Defining It, Finding It, Collecting It," *Museum News* (January–February 1982), 33–40.

25. "Boston's African Meeting House"; although the National Park Service provides much of the financing for the Meeting House, the site is administered locally.

26. Joy Ford Austin, "Their Face to the Rising Sun: Trends in the Development of Black Museums," *Museum News* (January–February 1982), 28–32; telephone interview with Joy Ford Austin, October 15, 1986.

27. The Historic New Orleans Collection has sponsored the publication of several books and booklets that concentrate on Afro-American history. Most notable of these are Elsa L. Schneider, ed., *Evidence of the Past: Primary Sources for Louisiana History*, and Ralston Crawford, *Music in the Streets*. They have recently received funds for the publication of a series of books on Louisiana history.

28. The *Tar Heel Junior Historian* is published three times a year by the North Carolina Museum of History and frequently features articles on black state and local history. The Spring 1986 issue, for example, contains an article by Alex Albright, titled "Breaking the Race Barrier: The Navy B-1 Band," on black musicians from North Carolina in the World War II navy.

29. All statistical information cited here is taken from our survey of museums unless otherwise noted.

30. Several historical journals might prove helpful, including *Journal of Negro History* and *Journal of Negro Education*. There are also several regional journals that are very useful, of which *Afro-Americans in New York Life and History* is one of the best. Also of interest is Darlene Clark Hine, ed., *The State of Afro-American History: Past, Present, and Future* (Baton Rouge: Louisiana State University Press, 1985)

31. Other minority visitors included Asians, American Indians, and Hispanics.

32. Rowena Stewart of the Philadelphia Afro-American Museum is attempting to solicit corporate funds to endow her museum for long-range exhibit development and institutional stability.

33. The Colorado State Historical Society uses a timeline to integrate blacks into the history of its region.

34. For an interesting and provocative article on the topic, see Thomas J. Schlereth, "Causing Conflict, Doing Violence," *Museum News* (October 1984), 45–52.

35. Zora Martin Felton, "An Afterword, 1984," in Susan K. Nichols, ed., *Museum Education Anthology* (1984), 85–86. See also the comments of Dennis A. O'Toole in the same article.

36. Zora Martin Felton, "An Afterword, 1984," 85–86.

37. Rex Ellis, "Black Programs: We've Learned a Great Deal Since the Summer of '79," *Colonial Williamsburg News* (July 1986), 5.

38. For an interesting look at EPCOT, see Alexander Wilson, "Walt Disney Returns Us to the Future," *Socialist Review* (August–September 1986), 112–19.

39. For a radical examination of contemporary museums, see Carol Duncan and Alan Wallach, "The Museum of Modern Art as Late Capitalist Ritual: An Iconographic Analysis," *Marxist Perspective* (Winter 1978), 28–51.

Tools, Technologies, and Contexts: Interpreting the History of American Technics

10

Joseph J. Corn

Enthusiasm for high technology characterizes our era. Spurred by anxiety over the declining competitiveness of American industry, particularly compared with the technical sophistication of countries like Japan, West Germany, and South Korea, this interest has focused attention not only on present and future policy regarding technology but also on past practice. More and more people have become interested in the history of technological change. Nowhere is this more apparent than in the rapidly increasing numbers of museums and historic sites that are preserving technical artifacts and interpreting them to the public.

Institutions exhibiting historic technologies vary greatly. They range from such vast facilities as the Smithsonian Institution's National Air and Space Museum (NASM), visited by thousands every day, to tiny one-room operations that annually attract a few hundred visitors to see their clocks, Victrolas, radios, or firefighting apparatus. There are public institutions, such as the California State Railroad Museum in Sacramento and the Chicago Museum of Science and Industry, and private ones, such as Philadelphia's Franklin Institute Science Museum and Mystic Seaport in Connecticut. Some specialize in the history of a particular technology or machine, such as the American Precision Museum (machine tools) in Windsor, Vermont, and the Museum of American Textile History in Lawrence, Massachusetts (textile machinery), while others interpret machinery along with a broad array of material culture, such as the Smithsonian's National Museum of American History (NMAH) and the Henry Ford Museum in Dearborn, Michigan. Some, like the Mercer Museum in Doylestown, Pennsylvania, with its broad collection of nineteenth-century tools and craft artifacts, illuminate a bygone era of work and production; others, such as the Computer Museum in Boston, devote their collecting and educational energies to recent history. Finally, while most of these institutions are traditional indoor museums, a few, such as Colonial Williamsburg in Virginia and Old World Wisconsin, actually use historical tools and equipment (usually replicas) in a re-created historical environment, seeking to entice and educate the visitor with so-called living history.[1]

Whatever their size or focus, these institutions invite one to scrutinize the tool-making propensity of human beings. Their exhibits bring us face to face with *Homo faber,* man the maker. Because the tools and machines they exhibit were constructed by human beings, we look at them with certain questions in mind: Why was a particular device invented and developed? How was it made and why? What was the context in which the object was used? How did it influence the culture in which it was adopted? It is rarely possible to answer these questions by looking at an object alone; even close scrutiny and handling will not answer some of them. For no matter how assiduously one tries to "read" an artifact's meaning or listen to what it "says" about itself and the past, one inevitably requires further information, some interpretation, usually from sources beyond the object.[2] Although the object is a text of sorts, we can seldom read that text very well without having some additional context. Indeed, in the case of tools or devices that are wholly unfamiliar, such as many hand tools that are no longer used, the object is virtually meaningless without a context.

This essay examines the ways museums and historic sites in the United States contextualize or interpret their exhibits of technology. Before beginning, I'll enter a few caveats regarding the scope of my remarks. Because of my long-standing interest in the history of transportation, I have given more emphasis to museums treating this subject than any other.[3] The essay also reflects my greater familiarity with institutions on the two coasts, East and West. Finally, my remarks must also be taken as those of one who has been involved with museums as an occasional curator and consultant but who is primarily a museum-loving academic and not a museum professional. My aim is to offer a critique of recent presentations on the history of technology in museums and not a complete account, either of the history of such museums or of their recent exhibition record.[4]

In the first section of the essay, I identify four styles of interpretation or presentation that are commonly encountered in such museums. I call these styles the internalist, the celebratory, the social historical, and the cultural historical. Each possesses its own strengths and weaknesses, and I treat some of these in my analysis. My four categories are meant to be heuristic aids to thinking about museum practice, not hard and fast definitions. There is considerable overlap among the various interpretive styles, and two or more are usually present in any single exhibition. In the second section of the essay, I examine some specific problems faced by museums interpreting the history of technology: what to do with very large technical artifacts; how to explain computers and other black-box technologies; and how to convey the insights of social history in the technology museum. The third and final section of the essay briefly compares the history of technology presented through exhibitions by museum curators with that written by academics.

Styles of Interpretation in the Exhibiting of Technical Artifacts

Although museums have definitely entered the age of interpretation, some exhibitions still leave artifacts to "speak for themselves." Occasionally, this works well, as in the National Museum of American History's "1876" exhibit, installed in the 1881 Arts and Industries Building at the Smithsonian.[5] This exhibit, mounted to commemorate the nation's bicentennial, re-creates some of the nineteenth-century exhibits of tools, machines, and other products shown at the Philadelphia centennial fair. Because such industrial exhibitions were not labeled or interpretated, the lack of any texts in the re-creation is historically accurate. It means, however, that visitors see many objects that they cannot identify. Hence visitors learn little from many of the individual objects in the re-created exposition, but from the plethora of material on display they can learn much about the variety and quantity of products in industrializing America, the pride contemporaries took in technological advance, the aesthetic of abundance, and the way industrial expositions encouraged these other factors.[6]

In most museum settings, however, the display of artifacts without interpretation considerably reduces the educational potential of exhibitions, with the public inevitably being the loser. Most museums today realize this and interpret their artifacts on display according to one or more of four interpretive styles.

Internalist. The traditional way of exhibiting technical artifacts, one that is still very common, may be called the internalist style. Objects are displayed according to their design, function, performance, or operating characteristics and without regard for intellectual, economic, social, political, technical, and other external influences that might have shaped them or, in turn, might have been stimulated by their existence. In other words, this style of interpretation presents the internal history of a class of artifacts, such as steam engines or washing machines. When done well, and particularly when machines can be shown operating, internalist exhibits help visitors to understand machinery *qua* machinery and to appreciate its technical evolution.[7] Often, however, internalist interpretations lack rigor and thoughtfulness and are little more than antiquarian. They provide a chronology of machines, accompanied perhaps by some genealogy as to how various devices are related to one another, but no true historical account that explains *why* they came into being when they did, looked like they did, or were used as they were.[8]

This antiquarian emphasis is most commonly found in smaller museums, particularly those focused on a single genre of technical artifact. The Briggs Cunningham Automotive Museum in Costa Mesa, California, is a 30,000-square-foot facility housing a moderate-size but important collection of vehicles gathered by former race-car driver, auto builder, and playboy Briggs Cunningham.[9] The cars are displayed as if they were parked on a street. While this is traditional in car museums, the Cunningham museum has allowed more space around the vehicles so that visitors may inspect or photograph them. The museum has even provided benches on which one can sit while contemplating some of the more outstanding examples of automotive machinery. Yet for those who are not auto buffs, the interpretation provides little help in focusing contemplation. The single label for each car, affixed to a pedestal in front or to the side of the vehicle, generally confines itself to reciting the year, model type, number of cylinders in the engine, horsepower, and kind of transmission.[10]

On the rare occasions when the texts at the Briggs Cunningham Museum go beyond statistical data, they merely hint at broader cultural interpretations and raise more questions than they answer. For example, the text for a 1929 Stutz four-passenger speedster provocatively notes that the car was "known as the safety-Stutz" because of its low double-drop frame, large hydraulic four-wheel brakes with vacuum boost, safety glass, and "noback" unit for hill holding. None of these features is defined or explained, but, this aside, the text leaves one with a number of questions. Was this the first car to have all of these features, and was it designed with safety foremost? Or did an imaginative advertising copywriter simply came up with a name, Safety Stutz, to sell the speedster? And was it in fact a safe car to drive? More important, what was there about the 1920s that prompted this concern for safety: Public opinion? An emerging consumer movement? Or the shakeout among automobile producers that significantly reduced the number of competitors? No other text in the museum even mentions safety. Because the interpretation of the Safety Stutz is so lacking in context, it teases visitors and ultimately insults their intelligence.

The internalist style dominates in automobile museums, as well as in many other institutions dealing with technology, for a couple of reasons. One is money. Many museums struggle along as nonprofit institutions and lack the funds to hire the kind of curators and historians who might move interpretation in other directions.[11] A second is that the individuals running such specialty museums often do not see their existing style of interpretation as a problem. These men (and virtually all of them are men) have frequently spent their lives working with or around the cars, trains, weapons, machine tools, or other kinds of artifacts to which the museum is devoted. Long experience and familiarity inevitably colors their intellectual approach to the objects under their custody. For car buffs like John W. Burgess, director of the Briggs Cunningham Museum and, as the museum's brochure notes, a "well known name in racing," the vehicles may well speak for themselves. Indeed, many of the men involved with such museums believe that to interpret the artifacts would be to lose the objectivity which is assumed to attach to recitations of engineering specifications or performance statistics.

The predominantly male practitioners of internalist history, by reifying the formal and performance aspects of automobiles or other kinds of technical artifacts, unconsciously perpetuate male power and domination. Their exhibits tend to exclude and mystify women, who are less likely than men to be interested either in specifics about horsepower and cylinder bores or in interpretations built around technical milestones and performance statistics. Such exhibitions implicitly validate physical power and competitiveness, qualities that traditionally reflect more the society of men than of women. Unless museums pay more attention to the imaginative, affective, and social aspects of the human-machine experience and unless they teach visitors how things work and why, they will not transcend the gender bias inherent in the internalist approach to the history of technology.

Celebratory.   Another interpretive approach commonly encountered in museums dealing with the history of technology is what I call the celebratory style. It links objects to themes of individual genius, national superiority, and technical progress. While the Briggs Cunningham Museum avoids such themes, at least at an explicit level, they may be encountered at other automotive museums and at many museums of technology generally.[12]

The celebratory style tends to be uncritical and usually misleading regarding the history of the particular technologies involved. Sometimes it flows from broad-based historical myths, such as the notion that invention is an act of solitary, inspired genius. Many exhibits celebrate the inventor of some device with a reverence that obscures a historical reality in which such breakthroughs seldom were the exclusive triumph of any single individual, nation, or culture. The celebratory style also dominates in exhibits treating the history of a particular company, especially if that firm sponsored the exhibition. The exhibits at the John Deere visitor center in Moline, Illinois, for example, are informative on the history of agricultural implements but distort the historical record by overemphasizing the role of the sponsoring firm, its founders, and its employees.[13]

In the noncorporate arena, the celebratory style frequently appears in extreme form in aerospace museums. Many of the exhibits at the best of these, the Smithsonian Institution's National Air and Space Museum, are still unabashed celebrations of flight. Indeed, historian Michael McMahon, in a 1981 review for *Technology and Culture*, described the museum as "largely a giant advertisement for air and space technology." [14]

The museum's "Milestones of Flight" gallery typifies this celebratory stance. The very name suggests that the history of flying machines is simply a path, always heading in the same direction, along which clear milestones of progress may be discerned. Embodying this Whiggish conception in architectural form, the "Milestones" gallery occupies the museum's most dramatic space, directly in the center of the building and rising six stories high, with one wall entirely of glass. In this space hang the Wright brothers' *Kitty Hawk Flyer* of 1903 along with Lindbergh's *Spirit of St. Louis* of 1927 and Chuck Yeager's Bell X-1 that in 1947 became the first plane to crack the sound barrier. On the floor are a few more milestone artifacts, such as the Apollo 11 command module that landed on the moon in 1969.

These craft are indisputably important in the history of flight, and the concept of milestones (or, better, of technological firsts) is not without some validity. Yet by isolating these few artifacts from those to which they are closely related and by not connecting them to the various military, economic, political, and social contexts that shaped them, the museum elevates these machines to veritable icons. It unabashedly celebrates them without raising any historical questions about their significance, let alone about the many antecedent failures and successes that made them possible.

Indeed, one of these failures sneaks into the "Milestones" gallery anyway, a backhanded testament to the inevitable political dimension of exhibits. The failure is symbolized by the 10-foot-long, steam-powered, unmanned *Aerodrome #5*, built in 1896 by Samuel Langley, a leading astronomer and secretary of the Smithsonian Institution. This unmanned craft flew nearly three-quarters of a mile on its longest sortie over the Potomoc, but this hardly constituted a milestone. For when Langley scaled up the machine to man-carrying size in 1903, the enlarged craft failed twice in its flight trials, the second time just a few days before the Wright brothers, at Kitty Hawk, North Carolina, succeeded brilliantly. Langley's failure was more than bad timing. His machine lacked an adequate control system and was unworkable in other ways.

Why, then, is *Aerodrome #5* in the "Milestones Gallery" at all? Politics. Although Langley's machines were not on the main line of aeronautical development, he did imprint his disappointment on subsequent Smithsonian exhibition policy. Until his death in 1906, he maintained that his 1903 machine was the first heavier-than-air craft that was *capable* of flying, a position his successors at the Smithsonian held for many more years. Needless to say, this angered the Wrights, who, although they wanted to give their *Flyer* to the Smithsonian, did not want it interpreted as the second machine capable of flight, even though it had been the first actually to fly. Because of the Smithsonian's position, the Wrights lent their plane to the Science Museum in London, where it remained until 1948, when Langley and most of the other principals to the Wright-Smithsonian controversy were long dead. None of these facts are revealed in the museum's labeling of *Aerodrome #5*, nor Langley's pursuit of his aeronautical research with a fifty thousand dollar grant from the War Department, arranged through a close friend.[15] The interpretation, then, ignores the significant political dimensions of the Langley story, aggrandizes his contribution to aviation history, and unwittingly diminishes the very meaning of the concept of *milestone* as an organizing theme for the gallery.

Other exhibits at the museum are not as blatant in their celebratory mindset, although one notices throughout the galleries a reluctance to be critical of aerospace development or to say anything unfavorable about flight or the aerospace industry. Such topics as the deliberate destruction of aircraft by engineers to gain data on structural safety or the emergence of sophisticated accident-investigation techniques, for example, both of which have provided valuable data for the design process, might instructively be dealt with in exhibits, though to be sure some of the relevant artifacts—pieces of wreckage, say—would be upsetting. Yet by virtually ignoring such subjects, the museum lines up ideologically as a promoter rather than an interpreter of flight. Just as the airline industry historically has avoided any discussion of safety in public and even today deploys a kind of doublespeak to avoid mentioning such words as *crash* or *accident* on board their planes, the museum, too, eschews an objective and critical voice on the subject.

Many factors contribute to the celebratory style, but three may be mentioned. First and most obviously, despite a century of trenchent philosophical and historical criticism of the idea, many Americans still equate technological advance with social progress. When a museum celebrates a machine in its collection or praises its inventors and builders, it reflects and perpetuates the myths of progress held by the general population. A second factor favoring the celebratory style flows from the significant support given museums by corporations with business interests in the field represented by the museum's artifacts.[16] Lockheed's or Grumman's donation of artifacts to the National Air and Space Museum does not necessarily mean they have influenced what appears in the interpretive texts. But such donations do affect museum managers, who tend to be sensitive to the perspectives and perceived needs of their aerospace-industry patrons. Because managers desire to continue good relations with such donors, they have fostered an interpretive climate that ensures that corporate and institutional sponsors are not offended. Whether the maintenance of such a climate requires outright censorship by curators or whether friendly persuasion suffices is not clear. What is certain, however, is that museums that focus on a narrow subject, particularly in the aerospace field, are probably more sensitive to the interests of their corporate donors than are museums that interpret a broader spectrum of objects.[17]

In aerospace museums there is often a third impetus to the celebratory style:

a desire to promote aerospace activities. This stems from the crusading zeal which has long been a part of the culture of flight. Many of the curatorial and administrative staff of such institutions (at NASM, fortunately, a decreasing number in recent years) flew for the military, worked as aerospace engineers, or held some other position in the broader aerospace effort. After entering the museum field, they tend to embrace the same proflight view as their colleagues who still work in the field. They are passionately airminded, as interested in the future of flight as they are in the history of the activity.[18] Indeed, the subject of aerospace probably generates a larger community of interest between those who interpret it and those who manufacture and use the artifacts than any other technological subject. These facts help explain why the directors of the National Air and Space Museum have included a former astronaut, engineer, space scientist, and fighter pilot and why the museum's interpretation historically has been so friendly to the aerospace industry and cause.

Social Historical. To academic observers, the celebratory and antiquarian styles of interpretation often seem uncritical and lacking in sophistication. The approaches most congruent with academic scholarship, using similar data and asking similar questions, are what I call the social-historical and the cultural-historical styles of interpretation. Shaped by the political upheavals of the 1960s and by developments in the social sciences, the new social history emphasizes the study of social groups and social structures, often employing quantitative methods. With an often explicit political motivation, it has also focused attention on groups heretofore ignored by historians and disadvantaged by society, such as women, blacks, and the working classes. Carried over into the museum, the new social history has sensitized curators to the diversity of American society and to the dangers of characterizing large segments of the population under such rubrics as *American* or *middle class*. It has also, as we shall see, altered the way technological artifacts are presented in exhibits.

A simultaneous trend, influenced by the same political developments as well as by the emergence of the new social history, has revived and given new meaning to cultural history. Using the anthropologist's broad definition of culture—all that a people think, do, and make—along with many of the anthropologist's tools and concepts, historians of culture have stretched traditional canons to bring heretofore neglected topics into their professional ken, such as sport, drinking and diet, etiquette, leisure activities, sexual behavior, and parades and other traditional rituals. Although much of this work might also be characterized as social history, here I make a distinction between work rooted in the specific study of particular social groups, which I call social history, and work that is more concerned with people's values, beliefs, symbol systems, and patterns of behavior, which I call cultural history. Although some exhibitions of technology draw upon the new social history, more often they are influenced by the new cultural history.

Social history has been most influential and successful in those institutions devoted in whole or in part to interpreting specific historical sites. Because they usually build their interpretations around artifacts surviving from a particular locale—including structures, such as factories, mills, and warehouses —they benefit handsomely from the social historian's ability to describe and understand discrete, identifiable populations, whether they be artisans, tradesmen, migrants, voters, consumers, or families. Exhibits rooted in some identifiable community are more able effectively to take into account patterns of community organization, social structure, and social dynamics.

At the Hagley Museum, located on the former site of the du Pont gunpowder works on the Brandywine River outside Wilmington, Delaware, the 1981 exhibition "Worker's World: The Industrial Village and the Company Town" used the museum's existing industrial buildings and historic structures, along with photographs and re-created boarders' rooms, to evoke the life of industrial workers from 1800 to 1920.[19] Walking through the various buildings and furnished rooms, visitors experienced the difference between the Spartan accommodations of a worker, the ample abode of a foreman, and the elegance of the mansion built by E. I. du Pont in 1803 and lived in by five generations of his family. In the restored Brandywine Manufacturers' Sunday School, visitors could also imagine what leisure was like in this nineteenth-century industrial village.

Because many of the structures in which black powder was manufactured are still in place on the site, along with some of the machinery used in the process, Hagley could effectively address not only the technical history pertinent to such artifacts but also social themes, such as industrial labor relations, class conflict, and work culture, all with reference to known individuals. Such topics, illuminated by the work of social historians in recent years, are difficult to interpret if all one has are apparatus, engines, or industrial machinery. Artifacts alone, as usually seen in an indoor museum, inevitably appear mute and impersonal. They seldom even hint at the social and cultural dynamics in which they at once time figured. At Hagley, however, the survival of the physical environment in which the machines were actually used, abused, and literally fought over, helps bring the worker's world to life and make an artifact-based social history both possible and accessible.

Not surprisingly, when "Worker's World" was packaged as a traveling show, the buildings and other traces of the natural habitat of Brandywine manufacture stayed behind. The traveling exhibit consisted of various small artifacts, such as hand tools and personal memorabilia, along with photographs and other graphic materials.[20] In this configuration the show lost much of its power. Distant from the physical remains of the worker's world and without the powerful presence of industrial artifacts in their natural setting, the traveling exhibit evoked the long-gone workers poorly. It tried, by using many large photographic blowups of work groups, buildings, and other images to simulate the work environment. Yet the photographic simulation, increasingly a cliché among exhibit designers, failed as an aid to recovering the historical experience of work. Unlike an old work site, which easily can become a stage for the re-creation or evocation of the life of work in the past, even if only in one's imagination, the photographic simulation tended to translate into one more modern bit of packaging to make the exhibit look good. That the well-illustrated book on the subject of the exhibition more effectively evoked the worker's world than did the traveling version of the show (though it, too, could not duplicate the experience of visiting Hagley and seeing the original exhibit) emphasizes the difficulty of dealing with the social history of technology in the traditional indoor museum.[21]

Although traditional museums have found it difficult effectively to incorporate social history into their technology exhibits, they have had little difficulty in providing a cultural context for their displays. In fact, the cultural historical style is today the most common and certainly the most successful style of interpretation.

Cultural Historical. Distinguished from the social historical by its broader topical interests and by its lack of focus on identifiable groups, the cultural-historical style has been adaptable to widely diverse subject matter and to museums of many different kinds. A small exhibit on agricultural technology at the Haggin Museum in Stockton, California, a combined art and history museum, typifies the cultural-historical style.

The exhibit honors Benjamin W. Holt, a Stockton man who perfected the Caterpillar tractor, but the installation is anything but celebratory. Rather, the texts, graphics, photographs, and selection of smaller artifacts set two large objects—a 1918 Holt Caterpillar tractor and a 1904 Haines-Houser combined harvester (also manufactured in Stockton)—into a broad cultural context. Besides explaining to visitors how these two large machines worked (a too often neglected topic in museums) and what distinguished them from previous tractors and harvesters, the exhibit clarifies some of the cultural and ecological reasons for Stockton's emergence as a center of technological innovation in agriculture. Holt's experiments with alternatives to wheeled tractors grew out of the inability of farmers to work the soft but extremely rich peat soil of the Sacramento–San Joaquim Delta. Horses, even when wearing wide, snowshoe-like "Tule shoes," sank into the earth, as did conventional tractors. In a city possessed of strong machine- and engine-building industries, called into being by Stockton's position as a river port for steamboats, mechanical experiments like Holt's were not unusual. And once he got his Caterpillar tractor into production, the heavy hauling requirements of Central Valley agriculture and of large water projects, both booming in turn-of-the-century California, guaranteed a regional market. In short, through a multifaceted approach to its major artifact, the exhibits manage to teach a great deal, not only about the Holt tractor but also about the region's economic life and culture.[22]

Whereas the Haggin Museum employs a cultural approach to interpret two large agricultural machines, Philadelphia's Franklin Institute Science Museum's exhibit "Shipbuilding on the Delaware" offers a cultural interpretation of a topic where the key artifact, a ship, could not fit into the museum. In its stead, a varied collection of models, naval architect's tools, photographs, dioramas, and other artifacts brilliantly relates the rise and fall of shipbuilding in the Greater Philadelphia area. The exhibit opens windows on the economic history of the region, the history of the ethnic groups that became shipbuilders, and the techniques of ship design and construction. "Shipbuilding on the Delaware" is also of interest in that it offers hands-on demonstrations of scientific principles relevant to ship design, such as buoyancy, center of gravity, and wave motion. These demonstrations, accessible and comprehensible to virtually anybody, further enrich an already excellent historical exhibit.

The National Museum of American History exhibition "Edison: Lighting a Revolution," opened in 1979, interprets in the cultural-historical style the beginnings of electric light and power. The exhibit displays a wide range of artifacts, including Thomas A. Edison's laboratory notebooks; the devices that comprised the "technical base" for electric power, such as batteries, generators, meters, motors, and lamps; a model of the Pearl Street Generating Station in New York; early electric consumer appliances; decorative pieces of aluminum produced by electricity; and many other objects, along with the traditional photographs and other graphics. The interpretation emphasizes that inventors, technologists, engineers, scientists, and entrepreneurs are often different people, each functioning in a different subculture with dissimilar goals and rewards. For instance, although electrical inventors rarely preserved experimental apparatus or prototype devices, some electrical promoters and entrepreneurs did collect and display relics from the new field, such as light bulbs. Exhibitions of such devices at the great industrial expositions, such the Chicago World's Fair of 1893, played a part in selling the public on the new technology. By alluding to such promotional exhibits, as well as to predictions about the future of electricity and other kinds of non-technical behavior, the NMAH show offers a valuable lesson on the relationship between culture and technological change. New technologies do not just come along when the time is ripe; they must be promoted and sold.[23]

Special Problems Interpreting the History of Technology in Museums

No matter the style with which museums interpret their technological artifacts, they face special problems. In "Edison: Lighting a Revolution," for example, the NMAH faced the problem of the very large artifact. Although electric-power generation was key to the lighting revolution, the museum could not exhibit a generating plant—it was simply too large. Many technological artifacts, particularly those developed since the Industrial Revolution, are similarly huge. Although many of our newer museums are also large, they have not grown enough to keep up with the increasing scale of technical artifacts. If they are successfully to interpret large artifacts, however, they must evolve better strategies and methods by which to present these objects; otherwise, they will by default become museums of small technology.

When objects are merely big, such as locomotives, museums can move a few examples into their galleries and at least suggest the history of the whole genre. If specimens are as significant as, say, the NMAH's *John Bull*, built in England in 1831 by Robert Stephenson and imported by Robert Stevens for the Camden and Amboy Railroad, or the Henry Ford Museum's Union Pacific *Big Boy* locomotive, an example of the largest steam engine ever built, the visitor can ignore the relative distortion of the railroad story created by having so few exemplars and rejoice over the mere survival of a few important machines. Inevitably, such large objects dominate their setting and imply an interpretive importance not necessarily equivalent to their size, but a much greater problem is the difficulty of contextualizing such behemoths. Their sheer visceral impact tends to upstage smaller artifacts in the vicinity, while any interpretation— whether internal or contextual—tends to get lost in their shadow.

After all, these engines are customarily exhibited in isolation from the monumental infrastructure that supported their use. In museums, locomotives usually are installed on a short piece of track without the network of cuts, bridges, tunnels, and viaducts that enable such machines to become a revolutionary mode of transportation. Locomotives in museums are also displayed without the coaling stations, water towers, roundhouses, or turntables that were essential to their operation and were part of the steam transport system.[24] I am not suggesting that museums create period-room settings for their steam engines, yet more effort must be made to contextualize these large machines.[25]

When the technological objects are bigger and heavier than locomotives and cannot be easily moved, let alone shoehorned into a museum, the problems are compounded. This arises with ships and virtually all the artifacts of civil engineering, such as bridges, tunnels, dams, and power plants. Museums wishing to interpret these artifacts have two options: to replicate the object in miniature or move the museum to the object.

The use of scale models of large artifacts in exhibits is very common, yet the practice has its critics. Some museum people believe only authentic historic artifacts should be exhibited and that a model, however faithful to the original, does not qualify as the real thing and therefore should not be displayed. This view seems unduly narrow, especially in the history of technology. Sometimes models are themselves historic artifacts—for example patent models and many ship models, which were often constructed as part of the design process. Similarly, the 1929 model of Edison's first generating station, displayed in NMAH's "Lighting a Revolution" and built on the occasion of the fiftieth anniversary of the electric light, had earned legitimacy as an historic object by the 1970s.[26] Even recently constructed models, I believe, have a place in museums, for they make exhibitions about large-scale machines or structures that much more educational. "Building Brooklyn Bridge, The Design and Construction, 1867–1883," another recent NMAH exhibition, commissioned models depicting some of John A. Roebling's earlier bridges, along with some illuminating the construction of the Brooklyn Bridge itself. Without these models, the original artifacts on display—engineering drawings, plans, photographs, and historical ephemera connected with the construction of Roebling's masterpiece—would have been less intelligible and certainly less interesting, especially for the nonspecialist. The models enabled visitors to visualize more easily the structure of the bridge and, in the case of a cross-sectional model of a caisson, permitted a glimpse of the "inside" of bridge construction.[27]

The second choice for interpreting the very large artifact is to bring the museum to the object. In recent years, increasing numbers of museums have been built at or in large artifacts, such as mills, factories, or ships. Lowell Industrial Park's use of the Boott Textile Mill Complex typifies the recent move toward interpreting industrial history *in situ,* using the original factory or plant environment as the museum. In the cavernous, low-ceiling space of the Boott Mill's weave room, for example, an operating loom at once conveys the noise, dinginess, and generally horrible conditions of the turn-of-the-century textile operative better than any number of looms, even if operating, could ever do in a pristine gallery space. The authentic, unrestored mill setting stands as a sobering corrective to an image of the past that has been sanitized of all grime, danger, and lingering echoes of labor.[28]

The expense of preserving the large artifacts of industrial civilization, even of simply stabilizing their decay, is staggering. In Lowell the mill and canal complex would not have been saved without the support of the federal government, whose National Park Service administers the historical park and has supervised the work of interpretation with sensitivity. In Long Beach, California, Wrather Port Properties, Ltd. has preserved two other large artifacts, the ocean liner *Queen Mary* and the gigantic flying boat the *Spruce Goose.* Yet the corporation's "Queen Mary and Spruce Goose Entertainment complex" demonstrates some of the problems that follow when interpretation is placed in the service of profit.[29]

The *Queen Mary,* launched in 1934, is the only surviving example of those great liners that once whisked passengers from Europe to America at more than thirty miles per hour. At 1,019 feet long and weighing 81,237 tons, the ship is still one of the largest moving artifacts ever built. Today it is permanently moored in its own small lagoon in Long Beach harbor. The ship is at once a hotel, a convention center, a museum, and a prime tourist attraction, part of what Wrather Port Properties, Ltd. bills as an "entertainment complex." Visitors to the hotel may spend a night in a former first-class stateroom on the ship and take their meals in one of the four restaurants on board. Most visitors, however, come merely to take the "Queen Mary Shipwalk," a self-guided tour of the ship and its exhibits.

Walking the decks of the gigantic liner evokes the sensations and experiences of ocean travel better than any book or conventional museum exhibit. Only a real voyage would be more instructive. The "Shipwalk" also exhibits well-done restorations of first-class, cabin-class, and tourist-class staterooms, plus various social rooms, including a first-class drawing room and a wonderful first-class children's playroom. All combine to give a sense of how distinctions of rank and wealth operated even amid the privileged group that sailed on transatlantic liners in their prejet heyday. Other exhibits interpret the ship's wartime service, when its posh furnishings and decorations were removed for the duration so that it could serve as a troop transport. These exhibits are handled professionally: the texts are informative, and manikins attired in civilian and Cunard White Star Line dress and uniforms give the various cabin settings and spaces further authenticity.

At the technical heart of the giant liner, however, in the engine room, interpretation and information give way to entertainment, and very poor entertainment at that. Visitors are subjected to a silly and totally unhistorical sound and light show dealing with an imaginary near collision on the high seas. As the cavernous and machinery-filled space darkens and the show begins, British-accented voices come over loudspeakers, warning of an impending collision. Spotlights flash on some of the engine controls, bells begin to ring, fake steam escapes randomly behind the audience, and a few steam valves spin wildly, as if operated by ghosts. An anonymous voice barks commands: "Full steam ahead," "Hard to port." "Aye, aye, sir," choruses an anxious voice in response. But in barely a minute, a happy ending: the collision is avoided and the show is over.

From the look on the faces of the people with whom I visited the *Queen,* this little drama failed as entertainment. More importantly, it taught one nothing about how more than eighty thousand tons of ship could be pushed through wind and wave at nearly the speed of an automobile. It also ignored the men who worked the machinery and their real worries—forget any thoughts of collision—as they sweated through arduous shifts in oppressive heat. Worst of all, the show gave a wholly false impression of the dangers of ocean travel. It ignored the liner's exemplary safety record: the *Queen* completed 1,001 voyages during its active career, steaming millions of miles with only one tragic incident. While voyaging in convoy at night under a blackout and radio silence during World War II, the ship accidentally hit a British destroyer which was out of formation and sliced the warship in two with serious loss of life. But even had the sound and light show been based on this true-to-life incident, one could fault an interpretation built around such an exceptional occurrence.

The occasionally frivolous and ahistorical interpretation aside, one leaves the *Queen Mary* feeling that the quest for profit need not be wholly antithetical to respect for the historical artifact. Visiting Wrather Port Properties' second attraction, however, is another story. The *Spruce Goose,* the two hundred-ton all-wood flying boat built during World War II by former movie mogul and air racer Howard Hughes, is interpreted in the most unrestrained celebratory style imaginable. The plane itself sits in a large domed structure, in semidarkness and lighted by luminous spots as if it were a priceless gem. In the texts around the craft, Hughes becomes a virtual god, an aviation visionary without peers or predecessors. The reality was otherwise. Hughes shared his era's preoccupation with large flying boats as the best means for intercontinental air transport, although by the late 1930s the eventual dominance of land planes in this activity could already be glimpsed. When it made a brief flight low over the water in 1947, Hughes' gigantic plane was already obsolete. None of this, however, is suggested by the hagiographical commentary.

The management of Wrather Port Properties, Ltd. is less interested in serious history than in making money, and to this end it has installed beside the plane what it calls Time Voyager. Billed as "a totally unique experience so breathtakingly real, that you believe that you are actually traveling through time," Time Voyager is in fact merely a slightly updated amusement-park ride. It has vibrating seats, electronic sound effects, projected images, and costumed flight attendants who perform some simple dance steps. Those who rode the Time Voyager with me appeared bored and somewhat mystified over the point of the whole thing. For besides the time lost experiencing the attraction, nothing about it suggested time travel. To an audience that knows how realistically films can depict the future, the hokey production did not live up to its billing.

It may not matter that much how well gigantic objects like the *Spruce Goose* or the *Queen Mary* are contextualized, for visitors easily understand what they are. The ship is clearly a ship, floating there in the water, and strolling its corridors and decks makes clear its opulence and its purpose as a carrier of passengers. Some technical artifacts, so-called black-box technologies, are not so easily understood simply by looking. The computer is the archetypal example. The exterior of a computer offers virtually no clue as to the machine's purpose or potentials. Interpreting this new genre of technology is the second problem faced by museums that requires consideration.

What interests us about computers is primarily the way they are insinuating themselves into our daily lives, work routines, and even thought processes, not to mention their centrality to industrial production, consumer goods, and military weaponry. These social and cultural aspects of the computer revolution and the information age have prompted many museums to install or to undertake planning for exhibitions on computers. Yet the challenge of making such exhibits historically meaningful is daunting. Although the outpouring of published material on the social and cultural aspects of the computer revolution is immense, no museum to my knowledge has yet grappled successfully with these social and cultural themes. The one museum devoted entirely to explicating the history of computation, for example, the relatively new Computer Museum in Boston, essentially ignores such issues. It displays its historic computing equipment well enough but gives visitors no sense whatsoever of the scope or limits of the ongoing computer revolution.[30]

Part of the problem with computers in a museum is the general one of how to provide social and cultural context. This can be done through texts, of course, but if artifacts cannot help tell the story, why do an exhibit? Yet exhibitions about computers may be poor vehicles for illuminating their cultural consequences. This is true in part because the computer is much more opaque and inscrutable than most other museum objects. A person looking at an ocean liner, fire engine, or metal-working lathe can glean certain understandings—or at least make certain informed guesses—about what the object was designed to do, what it did, and even how well it performed its intended task, even by looking at the nonoperating machine. This is not true of a computer. Looking at a IBM 1401, for example, an all-transistorized machine that in 1958 was the first to sell well commercially, an observer can tell nothing about what it actually did or how fast it performed its actions. To be sure, a visitor to a museum encountering an unlabeled peavey or a froe, implements once used by lumbermen and by barrel makers, respectively, might be equally puzzled. Indeed, the average person would probably be more likely to guess that the computer was a computer than to guess the function of the two older implements. Yet once one knows that the peavey was used in lumbering, visual scrutiny of the object can provide more information, such as clues as to how the tool was used by woodcutters. This is not true of the computer; knowing that it was used by an insurance company, say, provides no clues about what it did for the firm, let alone how it transacted those operations.

The essential difference between the computer and most if not all precomputer technologies is that what one sees is much less important than what one does not see. It is not just that all computers look about the same on the outside. The computer's insides, too, are not visually revealing, even to an expert. This is because the heart of the machine, or, better, its brain, is for all intents and purposes invisible. We cannot see the programming code, embodied mainly in the computer's software, that configures the machine as a word processor, number cruncher, inventory monitor, design aid, or any of a host of other devices. All we can see are the tapes, disks, or floppies on which the program code resides. But looking at such artifacts directly, without a computer and the mediation of a cathode-ray tube or printer, is uninformative in the extreme. Unlike the peavey, which *is* informative to look at, the program that gives a computer life is not. To the extent, then, that computers are defined by their software, they are without much meaning, especially if exhibited in the traditional way: just sitting mute and inoperative on the gallery floor.

It follows that computers must run (or be run by their software) in a history exhibit if visitors are to learn much more about them than their size, color, and external configuration. The Computer Museum has installed a whole gallery full of interactive personal-computer (PC) exhibits, but these machines illuminate present-day computer potentials, not those of the past. The museum does not operate any of its historical computers.[31]

Paradoxically, it may not matter *which* computers museums run because of another unusual trait of these machines: they are by definition simulative devices. Their programs are symbolic constructs, always simulating some kind of other reality. This opens up an interesting interpretive possibility and problem. If the historic reality one seeks to interpret is itself a simulation and if one's re-created simulation is indistinguishable from the original, what happens to the line between simulation and reality, between artifact and interpretation? Does it matter at all if one displays the "real" thing? Consider a hypothetical case in which a museum wants to exhibit one of the first computer games, Space War, written by student hackers at MIT in 1961. Originally the game was coded onto paper tape that ran on a mainframe. If the tape survived today, it would no doubt be too fragile to run; in any case, the mainframe has long since been junked. Copies of Space War exist, however, for as the technologies for entering data into computers changed, people copied the program first onto magnetic tape, then onto magnetic disks, and most recently onto the familiar diskettes, from which many exact clones have been produced. One of these would be what our hypothetical museum would run were it to simulate the historic game.

Yet anybody who played the game in 1961 on the MIT mainframe would have a hard time telling the difference were he to play now on a PC. The PC version might be faster or slower; the size, shape, color, and resolution of the screen on which the action occurred might look different; and the tactile qualities of the game—the joysticks, or control devices—might vary. But such differences might easily be minimized or altogether eliminated. The modern simulation of the historic artifact, then, would become indistinguishable from the original. What this portends for museums that have until now collected and exhibited only authentic historic artifacts is not clear. It seems certain, however, that the introduction of interactive computer exhibits will further blur the once definitive line between original artifacts and latter-day interpretations.

Along with the problems of the large artifact and of interpreting the computer, museums of technology have a third problem that I want briefly to consider. This is a problem attendant to the doing of social history in such museums. As curators increasingly choose to provide a social context for their exhibits of technical artifacts, they often further confuse the difference between the simulative and the real. Thus in many recent exhibits the artifacts of interpretation, as they might be called, such as the large photoreproductions used to simulate the environment in the traveling version of "Worker's World," become more important than the historic objects that are being interpreted. Increasingly, exhibitions seem to achieve their effects through a density of interpretive artifacts—through their theatrical staging, as it were—rather than through the display of historic things.

To suggest the range of this practice, let us consider two exhibitions. In the first, the interpretation in effect itself became the exhibit; original objects were marginal to a visitor's experience. In the second, the interpretation, while educational and interesting, did not illuminate the historical artifacts on view in the museum.

"Perfect in Her Place," a 1981 exhibition at the NMAH, examined female workers engaged in a wide range of nineteenth-century industrial occupations. Its interpretive texts were sensitive to the harsh work conditions endured by women and, along with the show's graphics—reproductions of contemporary line drawings showing female workers—taught visitors much about the varied work roles performed by a group that has been largely ignored by museums. The exhibit proved an instructive essay in social history. Yet "Perfect in Her Place" contained few artifacts of historical interest or significance. The sewing machine and the shuttles displayed in the exhibit, for example, had presumably been used by women but otherwise were well-known and ordinary things. The exhibit contained no example of the larger machines operated by women in the nineteenth century, such as the coining press illustrated in the exhibition catalog.[32] Furthermore, the objects shown were essentially mute about the subject of the exhibit; looking at them, in other words, did not reveal much about the conditions of women's work or about the effects of technological change on the nature of that work. The objects functioned partly as mere illustration and partly to validate the fact that this was a museum exhibit. The heart of the exhibit was on-the-wall text and reproductions of woodcuts and other graphics depicting women working as spinners, cartridge loaders, or any of a dozen other industrial tasks. But reading this book-on-the-wall in the gallery was much less enjoyable and informative than reading the more comprehensive catalog later.

At the California State Railroad Museum (CSRRM) in Sacramento, opened in 1981, an excellent large and well-restored collection of railroad cars and locomotives is in no way dominated by interpretation. Quite to the contrary. Here the problem is that the interpretation, keyed to the personal dimension of railroading and built around appropriately costumed manikins of brakemen, conductors, and other railroad workers, with taped accounts by railroad veterans, sheds little light on the locomotives and rolling stock that comprise the museum's collection. It is as if there were two parallel but unconnected exhibits. One deals with social history and is made up mainly of what I've called artifacts of interpretation (the manikins and taped recollections); the other is about trains and is thinly interpreted, with brief labels mostly in the internalist style.

In part the thin interpretation of railroad hardware reflects curatorial choice. The museum's staff deliberately opted to deemphasize machinery and to focus on the personal dimension of railroading so as to appeal to the broad public whose tax dollars paid for the museum.[33] As a consequence, even though unsystematic in its approach, the museum does a better job of evoking the social history of railroading than any similar institution. In exchange, visitors get little help in understanding the large artifacts on display, and virtually none of the interpretation links individuals or special categories of persons, such as brakemen, to specific locomotives or railroad cars.

The challenge posed by the installation at the CSRRM, by "Perfect in Her Place," and by other recent exhibitions on social history, then, is to figure out ways that museums of technology can interpret history *through* the objects that dominate their collections. Clearly, we want to know more than museums have traditionally told us about the men and women who designed, built, operated, maintained, or were affected by technology, whether it is railroad cars or sewing machines. We now accept as a truism that technology cannot be understood without reference to the society in which it developed, that a society's values, work styles, and even politics are embedded in the artifacts themselves, there to see if we only are helped to look. But if museums are moving away from the interpretation of things toward the interpretation of lives, as curators sometimes characterize this trend, they must become more inventive in using real *objects* to explore these human dimensions. It is, after all, museums' expertise as collectors, custodians, and exhibitors of historic artifacts that makes them unique as institutions.

Museum History and Academic History

As a general proposition, it has been only the historian-curator in the museum who has worried about the problems of interpreting history through artifacts. Most historians in the academy have tended to pursue their social or cultural questions (or any other kind) about the past with a bias toward written sources. To be sure, there has been much fruitful interchange of late between the academy and the museum, with many Ph.D.-holding historians moving into curatorial positions and asking new questions of artifacts, while individuals with museum experience have entered the university world to raise the academic's consciousness of material culture. Yet the curators' exhibitions and the academics' histories offer quite different views of the past. These are not interpretations in conflict so much as simply different, the inevitable consequences of the differing institutional environments that nurture them.

To get some sense of how museum and academic history of technology diverge, let us briefly compare the kind of topics popular in recent academic historiography with those on which museum exhibitions have been mounted. A sampling of the former would include the relationship between science and technology, the emergence of industrial research laboratories, the growth and development of large-scale technical systems, and technology transfer. On these subjects, scholars have generated a rich and voluminious discourse, publishing many important articles and monographs.[34] Although individual curators in museums have been interested in these subjects and a few have written about them, none has mounted an exhibition entirely focused on any of them. Rather, curators choose quite different topics for their exhibits. Generally, exhibits fall into two types, as a few titles will suggest. The first type takes its organizing principle from the kind of objects displayed, as was true of "A Wonderful Invention: A Brief History of the Phonograph from Tinfoil to the LP," a 1977 exhibition on phonograph technology at the Library of Congress, or "The Queen of Inventions: Sewing Machines in American Homes and Factories, 1850–1920," a 1986 show at the Slater Mill Historic Site in Pawtucket, Rhode Island. The second type, more synthetic and keyed to the academic historian's way of delimiting topics, centers on the technology related to some large event, human activity or historic period. Representative exhibits would include the NMAH's 1986 show "At Home on the Road: Autocamping, Motels, and the Rediscovery of America" or its 1976 "Person to Person," an exhibition on the occasion of the one-hundredth anniversary of the telephone. To be sure, such exhibitions often allude in their interpretations to themes beloved of academics, such as the science-technology relationship, the emergence of research and development, or technology transfer. But such themes, and this is my point, are rarely the main subjects of exhibitions.[35]

Two factors explain the differing emphases in the publications of academics and the exhibitions of curators: the three-dimensional and nonverbal nature of exhibitions and the popular mission of the museum. As has been suggested throughout this essay, artifacts impose (or should impose) some broad limits on the kind of history a curator treats in an exhibition. So, too, does curators' production of exhibits for institutions, which, unlike universities, need first to attract visitors and then (and this is related) to entertain them as well as instruct them. Moreover, the visitors to a museum come from a broad spectrum of age groups and backgrounds, and curators want to communicate with all of them. University scholars, however, at least in their written work, need only communicate to a highly educated, specialized, and often quite small audience.

It follows that many of the ideas or topics considered important by academic historians of technology would be very difficult, if not impossible, to make into successful artifact-oriented exhibits. An exhibit on the changing relationship between science and technology would be unlikely to be as effective as an article or book on the same subject. To be sure, a curator could easily find objects to exhibit: a cotton gin or machine tool could make the point that much technology has emerged from empirical, nonscientific problem solving, while a radio or computer could illustrate technologies that owed much to theoretical advances in physics. The curator also might display scientific apparatus, laboratory notebooks, preprints of important scientific articles, and photographs of scientists who worked on problems that affected the development of radio or computers. But such artifacts could not convey very much about the intellectual content, let alone the thought processes of those individuals, knowledgeable in physics theory, who developed such electrical technology. Most important, such artifacts would require considerable explanation through text if they are to illuminate the central theme of the exhibit, the *changing relationship between science and technology over time*. The lack of evocative objects and the abstraction inherent in the topic, then, make our hypothetical exhibition an unlikely one. In short, not all historical topics may be suitable for museum treatment; the relationship between science and technology, for example, may simply be too academic.

There are many topics, however, that curators in museums of technology can treat more effectively than academics in books. The cultural style offers a multitude of as yet barely explored possibilities for the interpretation of technical artifacts. Take the automobile, for example, an object that museums have barely started to interpret. Despite the many specialized automobile museums and the impressive car collections at major history museums, there have been few exhibits *on* the automobile; rather, we have had many exhibits *of* automobiles. We need exhibitions that do more than arrange shiny vehicles for the visitor's visual delectation and label each with a short text.[36] Automobiles should be displayed not just as aesthetic objects but as evolving complexes of subsystems and mechanical components. Some should be disassembled for display, their pieces interrelated and interpreted. By explicating how cars are constructed and put together, such an exhibit—through careful and imaginative interpretation—could help visitors better to understand not only an important technological artifact but much twentieth-century cultural history as well.

Although a cultural history of the automobile that took cognizance of technological change would also make a good book, nobody has written it. In any event, my hypothetical exhibition would do what no book could ever do. It could show visitors the technical evolution of the car and some of the ways that evolution has reflected and been affected by American culture. It would do this by displaying real cars, without which no understanding of automotive history is possible. In showing "pieces of the true cross," as former NMAH Director Brooke Hindle has called authentic historic objects,[37] my exhibit would also remain true to the museum's unique heritage as a repository of three-dimensional artifacts. We know that people like to see such things, and there is no reason why, with suitable interpretation, visitors could not glean insights from the objects that could never be had from books. Yet if a museum exhibition piques visitors' curiosity about the history of technology and nudges them toward books, a goal that historian Eugene Ferguson long ago claimed for the museum, academic historians would be the last to complain.[38] The interpretation of tools and technology in context demands the labors of *both* museum scholars and their academic colleagues.

NOTES

1. On living history generally, see Jay Anderson, *Time Machines, The World of Living History* (Nashville, 1984). For developments in an area where technological change has had profound social consequences, see Darwin P. Kelsey, "Outdoor Museums and Historical Agriculture," *Agricultural History* 46, no. 1 (January 1972), 105–27.

2. I do not mean to deny that close study of artifacts can contribute immensely to our understanding of technical and cultural history. Through the study of objects, scholars have given us many new insights into various subjects, such as the history of musket manufacture, mass production in industry, locomotive construction, and machine tool development. For a recent study that owes much to artifact study, see, David A. Hounshell, *From the American System to Mass Production, 1800–1932: The Development of Manufacturing Technology in the United States* (Baltimore, Md.: Johns Hopkins University Press, 1984). See also Michael E. Workman, "The Artifact as Evidence: So What?" *Technology and Culture* 27, no. 1 (January 1986), 118–20.

3. Because Mary Blewett has written a chapter for this volume on industrial museums, I have paid little attention to the history of manufacturing technology as presented in American museums.

4. There is considerable literature on the history of technical museums and on specific exhibits treating the history of technology. For the history of technical museums and a comprehensive bibliography on the history of technology in museums, see Bernard S. Finn, "The Museum of Science and Technology," in Michael Shapiro, ed., *The Museum: A Reference Guide* (Westport, Conn.: Greenwood Press, 1989). Extended reviews of exhibits on the history of technology have appeared in *Technology and Cul-*

ture since 1968 and provide an excellent source for tracing what museum historians have been doing for the past twenty years; many of these reviews are cited below. For the first of them, see Eugene S. Ferguson, "Hall of Power Machinery, Museum of History and Technology," *Technology and Culture* 9, no. 1 (January 1968), 75–85; see also Thomas W. Leavitt, "Toward a Standard of Excellence: The Nature and Purpose of Exhibit Reviews," ibid., 70–75.

5. In a major sense, of course, *all* exhibits are interpretive. The mere act of preserving and displaying artifacts in an environment or setting not original to them constitutes interpretation. Among the messages implicit in such presentations is that the objects are interesting or valuable. When a series of similar objects, such as steam engines, is displayed together, particularly if they represent different periods, the public tends to "read" them as conveying a message of progress, social as well as technical. For a critique of "1876," see W. David Lewis, "Exhibit Review, The Smithsonian Institution's '1876' Exhibit," *Technology and Culture* 18, no. 4 (October 1977), 670–84.

6. The Smithsonian also published a major catalog for the exhibition: Robert C. Post, ed., *1876: A Centennial Exhibition* (Washington, D.C.: Smithsonian Institution Press, 1976).

7. Brooke Hindle has long argued that the operation of historic machines, or even replicas, is essential to conveying the historical meaning of such artifacts. See, for example, Brooke Hindle, "Museum Treatment of Industrialization: History, Problems, Opportunities," *Curator* 15, no. 3 (1972), 209, 211–16.

8. Steven Lubar used the terms *chronological* and *genealogical* in his "Exhibit Review, The Computer Museum, Boston, Massachussetts," *Technology and Culture* 27, no. 1 (January 1986), 99.

9. Unless noted to the contrary, my comments on museums and exhibitions are all based on personal visits in 1986 or earlier.

10. In a seminal 1973 article, George Basalla linked this kind of statistical presentation to "technological progressivism," the belief that increases in quantifiable matters, such as "size of cylinder bore, horsepower, speed," were measures of social progress. "Museums and Technological Utopianism," *Winterthur Conference Report* (1973), 357.

11. Addressing a somewhat different issue, John H. White, Jr. claims the story of railroad museums in the United States may be characterized in two words: no money. See his "The Railway Museum: Past, Present, and Future," *Technology and Culture* 14, no. 4 (October 1973), 606.

12. For a good analysis of what I call the celebratory style, see Howard Learner, *White Paper on Science Museums* (Washington, D.C.: Center for Science in the Public Interest, 1979), 3–4, 26–30.

13. Personal visit to John Deere corporate headquarters, 1976. For an account, also dated, of a similar kind of exhibition, see the review of the Little Red Shop, a museum of textile machinery operated by the Draper Division of North American Rockwell in Hopedale, Massachusetts, by James C. Hippen: "Industrial Textile Machinery: Five North American Museums," *Technology and Culture* 10, no. 4 (October 1969), 570–86.

14. "The Romance of Technological Progress: A Critical Review of the National Air

and Space Museum," *Technology and Culture* 22, no. 2 (April 1981), 281–96. I have also commented critically on the museum in *The Winged Gospel: America's Romance with Aviation, 1900–1950* (New York: Oxford University Press, 1983), ch. 7.

15. The best account of the Wrights' dispute with the Smithsonian is Tom D. Crouch, "The Feud between the Wright brothers & the Smithsonian," *American Heritage of Invention and Technology* 2, no. 3 (Spring 1987), 34–46.

16. Learner, *White Paper*, 26–30.

17. Some museums have been more than merely sensitive to the interests of corporate America and have served as miniexpositions for industry. They have taken exhibits conceived and created by corporations and installed them without modification in their own galleries. In such cases the museum has delegated its control over content and interpretation and can hardly complain, though its status as a nonprofit educational institution might well be questioned. For museums with their own collections, particularly if they cover a field broader than a single industry, it should be possible to manage relationships with corporate donors without becoming captive to industry interpretations. See, generally, Learner, *White Paper*, 26–30, 41–45.

18. For a discussion of the early history of airmindedness and the culture of flight, see Corn, *The Winged Gospel*.

19. For a brief discussion of Hagley's approach, see Tracey Linton Craig, "Delicate Balance," *History News* (May 1982), 17–21.

20. I saw the exhibition at the Henry Ford Museum in Dearborn, Michigan.

21. Glenn Porter, *The Worker's World at Hagley* (Greenville, Del.: Eleutherian Mills–Hagley Foundation, 1981).

22. See also the Haggin Museum, *Holt Memorial Hall* (n.p., n.d.).

23. See also the exhibition catalog: Bernard S. Finn, *Edison: Lighting a Revolution, The Beginning of Electric Power* (Washington, D.C.: Smithsonian Institution, 1979), especially 45, 56–57.

24. The installation of the *John Bull* at NMAH, near the entrance to the museum's exhibit "Engines of Change," places the locomotive on an early iron-truss bridge, thereby showing visitors a small piece of the railroad system's infrastructure. The California State Railroad Museum in Sacramento also has installed its Virginia and Truckee locomotive on a bridge, an 1884 iron truss, and its *Governor Stanford*, the first locomotive of the Central Pacific, in an operalike setting, a fake mountain habitat that is supposed to represent the railroad's construction through the Sierra Nevada.

25. Aircraft are often displayed in hangars or on the tarmac of an airfield, though I've never seen an aerospace museum interpret or even call attention to such ground-based facilities. Judging by prevailing aerospace-museum interpretation, most staff members in such institutions hardly see anything that happens on the ground.

26. Finn, *Lighting a Revolution*, 54. The argument against exhibiting models because they are not real historic objects is of course much stronger when the models are built expressly for a modern exhibit rather than when they are old and have some historical relationship to the original artifact.

27. For an overview of the exhibit, see the exhibition catalog: Robert M. Vogel, *Building Brooklyn Bridge: The Design and Construction, 1867–1883* (Washington, D.C.: Smithsonian Institution Press, 1983). Other successful deployments of scale models include an HO-gauge scale diorama of a western logging railroad at the Cali-

fornia State Railroad Museum, depicting the difficult terrain in which geared logging locomotives operated; a large model of a nineteenth-century Mystic River shipyard at Mystic Seaport; and models of Oliver Evans's automated flour mill, a typical early-nineteenth-century cotton mill, a gunpowder stamping mill, and other early industrial installations in the introductory exhibit at Hagley.

28. Writing in 1973, historian George Basalla described the apogee of sanitized exhibition practice: "The Mill," located at the New York corporate headquarters of Burlington Industries. The visitor to the Burlington exhibit encountered a "mill," where, in Basalla's words, he "finds white floors, white machines, and a mirrored wall. The amplified sounds of textile machines initially hide the fact that the moving machines, strung with brilliantly colored threads, are not producing fabric. In this technological paradise there are no human beings, or models of them, to spoil the effect of complex machinery working by itself to give mankind the gifts of Burlington Mills." Basalla, "Technological Utopianism," 361.

29. For information about this facility, see *Guide Map, Queen Mary and Spruce Goose, and introducing Time Voyager* (n.p., n.d.), 2.

30. See Lubar, "The Computer Museum," passim.

31. No matter what curators intend, the rapid pace of obsolescence in the computer field will quickly transform such exhibits into historical ones. Museums and science centers installing interactive exhibits on computers might therefore plan for this fate and add some historical interpretation as a hedge toward that inevitable day when their machines are no longer state of the art.

32. See Deborah J. Warner, *Perfect in Her Place, Women at Work in Industrial America* (Washington, D.C.: Smithsonian Institution Press, 1981).

33. John H. White, Jr., "Exhibit Review, The California State Railroad Museum: A Louvre for Locomotives," *Technology and Culture* 24, no. 4 (October 1983), 644–54.

34. For a thorough analysis of what academic historians of technology have been doing over a twenty-year period ending in 1980, see John M. Staudenmaier, S.J., *Technology's Storytellers: Reweaving the Human Fabric* (Cambridge, Mass.: MIT Press, 1985).

35. Relative to this point, it is helpful to remember that curators in history museums take a stance toward their audiences that is analogous to the way professors view freshmen or sophomores, and as a result both offer broad surveys rather than specialized or in-depth treatments. In art museums there is a tradition of what might be called the monographic exhibition, a more specialized, often exhaustively documented production, but so far history museums have mounted few shows directed at specialists.

36. Interestingly, art museums have led in this area. As early as the 1940s the Museum of Modern Art in New York mounted small exhibitions on cars, while more recently we have had a major exhibition of cars, "Automobile and Culture," at the Museum of Contemporary Art in Los Angeles in 1984. See also the catalog-book: Gerald Silk, ed., *Automobile and Culture* (New York: Abrams–Los Angeles Museum of Contemporary Art, 1984).

37. Brooke Hindle, "How Much Is a Piece of the True Cross Worth?" in Ian M. G. Quimby, ed., *Material Culture and the Study of American Life* (New York: Norton, 1978), 5–20.

38. Ferguson, "Hall of Power Machinery," 85.

Machines, Workers, and Capitalists: The Interpretation of Textile Industrialization in New England Museums

11

Mary H. Blewett

The job of interpreting industrialization is challenging and complex. The story needs to include the development of industry as a phase in the ongoing evolution of American capitalism, but it should also capture the rich and changing interactions among the worker, the manager, the machine, and the market. It should choose vivid incidents from local history to ground an exhibit firmly in the specifics of place and time. And it should exploit the wealth of research in social history produced over the last two decades to illuminate the human face of industrialization.

Museums that interpret the history of industrialization can use the textile-history institutions of New England as models that offer examples of both the opportunities and the dangers of trying to recapture the industrial world of the past. These private and public museums present the experiences of workers and industrialization as central themes in American history and link the early textile-factory system to American economic development and to regional economic resurgence in the 1970s and 1980s. Their interpretive models have varied over time from industrial development as a solution to production problems to earnest efforts to present industrialization as a social experience. Much of the interpretation and planning for new exhibits in the 1980s successfully uses social history to explore the experience of industrial workers and the effects of technology on society. Yet most exhibits assume industrialization to be a cyclical and progressive force without examining the economic and social implications of industrial capitalism as a system.[1] Seldom do they view industrial capitalism as a social and economic system with explicit links between the past and present, or situate economic growth in a regional, national, and even global context, or connect it with the production process in other localities and industries. The few exceptions deserve attention for succeeding in interpreting specific events in local economic history as part of an overall system that drives industrial development.

My decision to confine an examination of workers and industrialization to museums of the New England textile industry rested on the institutional richness of the region, the opportunities for comparisons, and the high level of physical expansion and interpretative activity during the past two decades. I observed exhibits, looked at archives, and interviewed directors and staff at the major public and privately financed museums of textile history in New England. I visited existing historic sites and museums (Slater Mill Historic Site in Pawtucket, Rhode Island, and the Museum of American Textile History, or MATH, formerly the Merrimack Valley Textile Museum, in North Andover, Massachusetts) as well as new sites (Lowell National Historical Park, Lowell, Massachusetts; the State Heritage Park sites in Lowell, Fall River, and Lawrence, Massachusetts; Charles River Museum of Industry in Waltham, Massachusetts; and the exhibit on Maine industry at the Maine State Museum in Augusta, Maine). I also considered the proposed Massachusetts Labor History Center and defunct projects (the abandoned Mill Village at Old Sturbridge Village, in Sturbridge, Massachusetts, and the exhibit of the Lowell Museum). Because all of these projects involved social historians as consultants, as museum personnel, and on teams of exhibit designers, they offer an unusual opportunity to evaluate whether social history provided exhibit designers and museum professionals with a new vision of the story of early industrial capitalism.

The new social history is an effort to demonstrate the powerful ways that social experience shapes work, politics, and ideology.[2] Its methodologies range from quantitative analysis of demographic data to the impressionistic reminiscences of oral history. Its fundamental focus in industrialization is on people as agents in making their own history. Its subjects are family, ethnicity, race, urban and rural life, gender and sex roles, mobility, and changing work and workplaces. Its vision is to link the past with the present through a systematic study of the changing experience of ordinary people. Social history has contributed to the understanding of industrialization by demonstrating its varieties of forms and the discontinuous and uneven process of industrial development. Social historians see workers as gendered and culturally distinct beings who bring their ethnicity, community values, traditions, and sense of place in family life to the job. Social experience complicates and enriches those relationships created by the mode of production, and social relations on the factory floor produce forms of collective behavior other than strikes and unions.

The past two decades of rising interest in the new forms of social history paralleled a number of economic and political changes for New England museums. The professional growth of museum staffs throughout the nation in the 1960s and 1970s benefited in part from the collapse of the academic market for historians and increased grant funds for new exhibits, notably by the National Endowment for the Humanities (NEH). NEH's insistence on including "consulting humanists" in the planning and implementation phases of grants produced connections between academic historians and museum personnel. New investment of public monies by the National Park Service and the Commonwealth of Massachusetts transformed urban policy from renewal by wrecker to revitalization through adaptive reuse. Although high costs for energy and high interest rates in the late 1970s created serious challenges for some New England museums, financial pressures on private museums were balanced by steady growth and seemingly endless funds for public developments at Lowell and throughout the Massachusetts State Heritage Park system. Like the process of industrialization itself, the interpretative programs of these museums are changing in response to new research in social history and to new economic and political developments in the region.

In addition to the new attention paid to the social implications of industrial development, one element seems common to most of the exhibit planning in New England textile museums: all attempt to trace the entire story of industrialization from the preindustrial setting through early industrialization to the mature factory system. Gone is the limited focus on the early nineteenth century or on one aspect of textile production or on one fiber (for example, cotton at Slater or wool at MATH). The ambitious overviews of the 1980s raise questions about how much space remains in the new exhibits for the rich detail of social life. The fundamental drive is to see textile production as the prototype for the national experience of industrial capitalism. Most museum interpretation argues that the textile industry became a model for and a forecaster of future industrial organization, mass production, and a high material standard of living in American society. As an integrated and centralized system of mass production, however, early textile manufacturing in Waltham, Lowell, Manchester, and Lawrence stands in sharp contrast to the decentralized and discontinuous development of other forms of pre–Civil War production and the persistence of hand labor. In addition, different models of paternalism in textile management within and outside New England suggest that a unilinear model does not hold in this industry for the nation or even the region.[3]

Despite a reluctance in many of the current exhibits to mention other historic sites by name (aside from British precedents, which are always mentioned as examples avoided by canny American entrepreneurs) or to provide the visitor with a clear regional sense of industrial development (specifically who borrowed and enhanced what organizational forms and technology from whom), one of the strengths of the New England museums is the variety of forms they take and the exploration of small-scale textile manufacturing in addition to large-scale factory production. Development can be traced from preindustrial methods at Sturbridge, Slater, Augusta, and MATH to early mechanization at Slater to the integrated factory at Charles River and MATH to large-scale production and its subsequent decline in the twentieth century at Lowell and Lawrence (MATH). The only missing element is a rural mill village, such as the one planned but abandoned by Old Sturbridge Village.

The absence of an exhibit on the factory village, owned and built in the New England countryside by a small textile company, is more than a missing piece from the complex puzzle of industrialization in textiles. It also means a gap in the social interpretation of technology and work. Facing intense pressure on its original site by ever-increasing numbers of visitors in the 1960s, Old Sturbridge Village sought to fill the void and encouraged researchers Theodore Penn and Richard Candee to re-create a textile-mill village as a living-history museum. Sturbridge purchased one thousand acres of land and acquired a stone mill, a mill owner's house, a tavern, and other structures from various New England locations. But the precipitous decline in visitation during the energy crisis year of 1973–74, rising interest rates and costs of labor, and the failure of even the 1976 bicentennial celebration to improve ticket sales led the Sturbridge administration to abandon the mill-village idea.[4]

Lost along with the restoration was the concept of the mill village as a force for change in technology and as a training ground of mechanics and skilled workers who left the village for the machine shops and technical schools of the industrial cities of New England. This interpretation of the place of the mill village in New England industrialization would have shifted the focus of the history of technology away from inventors and managers like Samuel Slater to the social system that generated mechanics and machines.[5] For historians of technology like Penn, a machine is more the product of a human mind embedded in a social system than the inevitable if problematic product of a line of technical development. This concept of the social context of technological change would have been unique to museum interpretation in New England but was lost along with the mill village at Sturbridge.

The emergence in the 1970s and early 1980s of the new social history in exhibits interpreting industrialization of New England textile production has largely taken the form of temporary exhibits or of overlays of comment by tour guides on the reactions of the community and workers to economic change. For example, the guides at Slater Mill borrow heavily from the work of Gary Kulik on the resistance of the community of Pawtucket and its workers to early water-power development and mechanization of textile production.[6] In fact, museum directors have engaged in an informal competition over which site can claim the first protest by textile workers. Recently, Michael Brewster Folsom, director of the Charles River Museum, located evidence to prove that the earliest known strike occurred in Waltham in 1821.[7] As a convenient social overview, Edward P. Thompson's model of the shift from the seasonal rhythms of rural life to industrial time discipline for factory workers is used at all New England museums, regardless of whether local experience confirms it.[8] The presence of mill villages and small-scale production along the Blackstone, Merrimack, Concord, and Charles rivers, among others, suggests a less-dramatic shift for the local labor market. Nonetheless, tensions between preindustrial experience and the coming of the factory system represent a major component of interpretation at many sites.

Social historians and museum professionals, who informally call themselves the New England Textile Mafia, have used textile-history museums to combine the history of technology and the history of industrial workers. They have operated as a consortium of specialists in American civilization, machine design, hydropower, and mill architecture.[9] Although they compete in the regional market for the industrial tourist, they serve as consultants to grant projects, prepare studies for exhibit designers, write and edit publications, and act as advisors to one another's institutions. They also have close connections with the Society for Industrial Archeology, the Smithsonian Institution, Hagley Museum, and other industrial-history museums. Some museum professionals have ongoing academic appointments or special relationships with local universities: Michael Folsom at Brandeis University, Patrick Malone of Slater at Brown University, and Thomas Leavitt and Laurence Gross of MATH at Merrimack College, Northeastern University, and Boston University. The former Lowell Museum and the Lowell National Historical and State Heritage parks have developed long-standing relationships with the state's University of Lowell. This regional cooperation and consultation is a particular strength of New England textile museums.

Technology and Culture in Maine

Most New England textile museums explain industrialization by viewing technology as a process and a part of a larger culture. This represents a critical reaction by technology and culture advocates against older exhibits that presented machines as works of art or simply as artifacts. The "Wool Technology and the Industrial Revolution" exhibit of Bruce Sinclair in 1964 at MATH and Paul Rivard's machine-shop exhibit in 1974 at Slater Mill pioneered this "technology and culture" approach. Both placed working machinery in spaces that not only suggest or actually reconstruct the mill or the work space but also demonstrate technical change and the historic process of industrialization. Both emphasize the influence of new machines on production and the evolution of technology and its influence on American economic development.

The "Made in Maine" exhibit at the Maine State Museum in Augusta, which opened in 1985, continues the technology and culture approach despite its intention to appreciate the work and lives of industrial workers in the nineteenth century as a supplement to the state's history and folklore of lumberjacks and mariners.[10] The exhibit is more an exploration of work places, machinery, and artifacts in the technology and culture tradition than an examination of the industrial experience of Maine people. Just outside the entrance to this new exhibit is another space intrepreting the sardine canning industry. A model of a female worker bends over a wooden table cleaning sardines and packing them into open tin cans; her hands are covered with bandages and her expression is grim determination. The success of this image raises the hopes of the visiting social historian about the interpretation of workers in the "Made in Maine" exhibit.

The exhibit is located next to the Maine State Capitol in a cultural building constructed in 1971. Paul Rivard, former head at Slater, came to the state museum in 1978 as director and began to plan the "Made in Maine" exhibit. The new exhibit depended primarily on donations and in-kind contributions from the Maine public. Incredibly, there was no increase in the operating budget of the museum to produce the exhibit, except for a special legislative appropriation for a new machinery collection. Yet the implementation was completed two years ahead of schedule.[11]

Rivard's alterations in the philosophy and organization of the museum, which he has termed "back to basics," represent a reaction against changes in museum management at Augusta, made in the late 1960s and early 1970s, that deconstructed hierarchy among museum staff and insisted upon relevance and abstract concepts as the basis of exhibits. Rivard resurrected the position of curator, began aggressively collecting machinery, and returned to a philosophy of allowing the artifacts to determine exhibit themes. His introduction of divisions of labor and increases in productivity provide an unself-conscious industrial analogy for museum management.[12] In spite of Rivard's defense of the new exhibit as social interpretation, it represents a continuation of his interest in the relationships between technology and culture. The definition of culture in the exhibit is limited to the technology and organization of industrial production.[13]

This technically and visually superb exhibit is organized around four workplaces: the home, the shop, the mill, and the factory. Each workplace is illustrated in room scenes encircling a central core that immediately grabs attention and diminishes the effect of everything else. In the center, a three-story woodworking shop of the 1850s has been restored, complete with water-driven turbine and fully operational power-transmission system.[14] This exhibit draws the visitor down a spiral walkway to watch the moving leather belts and view the cross section of machinery and structural components—all surrounded by a glass barrier. The restoration dominates the exhibit design: everything else seems a sideshow. But in contrast to the woodworking shop's glass-encased and frozen machinery, Rivard's 1974 machine shop at Slater (powered by the more primitive technology of the water wheel) provides a chance for an interpreter to run the various machines and the potential to explore the social atmosphere of the shop. The re-creation of the wood-working shop in Augusta does not provide the same chance to explore a work experience. I observed the hazards in the separation of the visitor from the workplaces by glass walls as one person tried to look closer to see more and bashed his head against the spotless glass. Earlier, in pointing out a detail to a companion, I bruised my knuckles the same way. Although a tribute to the visual appeal and maintenance of the exhibit by the museum staff, the pristine glass symbolized the barriers in the exhibit between people and things.

The textile-production section of "Made in Maine" is divided into domestic winding and tape weaving, a fulling mill, early mechanization of carding and spinning, and the weave room of an integrated factory. The links between the four stages of textile industrialization are lost in the exhibit design (the 1820 kitchen of a home weaver is followed by the 1880 parlor of a dressmaker), and the reasons for the changes in the organization of textile production are insufficiently explained. The labeling of the exhibit is minimal, and tour guides are not available. As the nineteenth-century industry that came to surpass even Maine lumbering in terms of value of product and the only example of factory work in the exhibit, textile production deserves a more coherent and prominent place in the interpretation.

Also missing is a sense of why industry in Maine grew so much. The exhibit ignores the role of capitalists as well as the state's connections with regional development in textiles.[15] For example, Maine daughters provided much of the work force for Massachusetts textile and shoe factories. How did these former migrants fare in factories in their own communities? There are no workers' words in the exhibit text. Their work experience and identities, for example, skilled male jack spinners and female weavers (without ethnic identification), are only briefly noted in the descriptions of machinery and comments on the work sites. Rivard's claim that the exhibit uses social history to recognize the role of women and children in Maine industry rests on brief mentions in the ex-hibit labels. Although the labels acknowledge that industrialization displaced home workers, they accept without question the balancing of that loss against the creation of new jobs and cheap standard products.[16] Disruptions, protests, and unions are absent even from the labels. Unlike some other exhibits on New England textiles, "Made in Maine" does not link the industrial past with the present economic system.

The weave room has seven power looms with differently patterned woolen cloth in the works, a drawing-in frame, a loom fixer's parts bin, and dim fifteen-watt filament bulbs in overhead lamps. This provides the interior for a handsome brick exterior wall with granite foundation and window lintels. But the weave room is silent, and the looms are marked "Please do not touch." Only one loom is run, and not for the average tourist. The more successful ar-rangement of an early carding mill one floor above (which seems unconnected structurally with the weave room) had a threaded jack spinner, two woolen cards, and plenty of lint on the ceiling and floors, but the space lacked life and motion and the synthetic sound is muffled and unconvincing. Elsewhere in the exhibit, simulated sounds for the blacksmith shop of hammering, filing, and quenching hot iron were more distinct and successful. Here in the weave room, I was lucky enough to attract the attention of one work-study student and summer guide with my clipboard and lengthy stay. As she responded to my questions and talked about her own experience working in a local textile factory and the similar experiences of her mother and brother, I finally felt in contact with working people. The museum exhibit badly needs more well-trained interpreters, preferably with industrial experience.

I left the exhibit impressed with the rich diversity of Maine industry and products, with the beauty and ingenuity of the exhibitry, and with the way the people of Maine had responded with contributions to the call to include industrial workers in the historic celebration of the state's past. But the overlay of social history was just too thin to illuminate the human side of industrialization.

Mill-Village Life at Pawtucket

Intensive efforts to plan and develop other new exhibits in the late 1970s and early 1980s provide clearer evidence of the influence of social history on museum interpretation than is found at "Made in Maine." Slater Mill Historic Site is a good example. An association interested in the collection and preservation of early textile machinery organized Slater Mill in 1921. Occasionally used for temporary exhibits of machine technology, the site of Samuel Slater's 1793 cotton-spinning mill became a public museum in 1955 and mounted its first exhibit in the early 1960's.[17] It acquired the 1810 Oziel Wilkinson Machine Shop next to the mill in 1966 and moved the Sylvanus Brown House (built in 1758) to the site five years later. The three structures sit on five acres along the banks of the swiftly flowing Blackstone River in downtown Pawtucket.[18] Together, they illustrate major elements in the process of early industrialization: the metal- and woodworking shops where Pawtucket artisans produced Slater's spinning frames, the wooden factory where children used water-powered machines to spin cotton yarn, and the households where men and women wove the yarn by hand into cloth marketed by Slater.

Slater Mill Historic Site interprets the Brown House as both a prefactory site for hand-spinning methods, which are demonstrated by tour guides, and as a location for outwork weaving, which used the yarn supplied by the mill. The house's sparsely furnished interior is based on an 1824 inventory of its contents, with a kitchen on the basement floor and three rooms above. When I visited the site, the tour guide ably explored the nature of preindustrial attitudes toward work and the sexual and generational division of labor in household production. She demonstrated, in the kitchen, the spinning equipment used for flax and wool, but the hearth was cold and the setting lifeless on a cool, rainy morning in June. A similar interpretation at Old Sturbridge Village, a recreated 1830 community, involved a glowing fireplace in a farmhouse kitchen where two women prepared food and dashed a churn, the contents of which stubbornly refused to turn to butter on that hot June afternoon.[19] In the Sturbridge setting, the spinning wheel and loom in the adjacent rooms seemed part of a system of household labor which appeared vital and continuous. The Brown House at Slater, now interpreted primarily as a domestic location of textile production, might combine preindustrial work and life more effectively by exploring a household composed of family and kin who ate, drank, slept, farmed, prayed, gave birth, and made cloth. Still, Slater Mill succeeds in placing its interpretation firmly within the larger context of a prefactory artisan community so well that the visitor's eyes search up and down the riverbanks for surviving signs of that early nineteenth-century village.

One of the sensory joys of Slater is the midbreast water wheel which powers the Wilkinson Machine Shop, located in a handsome stone mill. Restored in 1980 by museum Director Patrick M. Malone, an expert in hydropower technology, the majestic wheel creates an atmosphere—as it turns slowly and its blades rise dripping with river water—that recaptures the measured pace of mechanical life in the early nineteenth century.[20] The soft clank of the gears sounds almost like church bells and reminds the visitor of the ambience of an early mill village. This successful use of one working machine to recapture the past without using exhibit labels represents a singular achievement.

The machine shop, the creation of former Director Paul Rivard, is an excellent reminder of the complexities of early industrialization, with its development of wood, metal, and machine-tool industries as well as cotton mills. The intent is to interpret a generic machine shop which repaired textile machinery in the late nineteenth century. In a large room crammed with interesting artifacts, another tour guide, dressed in nineteenth-century-style work clothing, dwelt on the difficulties and dangers of the machine operations and the need for skilled mechanics.[21] Most of the machines, however, did not work (some are now considered too dangerous to run for visitors), but those that did were fascinating. In general, however, the site gave little sense of how the shop and its crew of skilled workers and apprentices functioned as a system. The shop interpretation might well explore the composition of a working class culture based on the artisan tradition in Pawtucket, a culture that produced functionally autonomous craftsmen who refused to work while the boss was watching them.[22]

Within Slater Mill itself the tour guide used the tower entrance and its surrounding memorabilia of Samuel Slater and scenes of early Pawtucket to

Wilkinson Machine Shop at Slater Mill Historic Site. (Slater Mill Historic Site)

summarize the work of former curator Gary Kulik on the community's reaction to Slater's innovations. This rich overlay of social interpretation of the initial experience of factory discipline and the local sources of protest illustrates Slater Mill's reliance on well-trained interpreters, since the main exhibit does not yet embody Kulik's findings. The visitor is led past machine after machine (the unthreaded mule spinner was particularly difficult to interpret), and the process of cotton textile manufacture is demonstrated through mechanical artifacts, only some of which work. As a result, opportunities to discuss a social interpretation of mill work are lost. One Slater guide was reluctant to grasp and stop the whirling flyer on a throstle spinning frame, even though children of ten and younger were required to do so in order to piece broken threads. Although understandable, this reluctance itself might have led to an exploration of the necessity of accustoming a child to factory discipline. Similarly, the guide also explained the danger of the "kiss of death" shuttle, but she did not explain the pressures of the piece rate system on the weavers, who devised this quick but potentially lethal way of changing the bobbins by sucking the thread through the eye of the shuttle and the lint into their lungs.

In addition to using machines to explain the process of textile production, Slater Mill's staff might interpret it as a space where five men, fifteen women, and fifty-two children worked together to spin yarn by water-powered machinery. How that was accomplished would amplify the story of the social experience of early industrialization. Or Slater Mill could decide to refocus its interpretation on just the spinning process and related operations as they developed in the eighteenth, nineteenth, and twentieth centuries and explore the social consequences of the shifts from spinning wheel to jenny to throstle to mules and rings, an emphasis in which the changing nature of the work force and the experience of mill work could be central.

An imaginative plan to reorganize Slater's exhibit of textile machinery (developed in 1981 by Gary Gerstle) recommended a chronological reorganization of textile technology to demonstrate changes in the system of production in three epochs (1780–1830, 1850–1890, 1880–1930) and a focus on social interpretation of the experience of mill work.[23] Gerstle's ideas on interpreting the essence of the Slater, or Rhode Island, system between 1780 and 1830 seem sufficiently challenging to support an exciting exhibit without extending the story to the later nineteenth century, when Pawtucket was outproduced by giant competitors in Lowell, Lawrence, and Fall River or to the economic and technological survival of Pawtucket industry in the twentieth century. But Slater Mill, which sees itself as a museum of the Blackstone Valley and depends on private and corporate contributions for its operating funds, regards the connections between its interpretation of Slater's achievements and the economic and political context of the region as vital to its future. This link seems to explain the unwarranted claims for Slater Mill's historic significance made in the 1985 script of a planned multimedia show written by Malone and media consultant Michael Schaffer: "Because it was here that the Industrial Revolution was first realized in America! . . . Slater's system was to become the model which all future industrial production in the country was to follow." [24]

Localism and fund-raising needs aside, the Pawtucket system of production of cotton yarn in a water-powered mill by child labor, a system dependent on hand labor and domestic weaving, was fundamentally different from and not the model for the large factories of Lowell, Lawrence, and Fall River. [25] The Rhode Island system successfully coexisted with the Waltham system (adopted at Lowell and Lawrence) of large corporations, integrated production, and a rural work force recruited to the city to live in company-owned boardinghouses. Interpretation of the contrasts between the two systems could tell a complex story of the survival of different forms of industrial production and would defy a progressive and unilinear view of industrialization.

Furthermore, the media show ignores Gerstle's view of the dominant influences of market competition and capitalist decision making on industrial production. Instead, it promises a continuation of twentieth-century economic vitality and diversified industry in Pawtucket based on the vigor of its machine technology and a skilled work force. This reliance on advanced technology and skilled workers represents the contemporary vision for regional economic growth of neoliberals and the high-technology industry in New England. But however unwelcome the comparison, the history of the region's textile industry and Pawtucket itself suggest that competition over market shares and managerial decisions to increase productivity (issues currently confronted by the high-tech industry) are more central to the dynamics of industrial capitalism. Samuel Slater, less a mechanic than a manager, faced these problems himself. [26] The attempt to link contemporary industrial resurgence in Rhode Island to the origins of the industrial revolution in Pawtucket ignores serious problems of power and control inherent to capitalist development and relevant to contemporary concerns.

Decisions to Deskill

Located on the town common in North Andover, Massachusetts, the Museum of American Textile History (Merrimack Valley Textile Museum until 1984) began in 1960 with a preindustrial collection of spinning wheels and looms from the North Andover Historical Society. Provided with an endowment and personal support by members of the J. P. Stevens family, the museum, under the initial direction of Hagley-trained historian Bruce Sinclair, defined its scope as early industrialization in woolen textiles from 1800 to 1850. [27] The museum with its archives and machinery collection was installed in a modern

1830-style brick building with a cupola and factory bell. Sinclair's permanent exhibit, "Wool Technology and the Industrial Revolution," which opened in 1964, confined its specialized story to a discussion of how technological changes in textile production in the Merrimack Valley served as a motive for industrial development.[28] Since 1975, however, the interpretation at MATH has shifted away from a technology-and-culture approach to an emphasis on the effects of the industrial process on people.

Even more recently MATH has become a nationally oriented museum with an inclusive interest in all aspects of textile industrialization. Thomas Leavitt, the museum's director since 1964, always viewed Merrimack Valley as a museum with national interpretive and collection responsibilities. In 1984 he persuaded the museum's board of trustees to rename the museum, widen its scope of activities to include all fibers used in American textile production, and begin planning for relocation to the former Pacific Mill Weave Shed in Lawrence.[29] This new direction has been supported by NEH grants to plan and implement a new exhibit and by financial and development support from the city of Lawrence and the Commonwealth of Massachusetts through the State Heritage Park System.[30] Ironically, the Massachusetts Labor History Center (proposed by the Governor's Executive Office of Labor in 1984) may materialize in Lawrence as part of a museum complex, shared with an institution originally financed by the family that operated J. P. Stevens Company, a notorious opponent of unions in the Southern textile industry.[31]

The tours at the North Andover site reflect the new orientation at MATH. Its public programs supervisor, Robert Brown, led our tour as a late-July stand-in for vacationing docents.[32] Brown's doctorate in American history and his extensive training in machine technology combine the best of the academic and the practical. MATH's reliance on well-trained, experienced interpreters who know their machinery is as central to its interpretative program as Slater's. A fifteen-minute video, *Homespun: Cloth Making in Early America*, on preindustrial methods of woolen production replaces half the museum's original permanent exhibit on the first floor, which now serves as space for temporary exhibits. But video cannot replace the touch and feel of preindustrial artifacts and methods, and one visitor expressed a special nostalgia for a large and an impressive jack-spinning machine which is now in storage.

The tour of the remainder of the permanent exhibit (renamed "Factory Labor: Shaping Work in America") demonstrates MATH's new inclusive approach by discussing: English precedents; developments at Slater, Waltham, and Lowell; the sources of merchant capital for New England textile production; and the Southern plantation system. A factory bell provides the focus for a discussion of time discipline, and the guide ran almost all of the machinery: a carding machine, jack spinner, woolen loom from 1876, and a Draper loom with automatic stop motion by drop wires, automatic bobbin changer,

Draper loom in the Museum of American Textile History. (Museum of American Textile History)

and pick counter. A bobbin that accidentally flew loose as it was discharged from the shuttle was a startling reminder of the dangerous working conditions in textile factories, which the guide discussed at length. The choice of these working machines and the interpretation of the changes they brought to the work process are the best in any New England museum and are a model for the others.

Attention throughout the tour to the changing sex and age composition of the work force for various jobs was marred only by the unwarranted assertion that skill meant male and high wages. In fact, skill definitions represent social choices by managers, and drawing-in girls, female menders and burlers, and female weavers and weave-room inspectors held skilled, well-paid jobs in the industry. Information on ethnic groups and labor protest is absent from the interpretation except when a particular guide decides to include it. The tour could easily be stretched to an hour; I would have preferred at least fifteen more minutes on factory work instead of the video on preindustrial methods. When questioned about labor protest, tour guide Brown asserted sadly that the success of textile unions was one reason the New England mills relocated to the South. This claim would have surprised the historically unorganized textile workers of Lowell, Lawrence, and Manchester.[33]

Curators Laurence Gross and Paul Hudon are currently planning for what they want to be the "exhibit of record on the development of factory labor in the United States" at MATH's new site in Lawrence.[34] The exhibit design features four workplaces: a weaver's shop, a water-powered carding mill, a small mid-nineteenth-century integrated factory, and a factory of the 1920–1950 period. Rejecting technological determinism, the focus of the exhibit, developed primarily by Gross and Hudon, is the changing nature of work as the result of human choice and decision. One fascinating element is the emphasis placed on contingency in industrial development through the suggestion that the carding mill might have been an alternate path to industrialization with the factory system. This water-powered mill mechanized one step in production but left the rest of the work process decentralized and the materials owned and (when finished) marketed by the worker. Unlike the carding mill in the "Made in Maine" exhibit, the interpretation planned at MATH suggests that centralized and integrated production financed by large capital represents only one option for early industrialization.

The overall interpretation in the planned MATH exhibit centers on workers, machines, and supervisors in the workplace, and the major theme is the de-skilling of workers by decisions which produced the mature factory system. There is, however, a curiously abstract quality to the planned exhibit. Based on the new national mission of MATH, the exhibit has abandoned a New England focus. It refers to but does not systematically discuss a specific and changing tradition of labor protest. Based on present planning, the 1912 Bread and Roses Strike in Lawrence will not receive the attention that it deserves as a local or regional event.[35] All workplaces are generic without specificity of time and place. Social history in the interpretation is limited to labor history of the shop-floor variety. Despite the historic importance of the textile factory as the first employer of women, the work force remains ungendered and culturally neutral. Despite the focus of interpretation on process and people, the lack of attention to social experience in the work place is startling. Missing are references to the social contexts of gender, religion, ethnicity, and family.

The interpretive text is focused on human choice and decision making through three recurring questions: Who makes the cloth? Who makes the rules? Who makes the money? But the setting of these important decisions and the persons who made them remain offstage in the exhibit, which seems thereby to avoid the question of why certain people in a capitalist system had the power to deskill the work process. Instead, interpretation focuses on the results of these choices in the form of altered work relationships and contexts. This theme of increasing productivity and profits by deskilling the work force is compelling and will be unique in New England textile exhibits. The exhibit planners have built into their interpretation an explicit consideration of present and future work practices as the product of human choices. But without an exploration of active worker responses in words and deeds as both contributing to and resisting changes in the work process, the danger in the final analysis is to create a victimization model. Nonetheless, as I left the present museum in North Andover and drove north to Interstate 495, a vista of Lawrence and its red brick clock towers, chimneys, and looming mills rose before me in the distance, illustrating the exciting vision of MATH's new direction.

The City as Museum

The interpretive planning at the Lowell National Historical Park (LNHP) is more successful in its concern for the social experience of industrialization. The tours offered by LNHP begin at the Market Mills Visitors' Center, located in a rehabilitated mill complex which most recently was the site of silk and carpet weaving operations.[36] Above the center, in federally financed elderly-housing apartments, live many former textile workers. The park's staff has encouraged them to participate in an oral-history project conducted by University of Lowell personnel and to form a mill workers' advisory committee to assist with park interpretation. The increasingly familiar sight of cleaned-up red brick walls, granite lintels, new windows, gaslights, and lavish landscaping reminded me of the standard "look" of many of the textile-history museums and rehabilitated mill sites in New England, but the LNHP's visitor center is within sight of functioning manufacturing concerns and run-down tenements, a reminder of the underside of the industrial past and present. The experience at Lowell is fundamentally an experience of scale.[37] The entire city is the museum.

The Lowell Park offers an orientation to its various tours with a small exhibit in the Visitors' Center and in an impressive media show. The National Park Service defines five interpretive themes: capital, machines, power, labor, and the industrial city.[38] The media show, "Lowell: An Industrial Revelation," demonstrates the successful collaboration of social historian Thomas Dublin and media specialist Michael Schaffer.[39] The colorful slide show explores both the social experience and the achievements and failures of American industrialization in Lowell. Ideological and technical links with the British textile industry are not, however, balanced by similar links with Slater and Waltham, leaving a wholly unwarranted impression of the singularity of Lowell's development. The claim that Lowell was the first great industrial city and the emphasis on the power of capital in the destiny of the city are better founded. The narrative then argues that Lowell's success stimulated imitation and competition throughout New England. Overproduction drove down the price of cheap cotton textiles and led to the decisions by capitalists in the 1830s and 1840s to cut wages in order to maintain dividends. Thus, according to the script, was born the cycle of conflict between labor and management in American industry. But more attention to the earlier tensions and turnouts at Pawtucket and Waltham would make conflict systemic to early industrial capitalism and remove the impression of the uniqueness of the 1830s strikes and the activities of the Lowell Female Labor Reform Association in the 1840s.

The excellence of the presentation on pre–Civil War Lowell owes much to Dublin's prize-winning book *Women at Work*. The fortunes of the industry after the Civil War are less well researched, and the narrative becomes a tale of intensive competition and market determinism for an explanation of the industry's decline. Nonetheless, the social aspects of late industrialism are captured through factory songs, examples of ethnic diversity, the influence of immigrant culture on the city, the successful Lowell strike in 1912 (correctly interpreted as an extension of the famous Bread and Roses Strike in Lawrence), scenes of capital flight during the Great Depression, and the demolition of many of the cotton mills.

One is left unprepared for the boosterist conclusion: Lowell's revitalization as ascribed to "a resurgence of local pride" and a "new spirit." One could more accurately explain the rebirth of Lowell as stimulated by forty million dollars in federal money for park development since 1978.[40] The rest is owed to state funds for a State Heritage Park devoted to the interpretation of hydropower technology in Lowell and to an expanding high-technology industry, notably the location in Lowell of the corporate headquarters of Wang Laboratories. Economic development and the speculative real estate market in Lowell

They Came To Lowell. Last year more than 500,000 visitors made Lowell, Massachusetts, a special destination... and found a working American dream. You can find it, too. Come to Lowell.

Book Passage To Lowell's Historic Mill District on an old-fashioned trolley and canalboat! On the Mill and Canal Tour you'll inspect the Guard Locks, meet gatekeepers in period costume, and explore a classic Lowell mill.

HISTORY FOR THE TAKING

By 1830, Lowell, Massachusetts, had become recognized as a model industrial community. And today, Lowell's back – a gateway to fun, history, and the dramatic story of America's Industrial Revolution. From the thunder of the original textile mills to the Merrimack River's rush, it's like stepping back into the 19th century.

Listen To A Live Performance of Mill Era songs and stories with folk artist Alex Demas. Dulcimers, banjos, fiddles and mandolins carry the tunes Tuesdays through Thursdays at 10:30.

For Tour Reservations or more information on the Lowell National Historical Park and Heritage State Park,

Meet The Mill Girls

Take in the multi-image slide show at the National and State Park Visitors Center. Discover the mills and the mill girls, the strikes, the struggles, the ruin, and the rebirth. It's all history for the taking – in Lowell.

Heritage State Park Waterpower Exhibit.

contact the Visitor Center, 246 Market Street, Lowell, MA 01852. Or call (617) 459-1000. Open daily 8:30-5:00. **"Come Share The Spirit Of Lowell."**

LOWELL
MASSACHUSETTS
HISTORY AT WORK

Wade Into Waterpower! New this year, in the historic Mack Building, is the exciting Lowell Heritage State Park Waterpower Exhibit. With hands-on working models of canal locks, actual turbines, an antique loom, and some fascinating personal history.

(Lowell National Historical Park)

in the 1980s illustrate the effects of the boom in tourism and services. Historic preservation and adaptive reuse for housing and business space have been the prime stimuli of economic activity in the region.[41] Former mill workers were wondering in amazement what would sell next. Despite ripples of anxiety in the high-tech industry (profits in decline at Wang and other computer concerns and general layoffs), no one at LNHP was pointing out that the historic lessons of competition and declining market shares in cotton textiles also apply to high tech.

The two major tours offered to the visiting public in the summer of 1986 were the Mill and Canal Tour and the Mill and Trolley Tour. Both proved intellectually challenging and physically exhausting, especially on one witheringly hot day in late July. Each is more than two hours, crammed with information, and delivered with spirit by a labor-intensive summer staff of college-age interpreters. The Mill and Canal Tour begins with an orientation to preindustrial economic activity and the chronological and geographic development of the major transportation and power-canal systems. Park interpretation has always assumed an audience of canal and hydropower enthusiasts. We rode an open-air electric trolley (circa 1905) to the central controlling gates of the power-canal system, the Swamp Locks, where a power launch takes the visitor up the Pawtucket Canal, the original transportation canal built in 1796. This refreshing boat ride passes derelict junkyards and operating industrial plants whose workers took a break and waved at the tourists. When the boat reaches the Francis Gate, it moves into the recently restored locking system. Disembarking, the visitor meets Enoch or Sarah Page, played by guides for the State Heritage Park. They use living-history techniques and the soft, melodic country accents of nineteenth-century New Englanders to explain the life of a gatekeeper and his wife in the 1850s and the routine of locking boats in and out of the canal. Their anecdotes also reveal the social hierarchy between the mill agents and their employees.

When the boat has been floated up in the lock chamber to the level of the Merrimack River, the launch proceeds into the source of all the water power, the ponding behind the major dam on thirty-two-foot-high Pawtucket Falls—not very impressive in dry summer weather. Entering the lock chamber at the Northern Canal Gatehouse (soon to provide a water-born circuit of the city) the tour leaves the boat and visitors enter an air-conditioned bus for a ride which skirts (without comment) the Acre, the first working-class immigrant neighborhood in the city. The bus delivers the tourists to the old Suffolk and Tremont Mill of the 1830s, recently the site of the Lowell Museum (1976–1981) and now the Wannalancit Office and Technology Center, where the State Heritage Park's major exhibit features water turbines.

Throughout the tour, the guide delivers a vast amount of information on hydropower engineering, the building of the granite-lined canals by Irish laborers using picks and shovels, the experience of the mill girls at work and in their boardinghouses, the time discipline of factory life, and the development of the family economy and child labor among immigrant workers. This attention to social life among industrial workers, however, is marred by a persistent technological determinism. Water power "makes money," machinery "makes money," factories "make money," but the labor of mill girls and immigrants never "makes money." An unintentionally insensitive statement by the guide that people were replaceable but that machines were not provoked looks of chagrin and anger from several visitors. After an intensive but superbly clear explanation of the workings of a water turbine, done with only the giant, rusty pieces of one pulled from the Wannalancit wheel pit by a previous mill owner, the tour rejoins the trolley for a ride through the city back to the Visitors' Center. The strengths of this tour lie in its exploration of the diverse environments of the industrial city: the river, the falls and the canals; locks, turbines, and gatehouses; the physical presence of nineteenth-century city offices, mills, agents' houses and boardinghouses; the ethnic neighborhoods, old and new, still distinguished by their tenements, shops, and churches with golden domes, neo-Gothic spires, and Romanesque facades.

The second major tour, the Mill and Trolley, is shorter and focuses more on the industrial work force.[42] Initially weighted down by the theme "How Machinery Changes People," the tour guide shifts away from technology to the now-familiar description of the mill-girl era in front of several restored boardinghouses adjacent to Boott Mill, the site of the National Park's major exhibit on work in the textile factory. Another exhibit planned for one of the boardinghouses will explore the social experience of the mill girls and their residences and attempt to link this space to the nearby factory and its prominent bell tower. A third will house an exhibit on immigration and ethnic life, and a fourth is scheduled to contain an exhibit on organized labor sponsored by the Central Labor Council and the AFL-CIO. In the summer of 1986, the beautifully restored exteriors, if a little too clean and unlived in, served as an impressive backdrop for verbal interpretation.

The guide used our walk across the trolley tracks and power canal and into the busy yard of Boott Mill to encourage us to imagine the closing of the gates at the beginning of the working day, which forced tardy workers to enter through the mill's countinghouse and confront their bosses. Our tour guide, the granddaughter of a Lowell mill worker, then began to draw upon her grandmother's stories and her training, based on the oral-history collection, to demonstrate the "problems" of the factory work force. Leading us up a winding staircase and into a very large and empty mill space that actually smelled like a mill—greasy, musty, stuffy—she demonstrated the process of cleaning and spinning cotton with simple illustrations and devices. We touched and pulled apart cotton yarn in various stages. The guide then explained the operation of a power loom, using a working machine, but she also commented on and responded to questions with information on piece work, speed-ups, automatic looms and the stretch-out, the kiss-of-death shuttle, and other experiences of textile workers. Unmentioned, however, were the ways in which the work process was itself shaped by workers through the values and culture that they brought with them to the mills each morning. The atmosphere of Boott Mill, the noise and motion of the working loom, and the description of the process of work produced so much visitor interest that the tour was late in returning to the Visitors' Center. Many visitors knew something about New England textiles or about industrial work; some were clearly enthusiastic in their appreciation of the guide's personal and technical information. Based on that response, a tour that focused solely on factory work in the later stages of industrialization and the response of the immigrant work force to changes in the work process would be popular with visitors, even without the Yankee mill girls' story.

The National Park Service decided to develop its major exhibit at the Boott Mill in a design by the Center for History Now,[43] for when the Lowell Museum closed its exhibit in 1981, the Park Service lost access to the working weave room at the Wannalancit, with its pounding machines, shaking floors, ferocious noise, and its Colombian workers. The weave-room exhibit at the Boott need not be interpreted simply as a noisy and unpleasant place to work. Instead, it could be explored as a workplace where the piece rate and the consequent need to avoid spoiled work and earn a living wage brought weavers, loom fixers, smash piecers, battery girls, bobbin boys, and other workers into a complex and systemic relationship with their machines and their supervisors, a relationship shaped by special languages, behaviors, and tensions. Spaces currently planned to interpret managerial decision making (an overseer's office adjacent to the weave room) and absentee ownership (a treasurer's office in Boston) could be used to address issues of who had the power to make policy on piece rates, labor costs, markets, and profits. Despite lip service by the LNHP staff to a larger vision, efforts to connect the historic parallels of the textile industry and the high-technology industries in New England seem limited to an interpretation of similarities in location and growth. Lessons on international competition, market shares, and the causes of decline will be left to the visitor to deduce.[44]

The Lowell Park planners and exhibit designers are also beginning to look beyond the walls of Boott Mill into the adjoining neighborhood of tenements, boardinghouses, schools, and streets.[45] They could use the memories of early-twentieth-century mill workers in the oral-history collection to develop the story of community life just outside the mill, a reminder that social life and working life are fundamentally connected. If these plans could be fully realized, the interpretation at the Lowell Park will involve social history as central to its interpretation of the industrial experience in textiles in a manner unparalleled at other New England sites.

Public History as Venture Capital

The Massachusetts Urban Heritage State Park System is intended to use historic preservation for economic revitalization. Financed by the state and supported by economic developers, the park system offers public money to enhance the abandoned industrial sites of cities like Fall River, Lowell, Lawrence, and Lynn. The program promises recreation and tourism to stimulate local services and rehabilitated buildings and mills to attract high-tech and light industries.[46] The weight of this mission for the Heritage Park System is a heavy burden for interpreting the industrial past. Most of the resulting interpretation subordinates this past to the public use of history as an incentive to future investment and development. The results at Lawrence are fascinating, but at Fall River they are appalling.

The focus at Lawrence, "The City of Workers," is the woolen textile industry and the Bread and Roses Strike of 1912. Pressure on the Heritage State Park staff by community groups, including the Bread and Roses Heritage Committee (composed of local-history buffs) and the children and grandchildren of mill workers (in addition to the well-known historic significance of the strike in American labor history), makes the use of a strike in this exhibit unique among exhibitions that boost local economic opportunity. The exhibit, which opened on Labor Day 1986, is housed in a restored 1847 boardinghouse situated along the North Canal and surrounded by a fascinating array of industrial wreckage and architecture, including the Pacific Mills with a functioning bell tower, the administrative headquarters of the American Woolen Company (the Wood Building), warehouses, abandoned railroad tracks, MATH's Pacific Weave Shed, and general decay.[47] But this atmosphere was to be swept away by landscaping, rehabilitation, and development under new plans. The focus of the Heritage State Park program on the use of public history for economic revitalization is specifically designed to obliterate the current aura of industrial decline around the park site.

The story of Lawrence is correctly placed within the regional development of textiles in New England, but the exhibit lacks working machines and the one workplace setting shows drawing-in, a textile job late to be mechanized. As skilled hand work, drawing-in (especially in the absence of a loom) is a curious choice to represent textile industrialization. A display of electronic graphics depicts the important differences among the various waves of immigrant workers to the city. Other strengths in the exhibit include a tenement kitchen as a social space where the family ate, bathed, and told stories of the old country while the children instructed their parents in the language and ways

Tenement kitchen in the Lawrence Heritage State Park. (Lawrence Heritage State Park)

of the new one. But this concept is not well supported by the artifacts, which are freshly polyurethaned, or by the reconstruction of the kitchen entrance, the steps to which are unmarred by human feet. Through the kitchen window, however, one can see out into a neighborhood filled with back porches, wash lines, and other tenements. Unfortunately, the immigrant kitchen area with its links to families, shops, and the larger ethnic community stands on its own without any interpretive connection to the adjoining exhibit on the strike of 1912. This separation ignores recent research that connects the foundations of strike activity to social networks of ethnicity and gender within the community and the region.[48]

The story of the Bread and Roses Strike is told vividly in a videotape narrated by a newspaper hawker who "was there." The events of the strike unfold through newspaper headlines and cartoons; photographs, including Lewis Hine's images; and some intriguing film footage of mill workers leaving their work. But much in the interpretation is troubling. The fundamental concern is that the 1912 strike happened in Lawrence (our strike!) and it was a success (it worked!). There is no interest whatever in the strategy and politics of the Industrial Workers of the World (IWW) or in the potential for industrial unions which the success in Lawrence heralded. Success in 1912, according to the exhibit, led to higher wages and unspecified "national reforms of workers' rights law." The Bread and Roses Strike stands, like the immigrant kitchen, by itself—in isolation from other instances of labor protest in Lawrence or in the region. The exhibit ignores evidence of the same success in Lowell in 1912, IWW activity in other cities, and the frightened reaction of New England textile managers, who raised wages throughout the region in 1912 to stave off additional IWW organization. In short, the 1912 strike ("it happened right here, in Lawrence") is presented as a symbol of the local can-do spirit awaiting venture capital.

In southeastern Massachusetts near Pawtucket, the State Heritage Park at Fall River overlooks Battleship Cove, a marine museum and permanent anchorage for World War II submarines and ships. The building's glass-curtained walls seem to have been designed primarily to draw the visitor's eye away from the graphic exhibit on Fall River as a textile city and out to the naval flotilla. There is little of interest here: the one loom is encased in plastic, frozen and untouchable. The graphics on the city and the mills are well presented, but the media show, "The Fabric of Fall River," is a one-dimensional celebration of the ethnic groups of Fall River with a pedestrian account of the rise of the industry (ascribed to "Yankee ingenuity, vision and drive") and little attempt to explain why Fall River was considered one of the most strike-torn cities in the nineteenth century.[49] The slide show, designed by media specialist Michael Schaffer, suffers from a lack of participation by historical consultants and concludes with a jarring moment depicting the "people" of Fall River (complete with the high school band) entertaining a foreign cruise ship drawn up in the cove. This disturbing image—will diving for coins be next?—is supposed somehow to demonstrate the vitality of the community to new industry. No dignity for former textile workers here.

A Masterly Plan

In contrast to the subordination of the industrial past to the development future in the State Heritage Park System is the Charles River Museum of Industry, located in the power plant of the former Boston Manufacturing Company mill complex on the banks of the Charles River in Waltham. Stripped of its steam-generation equipment, the power plant possesses the dizzying dimensions of the late Roman basilica—a truly awe-inspiring space and a challenge to exhibit design.[50] The Charles River Museum leases its space from the owners of the Francis Cabot Lowell Mill elderly-housing complex developed with federal housing funds by the Gordon Charles River Falls Company. The current NEH-financed exhibit on textiles consists of graphics on the development of the Boston Manufacturing Company, the first integrated factory in New England, and stretches along the rehabilitated corridors of the old textile mill.

The mill complex winds along the banks of the sluggish and verdant Charles River. The river proved such an inadequate source of water power for expansion that company capitalists began a survey of alternative sites, a search leading to the Pawtucket Falls on the Merrimack River and the establishment of Lowell. Among the interpretative strengths at Waltham are the articulated links with other textile museums.[51] Organized in 1980, the Charles River Museum is just beginning to implement its master plan, developed primarily by director Michael Folsom, lecturer in American Studies at Brandeis and editor of the MIT Press's Documents in Industrial History Series. The main themes are labor, ingenuity, and enterprise. This stunning and ambitious interpretation of industrial life in the Waltham area insists in a unique way on seeing the slave economy of the Cotton South as integral to the textile factory system of New England and regarding cotton textiles as only one historic component in regional industrial development.

The museum's novel purpose is to interpret the Industrial Revolution as a coherent, comprehensive, and systematic whole. Like Slater, the Charles River Museum situates the origins of the textile factory in a context of development in other Waltham industries: machine tools and watch manufacturing. Unlike Slater, however, this museum plans to pursue industrial development out of the textile story and into the mass production of watches, automobile manufacturing, and the development of electronics in the Waltham area. This thematic scope permits interpretation to encompass contemporary issues of American industry and comment freely on the links between past and present. Such a broad approach to industrialization reflects the actual diversity of Waltham's industrial experience as well as serves the sources of the museum's operating and exhibit costs: local developers, the Raytheon and Honeywell corporations, and the Commonwealth of Massachusetts through the State Heritage Park program.[52]

The museum's interests also involve the collection of community history by Waltham residents, including union halls and ethnic clubs, and a unique concern for the effects of industrialization on rural areas as well as city life. The master plan takes up issues which suggest the potential for an unusual confrontation with major issues of industrial capitalism as an economic system. For example, interpretation planning situates all industrial development within a market context, explores the sources of capitalization, and considers issues of contemporary public policy. The first exhibits will be on power generation, watch manufacturing, and machine tools, but the master plan promises a working model of the integrated system of textile manufacture, pioneered at the Boston Manufacturing Company in 1814 and copied as the Waltham-Lowell system in the major urban centers of New England textile production. The achievement of the master plan at Charles River stands as a model of inclusive vision for all museums that interpret industrialization and workers as part of a system that transcends place and era.

Conclusion

An overview of various New England sites demonstrates both the uneven handling of social experience in the interpretation of textile industrialization and some hesitancy in seeing industrial capitalism in systemic ways that apply to contemporary American economic problems. The technology-and-culture approach persists, while other museum professionals and exhibit designers are struggling to combine an interpretation of the changing nature of the process of production with approaches that reflect human scale and contingency. In doing so, some of the textile-history museums of New England are developing new models of interpreting workers and industrialization that use new research in social history and point in exciting new directions. Museums and exhibit planners who plan to interpret industrial growth would do well to begin their model building with a look at the achievements in New England in applying historical scholarship to interpretation and in situating industrial experience in a social framework.

This review of the diverse exhibits in these New England museums also indicates another potential for interpreting workers and industrialization.[53] Much of the experience of industrial capitalism in textiles, as perhaps in other industries, was regional, not local: the sources of capital, the development of technology, the exploitation of water power, the recruitment of the work force, and the sharing of markets. The important trade associations, such as the New England Cotton Manufacturers' Association, represented coalitions of regional interests, which often determined joint policy on wages, markets, and labor unrest. Worker protest also took regional forms beginning with the New England workingmen's associations and early protest by female textile operatives which continued in the organizational strategies of the Knights of Labor, the craft unions of the American Federation of Labor, the Industrial Workers of the World, and the Congress of Industrial Organizations.

In the future, museum directors and exhibit designers might try to make the region part of their interpretive focus. They should continue to use informal consultation and formal activities, such as the Lowell Conference on Industrial History, to explore the ways in which textile manufacturing and its work force transcended the local community, assumed various and powerful forms of regional organization, and influenced national development. Connections as well as differences among the great textile cities of Fall River, Manchester, Lawrence, and Lowell deserve interpretation in exhibits, conferences, and publications. New England textile-history museums have already demonstrated by their past achievements that their professionals have the vision and talent to make that happen.

Acknowledgments

My thanks to Patrick Malone, Theodore Z. Penn, Michael Brewster Folsom, Thomas Leavitt, Robert Weible, Laurence Gross, and Paul Hudon for their generosity with their time and with the files of their institutions. Thanks also to Peter Blewett, Ava Baron, and Richard Butsch for making the exhibit visits in 1985 and 1986 stimulating and companionable. A shorter version of this paper was presented at the Lowell Conference on Industrial History in November 1985.

NOTES

1. My analysis of the interpretation of textile production by New England history museums was influenced by a comment from Mike Wallace at the Lowell Conference on Industrial History in November 1985, published as "Industrial Museums and the History of Deindustrialization," *Public Historian* 9 (Winter 1987), 9–19.

2. For recent definitions of the new social history designed for use by museum specialists, see James B. Gardner and George Rollie Adams, eds., *Ordinary People and Everyday Life: Perspectives on the New Social History* (Nashville, Tenn.: American Association for State and Local History, 1983).

3. For differences in nineteenth-century industrialization, see Paul G. Faler, *Mechanics and Manufacturers in the Early Industrial Revolution: Lynn, Massachusetts,*

1780–1860 (Albany: State University Press of New York, 1981); Alan Dawley, *Class and Community: The Industrial Revolution in Lynn* (Cambridge, Mass.: Harvard University Press, 1976); Sean Wilentz, *Chants Democratic: New York City and the Rise of the American Working Class* (New York: Oxford University Press, 1984); Susan E. Hirsch, *Roots of the American Working Class: The Industrialization of Crafts in Newark, 1800–1860* (Philadelphia: Temple University Press, 1978); Bruce Laurie, *Working People of Philadelphia, 1800–1850* (Philadelphia: Temple University Press, 1980); Philip Scranton, "Varieties of Paternalism: Industrial Structures and the Social Relations of Production in American Textiles," *American Quarterly* 36 (1984), 235–58; Charles G. Steffen, *Mechanics of Baltimore: Workers and Politics in the Age of Revolution* (Urbana: University of Illinois Press, 1984); Mary Blewett, *Men, Women, and Work: A Study of Class, Gender, and Protest in the New England Shoe Industry, 1780–1910* (Urbana: University of Illinois Press, 1988).

4. Gary Kulik, Roger Parks, Theodore Z. Penn, *The New England Mill Village, 1790–1860* (Cambridge, Mass.: MIT Press and Merrimack Valley Textile Museum, 1982). On the surviving mill village at Harrisville, New Hampshire, see John Borden Armstrong, *Factory Under the Elms* (North Andover, Mass.: Museum of American Textile History, 1985).

5. Interview with Theodore Penn, July 24, 1985.

6. Gary Kulik, "Patterns of Resistance to Industrial Capitalism: Pawtucket Village and the Strike of 1824," in Milton Cantor, ed., *American Working Class Culture: Explorations in American Labor and Social History* (Westport, Conn.: Greenwood Press, 1979). Slater Mill's use of Kulik's work on the reactions of Pawtucket citizens to early industrialization confirms Jonathan Prude's definition of conflict as the very essence of industrial change. See *The Coming of Industrial Order: Town and Factory Life in Rural Massachusetts, 1810–1860* (Cambridge, England: Cambridge University Press, 1983), xi.

7. Interview with Michael Folsom, July 18, 1985.

8. E. P. Thompson, "Time, Work-Discipline and Industrial Capitalism," *Past and Present* (December 1967), 56–97. For a sense of a gradually shifting concept of time and work discipline, see the description of the weaver's shop in the proposed exhibit at MATH, draft of an NEH grant proposal for an exhibit, "A Necessity of Life: The Path of Textile Factory Production," October 1985, MATH Files.

9. Interview with Theodore Penn, July 24, 1985; Patrick Malone, June 28, 1985.

10. Introduction, Paul E. Rivard, *Made in Maine*, (Portland: Maine State Museum, 1985).

11. Site visit, July 22, 1986.

12. "Made in Maine" issue, *Broadside* (Fall 1985), Maine State Museum.

13. Paul E. Rivard and Marilyn Norcini, "Made in Maine," *History News* (November 1985), 7–12, especially 9, 11.

14. Among the various work sites are a kitchen, a dressmaker's parlor, carding mill, and many shops that produced rifles, shoes, furniture, metal, and wooden goods. The weave room of a textile factory is the only mature industrial site interpreted.

15. The exhibit catalog *Made in Maine*, mentions the development of water power in Maine as a result of the overdevelopment of sites in Massachusetts and Rhode Island

and pays some attention to comparative regional industrial development and the sources of capital for a few industries. In the exhibit text, the economic development of Maine industry in the nineteenth century is viewed from within the state.

16. Rivard's insistence that the new exhibit has "a strong social perspective" and has "achieved social relevance," is unconvincing; see Rivard and Norcini, "Made in Maine," 9, 12.

17. For a 1969 critique of the use of machinery as uninterpreted artifact at Slater Mill, see James C. Hippen, "Industrial Textile Machinery: Five North American Museums," *Technology and Culture* 10 (October 1969), 570–86.

18. Theodore Z. Penn, "Exhibit Review: The Slater Mill Historic Site and the Wilkinson Mill Machine Shop," *Technology and Culture* 21 (January 1980), 56–66.

19. Visit to Slater Mill, June 1985 and Training Manual for Tour Guides, Slater Mill Historic Site, June 1985, Slater Mill Files. Visit to Old Sturbridge Village, June 1981.

20. The wheel pit of the Wilkinson Mill is unlabeled and interpreted only by the tour guide, a marvelously successful decision made by Director Malone over the objection of some of the consultants to an NEH planning grant completed in 1977. See Final Report, "Industrial Power in Nineteenth-Century America," October 26, 1977, p. 9, Slater Mill Files.

21. Familiarity with industrial history will enhance a visitor's appreciation of exhibits, but ordinary visitors must take the exhibit at face value. For an appreciation of Slater Mill from the first viewpoint, see Penn, "Exhibit Review," 61–66.

22. David Montgomery, "Workers' Control of Machine Productivity in the Nineteenth Century," *Labor History* 17 (Fall 1976), 485–509.

23. Gary Gerstle, "Looking Ahead: A Plan for Rearranging the Machinery and Revising the Tour in the Slater Mill," September 23, 1981, Slater Mill Files. Curator Stephen Victor in a 1979 NEH planning-grant application had previously argued for reorganizing the exhibit on textile machinery. See "Machines and Workers in the Textile Industry," NEH planning-grant application, November 11, 1979, Slater Mill Files. The scope of Victor's plan rested on an overall interpretation of "the textile industry in the United States from 1790 to the present" and its effects on New England and American society, with special attention to the "human response to technology in the textile industry." This document seems to mark a major shift at Slater from a concentration on early industrial development in the Blackstone River Valley to an inclusive and general interpretation of the industrial revolution in textiles. For the mixed reactions of consultants to Victor's proposals, see Herbert Gutman to Steve Victor, August 20, 1980; Ted Penn to Steve Victor, n.d. especially the injunction to "Simplify! Simplify!"; Laurence F. Gross to Stephen Victor, August 12, 1980; in Correspondence re NEH Conference, Summer 1980, Slater Mill Files.

24. "Pawtucket—Cradle of American Industry," a May 10, 1985, script for a Slater Mill slide show, Slater Mill Files. Interpretation at Slater Mill recognizes the many negative aspects of industrial development: flooded farmland and ruined fishing, recurrent depressions and strikes, fierce competition, and the inevitable rise of rival centers of textile production, Training Manual, June 1985, Slater Mill Files. The Slater staff has recently collected oral history, recruited former weavers and knitters to help explain the work experience and keep the machines going, and gathered and performed work

songs. Slater has published several regional guidebooks on historic industrial structures: Gary Kulik, *Rhode Island Textile Mills*, (Pawtucket, R.I.: Slater Mill Historic Site, c. 1979); Patrick M. Malone, et al., *Guidebook: Rhode Island and Southeastern Massachusetts Excursion* (Pawtucket, R.I.: Fifth Conference on the Conservation of the Industrial Heritage, 1984). In accordance with Jonathan Prude's work, this series could be extended to the connections between Slater's innovations and the persistance of rural textile production in New England.

25. Paul Rivard argued that gradual and discontinuous change was central to early industrialization in *The Home Manufacture of Cloth, 1790–1840* (Pawtucket, R.I.: Slater Mill Historic Site, 1974).

26. For a recent example of neoliberal economic analysis, see Bart Ziegler, Associated Press, "Experts Explain Bay's State's Economic Revival," *Lowell Sun*, July 14, 1986. On Slater, see Paul E. Rivard, *Samuel Slater: Father of American Manufactures* (Pawtucket, R.I.: Slater Mill Historic Site, 1974).

27. J. Bruce Sinclair, "The Merrimack Valley Textile Museum: A New Institution for an Important Aspect of American History," *Transactions, 1956–1963* of the Colonial Society of Massachusetts 43 (Boston 1966), 406–16, and Caroline S. Rogers, "The Merrimack Valley Textile Museum," *Shuttle, Spindle and Dye-Pot* 1 (November 1969).

28. *Wool Technology and the Industrial Revolution* (North Andover, Mass.: Merrimack Valley Textile Museum, 1965); Ian Quimby, "The Specialized Museum: A Case Study," *Museum News* 44 (January and March 1966).

29. Thomas W. Leavitt, "Merrimack Valley Textile Museum," *Technology and Culture* 8 (April 1967), 204–6. Leavitt also helped to pioneer the idea of raising standards of excellence at museums by reviewing exhibits, "The Need for Critical Standards in History Museums Exhibits: A Case in Point," *Curator* 10 (June 1967), 91-94; "Towards a Standard of Excellence: The Nature and Purpose of Exhibit Reviews," *Technology and Culture* 9 (January 1968), 70–75. He has also supported important conferences on the history of the American textile industry and industrialization, and the museum has maintained an active program of publication on textile history in association with Boston University and MIT.

30. *Museum of American Textile History News* (Fall 1985; Winter 1985; Winter 1986).

31. Correspondence with Executive Office of Labor re advisory committee to study the feasibility of a labor-history museum in Lawrence, 1985–1986, in possession of the author.

32. Site visit, July 31, 1986.

33. Research on Lowell suggests that strikes and resistance among textile workers were frequent but that unions were weak until the late 1930s, well after most of the mills had closed or departed to the South. See Mary H. Blewett, ed., *Surviving Hard Times: The Working People of Lowell* (Lowell, Mass.: Lowell Museum, 1982).

34. Draft of an NEH grant proposal, "A Necessity of Life: The Path of Textile Factory Production," October 1985, Files of MATH. See also Laurence Gross, "Workers and Artifacts: New Uses, New Purposes," *Proceedings, Industrial Heritage '84* 2 (Fifth International Conference on the Conservation of the Industrial Heritage), 63–69. I am

grateful to Tom Leavitt, Larry Gross, and Paul Hudon for sharing with me a copy of their grant proposal and exhibit design in progress. Historical consultants to the new exhibit plan included Herbert Gutman, Gary Gerstle, Jonathan Prude, Philip Scranton, and Barbara Tucker, *MATHNews* (Winter 1985).

35. For the Lawrence Heritage State Park treatment of the 1912 strike, see below.

36. Site visit, July 24, 1986. For the original plan recommending the park, see *Lowell, Massachusetts, Report of the Lowell Historic Canal District Commission to the Ninety-Fifth Congress of the United States of America* (Washington, D.C.: Government Printing Office, 1977) referred to locally as "the Brown Book." In 1987, 850,000 people visited the park; its staff expects one million visitors by 1990.

37. Federal financing of the development of interpretation at the Lowell Park has also been large scale: $410,000 for interpretation planning at major exhibits in the Boott Mill and $145,000 at a restored row of boardinghouses and $2 million for the exhibits. Interview with Lowell National Historical Park historian Robert Weible, August 1, 1986.

38. The choice of these five themes represents a flexible policy, adopted by the Park Service staff, that has proved unusually responsive to strong pressures from the academic and local communities, both of which have shared actively in the development of interpretation, especially the important decision to interpret post–Civil War experience. Criticism of the park's interpretation has come largely from the political left, as the business community, apparently content with the economic stimulus of local development, has been silent on ideological issues concerning industrial capitalism. Interview with Robert Weible, October 2, 1985. Weible has written thoughtful internal memos on interpretation (see files of the LNHP) and important papers on the park's development which indicate his concern with the issues raised by the new social history. See Robert Weible, "Lowell: Building a New Appreciation for Historical Place," *The Public Historian* 6 (Summer 1984), 27–38; "Lowell National Historical Park and the Evolution of a Community's Historical Identity," paper presented at the 1983 OAH conference; "Programming Public History at Historic Sites and Museums in the 1980s," paper presented at the 1986 New England Archivists meeting. For an excellent critical analysis of the uses of the city's history in the development of the LNHP, see Loretta Ryan, "The Remaking of Lowell and Its Histories, 1965–1982," paper read at the Lowell Conference on Industrial History, November 1985.

39. Early planning for interpretation involved social historian Tamara Hareven, who helped organize the first (1980) in a series of annual conferences on Industrial History sponsored initially by the Lowell Park and the Lowell Historic Preservation Commission and now by the Tsongas Center for Industrial History. For concerns about the nature of interpretation at Lowell, see Mary Blewett, "Lowell: The National Park Service Meets the Working People of Lowell," *Labor and Community Newsletter* 1, no. 2 (August 1979), 2–3; David Sylvester, "Lowell's Labor's Lost," *The Progressive* (July 1981), 34–35; and Brian Mitchell, "Interpreting American Industrial History: The Lowell National Historical Park's General Management Plan—An Overview," *International Labor and Working Class History* no. 21 (Spring 1982), 69–72.

40. *Lowell Sun*, July 17, 1986.

41. For an overview, see Michael Wallace, "Reflections on the History of Historic

Preservation," in Susan Porter Benson, Stephen Brier, and Roy Rosenzweig, eds., *Presenting the Past: Essays on History and the Public* (Philadelphia: Temple University Press, 1986), 165–99.

42. The interpretation on this tour answers in part the 1982 critique by Paul Hudon of the lack of social history in the Lowell tours, "Exhibits: New Lowell Experiments," *Museum News* (November–December 1982), 71–75.

43. Social historians Avi Decter and Shomer Zwelling direct the exhibit design team at the Center for History Now.

44. The Center for History Now, "Boott Mill Exhibits: A Conceptual Plan," January 1986, Files of LNHP, and interview with Robert Weible, August 1, 1986.

45. Kathleen Bond, "A Preliminary Report on the Demography of Boott Mills Units #33–48, 1838–1942," 1986, Files of LNHP.

46. "Labor's Legacy," Calendar Section, *Boston Globe*, August 28, 1986, and brochures published by the commonwealth of Massachusetts, "The Spirit is Working: Lawrence" and "Massachusetts Heritage State Parks," 1986.

47. Site visit, September 1, 1986.

48. See the recent work of Ardis Cameron on the 1912 strike as a network of neighborhoods and activist women, "Bread and Roses Revisited: Women's Culture and Working-class Activism in the Lawrence Strike of 1912," in Ruth Milkman, ed., *Women, Work and Protest* (Boston: Routledge and Kegan Paul, 1985), 42–61, and of Dexter P. Arnold on the strike as an ethnic and regional event, " 'A Row of Bricks': Worker Activism in the Merrimack Valley Textile Industry, 1912–1922," doctoral dissertation, University of Wisconsin, 1985.

49. There is little indication that historical consultants Donna Huse, Steve Dunswell, Patrick Malone, or Philip Silvia influenced the Heritage State Park interpretation at Fall River.

50. Site visit and interview with Michael Folsom, July 18, 1985. The location is 154 Moody Street, Waltham.

51. Charles River Museum of Industry, *Master Plan for Exhibits and Programs* (Waltham, Mass., 1983), 4–7.

52. For a short account of the museum's development, see "Waltham: Fundamental to Industrial America," *Waltham News-Tribune*, November 13, 1984, Charles River Museum Files. See also the Charles River Museum of Industry newsletter *Shoptalk* (Fall 1985 and Spring 1987).

53. For a different view of industrial-history research and interpretation, see T. Allan Comp, "The Best Arena: Industrial History at the Local Level," *History News* (May 1982), 8–11.

History Museums and Material Culture

12

Thomas J. Schlereth

The relationship between American history museums and material-culture studies is both an old and a new one. It is old in the obvious sense that the collection, preservation, and display of artifacts has been a traditional task of history museums. It is new in that the term *material culture* has been in use only since the late nineteenth century,[1] when anthropologists first employed the phrase in an effort to distinguish three types of cultural data: ideational (found usually in oral or written data), sociological (documented by fieldwork observation of human behavior, such as child rearing or kinship patterning), and material (found in the work of people, such as ceramics, tools, houses, and the like).

In the twentieth century, the meaning of *material culture* has undergone various redefinitions and reformulations.[2] Perhaps most striking is that, in the past decade, the term has gained growing currency among researchers in the arts and humanities. Its diverse advocates now include art historian Jules Prown; folklorist Henry Glassie; technology historian Brooke Hindle; Kenneth Ames, a scholar in the decorative arts; and archaeologist James Deetz. In Deetz's estimate, *material culture* can be defined briefly as "that segment of man's physical environment which is purposely shaped by him according to culturally dictated plans."[3]

Such a definition underlies this essay. Nevertheless, *material culture* is not the only nomenclature favored by historians who study artifacts in the museum or in the academy. Canadians prefer the term *material history,* as in the title of the *Material History Bulletin*, a journal published by the National Museum of Man in Ottawa.[4] "Material history," writes Gregg Finley, "refers to both the artifacts under investigation and the disciplinary basis of the investigation."[5] In addition, the phrase *material life* (or its sometime synonym, *material civilization*), has been used by both French and American historians. Economic historian Fernand Braudel's stated attempt to devise a label that would be an alternative to the word *technology* but would "maintain a bridge to the material culture of anthropology and archaeology" and yet still convey an overview of "an economic culture of everyday life" is one source of this term.[6] Another is social historian Cary Carson, director of research at Colonial Williamsburg, who sees the study of material life as involving object research on social institutions and social relations because "artifacts serve on one level as the devices that men and women have always used to mediate their relationships with one another and with the physical world."[7]

Elsewhere I have assessed the assets and liabilities of these three terms, recognizing that each is problematic in certain ways and that each betrays certain scholarly predilections, institutional affiliations, and intellectual temperaments of proponents.[8] Here I prefer the label *material culture* for several reasons: common use in several disciplines in both the humanities and social sciences; a historical lineage of scholarship dating back to the nineteenth century; evocation of both human behavior and belief; embodiment of the culture concept; and an increasingly widespread usage, at least in the past decade, among both "museum historians" and "academic historians."[9]

In order to understand the history of American material culture as a scholarly enterprise, I once divided it (see the table) into three chronological phases: a collecting or classifying period (1876–1948); a descriptive or connoisseurship era (1948–1965); and an analytical or explanatory period (1965–present). To be sure, the three periods overlap and were never as distinct as my Procrustean outline might suggest. For example, the earlier interest in collecting artifacts and arranging them in appropriate topologies has continued with vigor into the present. Similarly, R. T. H. Halsey, L. V. Lockwood, and others occasionally practiced the careful connoisseurship of material culture evidence before World War II. Important analytical studies by J. Kouwenhoven, C. M. Watkins, and J. B. Jackson also appeared before the mid-1960s. The classification scheme nevertheless provides a shorthand to the history of material-culture research. If one examines the biographies of the scholars I claim to be representative of their time, one finds that almost three-fourths of the key contributors to the American material-culture movement had some museum experience.

This essay assesses the complex and reciprocal relationship between museums and material culture, focusing particularly on the past two decades. Using the three categories of the classification scheme—collection, description, and interpretation—it asks how material-culture research has affected public presentations in museums as well as how history-museum presentations and programs have influenced the public's understanding of the scope and significance of object research. It concludes with some observations on the future course of material-culture studies and American-history museums.

The Shifting Paradigms: A Brief Historical Overview of Material Culture Studies in America

Characteristics	Age of Collecting (1876–1948)	Age of Description (1948–1965)	Age of Analysis (1965—)	
	I	II	III	IV
Pioneering Scholars	J. Henry	J. C. Harrington	B. Hindle	D. Kelsey
	C. Dana	L. Jones	C. Hummel	H. Marshall
	C. Wilcomb	C. Watkins	I. Noël Hume	C. Carson
	W. Nutting	J. Kouwenhoven	D. Yoder	S. Bronner
	G. Goode	T. J. Wertenbaker	P. Lewis	M. Jones
	W. Appleton	F. Kniffen	W. Roberts	J. Prown
	L. V. Lockwood	J. B. Jackson	G. Kubler	M. Leone
	I. Phelps Stokes	C. Peterson	J. Schlebecker	J. Vlach
	H. Cahill	J. Cotter	E. Dethlefsen	J. Anderson
	S. Clark	J. Downs	A. Gowans	P. Marzio
	H. DuPont	E. Ferguson	A. Garvan	C. Gilborn
	R. T. H. Halsey	W. Whitehill	A. Ludwig	K. Ames
	H. Mercer	C. Montgomery	J. Deetz	R. Cowan
				C. Kidwell
				R. Trent
				H. Glassie
Typical Intellectual Emphases	Historical associationism; primacy fascination; search for artistic uniqueness	Cult of connoisseurship: taxonomy fascination; search for American uniqueness	Vernacularism, typicality, methodology fascination; search for artifact's evidential uniqueness	
Principal Research Concerns	Collecting, salvaging, preserving, hoarding high-style, unique, or elite artifacts	Preparing descriptive typologies, chronologies, classification systems of artifacts	Seeking to use artifacts to analyze human behavior in societal context	
Interests in Artifacts and Artifact-Makers	Objets d'art: an artiste creating art	Results of craft processes: a technician working in a tradition of artisanry	Consumer goods and services: a citizen involved in community life	

Main Disciplinary Specialties	Art history, architectural history; anthropology, archaeology	History of technology; folk art and folklife studies; cultural and historical geography; cultural history; historical archaeology	Social history: industrial, commercial, experimental archaeology; museum studies; social and environmental psychology; folkloristics; cognitive anthropology
Professional Institutions	The Walpole Society; College Art Association; Society of Architectural Historians	Society for History of Technology; Decorative Arts Society; American Association for State and Local History	Pioneer America Society; Society for Industrial Archaeology; Society for a North American Cultural Survey
Research Centers Established	Smithsonian Institution; Colonial Williamsburg; Index of American Design; Henry Ford Museum	Winterthur Museum-University of Delaware; Cooperstown Program SUNY-Oneonta; National Park Service Index of Early American Culture	George Washington University; University of Pennsylvania; American Folklife Center; Boston University; Indiana University
Typical Serial Publications	*Antiques; The Antiquarian; Art in America*	*Technology and Culture; Winterthur Portfolio* (annual); *Pennsylvania Folklife; Contributions from MHT*	*Material History Bulletin; Winterthur Portfolio* (quarterly); *ALHFAM Bulletin; Journal of Interdisciplinary History; Journal of American Culture*
Historiographical Assessments	W. Kaplan, "R. H. Halsey: An Ideology of Collecting American Decorative Arts" (1980)	C. Montgomery, "Classics and Collectibles" (1977)	S. Bronner, "Concepts in the Study of Material Aspects of American Folk Culture" (1979)
Representative Publications	I. Lyon, *Colonial Furniture of New England* (1891)	J. Kouwenhoven, *Made in America* (1948)	H. Glassie, *Folk Housing in Middle Virginia* (1975)
	C. Wissler, "Material Cultures of North American Indians" (1914)	J. Lipman, *American Folk Art* (1948)	L. Ferguson, *Historical Archaeology and the Importance of Material Things* (1977)
	H. Mercer, *Ancient Carpenter Tools* (1929)	S. Giedion, *Mechanization Takes Command* (1948)	K. Ames, *Beyond Necessity* (1977)
	F. Kimball, *Domestic Architecture of the American Colonies* (1922)	C. Montgomery, *American Furniture: The Federal Period* (1966)	M. Jones, *The Hand-Made Object* (1975)
	R. Burlingame, *March of the Iron Men* (1938)	A. Gowans, *Images of American Living* (1964)	P. Benes, *The Masks of Orthodoxy* (1977)
			J. Fitchen, *The New World Dutch Barn* (1968)

History-Museum Collecting: Gathering Material Evidence

Most American history museums acknowledge the collection of the physical past as one of their functions. In this century, and particularly since the 1950s, they have become the major repositories for most extant, moveable, pre-1850 American artifacts. Thus anyone pursuing object research on a pre–Civil War historical topic must work in museum collections. As a result, the future of a large segment of material-culture studies, be they communicated in essays or exhibits, will be determined by the content of American history-museum collections. Although historical archaeology may add some objects, collections of pre-1850 data are now largely closed. Curators' preferences, donors' demands, museum size, conservation practices, and collecting fads have shaped the surviving evidence.

The utility of historic-museum object collections is limited. Often the provenance of objects within the museum's confines is not known. Their historical and cultural contexts have vanished or were never recorded. For example, tools have been separated from the craftsman and his tool chest or kit, from the shops where they were used, and from the products fabricated with their help. "Out of site" can mean "out of sight." Without a documented context, many artifacts remain little more than historical souvenirs. History museums are not the only institutions saddled with anonymous artifacts. The material-culture holdings of many anthropological museums, as Nan Rothschild and Anne-Marie Cantwell have shown, are similarly problematic.[10] History-museum exhibitions might, however, introduce the public to what it does not know about their holdings. Visitors would, I think, welcome such intellectual candor and learn much from it. An extended discussion among museum historians about the research problems of their previously gathered collections would be a contribution to material-culture methodology.

The public would also profit from knowing more about the fecklessness of material-culture survival and what this means for historical interpretation. More research should be done on the complex process of selection by which some artifacts survive and others perish. In their interpretation of the past, history museums must attempt to establish some quantitative sense of what has been lost in relation to what they have saved.[11] We have no adequate awareness of how wide the gap is between the former reality of the physical past and its present reality as extant objects in our collections.

More accessibility for scholars and the interested public to museum collections and techniques for their verification is a must for the mutual sophistication of both history-museum interpretation and material-culture research. Unlike most documentary data stored in libraries and archives, material-culture evidence cannot be easily duplicated, microfilmed, published, or made widely available to other scholars for further interpretation and verification. Most historical institutions do not engage in regular object-study loans, as is common among anthropology and science museums. Nor is there any adequate finding of aid to material-culture collections comparable to the National Union Catalogs of Books, Serials, and Manuscripts.

Recently, Wilcomb Washburn proposed reducing many artifacts now in museum collections to photographs, drawings, and other more portable, quantitative, and storable forms of data as a way to improve access. Such extracted evidence would then permit the disposal of many, although not all, preserved objects.[12]

Modern artifacts—computers, holography, video discs—may assist in duplicating and manipulating material culture in research inquiries involving large aggregates of data, as the efforts of several history museums (St. Mary's City, the Strong Museum, Plimoth Plantation, Sleepy Hollow Restorations, and the Smithsonian Institution) have suggested. Robert Chenall's scheme, *Nomenclature for Museum Cataloging: A System for Classifying Man-Made Objects* (1978), first developed at the Strong Museum in Rochester, continues to prompt useful debate about this issue in the methodology of material-culture research and collection management.[13]

Finally, history museums that claim to cover all of American history must confront the question of contemporary material culture. Yet many refuse, because of limitations of space and time, lack of personnel and funds, and the complexity of selection and documentation. The first two objections are real but not insurmountable. The third is pertinent to the interrelation of material culture and the history museum. Many historians, in the academy and in the museum, have been reluctant to become aggressive, purposeful collectors. Instead they are content to wait and accept whatever objects or documents chance happens to place into their hands. This laissez-faire policy of collecting leaves the selecting of the material-culture evidence to private collectors, antique promoters, and collectible entrepreneurs.

A cadre of material-culture researchers would have it otherwise. They argue that history museums should take an active, deliberate, analytical approach to the collection of contemporary objects. Some espouse the program developed by the historical museums of Sweden called SAMDOK (an acronym for the Swedish word *samtidsdokumentation,* or "same-time documentation"); others promote the work of American projects, such as the Society for the North American Cultural Survey or the Contemporary Collections of the American Folklife Center.[14] At least a few museums, including the Oakland Museum and the National Museum of American History, have followed this lead and have revised their collection policies to recognize the historical present.[15] Such purposeful collecting can reduce the bias that makes the study of material culture a kind of Whig history in which it is assumed that certain artifacts were destined to survive.

Because museums' collections of past objects are currently so unrepresentative, Dell Upton has argued that the best samples of material-culture evidence are "contemporary artifactual landscapes" that still exist outside the museum in their full density and complexity. He similarly points out that study of objects being fabricated and used right now—if the testimony of their makers and users is also collected and studied—may offer the most potential for theoretical and methodological advances in material-culture analysis. Only by careful collecting of present-day objects can museums ensure that their collections will be seen as useful by future scholars.[16]

Contemporary collecting can also make it easier for exhibits and other public presentations to connect past and present. A few material culturists have gone even further and have used exhibits on recent American history to collect additional contemporary material culture. For example, in three important exhibits, David Orr interpreted artifacts of the Vietnam War, Barbara Riley placed modern consumerism in historical perspective, and Joan Siedl and Nicholas Westbrook examined the history of mail-order catalogs.[17]

History-Museum Connoisseurship: Describing Material Evidence

Although many history museums have resisted collecting contemporary data on a large scale, they have paid increasing attention to the care and classification of their collections. This curatorship of artifacts has been principally a task of authentification, classification, and conservation. As such, this involvement with material culture has been principally descriptive, emphasizing connoisseurship and conservation, rather than analytical.[18]

Those in charge of artifacts in natural-history, physical-science, or anthropology museums are usually called scientists, whereas the comparable person in most American history museums is generally identified as a curator, not as a historian. This identification has often isolated the curatorial staff of many history museums from the American history profession, which became increasingly entrenched in the nation's colleges and universities in the late nineteenth and early twentieth centuries.[19] Excluded from the associations, conferences, and journals of the American history establishment, historians in museums understandably took little interest in the historiographical concerns, methodological techniques, and theoretical models erected by those who claimed to speak for the "history profession." Many history-museum curators, whose job descriptions focused on connoisseurship and conservation, therefore had little time or inclination to make original contributions to historical research. Some came to see themselves as essentially librarians or archivists maintaining objects for the use of other scholars or the museum staff who mounted exhibits.

The "compiler-describer-collector," as Cary Carson calls this type of artifact scholar, has both advanced and retarded material-culture research. Their principal labor has been to explain why man-made objects look as they do. All have a common devotion to objects as both starting points and destinations for their scholarship. But, as Carson notes, "however far afield they forage in written records, graphic sources, and oral histories to collect information they deem useful, they always come back to the object—literally—of their quest." Yet, continues Carson, the collector-compiler-describer "provides an essential preliminary service without which there can no more be a history of material life then there could be economic history without reliable statistics or biography without authentic personal papers." [20]

Those principally concerned with taxonomic questions have enriched object studies in several ways. One early experiment in developing a comprehensive methodology for describing and cataloging an enormous number of artifacts was the Index of Early American Culture at the Winterthur Museum. It was based on the principles of the human relations area files developed by anthropologist George Murdock and codified in the *Outline of Cultural Materials* (1950).[21] The published object checklist and the study collection are formats that history museums have occasionally borrowed from their counterparts in the art museums to describe and delineate classes of objects. Numerous exhibit catalogs exemplify this approach, as do comprehensive study collections, such as the one on permanent display at the Strong Museum in Rochester, New York.

Historians at American museums have also augmented the techniques of object description. In the past decade there have been several attempts to develop strategies that could be claimed as indigenous to material-culture research. E. McClung Fleming's artifact primer of four operations (identification, evaluation, cultural analysis, interpretation), Jules Prown's three-stage model (description, deduction, speculation) and, Robert Elliot's five-stage exercise (material, construction, function, provenance, and value) are examples of this quest.[22]

While connoisseurship and conservation do not normally have a public face (such work is done in offices and laboratories out of sight from a museum's public areas) they have an effect on public presentation of material culture. Called "object fetishism" by its critics, "object primacy" by its advocates, the reverential treatment often accorded single objects by curators is translated to museum visitors in what might be called "the enshrinement syndrome." For example, a West Virginia post office that had been neglected for more than one hundred years was dismantled and rebuilt in the National Museum of History and Technology (now the National Museum of American History). As Harold Skramstad notes, by moving this artifact into the museum it became, instantaneously, a revered national treasure—so revered, in fact, that there was serious talk of removing the original shutters and replacing them with exact replicas since the originals contained carvings of the names of Civil War soldiers: safe so long as the structure was neglected, but in serious jeopardy once it was securely in the museum. The ennobling effect of the museum environment affects not only visitors, but staff perceptions as well. When asked what great historical treasures the museum possessed, one curator at the National Museum responded that anything was a national treasure simply by being in the collection.[23]

Kenneth Ames points out other dangers of an overemphasis on merely describing objects: creator worship (concern for who made it or an exhaustive study of an object's maker rather than its user); primacy fascination (concern for who made it first or a high valuation being automatically assigned to an artifact's novelty or innovative elements); and excessive normative evaluation (asking what it is worth on the artifact market as opposed to its possible social, cultural, or ideological significance). Ames also alludes to another issue that history museums and material-culture studies must address: How representative is the material evidence that has been collected? How many instances of an object on display are to be found in a history museum's collections behind the scenes? How many exist in other museum collections? How many are one-of-a-kind? How many were truly commonplace in their time?[24]

Historians who espouse the use of material-culture evidence in order to counter the biases of documentary and statistical sources must also recognize its methodological limitations. The charge that many verbal records of American history have been generated by a small group of mostly white, mostly upper- or middle-class, mostly male, mostly urban, and mostly Protestant individuals could also be levied against many history-museum collections.[25] The influx of social-history topics (for example, demographic history) and techniques (for example, quantitative methods) into both material-culture research and history-museum interpretation may further alert us to the liabilities imposed by the gender, race, ethnic origin, and socioeconomic status of the makers and users of objects.[26]

History-Museum Interpreting: Analyzing Material Evidence

Over the past two decades, history museums and material culturists have gradually acknowledged the need to move beyond the simplistic claim that objects were important in and of themselves. Museums have had to interpret as well as gather and describe objects. National Endowment for the Humanities funding requirements made *interpretation* a buzz word among museum professionals in the 1970s. The American Association for State and Local History and other organizations sponsored seminars on museum interpretation throughout the United States. Book reviewers of studies in American material culture demanded "explanatory models." Manifestos for a new analytical vision of artifact research appeared. Theorists claimed that to achieve intellectual substance and academic respectability, defensible techniques and theories had to be applied to the material-culture evidence that previous generations had collected and classified.

Institutionally, North American history museums contributed to this effort by publishing two of the three material-culture journals in North America: *Winterthur Portfolio: A Journal of American Material Culture* by the Winterthur Museum and *Material History Bulletin* by the National Museum of Man.[27] Numerous national and international conferences on the subject also received strong museum sponsorship and support.[28] Institutions, such as the Smithsonian, established fellowships in material-culture research, and occasionally a museum, such as the Colorado State Historical Society, advertised for a curator of material culture.[29]

Intellectually, North American history museums have only begun to explore the explanatory power of the artifact. While several provocative advances (reviewed below) have been made at large institutions, the present state of the art in object interpretation in historical explanation is still largely derivative. But this was also the case within the multidisciplinary material-culture movement as a whole. In material-culture theory, students of the object have been consumers rather than producers. In an assessment of how widespread and diverse this borrowing has been, I once came up with several conceptual positions on which American material-culture scholarship was modeled.[30] One might ask: What role have history museums played in the development or diffusion of these explanatory paradigms? Which of these intellectual frameworks have been most influential in contemporary history-museum interpretation?

One way of answering the last question is to dismiss two material-cultural approaches—the structuralist and the behavioralist—that have been least congenial to historians working in museums.[31] Although the monographic literature applying structuralism in material-culture research is growing, the theory has yet to inform a major history exhibition. Similarly, the behavioralistic approach advocated by Michael Owen Jones surfaces principally in folk art and craft demonstrations.[32] History museums have, however, benefited from and contributed to four other identifiable forms of material-culture interpretive theory: national character; functionalist; cultural reconstructionist, and social history.

The national-character approach to material-culture interpretation uses particular objects to explain the collective ethos of an entire nation. Its advocates have produced such classics as John Kouwenhoven, *Made in America* (1948); Alan Gowans, *Images of American Living* (1964); Alan Trachtenberg, *The Brooklyn Bridge: Fact and Symbol* (1964); and Daniel Boorstin, *The Americans* (1958–1973). Its manifestation in the history museum can be documented in several blockbuster exhibitions mounted at the time of the nation's bicentennial. For example, the National Museum of American History made American pluralism the chief American character trait in its "A Nation of Nations" exhibit. Although this focus on the collective character is most frequently applied to explain the total national experience (particularly by demonstrating what is "American" about American artifacts), it has also informed permanent gallery installations on a regional level (for example, the New York State Museum's plans for its Upstate Gallery) and a local level (for example, the Fort Worth Museum of Science and History "Images of Fort Worth").

In the New York State Museum's permanent gallery, the museum historians plan to organize part of their artifact assemblage around a sense of self-definition by opposition ("We are what New York City is NOT") to demonstrate how upstate New York historically has had a distinctive regional identity, one claiming to be nonmetropolitan, rural oriented, and independent. In the Fort Worth exhibit, curators attempt to prove that Fort Worth is the state's "Texasmost" city by documenting its several "border lives"—as a frontier line in the 1850s, a cattle kingdom in the 1870s, a commercial gateway to the West in the 1890s, to meatpacking after 1910, to the West Texas oil fields in the 1920s, and to the aviation industry of the 1940s—as emblematic of "Texasness" as a whole.[33]

A national-character approach, whether communicated in monographs or museums, can be prone to the fallacy of progressive determinism, a tendency that has been enormously influential in both American-history and material-culture research. Often the American past is depicted as one material success after another in an ever-upward ascent of more goods and services for all the nation's citizens. George Basalla and others have traced this tendency in the history of technology and in technical museums. Such museums, notes Basalla, are often dominated by a "technological cornucopia" mentality in their celebration of American progress. Michael Ettema sees the same problem in the American decorative arts, as does Dell Upton in American vernacular architecture.[34] Examples of this perspective's influencing exhibits would be those at the National Air and Space Museum and "In Praise of America: American Decorative Arts, 1650–1830," mounted in 1980 by the National Gallery of Art.[35]

A national-character emphasis in a history-museum exhibition need not be uncritical or insensitive to changes that were unsuccessful or to points of view that did not prevail. Exhibits around several 1980s historical anniversaries— the opening of the Brooklyn Bridge, the completion of the Statue of Liberty, the ratification of the U.S. Constitution, the adoption of the national flag, the opening of Ellis Island—could explore not only the continuity and consensus surrounding these national symbols but also the complexities, contradictions, and controversies they have engendered among Americans, whom historian Michael Kammen has aptly described as a "people of paradox."[36]

Even a minor revision of a traditional national-character exhibit can promote more sophisticated understanding of nationhood and a more perceptive understanding of the national past. When an exhibit is different in tone, subject matter, or point of view from what they expect, visitors will be surprised and take notice. For instance, Barbara Clark Smith of the National Museum of American History has suggested revising its exhibit "The Star Spangled Banner" by alternately playing a traditional nineteenth-century rendition of the national anthem and Jimi Hendrix's 1960s version of the song. Many visitors would be taken aback, but they would also think critically about the presentation.[37]

A special interest in the material culture of technics unites the advocates of national-character research (who see such artifacts as skyscrapers, assembly lines, balloon-frame houses as quintessentially American) and those who follow a functionalist interpretation. Functionalists hold that culture is primarily a means of adapting to environment, with technology being the primary adaptive mechanism. With strong advocates in fields of cultural anthropology, the history of technology, and folklore, the functionalists in material-culture research are especially concerned with explaining two processes: how an object was "worked" (how its maker acted in order to make it) and how the object itself "works" (how it actually functions in a sociocultural context).[38]

History museums with institutional ties to natural-history collections often have a strong functionalist orientation that is evident, for example, in the use of habitat groups to show stages of economic evolution and the development of technological skills. Many American Indian history museums, despite recent calls for broader interpretation, have a similar focus.[39] The ubiquitous craft demonstrations found at practically all outdoor living-history sites and agricultural museums are often other examples of functionalism. Finally, the approach is personified in such organizations as SWEAT (Society of Workers in the Early American Trades) and, of course, in the ever-proliferating reenactment movement.[40]

Although history museums have become enormously proficient in demonstrating how an artifact was actually worked—Old Sturbridge Village and Conner Prairie Settlement, for example, pride themselves on their accurate replication of the processes of how things were made—most history sites and exhibits pay less attention to how objects functioned in a social, cultural, or political context. The traditional emphasis of so much material-culture research on the makers of objects rather than the users encouraged this neglect. Moreover, the extensive literature on this the second half of the functionalist equation (that is, the magical, religious, regional, national, social, and ideological functions of artifacts) has received only limited attention from museum historians.[41]

Historians, sensitive to how ideologies function, recognize that objects mediate power relationships between people. Artifacts do have politics.[42] And curators, interpreting government buildings, churches, civic structures, recreational spaces, public sites, and history museums, must not neglect this important function of material culture, past and present.

Functionalists are eager to demonstrate that material culture reflects the rationality and practicality of participants in a culture. A person's description of his own motives often helps the researcher establish a functional explanation. Thus oral-history fieldwork is a frequently employed research tool. But often such information is not available. Then the researcher is left to probe "the mind of the maker," particularly the functional sequence that existed in the fabrication and use of an artifact.

In order to explore the cognitive processes involved in the production of past material culture, researchers in a number of American history museums have engaged in "experimental or imitative archaeology." Experiments in seventeenth-century brewing have been done at Plimoth Plantation and in early-nineteen-century kiln construction and ceramic manufacture at Old Sturbridge Village.[43] In a summary of such research, Jay Anderson notes that "experimental archaeology was developed as a means of (1) practically testing theories of past cultural behavior, especially the technological processes involving the use of tools, and (2) obtaining data, not readily available from more traditional artifact and historical sources." [44]

A strict functionalist interpretation of material culture can exaggerate human efficacy. The aura and physical presence of certain types of things still so tangibly present centuries after their actual making can seduce the researcher into overemphasizing what anthropologists call "the culture of agency"—the self-defining or self-assertive activities of their original makers. The history that is written or exhibited from such material culture is prone, therefore, to champion only the activities of the movers and shakers of the past. More triumphs than tragedies survive in the extant physical record.

Functionalist-oriented exhibits in museums often promote a view of history as a story of success and achievement. For example, the Cooper-Hewitt Museum's 1986 exhibit "Milestones: Fifty Years of Goods and Services" chronicled five decades of consumer "small wonders and big deals" without much attention to consumer fraud, protection, or rejection.[45] Such exhibits usually neglect the downside of human life, common to us all but not commonly depicted. For example, in many living-history farms there is little material culture that helps a visitor experience something of the isolation, monotony, or loneliness of a frontier prairie existence.

In these contexts, documentary and statistical records (rather than the artifactual) may prove especially helpful to the researcher since people could and did write about the dark and unpleasant side of their existence; that is, the uncertainties, the false starts, the halfway measures, the intentions that failed. But object study also requires analyses of material-culture pathology so that we might know more about what things, in various historical periods, did not work, which consistently broke down or were quickly junked in favor of other products. Since most of the American material-culture history studied to date has been (like so much of American written history) the history of winners, more appreciation of the losers (people and products) might be a valuable corrective.

John Demos, for example, notes that *New England Begins: The Seventeenth Century*, an exhibition and three-volume catalog produced by the Department of American Decorative Arts and Sculpture of the Boston Museum of Fine Arts (BMFA), depicts New England settlers as uncommonly active, effective, and forceful in coping with the circumstances of their lives.[46] This viewpoint contrasts sharply with a generation of scholarly opinion on seventeenth-century New England life, which has emphasized the unanticipated and the unwelcomed effects of seventeenth-century life in a new environment. Americans arrived with plans, expectations, and assumptions as to what they were about, but environmental circumstances transformed most of these.[47] The artifacts analyzed by the BMFA research team of archaeologists, decorative-arts specialists, and social historians lead to a quite different conclusion. New Englanders were in control of their lives and their actions, artifice, and artifacts show them so.

A number of cultural anthropologists, folklike scholars, historical archaeologists, and historic preservationists take what might be called a "cultural reconstructionist" view of material culture. This approach is evident in small institutions like Turkey Run Farm in Virginia and larger operations such as Historic New Harmony in Indiana. Cultural reconstructionists believe, with varying degrees of fervor, that the past is real, that much of its reality can be resurrected, often physically rebuilt, through patient empirical research. Their imperative is no less than to document, study, and communicate as holistic a view of the past as is possible. In this attempt at reconstructing a total sense of the past, artifacts are seen as vital building blocks.[48]

American historical reconstructionists have found certain pasts more in need of rebuilding than others. To date, most of their work has focused on America's preindustrial craft villages, rural agrarian communities, and military garrisons. Deliberate utopian ventures constitute an inordinately large proportion of American cultural-reconstruction interpretations. There are more Shaker villages in the United States than there are Shakers. Unfortunately, the acute social and religious radicalism (and ostracism) of these and other dissenters (now ironically organized into the National Historic Communal Societies Association) is never adequately portrayed in many twentieth-century restorations of their lifestyles. The once bitterly maligned countercultures of earlier eras have been homogenized into respectable middle-class cultural establishments.

Although cultural reconstructionists may seem more intent on historic preservation than historical analysis, their approach is strongly research oriented. In their background preparation (and sometimes in their exhibits) extensive documentary, statistical, and especially archaeological evidence is usually examined before an interpretive framework is articulated. This analysis is revised as new data become available. Although such an approach is used by some historic-house museums and historic sites, the paradigm finds its largest following in outdoor living-history museums.

Plimoth Plantation represents the epitome of the cultural-reconstructionist model, since, as is stated in its mission statement, its goal is to re-create a complete portrait of life in the colony in the year 1627. Its staff has painstakingly researched every detail of clothing, speech, work habits, house construction, furnishings, diet, livestock, and family life. Interpreters bring these details to life by acting out roles of settlers. Because the museum is stocked entirely with reproductions, visitors are encouraged to open cupboards, sit on benches and pick up food containers. The result, unlike many overtidy, immaculate, and manicured outdoor villages, is a decidedly unromanticized view, complete with the filth, hard labor, and lack of privacy typical of the early seventeenth century. The museum's planners have made every effort to avoid presenting the Pilgrims as the courageous and visionary founding fathers celebrated in modern folklore. Indeed, Pilgrim lives seem restricted, difficult, and mundane; the reconstruction of their past lifestyle strikes one as sensitive, convincing, and accurate.

And yet, as Michael Ettema has argued, the restoration gives few clues about why it is important for us to know that information. Because this "time travel" approach allows for no anachronistic questioning about life after 1627, the past is severed from the present. Ettema writes:

> The visitor is discouraged from questioning how social and material conditions in the Plimoth colony contributed to the social and material conditions we face in the present. But then, the role-playing interpreters would not be allowed to address such questions anyway. Theoretically, visitors might at least explore the social and cultural relations of Plimoth in 1627, but in practice, the very success of the reconstruction militates against it. The complete and seductive nature of the recreated material environment leads the visitor only to explore what can be seen and touched. The history of life in Plimoth becomes the history of its material conditions. Modern people may find such a technologically crude environment appealing in its rusticity or appalling in its backwardness, but in any event the primary conclusion most will draw is that progress has brought us many material comforts. Through its elaborate and enjoyable scheme, the Plantation simply reinforces the ideas that modern technology results in a superior existence and that it is the only logical course for humanity. The only real choice in life is to sustain progress, and that is best done materially.[49]

Outdoor living-history museums tend to pay attention to the spatial and environmental contexts of material culture. They are interested in various landscape features (particularly houses and barns) and how such artifacts depict cultural adaptations across space. An assumption, sometimes explicit, sometimes not, underlying much of their research is a concept of regionalism, especially the idea that a region's diverse material culture is, at its core, integrative; that is to say, all the culture manifested in a region's material culture can be considered to be an integrated whole.[50]

Cultural reconstruction, despite its many adherents in history museums and material-culture research, is not without its pitfalls. An obvious dilemma is its tendency to present the past as static. Uniformity and homogeneity can also characterize these interpretations, particularly if the material culture of those outside its mainstream—laborers, slaves, women, agitators—is underrepresented in a museum's collections. An example of a history museum's overcoming this problem is a 1979 New York Gallery Association exhibit at the Cooper-Hewitt Museum, "Resorts of the Catskills," which used cottage architecture, hotel advertisements, and promotions for resort activities directed at various ethnic and racial groups to explain different views of vacationing, nature, ideas of leisure, and experiences of ethnic identity.[51] Finally, perhaps because of the romantic but influential notions of early cultural reconstructionists, such as Jared Van Wagener and Henry Chandlee Forman, who viewed the past as primarily a harmonious agrarian existence that was supposedly destroyed by technology and urbanization, the approach has never been applied in any systematic way to urban material culture.[52]

Perhaps material culturists with a social-history orientation will one day make significant contributions to urban-history museums. A number of American city museums—for instance, Cincinnati, Brooklyn, Chicago, Pittsburgh —are attempting to analyze urbanization as a cultural process. They are also committed to exploring the material-culture ramifications of the social-history agenda: widening the conventional parameters of historical study to include day-to-day experiences (working, child rearing, schooling, play, marrying, dying) of large aggregates of the population (minorities, women, workers, ethnic groups) that have previously been excluded from many museum interpretations.

Social historians and certain students of material culture have much in common: a mutual concern for historical explanation of human behavior over time and place; a wish to challenge the older view of history as solely past politics; an interest in the heterogeneity of the American people and their life ways; and a desire to expand the traditional boundaries of American historical scholarship. Each frequently has been considered by other historians as a maverick approach to the past, yet each has claimed to hold a key to a more democratic and populist history.

Several topical areas—residential spaces, domestic life, women and children, working and workers, life cycles, and community landscapes—have been of interest to researchers with a social-history orientation working in history museums and material culture.[53] Social history's interest in the everyday lives of ordinary people, plus its concern for a higher degree of representativeness in the evidential basis of all historical explanation, has been its major influence in history museums. Such interest has been evident in exhibits dealing with workers (the Essex Institute's "Life and Times in Shoe City: The Shoe Workers of Lynn"), women (the Strong Museum's "Light of the Home"), and immigrants (the Balch Institute's "Freedom's Doors").[54] Significant social-history exhibits have also dealt with life-cycle history, from infancy and childhood (the Strong Museum's "A Century of Childhood") to death and mourning (the Museums at Stony Brook, "A Time to Mourn").[55] Adolescence and senescence still await comprehensive history-museum interpretation.

Among some material-culture students, social history has helped foster an increasing self-consciousness about methodological strategies: What type of data (written, statistical, oral, artifactual) produces the highest degree of causal explanation? How does the historian of objects measure change and depict it intelligibly to a public audience? Which questions that are worth asking about past human behavior are answerable with material culture?[56]

Social historians have frequently asked about the causes and consequences of human conflict, but neither history museums nor material-culture studies have yet offered convincing explanations in response.[57] To be sure, military conflict is well represented in museum material-culture collections, exhibits, and battlefield sites, but domestic conflict and violence in the American past receive little notice. Violence in America has taken racial, ethnic, labor, political, religious, and personal forms. Courtrooms, city halls, police stations, factory gates, prisons, arsenals, houses, and town squares have been the artifacts where such individual and group conflicts as Indian-white confrontations, ethnic rivalries, religious vendettas, clan feuds, urban riots, agrarian uprisings, and labor struggles took place.

So far, only a few museums and scholars have collected and interpreted the material culture of this aspect of the American past.[58] There are several reasons for this. One is professional. Social, as opposed to political, conflict has been a topic of interest to American historians for only a few decades.[59] Some are practical. Many museum staff members and their boards of trustees worry how visitors will react to presentations on ethnic tensions or religious conflicts.[60] Some are political. Some museum historians, like some social historians, avoid issues of conflict because they are uncomfortable with questions of power. Here the broader criticism leveled against social history by Eugene Genovese and Elizabeth Fox-Genovese and others applies. In their quest to understand group behavior, social historians often ignore relationships between groups. Like much social-history writing, therefore, social history as presented in museums is depoliticized. We may learn much about the details of everyday life, but not, as Genovese and Fox-Genovese put it, "who rides whom and how" in the political and economic arena.[61]

Nevertheless, several museum exhibitions have attempted to present well-balanced interpretations of conflict and violence. The Allen County–Fort Wayne Historical Society in Indiana and the Mississippi State Museum faced squarely the issue of how to exhibit the influence of the Ku Klux Klan in their regions. Both made appropriate use of controversial Klan artifacts in their exhibits. The Minnesota Historical Society's "Where Two Worlds Meet" grappled with the cultural conflict inevitable in the seventeenth-century French and Indian fur trade. The National Museum of American History made conflict, along with two other themes (everyday life and diversity), a central interpretive skein of its new "After the Revolution" installation. The curators depicted the rapidity and ubiquity of change in an era (1780–1800) that most of the American public now regards as static, almost mythic. Persuaded that all change involves conflict, the museum historians researching and presenting this exhibit sought to show how "fundamental transformations in family dynamics and living spaces, in patterns of work and consumption, and in how communities organized themselves characterized this time." [62]

Social history's most significant influence on American history museums has been in prompting reinterpretation of the material culture of domestic life. For example, the social-history possibilities of the period room have been explored. Permanent and temporary exhibitions on American domesticity, particularly in the nineteenth century, have made significant contributions to the work of both material-culture students and social-history researchers.[63]

The social-history approach to history-museum interpretation and material-culture research has enjoyed wide acceptance. Young scholars trained in the 1960s and 1970s are particularly attracted to its explanatory potential. Many of these men and women took advanced degrees in social history and instead of pursuing careers in academic institutions joined the staffs of American history museums. The full effect of this important occupational shift and intellectual reorientation probably will not be known for another decade or two. I would suggest, however, that its ramifications for more sophisticated museum interpretation and more rigorous artifact study are auspicious.

History Museums and Material Culture: Future Possibilities

What else might be ventured as to the future of material culture in the history museum? In conclusion, I want to discuss: (1) possible topics for future museum exhibits; (2) aspects of the relationship between museums and material-culture scholarship in the next decade or so; and, (3) the growing interest, among both historians in the academy and in museums, in the theory and practice of the history exhibit as a distinct mode of communication. With regard to topics that might be opportunities for further studies, I would propose that consumerism, foodways, childhood (already in vogue), recreation, and creativity will be subjects of mutual interest.[64] On the last topic, the historical origins, dimensions, and ramifications of human innovation and invention, we are already seeing research combining traditional documentation and material-culture evidence.[65] If the current arguments of Jules Prown and Dell Upton are heeded, there will be a return—despite the influence of the social-history juggernaut—to elite material culture, particularly high-style decorative arts, architecture, and fine arts. The strategy suggested here (at least by Upton) is to study high-style objects along with common material culture in a total "landscape approach" to artifact research.[66] An exemplar of this concept in history museum exhibition was the cooperative interpretation of the Lambert Castle–Botto House program "Mill Owner/Mill Worker," in Paterson, New Jersey.[67]

Although there is renewed interest in material-culture scholarship among some anthropologists, it remains to be seen whether or not the founders of the movement (or their museums) will make any serious claims to take over as its institutional or intellectual home base.[68] It is also difficult to predict the institutional future of the American material-culture movement. Some, like James Deetz, suggest it could be lodged in universities within multidisciplinary programs called departments of material culture.[69] Others argue for its organization through a consortium of history museums (with university affiliations) concentrating their efforts regionally or chronologically.[70]

If history museums are to play a larger role in material-culture research, they need to amplify their voice in the scholarly forums that cover the field. An alarming trend, however, prompts doubt about whether this will happen. In the 1984 American Association for State and Local History national survey of the history-museum profession, institutions were asked to identify their most important concern. Fund raising and public relations ranked first for almost half of them (43.1 percent), with management, preservation, conservation, and acquisition of collections next in order of priority. In contrast, those activities related to the interpretation of material culture ranked lowest: exhibits (2.2 percent), publications (2.0 percent), educational programs (1.8 percent), improved interpretation (1.3 percent). Most worrisome of all, research ranked last with only 0.2 percent of the respondents listing it as their major concern.[71]

In surveying the major national journals of the history-museum field over the past decade, one is struck by how few articles address methodological or conceptual issues in material-culture research.[72] However, a parallel review of the two American material-culture publications indicates a similar neglect of the museum interpretive potential of artifacts. Whereas these journals review material-culture scholarship when published in book form, only hesitantly have they or the history-museum journals been willing to establish a systematic policy of exhibit review and evaluation. Peer review of exhibits is an absolute necessity if material-culture scholarship in museums is to advance.[73]

What are occasionally reviewed in both material-culture and history-museum publications are exhibition catalogs. Although a thorough study of the catalog as a device for the communication of material-culture research has yet to be written, the genre is maturing as a standard vehicle for disseminating scholarly analyses of artifacts. In this sense, certain catalogs have become helpful reports of work-in-progress or, where their data have been fairly comprehensive, useful reference tools for the material culturalist's library.[74] A few daring scholars have used the medium to speculate about the interpretive message of artifacts in a wider cultural context.[75]

The problems and potential of the medium that generated the two-dimensional catalog—that is, the three-dimensional history exhibit—deserve much more serious research. Literature concerned with exhibition process has been largely left to art critics, whose primary interest lies with individual objects, or to social scientists, whose concern is more with behavior patterns of the visitor than with the exhibit as a complex artifact. Instead we need studies that view the history-museum exhibition as a type of publication and that recognize the selective arrangement of artifacts and other related information in a public display to be a museum's special mode of communication. Such displays are one of the media for exploring the intersections of material culture and its larger constellations of meaning. As Harold Skramstad observes, "perhaps more than anything else a museum's exhibition environment is an accurate index of its attitude toward material culture."[76]

We have had some preliminary discussion of the history exhibit as a distinct form of cultural discourse. Nicholas Westbrook and others have suggested that the complexities of the exhibition processes be given wider public acknowledgement.[77] Fath Davis Ruffins argues that we need to think of every exhibition as a spatial, often nonlinear, interactive, visual form, a complicated material-culture assemblage that is more than the sum of its parts. In her estimate, every exhibition is an approximation of the past and should therefore be best thought of as a "metaphor about the past," as well as a "cultural argument" in the present.[78] Finally, as Barbara and Cary Carson have proposed, one might think of the historic house, site, or setting as a material-culture theater furnished with appropriate and accurate artifacts, where what Rhys Isaac, in *The Transformation of Virginia*, calls "historical dramaturgy" might be enacted either by visitors or for them.[79]

These historians regard the history-museum environment as a public forum where the exploration and evaluation of material culture can be presented in both an intellectually stimulating and visually legible manner comprehensible to a wide audience. They see exhibits as cultural arguments that are the vehicles for communicating the best insights of material culture research. They recognize that those who study material culture have a mission that includes but also extends beyond the marshaling of objects or the description of artifacts. The mission—to integrate the three-dimensional remnants of our past with documentary, oral, and statistical resources—remains an engaging future task for both museum and academic historians.

Brooke Hindle, a scholar who has contributed to both institutional contexts, is optimistic about the future of material culture in the history museum. Although written a decade ago, his words still hold true. "The mission," he notes, "is a great one. Even the beginnings registered so far are exciting. They point to the fulfillment of the deep-running need of this generation and those to come for a better history of their past that is both true and useful. It will be truer and more useful than the present histories," concludes Hindle, "precisely because its abstractions will be tied by an intricate web to the real world of material culture." [80]

NOTES

1. For example, in 1875, A. Lane-Fox Pitt-Reviers, in his essay "On the Evolution of Culture," urged his fellow anthropologists to consider material culture as "the outward signs and symbols of particular ideas in the mind." See J. L. Meyers, ed., *The Evolution of Culture and Other Essays* (Oxford: Clarendon Press, 1906), 6.

2. A sampler of these definitions can be found in Thomas J. Schlereth, "Material Culture and Cultural Research," in Thomas J. Schlereth, ed., *Material Culture: A Research Guide* (Lawrence: University Press of Kansas, 1975), 2–5.

3. James Deetz, "Material Culture and Archaeology—What's the Difference?" in Leland Ferguson, ed., *Historical Archaeology and the Importance of Material Things* (Columbia, S.C.: Society for Historical Archaeology, 1977), 10.

4. Statements of definition for the *Material History Bulletin* are found in its first issue, 1 (1976), 3, and in issue 13 (Fall 1981), 2. See also Robert D. Turner, "The Limitations of Material History: A Museological Perspective" *Material History Bulletin*, 20 (Fall 1984), 87–92. The University of New Brunswick in St. John offers a diploma in material history in its master's-degree program.

5. A. Gregg Finley, "Material History and Curatorship Problems and Prospects," *Muse* 111, no. 3 (Autumn 1985), 34.

6. Quoted by A. Hunter Dupree, "Does the History of Technology Exist?" *Journal of Interdisciplinary History* 11, no. 4 (Spring 1981), 585.

7. Cary Carson, "Chesapeake Themes in the History of Early American Material Life," paper presented at "Maryland: A Product of Two Worlds" Conference, St. Mary's City, Maryland, May 19, 1984, pp. 6, 9.

8. Thomas J. Schlereth, "Material Culture or Material Life? Discipline or Field? Theory or Method?" in Gerald Pocius, ed., *North American Material Culture Research: New Objectives, New Theories* (St. John's, Newfoundland: Institute for Social and Economic Research, 1989).

9. E. McClung Fleming, "The University and the Museum, Needs and Opportunities for Cooperation," *Museologist* 111 (June 1969), 10–18.

10. Anne-Marie E. Cantwell and Nan A. Rothschild, "The Research Potential of Anthropological Museum Collections," *Annals of the New York Academy of Sciences* 376 (December 1981), 1–7.

11. John E. Fleming, director of the Afro-American Museum, recognizes this in his recent survey of artifact collections at thirty historical institutions; see his essay "Taking Stock of Afro-American Material Culture," *History News* 40, no. 2 (February 1985), 15–19.

12. Wilcomb Washburn, "Collecting Information, Not Objects," *Museum News* 62, no. 3 (February 1984), 5–15.

13. Sandra Elkins, "What's in a Name?" *History News* 40, no. 8 (August 1985), 6–13.

14. Goran Rosander, *Today for Tomorrow: Museum Documentation of Contemporary Society in Sweden by Acquisition of Objects* (Stockholm: SAMDOK Council, 1980); Maria Papageorge, "Collecting the Present in Sweden," *Museum News* 60 (September–October 1981), 13–18; John Rooney et al., *This Remarkable Continent: An Atlas of United States and Canadian Society and Cultures* (College Station: Texas A&M University Press, 1982).

15. L. Thomas Frye, "The Recent Past Is Prologue," *Museum News* 53 (November 1974), 24–26; Candace Floyd, "Too Close for Comfort," *History News* 40, no. 9 (September 1985), 9; Edith Mayo, "Connoisseurship of the Future," in *Twentieth-Century Popular Culture in Museums and Libraries*, 13–24.

16. Dell Upton, "The Power of Things: Recent Studies in American Vernacular Architecture," in Schlereth, *Material Culture: A Research Guide*, 72. For an oral-history study investigating the significance of material possessions in contemporary family life, see Mihaly Csikszentmihatyi and Eugene Halton-Rochberg, *The Meaning of Things: Domestic Symbols and the Self* (Cambridge: Cambridge University Press, 1981).

17. David Orr and Mark Ohno, "The Material Culture of Protest: A Case Study in Contemporary Collecting," in F. E. H. Schroeder, ed., *Twentieth-Century Popular Culture in Museums and Libraries* (Bowling Green, Ohio: Bowling Green University Popular Press, 1981); 37–54; Barbara Riley, "Contemporary Collecting: A Case Study," *Decorative Arts Newsletter* 4 (Summer, 1978), 3–6; Nicholas Westbrook and Joan Siedl, *The Wishbook: Mail Order in Minnesota—An Exhibition of the Minnesota Historical Society* (St. Paul: Minnesota Historical Society, 1978).

18. Charles Montgomery, "Some Remarks on the Practice and Science of Connoisseurship," *American Walpole Society Notebook* (1961), 7–20.

19. David Nicandi, "Museums, Scholars, and Popular History," *Pacific Coast Forum* 3, no. 4 (1978), 25–29.

20. Carson, "Chesapeake Themes," 77. For a Canadian discussion of this issue, see Gregg Finley, "Material History and Museums: A Curatorial Perspective in Doctoral Research," *Material History Bulletin* 20 (Fall 1984), 75–79, and Finley, "Material History and Curatorship," 36–39.

21. Anthony Garvan describes the index and its anticipated application to material-culture research in his essay "Historical Department in Comparative Culture Study,"

American Quarterly 14 (Summer 1962), 260–74. On the potential of a more recent research tool being developed at the Smithsonian, see Rita Cipalla, "The Video-Disc Advantage," *History News* 40, no. 8 (August 1985), 18–21.

22. E. McClung Fleming, "Artifact Study: A Proposed Model," *Winterthur Portfolio* 9 (June 1974), 153–61; Jules D. Prown, "Mind in Matter: An Introduction to Material Culture Theory and Method," *Winterthur Portfolio* 17, no. 1 (Spring 1982), 7–10; Robert S. Elliot, "Material History—Testing a Method for Artifact Analysis," *Material History Bulletin* 20 (Spring 1986), 5–14.

23. Harold K. Skramstad, Jr., "Interpreting Material Culture: A View From the Other Side of the Glass," in Ian M. G. Quimby, ed., *Material Culture and the Study of American Life* (New York: W. W. Norton, 1978), 180.

24. Kenneth Ames, *Beyond Necessity: Art in the Folk Tradition* (New York: W. W. Norton, 1977), 297–301.

25. On the political biases of artifact display and museum interpretation, see Michael Wallace, "Visiting the Past: History Museums in the United States," *Radical History Review* 25 (October 1981), 63–100; Mark P. Leone, "The Relationship Between Artifacts and the Public in Outdoor History Museums," *Annals of the New York Academy of Sciences* 376 (December 1981), 301–13.

26. Thomas J. Schlereth, "Social History Scholarship and Material Culture Research," *Journal of Social History* 16, no. 4 (June 1983), 111–43; Shomer Zwelling, "Social History Hits the Streets," *History News* 35, no. 1 (January 1980), 10–12.

27. The third scholarly publication, *Material Culture*, is published by the Pioneer Society of America at Transylvania University in Lexington, Kentucky.

28. "Canada's Material History—An International Conference," sponsored by the National Museum of Man, Ottawa, Ontario, March 1979; "Material Culture and the Study of American Life," sponsored by the Winterthur Museum, Winterthur, Delaware, March 23, 1980; Simon Bronner, ed., *American Material Culture and Folklife: A Symposium* (Cooperstown, N.Y.: Cooperstown Graduate Associate Proceedings, 1981); "Material Culture, A Conference," sponsored by the Bay State Historical League, Bradford, Massachusetts, June 20–22, 1980; North Carolina Department of Cultural Resources, "The Material Culture of Black History: Problems and Methods," Durham, North Carolina, December 13, 1980; "North American Material Culture Research: New Objectives, New Theories," sponsored by Winterthur Museum–Memorial University of Newfoundland, St. John's, Newfoundland, Canada, June 19–21, 1986.

29. The curator of material culture at the Colorado Historical Society administers "the material culture department of CHS with responsibility for planning, developing, implementing and supervising programs to aid in the cultural and historical heritage of Colorado." *History News* 35, no. 5 (May 1980), 19.

30. Thomas J. Schlereth, *Material Culture Studies in America* (Nashville, Tenn.: American Association for State and Local History, 1982), 32–75. Peter Rider has applied the topology to Canadian scholarship in his essay "Concrete Clio: Definition of a Field of History" *Material History Bulletin* 20 (Fall 1984), 93–94.

31. For a detailed discussion of the structuralist and behavioralistic approaches to material-culture research, see Schlereth, *Material Culture Studies in America*, 55–57 and 58–63.

32. Henry Glassie's *Folk Housing in Middle Virginia: A Structural Analysis of His-*

toric Artifacts (Knoxville: University of Tennessee Press, 1975) is an example of American structuralism; on behavioral approaches to material culture, see Michael Owen Jones, "Bibliographic and Reference Tools: Toward a Behavioral History" unpublished paper presented at the American Association for State and Local History Folklore Conference, New Orleans, September 4–6, 1980.

33. Patrick Norris, "A Primer of Place," *History News* 40, no. 6 (June 1985), 11–16.

34. George Basalla, "Museums and Technological Utopianism," in Ian M. G. Quimby and Polly Anne Earl, eds., *Technological Innovation and the Decorative Arts* (Charlottesville: University of Virginia, 1974), 360; Michael J. Ettema, "History, Nostalgia, and American Furniture," *Winterthur Portfolio* 17, nos. 2 and 3 (Summer and Autumn 1982), 135–44; Upton, "Power of Things," 72.

35. Wendy Cooper, *In Praise of America: American Decorative Arts, 1650–1830* (New York: Alfred A. Knopf, 1980).

36. Michael Kammen, ed., *The Contrapuntal Civilization: Essays Toward a New Understanding of the American Experience* (New York: Thomas Y. Crowell, 1971) and *People of Paradox: An Inquiry Concerning The Origins of American Civilization* (New York: Alfred A. Knopf, 1973).

37. Barbara Clark Smith, paper on the National Museum of American History exhibit "After the Revolution" presented at the Organization of American Historians annual meeting in Los Angeles, April 1984.

38. Richard Dorson, *Folklore and Folklife* (Chicago: University of Chicago Press), 20–21; Simon Bronner, "Concepts in the Study of Material Aspects of American Folk Culture," *Folklore Forum* 12 (1979), 145–46; Siegfried Giedeon, *Mechanization Takes Command* (New York: Oxford University Press, 1948); Lynn White, *Medieval Technology and Social Change* (New York: Oxford University Press, 1964); Carl Condit, *The Chicago School of Architecture* (Chicago: University of Chicago Press, 1964); Warren Roberts, "Folk Architecture in Context: The Folk Museum," *Pioneer American Society Proceedings* 1 (1973), 34–50.

39. On American Indian museum interpretation, see David Lowenthal, *The Past Is a Foreign Country* (Cambridge: Cambridge University Press, 1985), 55, 278, 276.

40. Data on SWEAT can be secured from its national headquarters: 606 Lake Land Blvd., Auburndale, FL 33823. On the reenactor movement, see Jay Anderson, *Time Machines: The World of Living History* (Nashville, Tenn.: American Association for State and Local History, 1984).

41. For a classic statement of an artifact's multiple functions based on Peter Bogatyrev, *The Functions of Folk Costume* (1937, 1971), see Henry Glassie, "Structure and Function, Folklore and the Artifact," *Semiotica* 7 (1973), 313–51. In his *All Silver and No Brass: An Irish Christmas Mumming* (Dublin: Dolmen, 1976), Glassie proposes several applications of the functionalist perspective.

42. Landon Winner, "Do Artifacts Have Politics?" *Daedalus* (1981), 121–36.

43. Jay Anderson, "Foodways Program on Living History Farms," in *Association for Living Historical Farms and Agricultural Museums Annual* 1 (1975), 21–23 and 23–26.

44. Jay Anderson, "Immaterial Material Culture: The Implications of Experimental Research for Folklike Museums," *Keystone Folklore* 21 (1976–77), 1–13; Robert

Saher, "Experimental Archaeology," *American Anthropologist* 63 (1961), 793–816; John Coles, *Archaeology by Experiment* (New York: Scribner, 1973).

45. The catalog *I'll Buy That* (New York: Cooper-Hewitt Museum, 1986) also celebrates the magazine *Consumer Reports*, which was celebrating its fiftieth anniversary in 1986.

46. John Demos, "Words and Things: A Review and Discussion of 'New England Begins,'" *William and Mary Quarterly* 40, no. 4 (October 1983), 584–97. See also Christopher M. Jedrey, "New England Begins: The Material Origins of American Culture," *Reviews in American History* 12 (September 1984), 363–71.

47. Bernard Bailyn, *Education in the Forming of American Society: Needs and Opportunities for Study* (Chapel Hill: University of North Carolina Press, 1960); Oscar Handlin, "The Significance of the Seventeenth Century," in James Morton Smith, ed., *Seventeenth-Century America: Essays in Colonial History* (Chapel Hill: University of North Carolina Press, 1959), 3–12.

48. For an extended discussion of this paradigm, see Mark P. Leone, "Issues in Anthropological Archaeology," in Mark P. Leone, ed., *Contemporary Archaeology* (Carbondale: Southern Illinois University Press, 1972), 19; Schlereth, "Material Culture Studies in America," 46–50.

49. Michael J. Ettema, "History Museums and the Culture of Materialism," in Jo Blatti, ed., *Past Meets Present: Essays About Historic Interpretation and Public Audiences* (Washington, D.C.: Smithsonian Institution Press, 1987), 62–85.

50. Fred Kniffen, "American Cultural Geography and Folklife" in Don Yoder, ed., *American Folklife* (Austin: University of Texas Press, 1976), 60, 63.

51. Alf Evers et al., *Resorts of the Catskills* (New York: St. Martin's Press, 1979) was the exhibition catalog.

52. Jared Van Wagener, *The Golden Age of Home Spun* (Ithaca, N.Y.: Cornell University Press, 1953); Henry Chandlee Forman, *Jamestown and St. Mary's: Buried Cities* (Baltimore, Md.: Johns Hopkins University Press, 1938).

53. Thomas J. Schlereth, "Material Culture Studies and Social History Research," *Journal of Social History* 16, no. 4 (June 1983), 111–43.

54. The Essex Institute, *Life and Times in Shoe City: The Shoe Workers of Lynn*; Harvey Green, *The Light of the Home* (New York: Pantheon, 1983); Gail Stern, *Freedom's Doors* (Philadelphia: Balch Institute, 1986).

55. Mary Lynn Stevens Heiningen, *A Century of Childhood, 1820–1920* (Rochester, N.Y.: Strong Museum, 1984); Martha V. Pike and Janice Gray Armstrong, *A Time To Mourn: Expressions of Grief in Nineteenth-Century America* (Stony Brook, N.Y.: Museums at Stony Brook, 1980).

56. Nicholas Westbrook, "Decisions, Decisions: An Exhibit's Invisible Ingredient," *Minnesota History* 45, no. 7 (Fall 1977), 292–96.

57. Thomas J. Schlereth, "Causing Conflict, Doing Violence," *Museum News* 63 (October 1984), 45–52.

58. For such exceptions, see Andrew Baker and Warren Leon, "Conflict and Community at Old Sturbridge Village," *History News* 41, no. 2 (March 1986), 6–11; David Crosson, "What's the Risk? Controversial Exhibits Challenge the Romantic Past," *History News* 36, no. 4 (April 1981), 17–19.

59. Richard Hofstader and Michael Wallace, eds. *American Violence: A Documentary History* (New York: Vintage Books, 1971), 4–20.

60. Candace Floyd, "Too Close for Comfort," *History News* 40, no. 9 (September 1985), 8–17.

61. Eugene Genovese and Elizabeth Fox-Genovese, "The Political Crisis of Social History," *Journal of Social History* 10, no. 2 (Winter 1976), 205–20.

62. David Crosson, "What's the Risk?" 17–19. Barbara Clark Smith, *After the Revolution* (New York: Pantheon, 1986), 2–4.

63. Dianne Pilgrim, "Inherited from the Past: The American Period Room," *American Art Journal* 10, no. 1, 5–23: Melinda Young Frye, "Charles Wilcomb, Museum Pioneer," *The Museum of California* 1, no. 5; Peter O'Connell, "Putting the Historic House into the Course of History," *Journal of Family History* 6 (Spring 1981), 28–40; Patricia West, "The New Social History and Historic House Museums: The Lindenwald Example," *Museum Studies Journal* 2, no. 3 (Fall 1986), 22–26; Roger B. White, "Whither the Urban Row House Exhibit? The Peale Museum's 'Rowhouse,'" *Technology and Culture* (January 1983), 76–90. On Minnesota's forthcoming installation, see, *A Home of Our Own: An American Dream—An Exhibit Scenario* (St. Paul: Minnesota Historical Society, 1986).

64. Neil McKendrick, John Brewer, and J. H. Plumb, *The Birth of a Consumer Society: The Commercialization of Eighteenth Century England* (Bloomington: Indiana University Press, 1982); Matyas Szabo, "The Use and Consumption of Things," *Ethnologia Scandinavia: A Journal for Nordic Ethnology* (1978), 107–18.

65. On material culture resources for the study of creativity, see Eugene Ferguson, "The Mind's Eye: Nonverbal Thought in Technology," *Science* 197 (1977), 827–36; Roger N. Shepard, "The Mental Image," *American Psychologist* 33 (February 1978), 125–37; Brooke Hindle, *Emulation and Invention* (New York: New York University Press, 1981).

66. Dell Upton, "Material Culture Studies: A Symposium," *Material Culture* 17, nos. 2 and 3 (Summer and Fall 1985), 86.

67. *Life and Times in Silk City: A Collaborative Museum Exhibition* (1984); see also John A. Herbst and Catherine Keene, *Life and Times in Silk City: A Photographic Essay of Paterson, New Jersey* (Paterson, N.J.: American Labor Museum, 1984).

68. Jane Powell Dwyer, ed., *Studies in Anthropology and Material Culture*, vol. 1 of the Haffenreffer Museum Studies in Anthropology and Material Culture Series (Providence, R.I.: Brown University, 1975), 5; Miles Richardson, *The Human Mirror* (Baton Rouge: Louisiana State University Press, 1974); Mark Leone, "The New Mormon Temple in Washington, D.C.," in L. Ferguson, ed., *Historical Archaeology and the Importance of Material Things* (Columbia, S.C.: Society for Historical Archaeology, 1977); Grant McCracken, "Clothing As Language: An Object Lesson in the Study of the Expressive Properties of Material Culture," in *Proceedings of the XIth International Congress of Anthropology and Ethnological Sciences*.

69. Deetz, "Material Culture and Archaeology—What's the Difference?" 11, 66.

70. Harvey Green, "Collecting Collectives: Collaboration in Collecting and Exhibiting," in *A Common Agenda for History Museums: Conference Proceedings*, ed. Lonn Taylor (Nashville, Tenn.: American Association for State and Local History, 1987), 50–53.

71. Charles Phillips and Patricia Hogan, "Who Cares For America's Heritage?" *History News* (September 1984), 12. On the growing tendency for museums to give priority to the conservation of artifacts over the interpretation of material culture, see

Charles Phillips, "To Educate or Conserve?" *History News* 40, no. 6 (June 1985), 7–10.

72. Exception to this would include Mark P. Leone, "Method As Message: Interpreting the Past With the Public," *Museum News* (October 1983), 35–41; James Deetz, "The Artifact and Its Context," *Museum News* 62, no. 1 (October 1983); Diane Douglas and Bernard Herman, "Theory and Artifact: An Interdisciplinary Approach Reshapes the Mendenhall Story," *History News* 39, no. 3 (March 1983), 32–35; Thomas J. Schlereth, "Five Pioneers of American Material Culture," *History News* 37, no. 9 (September 1982), 28–32.

73. Thomas W. Leavitt, "Toward A Standard of Excellence: The Nature and Purpose of Exhibit Review," *Technology and Culture* 9 (January 1968), 70–75, and "The Need for Critical Standards in History Museum Exhibits: A Case in Point," *Curator* 10, no. 2 (June 1967), 91–94. A recent model review is Richard L. Bushman, "Regional Material Culture: A Review of 'The Great River: Art and Society of the Connecticut Valley, 1635–1820,' " *William and Mary Quarterly* (April 1986), 245–51.

74. Cooper, *In Praise of America*.

75. Some recent museum catalogs in this class are Kenneth Ames, *Beyond Necessity: Art in the Folk Tradition* (Winterthur, Del.: Winterthur Museum, 1977); Robert Trent, *Hearts and Crowns: Folk Chairs of the Connecticut Coast, 1720–1840, as Viewed in Light of Henri Facillon's Introduction to Arts Populaire* (New Haven, Conn.: New Haven Colonial Historical Society, 1977); Barbara Ward, ed., *Silver in American Life: Selections from the Mabel Brady Garvan and Other Collections at Yale University* (New York: American Federation of Arts, 1979); Peter Benes and Phillip C. Zimmerman, *New England Meeting House and Church, 1630–1850* (Boston: Boston University Press, 1979); Herbert W. Hemphill, Jr., *Folk Sculpture, U.S.A.* (Brooklyn, N.Y.: Brooklyn Museum of Art, 1976); Robert St. George, *The Wrought Covenant: Source Materials for the Study of the Craftsmen and Community in Southeastern New England, 1620–1700* (Brockton, Mass.: Brockton Art Center, 1979); John Michael Vlach, *The Afro-American Tradition in the Decorative Arts* (Cleveland: Cleveland Museum of Art, 1978); Howard Wright Marshall, *Buckaroos in Paradise: Cowboy Life in Northern Nevada* (Washington, D.C.: Library of Congress, 1980); Pike and Armstrong, *A Time to Mourn*.

76. Harold Skramstad, "Interpreting Material Culture," 175–76.

77. Westbrook, "Decisions, Decisions"; Jay Anderson, "Living History: Stimulating Everyday Life in Living History Museums," *American Quarterly* 34, no. 3 (Summer 1982), 289–306.

78. Fath Davis Ruffins, "The Exhibition As Form: An Elegant Metaphor," *Museum News* 64, no. 1 (October 1985), 54–59.

79. Barbara G. Carson and Cary Carson, "Things Unspoken: Learning Social History Through Artifacts," in James B. Gardner and George Rollie Adams, eds., *Ordinary People and Everyday Life* (Nashville, Tenn.: American Association for State and Local History, 1983), 185–86.

80. Brooke Hindle, "How Much Is a Piece of The True Cross Worth?" in *Material Culture and the Study of American Life*, 20.

Notes on Contributors

Mary H. Blewett has taught history at the University of Lowell since 1965. Her most recent work on the social history of New England industrialization is *Men, Women, and Work: Class, Gender and Protest in the New England Shoe Industry, 1780–1910* (1988). She has also been active in the Lowell Historical Society and the Lowell Museum and has collected oral history for and served as an interpretive consultant to the Lowell National Historical Park.

Joseph J. Corn is a senior lecturer in the History Department at Stanford University, where he teaches courses on material culture and the history of technology. He has been a consultant and guest-curator for various museums and most recently co-curated "Yesterday's Tomorrows: Past Visions of the Future" for the Smithsonian Institution. His books include *The Winged Gospel: America's Romance with Aviation* (1983) and *Imagining Tomorrow: History, Technology, and the American Future* (1986).

Spencer R. Crew is curator in the Division of Community Life in the Department of Social and Cultural History at the National Museum of American History, Smithsonian Institution. He is curator of that museum's exhibit "Field to Factory: Afro-American Migration, 1915–1940." He previously taught at Douglass College of Rutgers University and the University of Maryland–Baltimore County.

Michael Frisch teaches in the History and American Studies departments of the State University of New York at Buffalo and is editor of *Oral History Review*. He has written extensively on urban and social history and has been active in public–historical museum interpretation and documentary media projects. He is the author of *A Shared Authority: Essays on the Craft and Meaning of Oral and Public History* (1989) and, in collaboration with photographer Milton Rogovin, is completing *Portraits in Steel*, an oral-history documentary of plant closings.

John A. Herbst has worked as an educator, curator, and historian with various museums and historical organizations since 1974. He has served as a trustee of two historic house museums and is active in the American Association for State and Local History and the Mid-Atlantic Association of Museums. Currently the executive director of the Historical Society of Western Pennsylvania, he also is a devoted gardener in Pittsburgh.

James Oliver Horton is associate professor of history and American civilization at George Washington University and director of the Afro-American Communities Project at the National Museum of American History, Smithsonian Institution. He has written many articles on Afro-American history and is co-author of *Black Bostonians: Family Life and Community Struggle in the Antebellum North* (1979). In addition to working with museums, his public history activities have included advising such television shows as ABC-TV's *Our World* and CBS-TV's *Sunrise Semester*.

Gary Kulik is editor of *American Quarterly* and assistant director of the National Museum of American History, Smithsonian Institution, where he also served as the chairman of the Department of Social and Cultural History from 1982 to 1987. The former curator of the Slater Mill Historic Site, he has worked in museums since 1975. He has written extensively on the social history of the American Industrial Revolution. This is his first venture into the history of museums.

Warren Leon has been at Old Sturbridge Village for ten years and is currently director of interpretation. Based on work in the village's Education Department and prior college teaching, he published a number of articles on history teaching and edited *The Small Town Sourcebook* (1979). His more recent writing has focused on museums and public history and has appeared in such journals as *History News*, *Museum News*, and *Journal of Social History*. He is a member of the steering committee of AASLH's Common Agenda for History Museums project.

David Lowenthal taught history and geography at Vassar College before becoming research associate and later secretary of the American Geographical Society. In 1972 he became professor of geography at University College London. His most recent book is *The Past Is a Foreign Country* (1985). His interest in history-museum presentations dates back to his much-cited "The American Way of History" (1966).

Barbara Melosh is curator of medical sciences at the National Museum of American History, Smithsonian Institution, and associate professor of English and American studies at George Mason University. She is the author of *"The Physician's Hand": Work Culture and Conflict in American Nursing* (1982), and co-author with Christina Simmons of "Exhibiting Women's History," in *Presenting the Past*, edited by Susan Porter Benson, Stephen Brier, and Roy Rosenzweig (1986).

John S. Patterson is associate professor of American studies and history at Pennsylvania State University at Harrisburg. He has written essays on Gettysburg for *Journal of Popular Culture* and *Prospects*. His work also has appeared in *American Quarterly*, *American Studies*, and *New England Quarterly*.

Margaret Piatt is assistant director of interpretation at Old Sturbridge Village. She previously held other positions at that institution and served as site manager for Historic Hudson Valley. She has presented workshops on living-history interpretation for the annual meetings of AAM, AASLH, ALHFAM, and other professional organizations. She has a special interest in the uses of theatre in history museums and has written and directed historical-drama scripts for many museums.

Roy Rosenzweig, associate professor of history and director of the Oral History Program at George Mason University, has consulted for many museums and community history projects and has produced and written historical documentary films. He is the co-editor of *Presenting the Past: Essays on History and the Public* (1986) and the author of *Eight Hours for What We Will: Workers and Leisure in an Industrial City* (1983). He is currently collaborating on a social history of Central Park.

Thomas J. Schlereth, professor and director of graduate studies in American studies at the University of Notre Dame, has written several books on the theory and practice of material-culture research. His most recent work in this field is *Doing Words and Things: A Cultural Historian's Craft* (1988). He is completing a study, *Everyday Life in Victorian America, 1876–1915*, to be published in 1990. He coordinates reviews of museum exhibits for *Journal of American History*.

Michael Wallace has written a series of essays on the presentation of history to popular audiences, two of which appear in Benson, Brier, and Rosenzweig, eds., *Presenting the Past: Essays on History and the Public* (1986). He serves as a consultant to the Museum of the City of New York, teaches at John Jay College (CUNY), and is currently writing a book on the history of New York City. He has been a director of the New York Public History Project.

Index